Discipleship That
TRANSFORMS

An Introduction to Christian Education
from a Wesleyan Holiness Perspective

JOHN H. AUKERMAN
General Editor

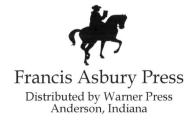

Francis Asbury Press
Distributed by Warner Press
Anderson, Indiana

Coordinator of Publishing & Creative Services
Church of God Ministries, Inc.
PO Box 2420
Anderson, IN 46018-2420
800-848-2464
www.chog.org

To purchase additional copies of this book, to inquire about distribution, and for all other sales-related matters, please contact:

 Warner Press, Inc.
PO Box 2499
Anderson, IN 46018-2499
800-741-7721
www.warnerpress.org

Cover and text design by Carolyn Frost.
Edited by Joseph D. Allison and Stephen R. Lewis.

ISBN-13: 978-1-59317-541-2

Library of Congress Cataloging-in-Publication Data

Discipleship that transforms : an introduction to Christian education from a Wesleyan Holiness perspective / John H. Aukerman, general editor.
     p.   cm.
    ISBN 978-1-59317-541-2 (pbk.)
    1. Christian education--Philosophy. 2. Holiness churches--Education. 3. Methodist Church--Education. I. Aukerman, John H.
    BV1464.D57 2011
    268'.87--dc22
                                          2011001510

Printed in the United States of America.

11 12 13 14 15 16 17 /EP/ 10 9 8 7 6 5 4 3 2 1

Dedication

This book is dedicated
to the thousands of students and parishioners
who enriched our understanding
of Christian education.

Table of Contents

Contributors vii

Preface ix

PART ONE: PRINCIPLES

1. Why This Book? 3
   By John H. Aukerman

2. Basic Theological Topics 13
   By Keith Drury

3. The Role of the Bible in Christian Education 23
   By Jerry Hickson

4. Jesus, the Master Teacher: Teaching That Transforms 29
   By Leon M. Blanchette

5. Overview of the History of Christian Education 41
   By John H. Aukerman

6. Educational Philosophy 57
   By Roger McKenzie

7. Premodern, Modern, and Postmodern Modes
   of Thinking and Being 75
   By Dawn Meadows

8. Human Development 87
   By John H. Aukerman

9. The Power of Story 97
   By John M. Johnson

10. Reaching Out and Bringing in Education,
    Evangelism, and the Nurture of Christian Faith 131
    By Sarah Blake

PART TWO: PLANNING

11. Administering Christian Education. 147
    By Roger McKenzie

12. Goals and Objectives in Christian Education 165
    By Roger McKenzie

13. How to Study the Bible 179
    By Jerry Hickson

14. Choosing and Evaluating Curriculum 191
    By Keith Drury

15. The Teaching-Learning Transaction. 203
    By Jane Kennard

16. Planning to Teach. 217
    By Jane Kennard

17. A Place to Teach: Educational Facilities 229
    By Kristin D. Longenecker Bullock

Part Three: Practice

18. A Church Cannot Not Teach. 245
    By Keith Drury

19. Do as I Do and as I Say: Intentional Discipleship. 257
    By Leon Blanchette

20. Camps and Retreats 267
    By Michael D. Sanders

21. Christian Education Across the Lifespan 281
    By John H. Aukerman

22. Meeting Special Needs in the Christian Education Setting 293
    By Sarah Blake

23. Why the Church Needs the Family. 309
    By Amanda Drury

24. Intercultural Education 321
    By Kristin D. Longenecker Bullock

25. Church and Public Education 333
    By Shannon New-Spangler

26. Contemporary Holiness Living. 345
    By Shannon New-Spangler and Brett A. Spangler

27. Christian Education in the Emerging Church 359
    By Jerry Hickson

28. Trends in Christian Education. 367
    By Jerry Hickson

Index 375

Contributors

John H. Aukerman, EdD (Ball State University). Professor of Christian Education, Director of Distance Education, Director of Outcomes Assessment, Anderson University School of Theology, Anderson, Indiana. Ordained, Church of God (Anderson). Chapters 1, 5, 8, and 21.

Sarah Blake, MDiv (Anderson University). Freelance Writer and Church Consultant. Chapters 10 and 22.

Leon M. Blanchette, EdD (Southern Baptist Theological Seminary). Associate Professor of Christian Education, Olivet Nazarene University, Bourbonnais, Illinois. Ordained Elder, Church of the Nazarene. Chapters 4 and 19.

Kristin D. Longenecker Bullock, MDiv (Anderson University). Ordained, Church of God (Anderson). Chapters 17 and 24.

Amanda J. Drury, MDiv and Doctoral Fellow, Timothy Scholar (Princeton Theological Seminary). Ordained, The Wesleyan Church. Chapter 23.

Keith Drury, MRE (Princeton Theological Seminary). Associate Professor of Christian Education, Indiana Wesleyan University, Marion, Indiana. Ordained, The Wesleyan Church. Chapters 2, 14, and 18.

Jerry Hickson, DMin (Fuller Theological Seminary). Senior Pastor, West Court Street Church of God, Flint, Michigan. Ordained, Church of God (Anderson). Chapters 3, 13, 27, and 28.

John M. Johnson, DMin (Ashland Theological Seminary). Associate Professor of Ministry and Missions, Director of Missions, Warner Pacific College, Portland, Oregon. Ordained, Church of God (Anderson). Chapter 9.

Jane Kennard, PhD (Trinity Evangelical Divinity School). Associate Professor of Christian Education, Mount Vernon Nazarene University, Mount Vernon, Ohio. Ordained, Church of God (Anderson). Chapters 15 and 16.

Roger McKenzie, PhD in Educational Studies (Trinity Evangelical Divinity School). Professor of Religion, Southern Wesleyan University, Central, South Carolina. Ordained, The Wesleyan Church. Chapters 6, 11, and 12.

Dawn Meadows, MATS (Asbury Theological Seminary). Instructor of Theology and Biblical Studies, Warner University, Lake Wales, Florida. Ordained, Church of God (Anderson). Chapter 7.

Shannon New-Spangler, MDiv (Anderson University). Senior Pastor, Harvest Point Church of God, Lordstown, Ohio. Ordained, Church of God (Anderson). Chapters 25 and 26.

Michael D. Sanders, DMin (Anderson University). Professor of Christian Formation and Campus Pastor, Warner University, Lake Wales, Florida. Ordained, Church of God (Anderson). Chapter 20.

Brett A. Spangler, MDiv (Anderson University). Chapter 26.

Preface

For more than twenty years, I have searched for an introductory Christian education textbook written with a view toward Holiness theology and practice. Failing in that, yet believing that such a text is desperately needed at our Holiness universities and seminaries, I decided to recruit a team of writers who could produce it.

The book you are reading is the result of that team's work. Most of the writers are professors in Holiness institutions of higher learning. A few from outside the academic community are nonetheless highly qualified Wesleyan ministers who are engaged in Christian education at the congregational level. So we believe this book has theological integrity.

We offer it to all colleges, universities, and seminaries in the Wesleyan Holiness tradition with the hope that it will help to educate the next generation of Wesleyan students. Our goal has been to produce a comprehensive text, yet one of manageable size. Therefore, each chapter is only an introduction to its topic; whole books have been written on each of these subjects. For this reason, most chapters conclude with a bibliography, "For Further Information," to help students find direction to additional resources.

We have given particular attention to appropriate use of Scripture, taking care to avoid reductionistic views and proof-texting. We believe that a proper understanding of the nature of Scripture is sorely needed in the twenty-first century and is essential for all Christian churches and schools.

John H. Aukerman,
General Editor
Anderson, Indiana
September 4, 2010

PART ONE

PRINCIPLES

CHAPTER ONE

Why This Book?

JOHN H. AUKERMAN

> Always live as God's holy people should,
> because God is the one who chose you,
> and he is holy. That's why the Scriptures
> say, "I am the holy God, and you must be
> holy too."
>
> —1 Peter 1:15–16

Why is this book needed? A large selection of high-quality Christian education textbooks is already available. What makes a Wesleyan Holiness approach to Christian education different from others? God has able teachers in many different Christian communions; haven't they already explicated the basic principles of the church's teaching ministry?

These are questions that the writers of this book asked themselves before beginning this volume. At the outset of this project, the writers had an extended conversation around the question, What makes a Wesleyan Holiness approach to Christian education different from other Christian approaches?

First, they did not believe that a Wesleyan Holiness approach is qualitatively better than any other. However, they understood that a Wesleyan Holiness approach to Christian education is *different from* other approaches in several respects. Their goal was to explore and explain those differences.

Second, the eleven team members agreed on the following points as their common understanding of a Wesleyan Holiness *perspective* on Christian education. To be sure, theologians would include many additional points in a description of Wesleyan Holiness *theology*, but that is not the purpose of this list. Rather, it sets forth the eleven team members' understanding of a Wesleyan Holiness perspective on the educational ministry of the church. It is written in the first person because these are the personal commitments of the team members, with additional commentary added to each point:

1. **We have a high view of the inspiration and authority of the Bible. We are not interested in inerrancy arguments; they are not built on solid philosophical foundations, and they lead only to unhealthy hermeneutics. We value and respect Bible knowledge, but mostly we see the Bible as the living, active Word of God that leads to a life of holiness.**

Our approach to Christian education is founded on an unshakable belief in the inspiration and authority of the Bible. The word *inspiration* literally means "God-breathed," and Wesleyans understand that God the Holy Spirit "breathed" the thoughts and ideas of the triune God into faithful writers, who made a written record of their observations and insights in Holy Scripture. So the Bible is a human record of human perceptions of God's creation and desire for relationship with humankind; the Bible is not a textbook of science, nor is it biography or history. It was written in a pre-modern, pre-scientific period with none of our modern assumptions or worldviews concerning science or history or anthropology or psychology or _____ (fill in the blank!). We affirm that the Bible is the "inspired Word of God" because it contains everything human beings need to know for salvation and holy living.

The writers of this book affirm the *authority* of the Bible. To be sure, there are many authorities in life: governments, schools, parents, teachers, institutions, judges, books, physicians, and psychologists, to name just a few. But all human authorities are subject to the highest Authority recognized by the Bible. Some Christians might put the Bible on an equal plane with other authorities, such as human intelligence, church officers and/or councils, or changing societal values. We do no such thing. We believe that all other authorities exist under the authority of the Bible, the sixty-six books of the Protestant canon. Whenever one of those authorities comes into conflict with the clear teaching of Scripture, the lesser authority must yield.

The team that developed this book has studied inerrancy arguments extensively and rejects all such attempts as unhelpful. First, inerrancy posits that the original manuscripts (the "autographs") of the Bible were inerrant, but none of those autographs are extant. Therefore, the case for inerrancy has no evidence. Second, inerrancy claims something for the Bible that its own writers dared not claim. Third, inerrancy holds that God took control of human writers and used them as mindless robots, much like people today use computers to send e-mails or cell phones to send text messages. Such a belief is contrary to the Bible's own teaching about the nature of human freedom and accountability. Fourth, inerrancy arguments tend only to divide believers, not unite them in love and holiness. And fifth, inerrancy arguments are just that, arguments that do not advance the kingdom of God. In fact, they bring argumentative Christians into disrepute in the world's eyes and harm the cause of Christ.

Because it holds a high view of the inspiration and authority of the Bible, this book values biblical knowledge, but not for its own sake. After all, an individual can read and even memorize the Bible without believing a word of it or being changed into the likeness of Christ. As Christian educators, we do not strive for the mere transfer of Bible knowledge from one person to another. People need to know the Bible so that they may believe that Jesus is the Christ, the only Son of the living God, and that believing they come to have life in his name (see John 20:30). Scripture explains how they may continue to grow in their relationship with the triune God as they approach a life of holiness—that is, a life wholly pleasing to God.

2. **We believe in the triune God and see God the Holy Spirit as the most active agent in spiritual transformation, with the human teacher constantly aware of the Holy Spirit as the primary teacher active in the classroom.**

This book is firmly rooted in the historic Christian understanding of one God in three persons: God the Father, God the Son, and God the Holy Spirit. This is a great mystery, and while we cannot fully comprehend it or explain it, we are committed to a Trinitarian understanding of God. Furthermore, without crossing the line into theological modalism, we note that the Bible identifies God the Holy Spirit as the most active agent in effective teaching. Some may see this point as debatable. Other believers of good will conclude that God the Father and/or God the Son are just as active in spiritual transformation. Nevertheless, we believe that Christian teachers are weak, fallible vessels at best, and in order for spiritual transformation and effective teaching to occur, teachers must maintain a constant awareness of and dependency on God the Holy Spirit as the primary teacher in the classroom.

3. **We are not satisfied with making holy individuals; we also seek to develop a holy people—the collective people of God. Thus we seek the transformation of the whole church—as a church—into a Christlike community. We believe that this is best accomplished when groups of believers meet to study, pray, and hold each other accountable.**

Holiness begins with the individual, but it must not end there. Personal holiness is necessary, but it is not sufficient. It is God's will to have *a holy people*, not just an aggregate of holy individuals.

The Enlightenment moved Western culture toward placing ultimate value upon the individual; we seek to move back toward the biblical concept of *peoplehood*. The actual word *peoplehood* came into use in the English language around 1899. It means "the quality or state of constituting a people; the awareness of the underlying unity that makes the individual a part of a people."[1]

Even though the word *peoplehood* is not in English translations of Bible, the concept existed in the minds of biblical writers and in ancient Near Eastern cultures. Significantly, the English Standard Version contains 2,752 uses of the word *people* but only 199 uses of the word *person*. One can readily discern the Bible's emphasis on groups of people rather than collections of individuals.

So the writers of this textbook promote the concept of *a holy people of God*. We believe that the church must become greater than the sum of its parts. In order to honor and glorify God, the whole people of God must be transformed into a holy, Christlike community.

4. **We believe that God works in all things and through all people for Kingdom purposes. Therefore we seek not only cooperation but unity with believers in non-Wesleyan Christian traditions.**

God is sovereign; God is not limited by any external forces; God works in all things for good. Sometimes God chooses to work even through those who do not believe.[2] Therefore, God surely works through believers in non-Wesleyan Christian traditions. For this reason, we seek fellowship, cooperation, and unity with all who are in Christ.

As stated previously, we do not consider Wesleyan Holiness to be better than other Christian traditions, but simply different from them. We hope that all Christ followers may be humble enough to learn from each other, even—and especially—from those who are seen as different.

God is so much grander, so much more glorious, so much more complex than human intelligence can comprehend, that surely God has truth in all streams of Christian thought. While this book is offered as a different perspective on the church's teaching ministry, our hope is that this different perspective will not further divide the body of Christ, but that it will in fact become a unifying force. If Christians of differing traditions can love one another, value one another, and learn from one another's experience, then perhaps there is hope for a revival of Christian unity in this century.

---

1. *Webster's Ninth New Collegiate Dictionary*, s.v. "Peoplehood."

2. See, e.g., Jeremiah 25, 27, and 43, where pagan Nebuchadnezzar is called God's servant.

5. **We are committed to the Wesleyan quadrilateral—we believe that truth is revealed and confirmed in scripture, reason, tradition, and experience. For us, scripture is the longest and strongest side of the quadrilateral—it carries more weight than any of the other three sides.**

Although John Wesley never used the term *quadrilateral* himself, many Wesleyan theologians have found it to be a convenient shorthand expression to summarize some large theological concepts. Note that a quadrilateral is any four-sided figure. Each side's length is independent of the other three, and each side may or may not be parallel with the opposite side. Any four-sided figure will do. Therefore, those who draw a square as representing the Wesleyan quadrilateral are mistaken. Nothing in Wesleyan theology says or implies that all four ways of apprehending the truth are of equal length or that the opposite sides are parallel.

In this postmodern era, it is difficult to know what truth is. Jesus promised his followers that they would know the truth (John 8:32), and the Wesleyan quadrilateral seems to be a reliable way to test various truth claims. If a proposition passes all four tests—that is, if it is biblical, reasonable, consistent with Christian tradition, and true to human experience—then one can safely accept it as being true. If it fails even one of these tests, the wise Christ follower would view it with skepticism. And if it fails the biblical test, the claim must be summarily rejected. This is what we mean when we say that Scripture is the longest and strongest side of the epistemological test.

6. **We believe that God actually offers "changing grace" to change us from what we are into what God calls us to be: fully devoted followers of Jesus Christ. We see salvation and sanctification less as the goal of the Christian life and more as the entrance into it.**

It has often been observed that "Amazing Grace" may be the most popular hymn in the world because human intellect will never plumb the depths of God's grace. But while many may end their experience of grace with the astounding fact that God really does love and accept them, Wesleyan Holiness theology goes a step further, toward "changing grace." So amazing is God's grace that God actually offers humans the ability to change.

Change is frightening, and many resist change. Psychologists have observed that many people prefer to remain in the familiar comfort of psychological distress than risk the unknown changes that health would bring. But the human condition calls for change. Sin is destructive and deadly, and "changing grace" allows a person to change. Note that the sinner does not effect the change; it is God who changes the sinful person into a saved person.

Salvation is just the first step to becoming a fully devoted follower of Jesus Christ. *Sanctification* is the second step. Again, it is God's "changing grace" or transformative power that sanctifies a believer. Yes, the believer must take a step toward God, accepting this life-changing gift, but it is still God who sanctifies. Unfortunately, the concept of sanctification is off-putting to many. Churches have preached and taught so many varied and even contradictory things about sanctification, leading to frustration and confusion among the ranks of the faithful.

Simply put, in both the Old Testament and New Testament, to be *sanctified* means to be "set apart" from others. As the concept developed historically, it came to mean that the "set-apart ones" became like the One to whom they had been set apart, that is, a set-apart believer became more and more like God.

How does sanctification work? Interestingly, the Bible offers several answers. For example, John 17:17–19 and 1 Thessalonians 5:23 imply that a believer might seek a deeper commitment in one single act of sanctification, what some believers refer to as a second definite work of grace. In contrast, the writer of Hebrews saw sanctification as an ongoing work of grace, a continuing experience.[3] The long controversy of how sanctification happens will not be settled here; suffice it to say that a Wesleyan perspective on Christian education holds that God's amazing grace changes sinful humans into saved and sanctified holy followers of Jesus Christ.

7. **We believe in prevenient grace, which has significant implications for our approach to ministry with children.**

The formal theological term *prevenient grace* may be better understood as "preceding grace," that is, grace that precedes a sinner's acceptance of Christ. It is the grace of God that stirs within a person before he or she makes a decision to follow Christ, the grace that makes that very decision possible. It assumes human free will to accept or reject God's offer of salvation. Thomas Oden defines prevenient grace as "the grace that begins to enable one to choose further to cooperate with saving grace. By offering the will the restored capacity to respond to grace, the person then may freely and increasingly become an active, willing participant in receiving the conditions for justification."[4]

The authors of this book see children as being made in the image and likeness of God (Gen 1:26f). At some time in the normal course of development (and nobody is exactly sure just when), children reach an age of accountability, a point at which they are aware of their sinful actions and attitudes and experi-

---

3. See Hebrews 2:11, "those who are being sanctified" (NKJV); also Hebrews 10:14, "those who are being made holy" (NIV). These versions were chosen because they correctly translate the Greek, showing the ongoing nature of sanctification (vis-à-vis the instantaneous nature).

4. Thomas Oden, *John Wesley's Scriptural Christianity* (Grand Rapids, MI: Zondervan, 1994), 243.

ence the need for salvation. Then prevenient grace becomes active. We do not mean to suggest that children can or should understand it, but that adults who work with children should view them the same way God does: as beings made in the image and likeness of God who are now being drawn toward repentance and salvation by God's own prevenient grace.

This theological approach to ministry totally rejects the idea that young children are totally depraved, and must repeat a verbal formula so they can be "saved." It rules out all attempts at manipulation of children; it refrains from frightening children with visions of hellfire and damnation; it avoids using peer pressure to force compliance to an assumed group norm. Rather, this approach treats children with all the respect and love due them as special creations in the image and likeness of God; it honors God's image in children by gently nurturing them in a community of Christian love; it introduces them to biblical concepts when they are developmentally able to receive them; and it walks with them right through their decisions to accept God's love, to move on to sanctification, and to develop into fully devoted Christ followers.

8. **We believe in human free will and in God-and-human cooperation in the growth process.**

This principle was implied in the previous statement, but it stands on its own. The battle between the Calvinist concept of predestination and the Arminian concept of free will has been raging for more than four centuries, and it will certainly not be settled here. Honest students of the Bible must admit that there are places in Scripture that seem to teach free will and other places that seem to teach against it. However, the writers of this book are on the side of Arminius, believing in human free will and in the reality—indeed, the necessity—of divine-human cooperation in the spiritual growth process.

It would seem pointless for God to have created sentient beings who did not have free will. In fact, God is the only One able to create creatures who can choose. (Human creations merely follow preprogrammed instructions: if this set of circumstances exists, a well-programmed computer merely responds in a predetermined way.) However, the very nature of God demands human free will as the basis for any genuine relationship with him. The fact that many choose not to obey God is evidence of their freedom of choice.

Taking this line of reasoning a little deeper, one can see that God is self-limiting when it comes to spiritual growth and development. Any believer has a full range of opportunity, but God does not force or even predetermine any particular individual's growth. God always initiates growth, but God then waits for our human response and decision. Little or no growth will take place without a divine-human partnership. If a Christian wants to remain at a certain level of faith, God allows that; but for every believer who chooses a deeper walk with Christ, God enables personal spiritual growth.

9. **We see the goal of Christian education/discipling as the transformation of lives toward Christlikeness for participation in the kingdom of God. This encompasses the Wesleyan emphasis on holiness and wholeness (not confined only to "spiritual" things) and the optimistic view of God's transformative work in the lives of individuals and society. Salvation is more than a ticket to heaven or giving intellectual assent to a list of theological propositions. As Christian educators, we can expect real on-the-street life change in the student.**

This statement carries several major theological themes:

a. We are primarily interested in discipling. This is in response to Jesus' command that his followers must make disciples as they go about their daily business. The familiar Great Commission given in Matthew 28:19f contains three participles: *going, baptizing,* and *teaching.* The only verb in the imperative mode is translated, "make disciples." An accurate translation of the Greek would read something like, "As you are going, make disciples of all nations, baptizing them in the name of the Father, and of the Son, and of the Holy Spirit, and teaching them to observe everything I have commanded you."

b. Jesus seeks the kind of disciples whose lives are transformed. It is not sufficient for a believer to say merely that "Jesus is my Savior"; believers need to come to the place where they can affirm with the apostle Paul that "Jesus is Lord" (1 Cor 12:3). When Jesus truly is Lord of one's life, the individual cannot remain the same; transformation will take place. One of the most dramatic instances of transformation is found in the world of insects, when a caterpillar spins a cocoon and emerges completely transformed as a butterfly. This kind of complete transformation is envisioned for emerging disciples of Jesus Christ.

c. Christian disciples must be transformed toward Christlikeness. Jesus said, "Whoever has seen me has seen the Father" (John 14:9). Extending this logic to human followers of Christ, one can conclude that a day will come in the life of a transformed believer when "whoever has seen her has seen her Lord." This is not to imply that absolute Christlikeness is likely, or even possible, for any human being. It is merely to assert that the goal of our growth is Christlikeness, and as transformation unfolds, the transformed disciple slowly and unmistakably exhibits more and more characteristics of the Christ.

d. This transformation occurs so that disciples might be effective participants in the kingdom of God, which is a present reality. Jesus taught that "the kingdom of God is in the midst of you" (Luke 17:21). He used the present tense verb, translated "is" (not the future, "will be"), and he used the plural "you" (the group, not the individual), meaning that God's kingdom was already present in the midst of Christian believers two thousand years ago. While some look only for a future kingdom, Wesleyan theology recognizes the present reality of God's reign in and among those who follow Christ.

e. There is no separation of life into sacred and secular realms; transformation toward Christlikeness affirms the essential unity of life. Rather than compartmentalizing a disciple's life, holiness draws the disparate segments into health and wholeness. A mature Christian believer is the same person on Sunday as he is on Monday. This is one of the marks of a disciple who is being transformed toward Christlikeness for participation in the kingdom of God.

f. Anyone who believes that the triune God is all-powerful and is currently reigning in physical space-time must hold an optimistic view of God's transformative work in the world. To be sure, terrible things are happening in human history, but God reigns and will ultimately triumph. The observant Christ follower will discern signs and seeds of kingdom transformation where others see only heartache and loss. For this reason, we know that the important task of discipling will not be in vain.

g. A Wesleyan Holiness theology for Christian education emphasizes the need to transform not only individuals but society. Individual life change is necessary but not sufficient. Individuals who are saved and sanctified must work together, under the leadership of the Holy Spirit, to transform society. They begin with their own social groupings in congregations, spread out to their local communities, and ultimately bring kingdom values to bear on society as a whole. Systemic evil is an unfortunate fact of human life, and the only antidote is societal transformation by God's reign.

h. Many believers see salvation primarily as their personal ticket to heaven; their salvation experience begins and ends with the self. This is a negative influence of the Enlightenment's emphasis on individualism. The writers of this book affirm their belief in heaven and the necessity of salvation to enter heaven, but we believe that the salvation experience is so much more than an individual guarantee of eternity with God. The experience of salvation is only the beginning of an exciting, lifelong journey of personal and societal transformation for kingdom purposes.

i. The writers of this book believe that salvation is much more than giving intellectual assent to a list of theological propositions. Some approaches to Christian life and ministry drill catalogs of beliefs into their people, as if right thinking will ensure their salvation. The folly of this approach is illustrated by the fact that the devil himself knows every right belief about God yet is by no means saved.

j. The only reliable evaluation of the church's educational ministry is change in the lives of students. When people repent of sin, accept God's gracious offer of salvation, and begin following Christ, change will be apparent in their behavior.

10. **We value a healthy balance of "being" and "doing." For example, we recognize that transformation is primarily in the heart of the believer and grows in great part through stillness and solitude and worship. All our "doing" is ultimately pleasing to God when it is that automatic response of a heart of love that is completely laid at the feet of Jesus. We believe that an inwardly transformed life will be missional and will intentionally and redemptively promote justice by combating social evils such as racism, war, poverty, and unjust discrimination wherever they are found.**

Just as it is impossible to separate a person into organs, bones, and blood and still have a living individual, there is no way to divide a person—or the Christian experience—into separate categories of "being" and "doing." Each influences the other: Who a person *is* shapes what a person *does*, and vice-versa. Therefore, the writers of this book reject teachings that lead to works-righteousness. While it is true that no amount of good works can save a sinner, it is also true that every genuine salvation experience will lead to good works. A Christ follower does not perform good works in order to please God but does them out of a heart of Christlike love that cannot look the other way when a need arises.

One category of "doing" that has often been overlooked concerns participation in issues of justice. The God revealed in the person and work of Jesus Christ is a God of justice, concerned that all of his children are treated properly. Wesleyan Christians believe that every inwardly transformed Christ follower will intentionally and redemptively promote justice by combating societal evils wherever they are found.

On a worldwide scale, these justice issues change from time to time. For example, current justice issues include racism, war, poverty, and women in ministry. We have an unwavering commitment to work against racism and poverty, to be sensitive to the needs of all who are affected by war (soldiers, civilians, terrorists, etc.), and to encourage the active ministry of women who are called by God and gifted for ministry.

But because these issues change, Christian educators must be quick to identify newly emerging forms of inequality and injustice. We must make the body of Christ aware of these needs. And we must teach disciples of Christ how to respond to these needs in effective, transformative ways.

CHAPTER TWO

Basic Theological Topics

KEITH DRURY

> ...you must teach only what is correct.
>
> —Titus 2:1

A Christian educator who says, "I just teach people and leave theology to others," would be like a math teacher saying, "I just teach students and leave the math to others." Theology and Christian doctrine provide the content of the church's teaching. *Theology* is the practice of disciplined, Spirit-guided reflection on God's revelation, while *doctrine* is the organized collection of beliefs based on the practice of theology. As such, the work of theology in the church leads to the formulation of Christian doctrine. Without theology and doctrine, Christian educators can be entertainers or babysitters, but they cannot be *Christian* educators. Knowing basic Christian doctrine and how to think theologically is critical for the Christian educator. This chapter provides a summary scan of the basic theological topics that Christian educators explore in depth in separate theology courses.

The Triune God

When Christians speak of "God," they refer to the triune God: Father, Son, and Holy Spirit, not just God the Father. While it is a common error in Sunday school classes to refer just to the Father as "God," this is not the Christian view; to Christians, God is one God in three persons—Father, Son, and Holy Spirit. The Son and the Holy Spirit are to be worshiped as God along with the Father. Jesus is not second-in-command or an assistant God but is "begotten of the

Father before all worlds, God of God, Light of Light, Very God of Very God, begotten, not made, being of one substance with the Father." And the Holy Spirit is not somewhere further down the chain of command but is "the Lord and Giver of Life who with the Father and the Son together is worshiped and glorified."[1]

The Christian church took several centuries to sort out and finally settle the question of the relationships in the Holy Trinity. The questions were perplexing: Was the Father the "real God"—Yahweh of the Old Testament? Was the Son, Jesus Christ, *like* God, or was Christ *"very* God"? If the Son were begotten, was he *made* by the Father with all the rest of Creation? Who then is the Holy Spirit? Was the Holy Spirit merely a manifestation or emanation of the Father and the Son, or was the Spirit *fully* God as well?

These early Christians determined that the divine persons were not separate. They are distinguishable, but not separate. If they were separate, Christianity would have multiple gods. Because the divine nature is infinite (inhabiting and transcending space and time) and because the Father has this divine nature, the Son has this divine nature, and the Spirit has this divine nature; they mutually indwell one another in time and space and beyond time and space.

For years Christians debated questions like these as they sorted out this greatest of all mysteries—the triune God. Eventually, Christians settled on a series of creeds that stated what orthodox Christians have believed ever since: God is one, but not one person. God is "One God in Three persons" as the early fathers Tertullian and Origen[2] put it. "One God" means "one divine nature" in three persons—the triune God: Father, Son, and Holy Spirit. Likewise, for Christians the Holy Spirit is not an emanation of God but is also a person—not an *it*. For example, the Nicene Creed states of the Holy Spirit, "who with the Father and the Son together is worshiped and glorified." Thus, for Christian educators God is one in three persons: the Father, Son, and Holy Spirit.

Creator

Christians believe that God is the "Maker of heaven and earth, and of all things visible and invisible." While creation is sometimes addressed under the heading of the Father, Christians believe the Son and Holy Spirit were also present and actively involved in creation.

Christians do not believe that creation just happened but that everything seen (and even what is not seen) is the handiwork of the triune God. Scripture does not describe *how* creation happened but *who* created it—the triune God.

---

1. Phrases in quotes, unless otherwise noted, are from the Nicene Creed, a profession of faith adopted in AD 325 by the first ecumenical council that met in the town of Nicaea in what is present-day Turkey.

2. In Alexandria and in North Africa respectively, Tertullian and Origen contributed early writings for believers in the second century AD.

God did it, however he did it. Christians may be interested in how it happened—fast or slow, trillions of years ago or more recently, but that is not the primary claim of Christian theology, for it only claims that whenever or however creation occurred, God is the "Maker of heaven and earth."

Creation is not just about this earth. Christians believe God created all of the heavens, all of the planets, all of the stars, all matter, all energy, electrons, protons, neutrons, quarks, even dark space that occupies the vast majority of the universe and all other matter, and energy still unaccounted for by physicists. When Christians say God is creator, they mean everything that *is* came from God's creative act. God made all that is seen and unseen, including angels—indeed everything that is not God was created by God.

Christians believe humans are a part of God's creation, not just that God created the original humans, or the first humans, but that he is the creator of all humanity. The subsection of theology that studies the nature of humanity is called *anthropology*.

Also under the head of creation is the doctrine of *providence*, a term theologians use to explain how God exercises his omnipotence and goodness in the creation. Here, too, is a place where theology addresses the troubling question of *theodicy*, which is the problem of evil and how a good God can allow evil in the world.

The Son, Jesus Christ

Christian theology gives special attention to the person and work of Jesus Christ—since Christians are not just *theists* but *Christians*. This study of the person and work of Christ in theology is called *Christology*. Christians believe Jesus Christ is the only-begotten Son of God. Jesus Christ was not created by the Father but was "begotten" and "like begets like." A human being begets a human being. Nature begets the same nature, not something different. To be made or created refers to or intimates a different nature. God begat Christ—like begat like, and very God begat very God. Christ was not begotten when he became a fetus in the Virgin Mary but was begotten "before all worlds." Jesus Christ is "God of God, Light of Light, Very God of Very God" and is "one substance with the Father."

This only-begotten Son of God "came down from Heaven" and was born of the Virgin Mary. Jesus Christ was not just a good man whom the Father adopted as his son; rather, he was the eternal Son of God who came down to become a fully human being in the Virgin Mary. Jesus was fully human and at the same time fully divine. He did not come as an apparition or ghost who merely appeared human, but was as human as anyone alive today. Thus, when Christians say that Jesus was "tempted in every way that we are" (Heb 4:15), they mean he was victorious over temptation as a fully human being. As the eternal Son, Jesus only operated out of his human nature in his earthly ministry. This is a particularly important doctrine for Christian educators seeking to inspire people to holy living. If people believe Christ was not fully human, his victory over temptation cannot be a model for them. But since he was fully human and lived a holy life as a human, he can, therefore, be a model of holy living. Christians today do not have any less power or grace available to them than Jesus Christ himself had in the first century.

The reason Christ came down was *"for us and our salvation."* God became human for the sake of humans. While on earth, Jesus was crucified under Pontius Pilate, suffered, and was buried, and on the third day he rose again and then ascended into heaven, where he sits at the right hand of the Father.

But that is not the end of the story, for Jesus Christ will "come again with glory to judge both the quick and the dead, and his kingdom will have no end." Christ existed before the incarnation, came to live and die as a human, rose again and ascended to heaven, and is coming again.

The content of Christian faith regarding Jesus includes Christ's past incarnation, death, burial, resurrection, and ascension and his future return when he will judge the living and the dead to establish his kingdom forever. This is the content of Christian doctrine regarding Jesus Christ. It is central to what the Christian educator teaches as "the gospel." It is not everything they teach, but *Christology* is the central focus of Christian theology.

The Holy Spirit

The study of the Holy Spirit is called *Pneumatology*. The third person of the Trinity sometimes draws the short straw among Christians, perhaps because they are obsessed with the past more than the present. Just as some Christians in Sunday school mistakenly think Jesus was created at conception, some Christians wrongly imagine that the Holy Spirit was created at Pentecost—as if he is the ghost of Jesus come back to haunt the church. Solid orthodox Christians believe otherwise. The Holy Spirit is "the Lord and Giver of Life" and was present at creation and is also very God as is the Father and the Son, and "with the Father and the Son together is worshiped and glorified." Christians worship the Father, the Son, *and* the Holy Spirit.

While worshiping the Holy Spirit along with the Father and Son may be of great interest to a worship planner, a Christian educator is especially interested in the work of the Holy Spirit that powerfully relates to the Christian educator's own work. Thus, the following list will delineate some of this work of the Holy Spirit that relates most closely to the Christian educator's work.[3] Since the work of the Holy Spirit is often overlooked, this will delineate some of his activities that especially relate to Christian education:

---

3. This list describing the work of the Holy Spirit is based on the descriptions appearing in Keith Drury, *Common Ground: What All Christians Believe and Why It Matters* (Indianapolis, IN: Wesleyan Publishing House, 2008), 124–27.

He draws: A Christian educator might imagine he or she can put together a clever program to attract people, but it is actually the Holy Spirit who draws people to God. The Holy Spirit is constantly carrying on an outreach program prompting the lost toward God and the church; the Christian educator's job is to join him in that ongoing work.

He convicts: No matter how powerful the teachers or preacher they cannot convince the world of sin; that is the Holy Spirit's work.

He sparks faith: Many Christians today imagine or even say they decided to believe on Christ, but they are wrong. A lost person does not have the power to decide for Christ. Humans are soil, and soil cannot create the seed of faith. Only the Holy Spirit can ignite the power to believe. Thus, Christian educators are constantly aware that they are not the primary agent in bringing people to Christ—the Holy Spirit is.

He gives life: With faith comes new life. It is the Holy Spirit who is "the Lord the giver of Life." Wesleyans are evangelicals to the extent that they believe a person can be born again; yet it is the Holy Spirit who raises the lost from death to life, converting them and making them new creatures in Christ.

He indwells: When persons are converted, the Holy Spirit comes to dwell inside them. They might say they received Christ, but more precisely, they mean that they received the Holy Spirit as they were united with Christ by the indwelling of the Holy Spirit. God the Holy Spirit is not out there or up there; rather, God the Holy Spirit is in here. When a teacher is trying to get something across to a Christian student, the teacher has an ally inside that person—the indwelling Holy Spirit who (one hopes) is trying to make the same point.

He comforts: Spiritual formation classes and small groups attempt to be a comforting communion for students weighed down by stress and pain. But this also is a primary work of the Holy Spirit. The Spirit brings spiritual balm to comfort believers. He binds where they are broken, soothes where they are troubled, and relieves pain. God the Holy Spirit is a person, and these are the acts of a compassionate person. When students leave a class feeling comforted, they are feeling the work of the Holy Spirit, who has been using the words and compassion of the body of Christ, the church.

He cleanses: The Holy Spirit cleanses from sin. The Spirit indwells all Christians but cohabits with some things that do not belong in the Christian's life. There are words, thoughts, or deeds that are alien to holy living. No matter how wonderful a teacher is or how powerful the accountability sessions of a small group are, God can do more than forgive a sinning Christian; it is the Holy Spirit who sets a person free—in a single moment or gradually over time. Either way, it is the Spirit's work. A teacher cannot educate sin out of a person's life, but the Holy Spirit can cleanse a person and set him or her free.

He fills: The Spirit filled the disciples, and he can fill believers today. In cleansing, the Spirit performs a ministry of subtraction; in filling and empowering, he performs a ministry of addition.

He teaches: The Holy Spirit is the master teacher of every Sunday school class and small group—and every human teacher is his assistant. He never misses a class, and he always comes prepared. A church might have gifted teachers and proficient Christian educators, but it is the Holy Spirit who invisibly leads his people into all truth and reminds his people of that truth later on. Teaching is a work carried on by the Spirit through, around, and beside (and sometimes in spite of) human teachers. Teaching is a *Spiritual* work.

All this and more is the work of God the Holy Spirit.[4] A Christian educator must understand the theology of the Holy Spirit not only as a set of propositions to teach but also as the driving power in the work of leading people to faith and nurturing them to holy living. Christian education is the work of the Holy Spirit as master Teacher, and Christian educators are the Teacher's aides.

The Holy Catholic Church

The theological study of the church is called *ecclesiology*. It is no accident that the Apostles' Creed speaks of the Holy Spirit and then immediately adds three beliefs about the church as follows: "I believe in the holy catholic church, the communion of saints, and forgiveness of sins." It is the Holy Spirit who creates the catholic (universal) church, the body of Christ. What is the church? The church is the body of Christ, the mystical community of followers of Jesus Christ concretely expressed in local churches. It is not merely some invisible theoretical construct but a real gathering of real people through which saving, sustaining, and sanctifying grace is made available by God to the world through the Holy Spirit. And how does one know a church is a real church? The tests for this (often called the marks of the church) are (a) the preaching of the pure Word of God, (b) the due administration of the sacraments, and (c) the community is rightly ordered.[5] It is not by accident that the very first thing mentioned in the creed after the three persons of the triune God is the holy catholic church, the universal body of Christ.

---

4. For a Pentecostal treatment of the role of the Holy Spirit, see Sylvia Lee, ed., *The Holy Spirit in Christian Education* (Springfield, MO: Gospel Publishing House, 1988).

5. While some Protestant theologians list anywhere from two to five marks of the church, most Wesleyan theologians agree with Thomas Oden's list of three. See Thomas C. Oden, *Classic Christianity: A Systematic Theology* (New York: HarperCollins, 1992), 717–19.

The Communion of Saints

The Spirit unites Christians of all races and languages around the world into one body of Christ. The Spirit creates a communion and fellowship of these disparate peoples that includes all those who have gone before and all those alive around the world today. "We are one in the bond of love." It is the Spirit who creates a caring compassionate church that teaches and reenacts the gospel and proclaims the forgiveness of sins by God's grace. Pastors and Christian educators cannot create a church; only the Spirit can do this work. However, where the church exists, it is a real gathering of believers in a concrete community. A person cannot claim to be in the church and be separated from a real community of believers. While not every person who gathers in a real assembly of believers may be a part of the body of Christ, all those who are in the body of Christ are a part of an actual assembly of believers. There are no solitary Christians.

The Forgiveness of Sins (Salvation, Sanctification)

The subsection of theology that focuses on a doctrine of sin is called *hamartiology*. What is sin? Is everything that falls short of absolute perfection sin? If so, then certainly a Christian must sin "every day in word thought and deed," for no one is absolutely perfect but God. Or when the Bible calls Christians to put away all sin, does it mean purposeful or premeditated willful disobedience to God? A Wesleyan hamartiology teaches that God's grace covers any lack of perfection in the Christian. It also teaches that God offers grace and power that is great enough to enable a Christian to love and obey God, and not commit purposeful and intentional sin. It may not be average Christianity, and it may at some times and in some places seem rare, but Wesleyan theology proclaims it is possible and should be urged for all Christians. This has been a special concern for churches in the Holiness Movement; however, it has been an ageless teaching of orthodox Christianity since the church fathers. The Christian educator's work is not just to educate people's minds so they know what is true and right; it is to disciple believers so they come to love God with all their hearts, souls, and minds, and love their neighbors as themselves. Christian educators are not just in the information business; they join God in a transformation business. The church cannot be satisfied with just teaching people to know what Christ has commanded. Christian education takes on Christ's commission to "teach them to do everything I have told you" (Matt 28:20).

In teaching on the forgiveness of sin, theologians often develop the doctrine of salvation, which is called *soteriology*. How can a person be saved? Will everyone be saved in the end, or are only some saved? How does salvation happen—in a moment or over time? Can one lose his or her salvation? How saved can a person be? These are the kind of questions to study in soteriology.

The beginning of the creeds states that the work of Christ is for "us and our salvation." Soteriology often starts from the bottom up, describing how a person seems to experience God's grace. This often results in a description or diagram called an *ordo salutis*—the order of salvation, which describes how this work seems to unfold. In a Wesleyan approach to soteriology, God is the primary player, though humans also play a role. Because of *the fall*, men and women cannot become righteous on their own. Humans are separated from God, and only God's grace can enable a person even to want to be saved. God has offered *prevenient grace*, which is "grace that goes before" that draws and enables humans to turn toward him. God has provided a way to *reconciliation*, through Jesus Christ. Through Christ's atoning death sins are forgiven. Humans can make peace with God and become a part of God's family. But the doctrine of salvation is about far more than forgiveness for sin; it is also about sanctification.

Wesleyans see the doctrine of *sanctification* as a subsection of soteriology. Many evangelicals today mistakenly think the doctrine of salvation is only about getting forgiven and receiving a ticket to heaven—being *justified*. Soteriology is not just about forgiveness or being born again (*regeneration*), but it also describes the transformation of a person into a Christlike individual. Thus, the doctrine of *full salvation* includes sanctification.

Sanctification is about transforming Christians into a people of God, not just giving out tickets to heaven. God's great plan of salvation is more than a label-switching operation—sticking a "saved" label on a formerly unsaved person. God's plan of salvation seeks to transform individuals so they become Christlike persons who are a part of a Christlike people, the holy church of God. Sanctification is for individuals, but it is also for the church, to make a holy people of God who lives as the body of Christ on earth. Christ did not call the church to go into all the world and make believers, but rather to make *disciples* of all nations (Matt 28:19). God intends actually to transform the thoughts, words, and deeds of his people so that they become like his only Son, Jesus Christ.

So, how does God plan to do this? How will he change people from what they are into an image of his only Son? God does this through the *means of grace*. The means of grace are the ordinary channels through which God mediates his grace and power. The means of grace include things like prayer, Scripture, the Lord's Supper, fasting, and so forth. Wesleyans do not see these things so much as disciplines or rungs of a ladder climbing up to holiness; that would only produce a works-righteousness resulting from self-discipline rather than through God's grace. The former might also make the person a proud Pharisee. Rather, the means of grace are channels through which God pours out his transforming grace to sanctify and change folks into a holy people. The primary means of grace are not solitary means but corporate—they are experienced in the church with other believers. God plans to turn a motley crew of human beings into an assembly of godly people who show to the world what Christlike living is in this present age.

Sanctification is a work of grace done in believers by God alone. Sanctification includes everything God does in us to make us more like Christ. It is God's work, not ours. Salvation (including sanctification) is a wholly owned work of God alone. A human's job is to put oneself under the influence of the means of grace so that God can change him—in a moment and over time—into an image of his Son, Jesus Christ. Through God's means of grace, he changes his people so that they "show the bright glory of the Lord, as the Lord's Spirit makes us more and more like our glorious Lord" (2 Cor 3:18). This is the romance of Christian education. It is joining the Holy Spirit in helping him to transform ordinary people into a holy people of God. It is lasting work. Virtually everything else passes away. Buildings crumble. Programs pass away. Denominations and organizations will all evaporate one day. Houses, cars, and motorcycles will all melt. Only the word of God and the souls of men and women will last forever. Christian education is joining with the Spirit to make a holy people of God who will abide with God in eternity forever and ever. What a wonderful life calling!

Resurrection of the Body and Life Everlasting

Theology begins before creation, with the eternal God, and moves through creation, the life, and work of Jesus Christ, and the person and work of the Holy Spirit; but it also looks to the future. The special study of future events in theology is called *eschatology*. Christian theology says life is moving somewhere. People are not circling around in an endless eddy of history with no end but are headed somewhere. When studying the person and work of Christ, Christian doctrine teaches that Christ is coming again to judge the living and the dead, so under that head is the *second coming* and *final judgment*. Near the end, the creeds confess belief in what happens in the end.

Christians believe that their bodies will be resurrected in the future, just like Jesus' body was. While some novice students wrongly believe, "When I die, my spirit goes to heaven and my body turns back to dust," that is not what orthodox Christian theology teaches. Christian theology teaches that everyone—Christians and unbelievers alike—will be resurrected to be judged (Rev 20:11–15). Christians have a high view of the body, so high that they teach that the body will some day be resurrected and in those bodies they will enter life everlasting. This is why Christian funerals (to the extent they are Christian) do not just talk about the departed as if they only live on in our memories. Christians believe in the resurrection because Christ himself was raised from the dead. Christian theology does not teach that Jesus' soul rose and floated around like a ghost for forty days. It teaches that Christ's actual body was missing from the grave and the resurrected body of Jesus had some continuity with the body of Christ before he was crucified. This raises all kinds of practical questions, but it has been orthodox Christian teaching for several thousand years and still is. The end of the story is not the grave but life everlasting. Christ's kingdom will be fully realized, and those who are a part of the family of God will live with God the Father, Son, and Holy Spirit forever and ever. Amen!

Conclusion

Christian educators study theology as they prepare for service in the church because theology provides the content of their teaching. A Christian educator who cares little about theology cares little about God and the gospel, for God and the gospel are the focus of theology. While the terms might seem mystifying at first, studying theology brings to the professional or volunteer Christian educator an understanding of what the entire business is all about and how it works. To understand the greatness of God and the person and work of the Father, Son, and Holy Spirit is to understand the primary content of the faith. If a Christian educator wishes to spend a life making disciples of God, then knowing God and his ways are critical to his or her work in the church.

CHAPTER THREE

The Role of the Bible in Christian Education

JERRY HICKSON

> Everything in the Scriptures is God's Word. All of it is useful for teaching and helping people and for correcting them and showing them how to live. The Scriptures train God's servants to do all kinds of good deeds.
>
> —2 Timothy 3:16–17

Wesleyans believe that the Bible is the Word of God and that Christian education is based on the revelation found there. This is a high view of the inspiration of the Bible. Christian education uses methods drawn from the social sciences, but at all times it is based on and is under the authority of the Bible. As Doug Pagitt describes it, the Bible is an "authoritative community member" rather than merely an historical document or storehouse of information.[1] "Our trust in the Bible does not depend on information that proves the Bible to be credible. We believe the Bible because our hopes, ideas, experiences, and community of faith allow and require us to believe."[2] While the Bible commands respect, care must be taken to avoid a form of idolatry.

---

1. Pagitt, *Reimagining Spiritual Formation*, 167–69.
2. Ibid., 168.

Some Christian statements of faith begin by affirming that the Bible is God's ultimate revelation of truth. Some Christian educators likewise begin with establishing the authority of the Bible and deducing other beliefs from this foundation. However, this route can lead to bibliolatry, the belief that Scripture is to be venerated or worshiped.[3] Wesleyans believe that a better starting place is the authoritative person of Jesus Christ.

Rather than building on a Bible that talks about Jesus, Wesleyan Christian education begins with the living Christ who is revealed in the Bible. In classic theological terms, "Christ is King and Lord of Scripture."[4] Christian art sometimes depicts Jesus holding out to us a Bible: a better image is an open Bible from which rises the form of Christ.[5]

> The ultimate, final authority is not Scripture but the living God himself as we find him in Jesus Christ. Jesus Christ and the message about him constitute the material norm for our faith just as the Bible is the formal norm. The Bible is authoritative because it points beyond itself to the absolute authority, the living and transcendent Word of God.[6]

Christian education must be profoundly biblical, but the focus is on Jesus Christ, not the Bible that reveals him to us.

As discussed in chapter 1, Wesleyans generally avoid using the concept of inerrancy to affirm the authority of Scripture. While arguments about inerrancy are common among Reformed traditions, including interdenominational groups like the National Association of Evangelicals and the Evangelical Theological Society, Holiness churches like the Church of the Nazarene and the Church of God (Anderson, Indiana) have defended the authority of Scripture in other ways.[7]

Those who hold the view of inerrancy claim that only the original manuscripts were faithful records of the inspiration of God. Since these manuscripts are not available, such an argument cannot be tested. More problematic is the implication that the Bible we have today is lacking in authority. If the authority of Scripture depends on its accuracy in every detail and if our current copies of the Bible have inaccuracies, then we cannot reliably base our Christian faith on the Bible. If we are to understand that the Bible is the Word of God, we need a

---

3. This practice is not entirely limited to Reformed traditions. The Articles of Faith for the Church of the Nazarene begins with the three persons of the Trinity before discussing Scripture (http://www.nazarene.org/ministries/administration/visitorcenter/beliefs/display.aspx). The Articles of Religion for The Wesleyan Church lead with a statement on the Bible (http://www.wesleyan.org/beliefs).

4. *Christus Rex et Dominus Scripturae* (Foster, *Streams of Living Water*, 231).

5. Foster, *Streams of Living Water*, 231.

6. Donald Bloesch, cited in Foster, *Streams of Living Water*, 231.

7. Dayton, "Battle for the Bible," 978.

concept of biblical inspiration that is more trustworthy than claims of inerrancy in the original manuscripts.[8]

Even more problematic is the other extreme viewpoint, which highlights the errors of the Bible. Donald Thorsen describes it this way:

> Some refer to this as an *errantist* view. To such people the Bible consists of a variety of legends, myths, and other types of oral traditions that were handed down to later generations who collected, edited, and preserved them in accordance with their contemporary questions and concerns…Of course, the extent of the Bible's errancy can be thought to extend far beyond matters of history, geography, and science. It may extend to spiritual and theological errors as well.[9]

Rather than asserting inerrancy theories (which tend toward mechanical inspiration) or errancy (which discounts the spiritual authority of the Bible), Wesleyans hold a more dynamic theory of inspiration. We believe that God inspired not the specific words of Scripture, or even the message itself, but the persons who wrote the Bible.[10] By virtue of their relationship with God, the Holy Spirit inspired their writings and gave them a unique authority. Over the years, the church has found these writings to be trustworthy. "The bulk of the Bible was given by God through men…the true theory must allow both the human and the divine element in the producing of the Bible."[11]

Thorsen well summarizes the orthodox Christian view of Scripture, which all Wesleyans would affirm: "Christians view Scripture as special revelation, inspired by God and authoritative with regard to matters of belief, value, and practice."[12]

Building on the Sure Foundation

More important than any theory of inspiration is our faithfulness in teaching the Bible. No other source provides an adequate authority or basis for Christian education. Teachers must continually strive to build their work on the truth of the Scriptures. Doctrinal systems, current events, and student interest have their place in lesson development, but only the Bible provides the authoritative basis for the teaching ministry of the church.

Christian education depends upon reliably "leading out" of Scripture what the Bible writers intended to say. (This process is called *exegesis*, from the Greek

---

8. Those who wish to study further on inerrancy or biblical inspiration should exercise discretion. Helpful resources include Dayton, "Battle for the Bible"; Rogers, *Biblical Authority*; and Rogers and McKim, *Authority and Interpretation of the Bible*.

9. Thorsen, *Exploration of Christian Theology*, 50–51.

10. This dynamic theory of inspiration is discussed in Stafford, *Theology for Disciples*, 47–49.

11. Byrum, "How Did God Inspire the Bible?," 4–5.

12. Thorsen, *Exploration of Christian Theology*, 41.

word meaning "to lead out.") Pastors and teachers must avoid the temptation to build lessons on their private agendas, "leading into" the Bible what they want it to say. (This process is called *eisegesis,* from the Greek word meaning "to lead in.") Educators must work diligently to let the Bible speak for itself rather than reading their own ideas into it. All scriptures that are used in a lesson must be interpreted in a manner that is faithful to their context (see chapter 13).

Some Christian educators seek to prove their points by citing a multitude of Scripture references. At times, this drifts into "proof-texting," citing verses that do not teach the desired point but simply use some term tangentially related to it. Better to develop a lesson with minimal mention of Scripture verses than to assert an idea and then embellish it with a series of Scripture verses that have little to do with it.

Two approaches to Scripture study are commonly used in Christian education. *Expository approaches* are usually based on a single passage of Scripture and draw their content from that text. *Topical approaches* begin with an idea or principle and then use more than one passage of Scripture to support it. These two approaches are significantly different in the way they use the Bible.

The best way to ensure biblical fidelity is to build a lesson around a single passage of Scripture. Expository methods may use additional passages of Scripture as cross-references, but the objective, framework, and content will be determined by the primary Scripture text. The lesson should offer relevant application to life issues, be age-appropriate, and use effective teaching methods. But the thrust and scope of the lesson is defined by the key passage of Scripture.

Topical approaches can be effective if careful exegesis is used. As we noted earlier, however, topical approaches to teaching the Bible are vulnerable to proof-texting and allow the teacher to neglect difficult topics. Topical approaches tend to highlight the Bible's relevance to life. On the other hand, topical approaches can produce lessons that are more relevant than biblical. If a topical approach is used, care should be taken to interpret carefully each scripture. The teacher should ensure that application being made is consistent with what that text says within its original context.

One trend among postmoderns is to emphasize reader response as a reliable method of interpretation, but Christian educators must be careful to preserve the original intent of Scripture. Discerning that intent is sometimes a challenge, but one dare not abandon all hope of objectivity. Reader response may well prove useful in small group study, where students are encouraged to draw personal implications from a passage under discussion. But in most circumstances, the educator is advised to steer a stricter course of exegesis.

Using the Bible responsibly includes fidelity to the entirety of the Scriptures. Christian educators must avoid leaning on one part of the Bible to the exclusion of the rest. This is often known as creating a "canon within a canon." The various writers and genres of the Bible are in tension at points, and biblical

Christian education must work within those tensions. Curriculum should be broad enough to cover Pauline and Johannine literature, Gospel and Torah. Individual lessons should refer to other parts of the Bible that support or contrast the message of the primary text.

While the primary goal is to effect life change in the learners, Christian educators should also attempt to instill basic biblical literacy. Learners are ill prepared to think theologically if they do not possess the basic data of the biblical narrative. Curricula must include the pivotal events of Bible history and the cultural context of those events.[13] Students should understand and appreciate the different types of literature found in the Bible. Faithful instruction in the biblical texts will require all of this.

A Word on Scripture Verse Markings

The Bible originally had no chapters and verses. Books were compiled as whole units, separate to themselves. As the canon was assembled, the Bible known today was developed. Centuries later, editorial work was done to assign chapter numbers and verse numbers to divide the books of the Bible into smaller units. Most modern translations render passages in paragraph form with little or no attention given to verse markings.

There is no sacred value to the numbers themselves or the spot where they are assigned. Sometimes, the location of these numbers interrupts the flow of thought of a passage. In these places, it is best to begin and end with the natural breaks in flow. As long as the contextual meaning of a verse is not violated, this is a more helpful practice than slavishly following the old verse divisions.

At times, the first word or phrase of a verse will be less than helpful to the core thought. In translating from one language (Greek and, especially, Hebrew) to English, certain constructions can be found that are not the norm in English. One example of these is the frequent use of conjunctive words, such as "therefore" and "and." Since these add little to the meaning of an isolated verse, these might be overlooked in lesson planning, especially when choosing memory verses.

Students of the Word

Those who aspire to be teachers of God's Word must themselves be students of it. The teacher's study of the Bible must go beyond merely scanning curriculum materials to prepare for the next lesson. Rather, teachers must be engaged in ongoing conversations with the Bible for their own spiritual enrichment.[14]

While Christian education looks to a higher authority than the Bible, it must at all times be faithful to God's Word. Bible knowledge is not the ultimate

---

13. Burge, "Greatest Story Never Read," 45–49.
14. See chapter 13 in this volume for help on developing a personal discipline of Bible study.

purpose of Christian education. But as we work to disciple learners, build their relationship with Jesus Christ, and transmit faithfully the Christian way of life, the Bible is a sure foundation for what we do.

Bibliography

Burge, Gary M. "The Greatest Story Never Read." *Christianity Today*, August 9, 1999, 45–50.

Byrum, R. R. "How Did God Inspire the Bible?" *Gospel Trumpet*, October 13, 1921.

Dayton, Donald W. "The Battle for the Bible: Renewing the Inerrancy Debate." *Christian Century*, November 10, 1976, 976–80.

Foster, Richard J. *Streams of Living Water*. San Francisco, CA: HarperSanFrancisco, 1998.

Pagitt, Doug. *Reimagining Spiritual Formation: A Week in the Life of an Experimental Church*. Grand Rapids, MI: Zondervan, 2003.

Rogers, Jack, ed. *Biblical Authority*. Waco, TX: Word, 1977.

Rogers, Jack B., and Donald K. McKim. *The Authority and Interpretation of the Bible*. San Francisco, CA: Harper & Row, 1979.

Stafford, Gilbert W. *Theology for Disciples*. Anderson, IN: Warner Press, 1996.

Thorsen, Donald. *An Exploration of Christian Theology*. Peabody, MA: Hendrickson Publishers, 2008.

CHAPTER FOUR

Jesus, the Master Teacher: Teaching That Transforms

LEON M. BLANCHETTE

> You will know the truth,
> and the truth will set you free.
>
> —John 8:32

There has been much discussion in many Christian education books about the validity of Jesus' serving as a model for teaching. Is it fair to set teachers up for potential failure by distinguishing Jesus as the perfect model to follow? One must ask if it is reasonable and realistic to expect others to teach as Jesus did. In an attempt to bring humor, as well as serious contemplation, to the conversation, Robert Branson, professor emeritus at Olivet Nazarene University and adjunct professor at Anderson University School of Theology, proposed the following top-ten list:

Top 10 Reasons Why Jesus Is Not a Good Example of a Master Teacher

10. His syllabus course demands were so difficult that most of his students dropped his class before it began.

9. His lessons were so difficult not even his closest followers understood.

8. His teaching techniques were not acceptable. He ridiculed his students and called them insulting names (e.g., "Get behind me, Satan.").

7. He talked over his students' heads. He intentionally misled them and hid his message.

6. When he gave his final exam, all of his students fled.

5. He was not a good role model. After all, he hung out with immoral people and associated with the outcasts of society.

4. He was a sexist. He didn't allow any women in his primary class.

3. He angered the assessment committee to the point that they wanted to kill him.

2. He refused to answer the questions of the accrediting body.

The number 1 reason why Jesus is not a good example of a good teacher: Most of his students died a horrible death because they believed what he said.[1]

While Branson's Top 10 list is meant to be humorous, he raises a legitimate concern about identifying Jesus as a model for teaching. Christian teachers do look at the behaviors, techniques, and philosophy that Jesus demonstrated through his teaching. Much of what Jesus did while living among humanity was to model how to live out one's relationship with God. That modeling included the way in which he taught. Branson makes this point clear when he says,

> Often Jesus is proclaimed as the "master teacher," or "perfect preacher," or the best in whatever field he is being used as an example. The logic flows from the idea that since he is God incarnate, he is perfect in every way. This is Docetism, which neglects Jesus' humanity. He is both fully God and fully human. Thus he is a good example as a teacher, but he was not totally successful in getting his ideas across; he was crucified. I think…that if Jesus was teaching in a modern university setting today, even in a Christian university, he would have been fired at the end of the first year. Some students would love him, others would detest taking a course from him, and his colleagues would be offended by his claims. In essence, I don't think that humanity… has changed that much since the first century.[2]

When identifying Jesus as a model for teaching, there are three areas that must be considered: why Jesus taught, how he taught, and what he taught. While much research and study have been conducted on what Jesus taught, the primary foci of this chapter are to give attention to why and how Jesus taught.

---

1. Robert D. Branson, private communication, November 6, 2003. Used by permission.
2. Robert D. Branson, e-mail message to author, February 12, 2010.

Why Jesus Taught

Before looking at how Jesus taught, it is imperative to understand his purpose for teaching. What were Jesus' motives for delivering his message to his students? Why would he spend so much of his short time in ministry to teach those who followed him? Jesus understood the power of teaching to transform lives. His primary purpose was not to deliver a new set of beliefs or to help his students acquire knowledge for the sake of intellectual achievement. His primary purpose was to transform the lives of his students. He knew that if they knew the truth, the truth would set them free (John 8:32).

It is significant that teaching became the avenue through which he chose to communicate truth. He could have chosen to write a list of dos and don'ts to be memorized and obeyed, and as long as one continued to be obedient to the rules, one's relationship with God would improve. Instead, he chose to teach through storytelling and other means that had a profound and personal impact on the lives of his students. He demonstrated that teaching had the power to change lives. The purpose of teaching has not changed. The goal of teachers must be to change the lives of students by communicating truth in a context of concern and interest in the student.

If Jesus stands as the model by which teaching strategies and successes are measured, then his focus on the student should also be primary in teaching today. It is not enough to teach students content. In particular, in Christian education, it must be the intention of teachers to make students the primary focus rather than the subject. In his DVD series *The 7 Laws of the Learner*, Bruce Wilkinson addresses this issue when he says, "I don't teach math; I teach students math."[3] The distinction here is one of focus. Is the focus on the subject or on the student? In every instance, Jesus' focus was on the student. Jesus valued every person with whom he came in contact. He knew that every person could be redeemed and reconciled to God. For this reason, he expressed his love for all persons who crossed his path by teaching them the truth that had the power to transform their lives. His love for his students did not allow him to let them stay where they were; rather, he challenged them to live more faithfully in their relationship with God.

It is also interesting to note that Jesus took upon himself the responsibility of making sure his students learned. He was unwilling to present the truth in a sterile, noncommitted manner and then allow his students to have a nonchalant attitude about the information. Jesus demonstrated that the teacher is responsible for doing everything within his or her power to help the student learn the information. The student has the option to accept or reject the truth, but it is the teacher's responsibility to help the student learn it. This means that the teacher must be creative and intentional about how the lesson is presented, and the

---

3. Bruce H. Wilkinson, *The 7 Laws of the Learner*, DVD. Atlanta, GA: Walk Thru the Bible Ministries, 1988.

true test of the effectiveness of the teacher is not whether the information was communicated, but rather whether the information was learned.

How Jesus Taught

The foundation for how Jesus taught can be found in his building of relationships with everyone with whom he came in contact. Everywhere Jesus went, whether in the fields, on a hill, or in the synagogue, at the grave of Lazarus, or at the well in Samaria, Jesus always built relationships with his students. Jesus understood that the most effective way to bring redemptive change to a life was through the establishing of relationships. This deep commitment to his students gave him the right to speak into their lives. Although the level and depth of relationship was different in each encounter, building relationships was essential to Jesus and his teaching.

As Jesus built relationships with his students, he recognized the need of the whole person. He refused to address the spiritual issues of a person's life without acknowledging the need of the whole person. There is more than one account in Scripture where Jesus addressed the physical and emotional needs before teaching the truth. His acknowledgement of the whole person as valuable, rather than as a problem to be conquered, is a demonstration that Jesus honored the *imago dei*, the image of God, in each person. Jesus' relationships with his students were holistic.

Methodology
Formal and Informal Teaching and Learning

Jesus' method of teaching is worthy of careful study. His methodology was closely linked to his compassion and love for his students. He allowed his students' circumstances to dictate the method he used to communicate a life-changing message. At times, the context called for a formal approach to teaching that led Jesus to preach the Word and call for obedience. Other times, his approach to teaching was much less formal and took place in the everyday moments of life. In the majority of teaching moments found in Scripture, Jesus chose informal methods of teaching as the most effective way of communicating deep truths to his students. These informal teaching methods included object lessons, parables, discussions over dinner, one-on-one conversations, and group interaction. Why is it that Jesus chose most of his teaching to occur as life was being lived?

When most people think about teaching, they automatically think of formal teaching; a classroom with tables, chairs, a lectern, a desk, a teacher who is the deliverer of knowledge, and students who are the recipients of that knowledge. The setting is controlled, and the curriculum is tightly organized. The weakness of this approach is that it is possible for the student to learn the data isolated from life experiences. The strengths of formal teaching are that specific outcomes can be identified, there is accountability for learned material, and a certain level of competence is achieved.[4] In addition, formal knowledge provides the foundation for future informal teaching. Formal education provides a good environment to learn important information, but it is a poor environment in which to learn information that leads to life-change. It is for this reason that Jesus chose to do most of his teaching in informal environments.

When people think about teaching, rarely do they consider what occurs in an informal environment. While formal teaching plays an important role in Christian education, informal teaching moments produce learning occasions that can lead to life-change. In their Taxonomy of Experiential Learning, Norman Steinaker and Robert Bell propose the following five levels of learning:

1. Exposure
2. Participation
3. Identification
4. Internalization
5. Dissemination[5]

In an attempt to simplify Steinaker and Bell's Taxonomy and make it applicable to Christian education, Perry Downs proposes the following revised stages:

Recall—I remember
Recall and Approval—I like
Recall and Speculation—I think
Recall and Application—I try
Recall and Adoption—I adopt[6]

These stages represent a movement from recalling information that has been learned without much understanding to understanding, application, and adoption into one's life. Downs notes that the deepest levels of learning, application and adoption, are best achieved through informal teaching.[7] This means that what typically takes place in the classroom, whether in school or church, can only achieve the lowest levels of learning unless intentional experiences are provided that allow for informal learning. Opportunities for informal teaching occur more often than opportunities for formal teaching, and these moments "allow the learner in varying degrees to participate to the extent that he can clarify,

---

4. Perry G. Downs, *Teaching for Spiritual Growth: An Introduction to Christian Education* (Grand Rapids: Zondervan Publishing House, 1994), 187.

5. Norman W. Steinaker and M. Robert Bell, *The Experiential Taxonomy: A New Approach to Teaching and Learning* (San Francisco: Academic Press, 1979), 3.

6. Downs, *Teaching for Spiritual Growth*, 38.

7. Ibid., 39.

assimilate and make meaningful, on the spot, the information and ideas being treated."[8] Informal learning is unstructured and focuses on learning through the experiences of life. The strength of informal learning is that it is mostly based on experience, which is also its weakness. There are times that one's experiences are wrong or incomplete, leading to inaccurate conclusions.[9]

Jesus' model and personal experience reinforces the idea that formal teaching is effective for teaching propositional truth, but when it comes to life-transformation, informal teaching is much more effective. Teaching as life is being lived is the most effective way to change a life. These teachable moments are significant, whether they are recognized as such or not. This truth can be seen when a child grows up and one day does or says something that looks and sounds just like her mother. What is done or said is exactly what she would do or say, and the realization of such can be terrifying. This frightening moment occurs because the information was learned without anyone formally teaching it, and yet as life is lived, a lesson has been learned.

Maybe it is time to re-evaluate the approach to education in the church. Most churches have chosen to follow a school model of education. Classrooms in many churches look like classrooms at local schools. If it is true that propositional truth is best communicated in a formal classroom environment, then the classrooms in our churches help to communicate the truths of Scripture that need to be learned. For this reason, formal education has a significant place and role in the educational life of the church. It is important to learn the stories of God's Word, and the classroom may be the best place for learning these stories. It must also be recognized that the purpose of the stories of the Bible is to teach students about God and how to live in relationship with him. It is not enough to know about God, students of the Word must know God. If nothing more is done than teaching the Bible story and attaching a moral lesson to the story, then a disservice has been done to the biblical text and to the student. Every story of the Bible has a truth to be learned and applied to life. Without application the story is no more than a story, perhaps another one of Aesop's fables. Here's the rub: application of the story rarely occurs in formal classroom settings. Application requires an opportunity to live out the truth in real life. Perhaps this explains, in part, why Jesus focused so much on informal teaching. He knew that this approach to teaching was effective in bringing about life-change.

Many scholars recognize that education in general, but specifically religious education, is best learned by the model of "walking in the shadow of parents who live out their teachings."[10] In a similar way that one's first language is learned not by deliberate teaching but through "surroundings, people, and

---

8. Lawrence O. Richards, *A Theology of Christian Education* (Grand Rapids: Zondervan, 1975), 237.

9. Downs, *Teaching for Spiritual Growth*, 188.

10. Donald Joy, "Why Reach and Teach Children?" in *Childhood Education in the Church*, ed. Robert E. Clark, Joanne Brubaker, and Roy B. Zuck, 6 (Chicago: Moody Press, 1986).

experiences," much of Christian education is learned through the everyday opportunities of experiencing life together as family.[11] If one had to choose between the formal approach to education provided through public and private schools and the informal education provided by parents as life is experienced, the schools would lose out every time.[12]

Parables

Among the many methodologies that Jesus used in his teaching was the use of parables. A parable is generally understood as an earthly story with a heavenly or spiritual meaning. Another way of understanding this is to recognize that a parable often takes an abstract thought and presents it in a concrete way. Jesus took concepts that were difficult to understand and process and presented them using common, everyday objects to make the truth understandable. There is an important technique to learn from Jesus at this point. Much of what is taught in Scripture can be difficult for many people to understand and comprehend, especially children and youth. Concepts such as love, salvation, sanctification, and grace can be very difficult concepts to process. Applying concrete examples and explanations to abstract concepts assists the student in learning the truth. An example of this can be found in a situation that occurs every Sunday in churches around the world when a salvation opportunity is offered to children. The standard phrasing includes "asking Jesus into your heart." For the average church going adult, this phrase makes total sense, but for the child whose world is very concrete the idea of asking Jesus into one's heart can be taken very literally. Understanding that the concept of salvation is an abstract thought and that children think in concrete terms provides an opportunity to use an alternative description or language for describing the process. An alternative way of describing salvation may include "asking Jesus to forgive your sin (of course, sin would need to be explained) and to come into your life and become your friend." These concepts resonate with children and make the experience meaningful and authentic to the child.

Following the Parable of the Sower, Jesus was asked by his disciples why he taught in parables (Matt 13:10). Jesus responded, "I use stories when I speak to them because when they look, they cannot see, and when they listen, they cannot hear or understand" (Matthew 13:13). Jesus, the master teacher, chose to confound those who were not truly interested in what he had to say. It seems that there were appropriate times not to make the truth clear; but for those who wanted to know, for those who had eyes to see, the truth was knowable, although not always easily. Jesus stretched his students to look a little closer and to dig a little deeper in order to find the truth.

---

11. Ted Ward, "The Teaching-Learning Process," in *Introducing Christian Education: Foundations for the Twenty-First Century*, ed. Michael Anthony, 121 (Grand Rapids: Baker Academic, 2001).

12. Donald Joy, "Why Reach and Teach Children?," 6.

This idea of stretching one's students and causing them to go further than they have gone before is consistent with a concept taught by Jean Piaget. Piaget, the father of cognitive development theory, proposed that learning takes place through the act of disequilibrium, an imbalance between what is known and newly acquired information, and a regaining of equilibration, a coming to conclusion about the newly acquired information.[13] When one encounters new information that seems at odds with previously understood information, the teeter-totter of knowledge tilts out of balance. This imbalance is so uncomfortable that one cannot continue without working through the information until balance occurs. One of three things must occur: (1) the new information is accepted and replaces previous information, (2) the new information is rejected, or (3) enough balance is found between the concepts that the person is willing to live with the conflict. Piaget proposes that this processing of imbalance is required for the advancement of knowledge. As the information is processed and resolution is achieved, equilibration occurs and so does learning.

As Jesus taught his students through parables, as well as through other methods, he constantly challenged them with new information. For those who "could not see" or "could not hear," the new information was rejected. For those who had "eyes to see" and "ears to hear," the new information was accepted and brought life-change. Parables have the power to work in the lives of people today in the same life-changing way.

Modeling

Telling people what to do is one form of teaching, but a more effective approach is showing them what to do. Recognizing the power of modeling, Jesus often showed his students how they were to live. According to the account in John 13, Jesus modeled for his disciples what it means to be a servant. The tradition at Passover was that the head of the family wash his hands in a basin as a symbol of purification before the Passover feast began. Instead of following this tradition, which would have been common knowledge among those in attendance, Jesus wrapped a towel around his waist, poured water into a basin, and began to wash his disciples' feet. Jesus said to them, "I have set the example, and you should do for each other exactly what I have done for you" (John 13:15). It is likely that the disciples never forgot what Jesus showed them.

In the *7 Laws of the Learner* video series, Wilkinson discusses the power of equipping through the use of modeling. Wilkinson gives an example of a mom teaching her daughter how to make a cake. He identifies five steps that are a part of this modeling process. The first step is to explain how to do it. At this point modeling has not occurred, only information has been transferred. The second step involves showing the child how to crack an egg and how to mix the

---

13. Rodger W. Bybee and Robert B. Sund, *Piaget for Educators*, 2nd ed. (Prospect Heights, IL: Waveland Press, 1990), 194.

ingredients; this is where the modeling begins. The third step involves the child and the parent performing the steps together with correction and encouragement along the way. The fourth step is allowing the child to do it herself as the mother watches. And finally, the child is able to do it by herself.[14] This process demonstrates the power of modeling. It is clear that the modeling approach requires an investment of time on the part of the mentor, but the benefits are significant.

It is no mistake that Jesus lived his life in such a way that if those who followed him were to live their lives as he did, they would be honoring the Father. Jesus not only told his students how to live, but he modeled it before them. Even when they would not listen or obey, he continued to model the way to live correctly. It's not surprising that after he left this earth to be with the Father, the disciples continued to live as he did with the leadership of the Holy Spirit. They may have forgotten some of the things he said, but they did not forget the things that he did.

Conversations

Throughout the Gospels, Jesus is found conversing with those whom he taught. It is through these conversations that Jesus built personal relationships with his students and by doing so was able to learn of their need and earn the right to speak into their lives. Among the many people with whom Jesus had conversations were the Samaritan woman, Nicodemus, Zacchaeus, and the rich young ruler. Jesus used conversations to share life with his students, and in the process, he dug deep into their souls. It could be said that the building of relationships was for the purpose of eventually meeting the needs of his students by sharing with them the truth that would set them free.

It seems that Jesus also recognized that as the teacher it was his responsibility to help his students learn. His attitude reflected that he did not believe his responsibility ended with the communication of information to his students. He saw it as his responsibility to help his students learn. As he conversed with his students, he provided ample opportunity for students to learn what he was teaching. Like the Samaritan woman he met at the well, the level of teaching deepened until the truth was finally understood. He never gave up on her, and he was unwilling to leave her with a misunderstanding of what he taught.

The art of teaching would be transformed today if teachers took on Jesus' attitude about teaching. No longer would there be boring lectures or teachers who are disconnected from their students with an attitude that says, "If they want to learn the material, it is up to them; my responsibility is to teach it." Instead, creative lessons would be taught that were designed to engage the student in learning. The many different learning styles would be acknowledged, and teachers would vary their teaching style. Students would be engaged with the

---

14 . Wilkinson, *7 Laws of the Learner.*

curriculum, and the classroom would become a place where true learning took place. No longer would learning be designed to assist students to pass a test with little concern for whether or not the information is absorbed. When teachers begin to recognize that building relationships with their students through engaging in conversations will have significant impact in student learning, and teachers begin to see their responsibility in helping their students to learn, education inside and outside the classroom will become an engaging and life-transforming experience for all involved.

Other Methods

Much of this chapter has focused on the importance of the methodology used by Jesus: formal and informal learning, parables, modeling, and conversations. Jesus was not limited to these forms of teaching alone. The truth is, the number of methods that Jesus used was only limited by the number of opportunities which he encountered. Jesus used symbols, questions and answers, miracles, and word pictures—whatever method was necessary to communicate the truth to his students.

Jesus is often found using symbols such as wine and bread, a coin, seed, and a pearl to teach deep truths that were otherwise difficult to understand. He also used a process that has become known today as the catechism. The word *catechism* means "a set of questions and answers about any subject."[15] Commonly, the catechism is a set of questions and answers that teach religious doctrine. Jesus often asked questions of his students which forced them to think through the concept and come up with more than the common "Sunday school" response. On many occasions, when Jesus was asked a question, he would respond with a question. It is clear that helping people struggle through a difficult concept and come to their own answer is a much more effective form of teaching than just giving the answer.

What Jesus Taught

While the method of teaching used by Jesus serves as a model for teaching, one cannot overlook the content of his teaching. Jesus never compromised the truth as he creatively taught his students. He wanted to be certain that his students knew the truth. Whenever questions were raised about something he did or said, especially when he was being challenged by the religious leaders, he constantly took his students back to the Word of God. He was often harsh with the religious leaders who should have known God's Word and often misunderstood it or neglected to live by it. Knowing the truth without applying the truth to life is not knowing the truth at all. Knowing the truth and living it is at the heart of what Jesus taught.

---

15. *Thorndike Barnhart Comprehensive Desk Dictionary*, s.v. "catechism."

When all was said and done, Jesus was most concerned that the truth he taught change the lives of his students. He was not consumed with the acquisition of knowledge for the sake of knowing. The purpose of his teaching was to allow the truth to change his students. When teachers put the needs of their students ahead of the acquisition of knowledge, their teaching will bring about life-change. When this occurs, then it can be said that they teach like Jesus, the Master Teacher.

Bibliography

Bybee, Rodger W., and Robert B. Sund. *Piaget for Educators*, 2nd ed. Prospect Heights, IL: Waveland Press, 1990.

Downs, Perry G. *Teaching for Spiritual Growth: An Introduction to Christian Education*. Grand Rapids, MI: Zondervan Publishing House, 1994.

Joy, Donald. "Why Reach and Teach Children?" In *Childhood Education in the Church*, edited by Robert E. Clark, Joanne Brubaker, and Roy B. Zuck, 3–22. Chicago: Moody Press, 1986.

Richards, Lawrence O. *A Theology of Christian Education*. Grand Rapids, MI: Zondervan, 1975.

Steinaker, Norman W., and M. Robert Bell. *The Experiential Taxonomy: A New Approach to Teaching and Learning*. San Francisco, CA: Academic Press, 1979.

Ward, Ted. "The Teaching-Learning Process." In *Introducing Christian Education: Foundations for the Twenty-First Century*, edited by Michael Anthony, 117–24. Grand Rapids, MI: Baker Academic, 2001.

Wilkinson, Bruce H. *The 7 Laws of the Learner*, DVD. Atlanta, GA: Walk Thru the Bible Ministries.

CHAPTER FIVE

Overview of the History of Christian Education

JOHN H. AUKERMAN

> Love the LORD your God with all your heart, soul, and strength. Memorize his laws and tell them to your children over and over again. Talk about them all the time, whether you're at home or walking along the road or going to bed at night, or getting up in the morning.
>
> Deuteronomy 6:5–7

Old Testament Roots of Christian Education

The deepest roots of Christian education reach all the way back to Abram and the covenant. Yahweh called this unknown man to leave his homeland and travel to a new home of undetermined location. He promised Abram that his offspring would be as numerous as the stars in the sky and that all the peoples of the earth would be blessed because of him.

This covenant was both national and personal—a sacred bond between the Hebrew nation and its God, and between each individual Hebrew person and God. Every descendant of Abraham had a lifelong obligation to God, to the family, and to the nation.[1] This obligation was communicated—taught—in the family. Perhaps they sat around a campfire, under a canopy of millions of

---

1. Gangel and Benson, *Christian Education*, 22.

twinkling stars, while parents told the story to their children, who would pass it on to their children, who in turn would tell their children: "My ancestor was homeless, an Aramean who went to live in Egypt. There were only a few in his family then, but they became great and powerful, a nation of many people" (Deut 26:5). Communicating the covenant was an informal process, never codified nor institutionalized. But it was very effective. It kept the story of God's covenant people alive through generation after generation, century after century.

Biblical scholars estimate that Abraham lived about 1,800 years before Christ (give or take a few centuries). By the time of Moses, ca. 1200 BC, Hebrew education had become formalized. The *Torah* (Law; Pentateuch; first five books of the Old Testament) meant far more to ancient Israel than the United States constitution means to Americans today. Few Americans, if any, can recite any major passage from the constitution, "but a Hebrew boy who scarcely walked heard and repeated the *Torah* until it was woven into the very fabric of his life."[2] The word *torah* itself "has the double meaning of both covenant and instruction,"[3] so it communicated a dual meaning to the Hebrew people—Yahweh's covenant with them *and* their instructional obligation. The heart of *Torah* was the Decalogue, the Ten Commandments (Ex 20:1–17), and after rehearsing it in Deuteronomy 5, Moses gave the *Shema* to the Hebrew nation:

> Listen, Israel! The LORD our God is the only true God! So love the LORD your God with all your heart, soul, and strength. Memorize his laws and tell them to your children over and over again. Talk about them all the time, whether you're at home or walking along the road or going to bed at night, or getting up in the morning. Write down copies and tie them to your wrists and foreheads to help you obey them. Write these laws on the door frames of your homes and on your town gates. (Deut 6:4-9)

Hebrew parents were to do three things: (1) love Yahweh, (2) memorize his law, and (3) tell their children. In the list of specific commands, Moses seems to have been telling parents to take advantage of every imaginable opportunity to talk to their children about Yahweh's laws. A key term in the Hebrew text of Deuteronomy 6 is *shanan*, which means to whet or sharpen. Parents were expected to whet the intellectual and spiritual appetites of their children, to sharpen their minds and souls, to be alert for "teachable moments so that instruction in the faith of Israel might be given."[4]

It was after Moses' death, during the time of Joshua, that the Hebrew nation first developed a philosophy of history, an attempt to explain why historical events unfolded as they did. Other peoples would attribute such events to natural

---

2. Ibid., 23.

3. Miller, *Story and Context*, 43.

4. Gangel, "Toward a Biblical Theology," 60.

disasters, beneficent or evil gods, political rulers, random chance, and so on. But the Hebrew people developed the philosophy that their God, Yahweh, was in control of all the events that took place in the whole world. This was the beginning of the teaching of *history as interpretation*, in which lists of names, dates, places and events are not as important as the meanings, the interpretation, of those names, dates, places, and events. This particular understanding of history arose during the time of Joshua, and the particular interpretation that Israel gave to history was religious in nature.

The next great movement in Hebrew education came during the monarchy (beginning ca. 1100 BC). Yahweh called and commissioned prophets to speak his word to the people and their leaders. The preaching and teaching of Isaiah, Micah, Amos, and the others brought a deepening of religious insight, an increase in fervor, a more intimate knowledge of God. The prophets proclaimed a high ethical standard, personal righteousness before Yahweh, and care for the poor, the sick, and the stranger. For the most part, however, their message fell on deaf ears.

During the exile (ca. 597–538 BC), the ministry of the prophets continued. However, a new teaching was introduced: that God comforts his people when they are hurting.

Following the return from captivity, during the fifth century BC, Israel developed its first formal schooling system, the synagogue. A synagogue was established at any location in which "ten adult Jewish men were present."[5] Beginning at the age of five years, boys learned the Hebrew alphabet and then memorized large portions of Scripture: "the Shema (Deut 6:4–9); the Hallel (Ps 113–118); the story of creation (Gen 1–5); the essence of Levitical law (Lev 1–8); and a personal text that began with the first letter of the child's name and ended with the last letter of his name."[6] The teachers were called rabbis, and they taught primarily by lecturing. Students memorized and recited the lessons. In the back-and-forth exchange between rabbi and student, something new in the history of education emerged: teaching through dialog.

Perhaps no other people group in human history incorporated education into life better than Israel did. The simple fact that Israel continues in existence today is testimony to the power of teaching. Parents told their nation's story to their children, who told their children, who told their children, ad infinitum. Israel's national identity has been maintained through wave after wave of foreign conquest: it has been fragmented, broken, beaten, exiled, humiliated, and was almost exterminated in the 1940s. But this one nation has always told its story to its children, and that powerfully effective act has been one of the forces that has kept Israel alive to this day. It would not be possible to calculate Christianity's debt to Hebrew education. The lessons learned from the Old

---

5. Bryan, *Relationship Learning*, 31.

6. Ibid., 31–32.

Testament, including its theological foundation, have shaped twenty-first-century Wesleyan Holiness churches in more ways than can be counted.

Jesus, the Master Teacher

Jesus established his ministry as one of teaching. To be sure, he also preached, but he was called "teacher" forty-five times in the New Testament.[7] Of himself, Jesus said, "You call me your teacher and Lord, and you should, because that is who I am" (John 13:13). His pattern was to teach groups of people—sometimes in a temple, sometimes in a synagogue, sometimes in a home, sometimes outdoors. He used methods such as stories, object lessons, and repetition; and he always gave a clear indication of the kind of response he expected from his learners. Of the 227 specific teaching situations in the four Gospels, 71 occurred in large groups and 156 involved small groups. (This might provide a clue about the relative value of teaching in large groups versus small groups and about why John Wesley's class meetings were so effective.)

Jesus made the most effective use of the small group in his training of leaders—the twelve apostles. He lived with them twenty-four hours a day for three full years as they traveled and ministered together. In effect, he established what many have called the first Christian camping program! The power of this kind of intensive teaching-learning is in its modeling of Kingdom living: Jesus lived the way he wanted his disciples to live, and almost all of them caught his lifestyle, values, attitudes, and theology. Numerous authors have analyzed Jesus' teaching techniques; the following list is compiled and adapted from the work of Georgiannna Summers.

1. **Jesus used what was at hand.** He used materials from the immediate environment. He used on-the-spot situations as illustrations of his points. He affirmed peoples' actions as examples. He looked people straight in the eye and used vivid, dramatic language. Examples: Mark 12:41–44; Luke 7:36–50.

2. **Jesus taught with stories.** He chose stories with which his audience could identify. He used action words. He involved his learners by asking pertinent questions. Examples: Matthew 25:1–13; Luke 14:16–24.

3. **Jesus used questions as a teaching technique.** He helped people recognize what they already knew. He added importance to a statement or idea. He encouraged his learners to think for themselves. He helped people to listen better and become more involved. He challenged and confronted people. Examples: Mark 11:27–33; Matthew 15:1–9.

4. **Jesus used scripture in his teaching.** He quoted scripture as his major authority. He often gave scripture a fresh interpretation. He showed

---

7. Ibid., 37.

scripture's relevance to daily living. He rephrased scripture for ease of remembering. He applied scripture to his own life. He turned to scripture as a personal resource for living. Examples: Mark 12:18–27; Mark 12:28–31.

5. **Jesus taught with authority.** He spoke out of his own experiences. He revealed his humanness. He shared his personal experience of God. He lived his words in action. Examples: Matthew 7:24-29; Matthew 4:1-11.

6. **Jesus called for commitment.** He issued a warm invitation. He asked direct questions. He shaped his call to the maturity level of his learners. He allowed people to say no. He explained the costs and rewards of discipleship. He gave specific assignments to his disciples and sent them out. Examples: John 8:2–11; John 21:15–17.

7. **Jesus was led by the Spirit and spent time in prayer.** He prayed for guidance in making decisions. He prayed for help in knowing what and how to teach. He reflected and evaluated experiences. He was renewed in prayer. He prayed as an example to his followers. Examples: Luke 5:12–16; Luke 6:12–13.

8. **Jesus learned about his audience.** He listened to their needs. He visited with them socially. He responded to their feelings. He learned about their ideas. Example: Matthew 8:5–13.[8]

Christian Education in the Early Centuries

The great educational need in the new Christian church was the re-education of converted Jews. Adults had been well-schooled in Hebrew theology, but they needed to learn the exciting new truths presented by the promised Messiah, Jesus of Nazareth. Therefore, early Christian education was mostly adult-centered, even though a few congregations provided teaching for children.[9]

One of the first theological needs of the young church was to define its beliefs. It accomplished this by formulating creeds, which were diligently taught to its members:

The Apostles' Creed (probably originated in the first century AD)

I believe in God, the Father almighty, creator of heaven and earth. I believe in Jesus Christ, God's only Son, our Lord, who was conceived by the Holy Spirit, born of the Virgin Mary, suffered under Pontius Pilate, was crucified, died, and was buried; he descended into hell. On the third day he rose again; he ascended into heaven, he is seated at the right hand of the Father, and he will come to judge the living and the dead. I believe in the Holy Spirit, the

---

8. Summers, *Teaching as Jesus Taught*. See also Horne, *Teaching Techniques of Jesus*.

9. Miller, *Story and Context*, 49.

holy catholic Church, the Communion of saints, the forgiveness of sins, the resurrection of the body, and the life everlasting. Amen.[10]

The Nicene Creed (AD 325, 381)

We believe in one God, the Father, the Almighty, maker of heaven and earth, of all that is, seen and unseen. We believe in one Lord, Jesus Christ, the only Son of God, eternally begotten of the Father, God from God, Light from Light, true God from true God, begotten, not made, of one Being with the Father; through him all things were made. For us and for our salvation he came down from heaven, was incarnate of the Holy Spirit and the Virgin Mary and became truly human. For our sake he was crucified under Pontius Pilate; he suffered death and was buried. On the third day he rose again in accordance with the Scriptures; he ascended into heaven and is seated at the right hand of the Father. He will come again in glory to judge the living and the dead, and his kingdom will have no end. We believe in the Holy Spirit, the Lord, the giver of life, who proceeds from the Father [and the Son], who with the Father and the Son is worshiped and glorified, who has spoken through the prophets. We believe in one holy catholic and apostolic Church. We acknowledge one baptism for the forgiveness of sins. We look for the resurrection of the dead, and the life of the world to come. Amen.[11]

These initial efforts to define beliefs morphed into a test of orthodoxy, and when Christianity became the official religion of the Roman Empire in AD 313, the creeds became law and forced the Christian faith into conformity with the nation-state. This continued until the Anabaptists insisted on the separation of church and state in the sixteenth century. And even though the United States is officially neutral with regard to religion, many Christians have difficulty separating their religious fervor from their patriotic love of country. Witness the presence of a nationalistic symbol, the American flag, prominently displayed in places of worship, Christian sanctuaries; also witness the proliferation of secular "worship" services on national holidays like Mother's Day, the Fourth of July, and Labor Day. (Perhaps Wesleyan Holiness churches would do well to rethink the symbols and activities they allow in sacred spaces).

By the fourth century, Christian education had assumed the form of preaching to catechumens.[12] A catechumen was someone who was learning the basics of Christian faith in preparation for baptism and church membership. The learn-

---

10. English Language Liturgical Consultation, "The Apostles' Creed." http://www.englishtexts. org/survey.html#theapostlescreed (accessed June 22, 2010).

11. English Language Liturgical Consultation, "The Nicene Creed." http://www.englishtexts. org/survey.html#thenicenecreed (accessed June 22, 2010).

12. Sawicki, *Gospel in History*, 112.

ing process was a strictly regimented three-year course of instruction culminating in a personally overwhelming experience, as described by Marianne Sawicki:

> Christian Initiation rituals had grown rather elaborate, even sensuous, and their power for effective communication can hardly be doubted. The men, women, and children who assembled on the day before Easter to be baptized had...several weeks of intense moral catechesis, prayer, and fasting. Their stomachs were empty as they prayed with the bishop and listened to scripture readings all night long. The bishop...blessed the icy cold running water in which they would be immersed. The men and the women separated and undressed completely...The bishop blessed two jars of oil: the oil of exorcism and the oil of thanksgiving. The first would be used as a kind of soap, and the second as a perfume.
>
> Each candidate for baptism was lathered with the exorcising oil, then went down into the water with a deacon. A presbyter standing by the water took hold of him or her, and three times asked the candidate to affirm belief: in God the Father, in God's Son, and in the Holy Spirit. After each affirming answer, the candidate's head was pushed under the water...
>
> The newly baptized Christians emerged from the cold water, dried off, and put on new white clothing...The neophytes were rubbed with the fragrant oil of thanksgiving...Then, for the first time, they celebrated the Eucharist together.
>
> The new Christians would have been told very little about the rituals... before they participated in them. Therefore the bishop's sermons at Easter, during Easter week, and for the Sundays until Pentecost were devoted to explaining the meaning and significance of these rites...
>
> During the centuries when Christians were persecuted and their meetings had to be kept secret, this kind of Christian Initiation promoted internal cohesion in the community and strong "horizontal" bonding...[13]

Perhaps new Christians in Wesleyan holiness churches of the twenty-first century would understand and appreciate the faith more deeply if their preparation and participation in baptism and Communion shared some commonalities with their fourth-century sisters and brothers.

As the centuries wore on toward the Middle Ages, the need arose for Christian apologists, scholars who defended the new Christian faith intellectually. They tried to convince nonbelievers of the truth of Christianity by a conscious union of Christian thought with secular philosophy. This was the beginning of a "scientific theology" held by many believers today: a cookbook approach to faith that teaches that if a Christian follows the right formula, then certain things will happen. An example would be a "scientific" approach to James

---

13. Ibid., 119–20.

5:14–15: "If you are sick, ask the church leaders to come and pray for you. Ask them to put olive oil on you in the name of the Lord. If you have faith when you pray for sick people, they will get well. The Lord will heal them, and if they have sinned, he will forgive them." To be sure, God heals the sick, but not always. A contemporary Christian with a black-and-white "scientific theology" is surely headed for spiritual difficulties.

Christian Education in the Middle Ages

This "period represents an all-time low for education in the Church, and the general neglect was reflected in the ignorance of the clergy."[14] With the advance of the so-called "barbarian invaders"[15] into Europe, Christianity was forced underground, resulting in the development of monasteries, where the faithful lived in relative peace and security. During these centuries, it was the monks who were chiefly responsible for maintaining the Christian faith. Education consisted of copying and recopying the Scriptures: students sat on hard wood benches in scriptoriums, from sunrise to sunset, writing one phrase of Scripture at a time as it was read aloud from the front of the room. "The monastic movement kept alive the unity of disciplined community, devotion, study, and work."[16] Because the common people could not read or write, the church relied on symbols, art, and drama to teach the tenets of the faith. However, the people knew so little Christian theology that they were "incapable of teaching their own children in the home."[17]

Gradually, the fame of certain monasteries spread, and students traveled hundreds of miles to study under a specific teacher. When the ancient Greek classics were rediscovered (e.g., Socrates, Plato, Aristotle, Euclid, Hippocrates), the European universities began to emerge. Eventually the liberal arts were recognized in two divisions: the *Trivium* (grammar, rhetoric, and logic) and the *Quadrivium* (arithmetic, geometry, music, and astronomy). The first doctoral degrees awarded were in law, medicine, and theology. Thus, the current American system of higher education traces its roots directly to the medieval universities that grew out of the teaching ministry of the church.

Renaissance and Reformation

In the thirteenth through the seventeenth centuries, humanism gained ascendancy. The fifth century BC teaching of Protagoras that "man is the measure of all things" had finally triumphed. Humanism is the philosophy that still dominates Western thinking today, and it is in direct contradiction with what Wesleyan Holiness churches believe about God, Christ, the Bible, the Christian

---

14. Smart, *Teaching Ministry of the Church*, 47.
15. Gangel and Benson, *Christian Education*, 106.
16. Miller, *Story and Context*, 49.
17. Smart, *Teaching Ministry of the Church*, 47.

life, discipleship, and holiness. It carries profound implications and challenges to every twenty-first-century Holiness preacher and teacher.

Partly as a reaction to the strong community orientation of the monasteries, this new era of humanistic thinking led the church to emphasize the direct relationship of the individual believer to God. Previous to this time, the concept of individual salvation was hardly mentioned (cf. the Philippian jailer in Acts 16, whose salvation was not individualistic but included his "whole house"). During the Renaissance and Reformation periods, churches wrote catechisms (lengthy catalogs of Christian doctrine) to ensure that every individual Christian held "proper" beliefs. Schools also were developed, primarily to teach literacy so common people could read the Bible (which had become available to them, thanks to Guttenberg's invention of movable type). The minister, who was typically the most highly educated person in the village, was the logical one to teach in these schools; therefore, the content of instruction was highly religious.

Christian Education in the Seventeenth and Eighteenth Centuries

The church remained the dominant force in the educational world as the Modern Era unfolded. Religion continued to be the primary course of study, and education was mostly for adults.

As the Industrial Revolution took shape, children in Europe were exploited as a free source of labor. "Many began at four or five years of age to work in the mines, the mills, and the brickyards."[18] They were forced to work six days a week, under harsh and inhumane conditions. For the children of England, their only day off—Sunday—became a day of freedom and delinquency as roaming gangs of vandals cruised the cities.

In 1780, Robert Raikes of Gloucester, England, protested the exploitation of children by starting the Sunday school. A social reformer, Raikes took children into his home on Sundays for eight hours of instruction. His curriculum was composed of the original "Three R's"—reading, 'riting, and religion. The schools grew: within four years there were two hundred fifty thousand students in Sunday schools. By 1785 the Sunday school had three major characteristics: strong lay leadership, a compassionate response to social evils, and a focus of study on the Bible. The sophisticates of society wanted nothing to do with Raikes's ruffians and delinquents. In the face of such stiff opposition from genteel society, the Sunday school remained a parachurch organization for more than thirty-five years.

In 1785, William Elliott established the first Sunday school in America on his plantation in Virginia, and by 1790 it had spread, attracting middle class children and a small number from the upper class. It was almost exclusively a lay movement: pastors in most denominations derided the Sunday school. However,

---

18. Henderson, *Model for Making Disciples*, 18.

parents discovered the convenience of having their children attend Sunday school while they themselves were in worship. Sunday schools moved gradually into churches as a result of middle class interest. Over time a particular school would become identified with a nearby congregation. Eventually the clergy recognized its potential as a growth force, and their attitude toward it began to change.

At about the same time, John Wesley had begun his efforts to reform the Church of England and introduced the now-famous class meetings. The emphasis was on discipleship, personal accountability, religious instruction, and evangelism. It was the one enthusiastic partner found by the Sunday schools. Wesley's evangelistic churches needed an educational system to carry their work forward, and they quickly incorporated the Sunday school. Those who looked with disfavor on the Sunday school also opposed the Wesleyan revival, and these two persecuted institutions became loyal partners in evangelizing England and America.[19]

Christian Education in the Nineteenth Century

The Sunday school continued to be led by laypeople, because most clergy outside of Wesleyan Methodism continued to view it with suspicion. It was, however, one of the few places where a woman could exercise public responsibility and leadership in nineteenth-century America. On another front, there were many important literary and musical developments in the United States in the 1800s, as Robert W. Lynn and Elliott Wright explain:

> In their prime, American reform movements sing…The Sunday school also sang. Knit together by common memories and even more by vivid expectations of a new future, the movement produced thousands of hymns and songs. The zeal captured in music and no less in stories, is both cause and result of the basic success of the Sunday school.
>
> The best known of all its songs came out of a novel published in 1860. *Say and Seal* was written by two sisters, Anna and Susan Warner, who managed to teach West Point cadets on Sundays as well as to produce best-sellers. Not surprisingly, the plot pivots around the doings of several persons involved in a Sunday school. A sweet girl named Faith Derrick is beloved by John Linden, a devoted Sabbath teacher. Among the scholars is little Johnny Fax…
>
> Central to the story of the triangle is young Johnny's declining health. Despite the ministrations of Miss Derrick and Linden, the boy seems destined to die. When Linden asks what he can do for the lad, Johnny holds up his bony arms to his teacher and says, "Walk—like last night." Linden picks up the feverish child and slowly walks back and forth and for a moment

---

19. Smart, *Teaching Ministry of the Church*, 50.

Johnny is quiet. Then he says, "Sing." Still rocking the frail creature in his arms, Linden begins a new song, one Johnny has not heard before. Faith hears every word clearly and distinctly:

Jesus loves me, this I know, For the Bible tells me so;
Little ones to him belong, They are weak but he is strong.

Jesus loves me—he who died, Heaven's gate to open wide;
He will wash away my sin, Let his little child come in.

Jesus loves me, loves me still, Though I'm very weak and ill;
From his shining throne on high, Come to watch me where I lie.

Jesus loves me, he will stay Close beside me all the way,
Then his little child will take Up to heaven for his dear sake.

A few minutes later...Linden turns to Faith and says, "We were permitted to show him the way at first, Faith, but he is showing it to us now." Johnny Fax dies.

The new song was set to music in 1861 by William B. Bradbury, who added the chorus, "Yes Jesus loves me...the Bible tells me so."[20]

It would not be possible to make an accurate assessment of the total impact of the Sunday school on American life and culture. Perhaps Lynn and Wright summarized it best when they wrote:

Succinctly put, the Sunday school is American Protestantism's training ground. Denominations have established hundreds of colleges and universities, but the Sunday school is the big school in matters religious for the Protestant people—originally and especially white people, though it has played a distinctive role in the religious experience and culture of black America. Compared to public education, Sunday school is marginal to American society, yet is an important little school in the rearing of the whole nation. The Sunday school is the big little school of the United States."[21]

In another important development, Christianity was once again at the forefront of educational innovation: the first graduate school in the United States was a seminary, opening its doors in 1808 in Andover, Massachusetts. Princeton Seminary was founded four years later. Princeton's curriculum consisted of the Bible in the first year of study, theology in the second year, and sacred rhetoric

20. Lynn and Wright, *Big Little School*, 68–70.
21. Ibid., 15–16.

(i.e., preaching) in the third year. This set the pattern for all seminaries' attitudes toward practical theology in general and Christian education in particular. Sadly, Christian education was not deemed important or relevant enough to be taught at the seminary level.

The nineteenth-century proliferation of seminaries repeated the Andover and Princeton neglect of Christian education. Most authorities tended to believe that Christian education might be studied by women and laypeople but certainly not by seminarians. Therefore, male seminary graduates wanted nothing to do with Christian education in general or the Sunday school in particular.

In spite of the seminaries' devaluing of Christian education, by 1800 the Sunday school in America had grown into a system of public day schools to teach literacy and religion to the nation's children (few Americans today know that the current public schools grew out of the Sunday school). Compulsory public education eventually became the law in all fifty states. Because the great American experiment included the separation of church and state—something new on the world political scene—and because people of all faiths are welcome in this country, religious instruction had to be dropped from the public school curriculum.

Catholics in America addressed the removal of religious instruction from public schools by creating parochial schools, which offered weekday instruction in literacy and religion. But Protestants allowed their children to attend the five-day-a-week public school and began teaching religion on Sundays for their members. As a result, the Sunday school was eventually incorporated into virtually every Protestant church in the United States.

Christian Education in the Twentieth Century

The Sunday school continued to grow and prosper during the first half of the twentieth century. In 1900, it had eight million students and one million teachers (the U.S. population was seventy-five million; so 12 percent of Americans were in Sunday school in 1900).

Early in the 1900s, William Rainey Harper was the major connecting link between Christian education and theological education. The founder and first president of the University of Chicago, he tended to blend theory and practice. He was a leader in systematic reflection on the pastor as educator, and his untimely death due to cancer in 1920 at the age of thirty set back the cause of Christian education in immeasurable ways.

The split between Christian education and academia renewed. Seminaries perceived Christian education as mere technique with no philosophical foundation and no substance. Only a small number of seminary professors attributed any validity to Christian education; it was conservative evangelicals who renewed and revitalized the teaching ministry of the church.

Sunday school reached its peak enrollment in 1969, with 40.4 million students, 19.9 percent of the population of the United States. Sunday school enrollment and attendance have been in steady decline ever since. Yet the Sunday school continued to have a powerful impact on many of those who participated. For example, when the United States faced its greatest constitutional crisis since the Civil War, vice president Gerald R. Ford was officially informed that Richard M. Nixon would probably resign the presidency and that he, Ford, would become president. Late that night, Ford and his wife Betty went to bed, and in his own words,

> We began to pray. "God, give us strength, give us wisdom, give us guidance as the possibility of a new life confronts us. We promise to do our very best, whatever may take place. You have sustained us in the past. We have faith in Your guiding hand in the difficult and challenging days ahead. In Jesus' name we pray."
>
> I concluded with a prayer from the fifth and sixth verses of chapter three of the Book of Proverbs: "Trust in the Lord with all thine heart, lean not on thine own understanding. In all thy ways acknowledge Him, and He shall direct thy paths."
>
> Fifty years before, I had learned that prayer as a child in Sunday school... It was something I said whenever a crisis arose.[22]

Even though Sunday school attendance is in a long-term decline, it continues to bear fruit for those who have participated in it.

In many ways, the twentieth century was a time of creating new ministries and formal organizations to promote Christian education. A few of the more notable educational ministries started in that century were the Religious Education Association (www.religiouseducation.net), Weekday Religious Education, vacation Bible school, Youth Fellowship, church camping, Youth for Christ (www.yfc.net), Young Life (www.younglife.org/us), youth ministry, children's ministry, Campus Crusade for Christ (www.campuscrusade.com), The LOGOS Ministry (www.thelogosministry.org), and the Navigators (www.navigators.org/us/).

Toward the end of the twentieth century, Christian educators paid new attention to adult education and senior adult ministry (e.g., www.sl50.org/), faith development across the life span (e.g., James Fowler, John Westerhoff, and others), and small groups. The real history of twentieth-century Christian education will not be written for many decades to come, but from this vantage point, it seems as if small-group ministries and age-level ministries might be taking the place that had been held by the Sunday school prior to the 1970s.

---

22. Ford, *Time to Heal*, 10.

Whither Christian Education?

The author of this chapter has no ability to see into the future, but it seems as if the twenty-first century ushered in a renewed emphasis on the Christian education of children. Children's ministry organizations, conferences, books, magazines, and training events have been proliferating for at least a decade, and it is at least possible that this century will create many exciting new ways to reach and disciple children, similar to the powerful work Robert Raikes did with them more than two hundred years ago.

It also seems as if a shift might be taking place within seminaries and Christian colleges. Generally speaking, there seem to be fewer professors of "Christian education" and more professors of "Christian formation" or "Christian ministries" or "specialized ministries." A 2010 search of the seven Wesleyan Holiness university and seminary Web sites represented by the writers of this textbook revealed that all of them listed professors of Christian ministry, church ministry, Christian formation, and so forth, but four of the seven were not using the term *Christian education*.[23] Perhaps this apparent trend toward newer terms may foreshadow a movement toward even newer forms of faith education for Christians in the current century.

---

23. No faculty with "Christian education" in their titles at Indiana Wesleyan University (Wesleyan Church), Southern Wesleyan University (Wesleyan Church), Warner Pacific College (Church of God), and Warner University (Church of God). Two professors of Christian education at Anderson University (Church of God) and Mount Vernon Nazarene University (Church of the Nazarene); and three at Olivet Nazarene University (Church of the Nazarene).

Bibliography

Bryan, C. Doug. *Relationship Learning: A Primer in Christian Education*. Nashville, TN: Broadman Press, 1990.

English Language Liturgical Consultation. http://www.englishtexts.org/survey.html (accessed June 22, 2010).

Ford, Gerald R. *A Time to Heal: The Autobiography of Gerald R. Ford*. New York: Harper and Row, 1979.

Gangel, Kenneth O. "Toward a Biblical Theology of Marriage and the Family." *Journal of Psychology and Theology* 5 (Winter 1977): 318–31.

Gangel, Kenneth O. and Warren S. Benson. *Christian Education: Its History and Philosophy*. Chicago: Moody Press, 1983.

Henderson, D. Michael. *A Model for Making Disciples: John Wesley's Class Meeting*. Nappanee, IN: Francis Asbury Press, 1997.

Horne, Herman Harrell. *Teaching Techniques of Jesus*. Grand Rapids, MI: Kregel Publications, 1971.

Lynn, Robert W. and Elliot Wright. *The Big Little School: 200 Years of the Sunday School*, 2nd ed. Birmingham, AL: Religious Education Press, 1980.

Miller, Donald E. *Story and Context: An Introduction to Christian Education*. Nashville, TN: Abingdon Press, 1987.

Sawicki, Marianne. *The Gospel in History: Portrait of a Teaching Church: The Origins of Christian Education*. New York: Paulist Press, 1988.

Smart, James D. *The Teaching Ministry of the Church: An Examination of the Basic Principles of Christian Education*. Philadelphia: The Westminster Press, 1954.

Summers, Georgianna. *Teaching as Jesus Taught*. Nashville, TN: Discipleship Resources, 1983.

CHAPTER SIX

Educational Philosophy

ROGER MCKENZIE

> My dear friends, you always obeyed when I was with you. Now that I am away, you should obey even more. So work with fear and trembling to discover what it really means to be saved. God is working in you to make you willing and able to obey him.
>
> —Philippians 2:12–13

Ted Ward got people's attention when he said that too often "Christian education is neither."[1] What is it about educational ministry that makes it both authentically Christian and appropriately formative so as to be genuinely educative? When it comes to approaches to education, there is no consensus on what ways are best. Though the following sounds like it could have come from a modern discussion of educational philosophy, Aristotle wrote it more than 2,300 years ago:

In modern times there are opposing views about the practice of education. There is no general agreement about what the young should learn either in relation to virtue or in relation to the best life; nor is it clear whether their education ought to be directed more towards the intellect than towards the character of the soul...And it is not certain whether training should be directed at things useful in life, or at those conducive to virtue, or at non-

---

1. Ward, "Facing Foundational Issues," 333.

essentials...And there is no agreement as to what in fact does tend towards virtue. Men do not all prize most highly the same virtue, so naturally they differ also about the proper training for it.[2]

The questions with which contemporary Christian educators are wrestling, though vitally important, are not new.

Why the Church Teaches

Clarifying why the church teaches is a vitally important first step toward a coherent educational ministry philosophy. The church teaches in response to Jesus' command in his great commission to "Go to the people of all nations and make them my disciples" (Matt 28:19). The goal of Christian education is mature discipleship in both the lives of believers and the church community. It is in the context of growing discipleship that persons develop the spiritual maturity to live faithfully and to make sense of their own life journeys. Only persons who are maturing as disciples can contribute significantly to the work of the church in transforming the world.

Jesus had an interesting and instructive conversation with a young man who thought that he had arrived at mature discipleship. When the rich young ruler asked Jesus about inheriting eternal life, Jesus described for him the requirements of the law. The rich young ruler claimed that he had kept all those commandments since he was a boy; it is interesting that Jesus did not dispute his claim. This young man had gone through the right steps, and it is likely that the religious community esteemed this young man for his religious practice. But deep inside, the young man must have known that there had to be more; maybe it was because of a growing awareness that his life was empty that he came to Jesus. Of course, when Jesus told him that there was, in fact, one more thing, "he went away gloomy and sad because he was very rich" (Mark 10:22). Jesus' message that he should go sell all that he had and give it to the poor and then come follow Jesus was more than he was willing to do. However, had such a young man shown up in most any contemporary church, he would have been esteemed for his moral lifestyle and, likely, put in a place of leadership even though his commitment to God was more façade than genuine.

Wesleyan theology rightly understands discipleship in terms of transformation; disciples must integrate faith into every area of their lives and express that faith through their lifestyles. The apostle Paul's description of maturing discipleship in Romans 12 involved a faith commitment expressed through sacrificial living; a level of commitment toward which the rich young ruler was not willing to strive. According to Paul, authentic Christian discipleship allows God, not only to change humans' statuses before him, but also to change people's thinking,

---

2. Aristotle, *Politics*, Vol. VIII:2.

thus allowing them to "know how to do everything that is good and pleasing to him" (Rom 12:2). In simplest terms, maturing disciples are becoming more like Jesus. Believers should express this quality of mature discipleship in their lives through practical holiness. Further, the attitudes and actions of God's gathered people as the church should reflect this maturing. For many people, the journey toward discipleship may begin before making a commitment to being a Christ follower; often in response to an invitation like Jesus gave to Andrew to "come and see" (John 1:39).

The Content of Christian Education

The Bible and the church's theology make up much of the content of Christian education. However, a Wesleyan approach to Christian education would be woefully incomplete if learning did not lead to a faith that is actively lived. Too often those assessing education have focused on what people know cognitively, often meaning what people can recite by rote memory. While some rote knowledge provides a base, it is inadequate as the goal. A much better appraisal of learning for Christian education is how people live, though it is admittedly much more difficult to measure. John Wesley's class meetings sought to hold disciples accountable for how they were living their faith. Influencing how people live requires an education that leads to transformation through the Holy Spirit.

There are five areas vital to helping people toward mature discipleship and transformed living. The first is Scripture. Wesleyans are people of the book. The Bible is central to the church's teaching ministry. Scripture provides both Christians and the church an important base of authority. The contents of Scripture are vital to maturing disciples, but disciples need to learn appropriate methods for studying and understanding Scripture.

Second is theology. Engaging in theological reflection is a natural response to careful study of the Bible. Therefore, helping people to think theologically is an important part of the church's educational ministry. Theological reflection leads to the third important area, tradition. Distinctives tend to emerge as people study Scripture and engage in theological reflection. In the late twentieth century, many churches drifted toward a generic kind of evangelicalism. But traditions matter and enrich the lives of disciples on their journeys. The distinctives of one group can enrich those in other groups as well. For example, the Holiness Movement has had a helpful influence on the larger Christian community than just those groups that would self identify as Holiness churches.

The fourth important area is lifestyle. The transformative work of God's presence through the Holy Spirit must be evidenced by believers' lifestyles. Mere agreement with a set of propositions is not an adequate faith response to the call to be followers of Christ. This Christian lifestyle is not lived in a vacuum, but in the fifth area, which is community. God adds those who are in Christ to his church. Living in community is part of how disciples learn, and Christians care one for another. In the context of community, disciples have the opportunity to become the persons that God intends that they be as they work to fulfill the kingdom mission in the world.

These five areas provide direction for shaping the content and culture of the church's teaching ministry. The next step is embracing a unifying philosophy for educational ministry that is capable of integrating the five areas as a foundation for transformative educational ministry practice.

Educational Philosophies

For centuries the church has both shaped and had its ministries influenced by educational philosophies. In fact, theories of education like progressivism, perennialism, essentialism, behaviorism, and educational humanism are foundational to understanding the variety of approaches to current Christian education practice.[3] Educational philosophies can seem quite complex, and sometimes they are. Yet these philosophies are really just means of organizing beliefs about how to understand and approach education. The components of an educational philosophy generally include the following: (1) the purposes for educating, (2) the nature of truth, (3) nature of learners, (4) perspective on the appropriate locus of authority in education, and (5) direction as to what constitutes appropriate approaches and methods. Too often the church has uncritically approached Christian education without operating out of an intentional philosophy of education.

Around the turn of the twentieth century, progressivism, according to George Kneller, "burst upon the educational scene with revolutionary force. It called for the replacement of time-honored practices by a new kind of education based on social change and the findings of behavioral sciences."[4] Progressivism challenged the time held traditions of the educational establishment regarding what to teach, how to teach, and the nature of learners. In response to progressivism, many other modern educational philosophies emerged. Because of the polarizing influence of progressivism, it makes sense to consider it first.

Progressivism

Progressivism is most closely associated with John Dewey, the influential educational philosopher of the late nineteenth and early twentieth centuries, though he was not the only early advocate of progressive ideas. Harold Burgess said, "John Dewey's philosophical doctrines and progressive proposals must be counted among the most significant of the factors which gave shape to the classical liberal model."[5] Progressivism challenged traditional educational

---

3. Knight, *Philosophy and Education*, 97–132.
4. Kneller, *Introduction to the Philosophy of Education*, 42.
5. Burgess, *Models of Religious Education*, 83.

practices in quite bold ways. According to Allan Ornstein and Daniel Levine, "Progressive teachers developed teaching styles and methods that emphasized students' own interests and needs. Their classrooms were flexible, permissive, and open-ended."[6]

One of the tenets of progressive education, according to George Knight, was the assumption "that children have a natural desire to learn and discover things about the world around them."[7] So, progressive educators shifted the locus of control away from teachers and administrators and more toward the learners. Choice was vitally important if meaningful learning were to occur. Michael J. Anthony and Warren S. Benson said, "To Dewey, human control of one's circumstances through the use of creative intelligence was a central focus of life"[8] and, therefore, was important in the learning process. With the focus on the child or learner, the role of teachers became capturing the interests and making those interests their beginning points as motivators for learning. In progressive approaches, the teacher functions more like an experienced travel guide rather than arbitrary director.[9]

Progressive educators hold that high levels of cooperation and democracy should characterize effective classrooms. Ornstein and Levine suggested, "For progressives children's readiness and interests and not predetermined subjects shape curriculum and instruction…They see teaching and learning as active, exciting, and ever changing processes."[10] The classroom was to remain connected to the culture and was to be a microcosm of the larger society.[11] Problem solving would be an important component of the curriculum. Therefore, according to Ornstein and Levine, progressive educators "generally condemned the following traditional school practices: (1) authoritarian teachers, (2) book-based instruction, (3) passive memorization of factual information, (4) the isolation of schools from society, and (5) using physical or psychological coercion to manage classrooms."[12]

Progressives challenged the view that education was merely the communication of the assembled truths articulated by previous generations. Dewey suggested knowledge "as modified action based on experience," according to Burgess.[13] Of course, one of the areas where this was most controversial in its application was in the church's teaching ministry.[14] Burgess outlined these

---

6. Ornstein and Levine, *Foundations of Education*.
7. Knight, *Philosophy and Education*, 100.
8. Anthony and Benson, *Exploring the History*, 331.
9. Knight, *Philosophy and Education*, 100–101.
10. Orenstein and Levine, *Foundations of Education*, 114.
11. Knight, *Philosophy and Education*, 101–2.
12. Orenstein and Levine, *Foundations of Education*, 114.
13. Burgess, *Models of Religious Education*, 83.
14. Ibid.

characteristics of progressive approaches to education, which also influenced the development of theological liberalism:

> (1) its willingness to give a considerable amount of self-directed freedom to individual learners; (2) its emphasis upon interest rather than punishment as the source of discipline; (3) its encouragement of overt, purposeful activity; (4) its focus upon growth factors in the child; (5) its classroom application of scientifically derived pedagogical principles; (6) its tailoring of instruction to different kinds and classes of children; and (7) its tendency to move beyond the classroom into the community—an attitude related to the progressive conviction that education is intrinsic to life itself, not merely a preparation for it.[15]

While problem solving was an important learning activity for Dewy, he did not advocate that learning would perpetually remain at that level, as did some of his followers. Kneller stated, "On the contrary, problem solving is a means by which the child is led from practical issues to the theoretical principles, from the concrete and sensory to the abstract and intellectual."[16]

Progressivism was influential as a philosophy, and it certainly did affect education practices. Yet progressivism remained more an innovative philosophy than a widely practiced coherent approach. Because of its revolutionary ideas, the responses to progressivism were numerous.

Perennialism

The focus of perennialism is on communicating the truths discovered and preserved by previous generations. Learners often encounter those truths through a curriculum based on great literature. Perennialism, as an educational approach, is a reaction against progressivism and other liberal approaches to education that emerged in the late nineteenth and early twentieth centuries; it reflected a desire to return to an emphasis on traditional approaches to education and the classic liberal arts. The philosophical rooting of perennialism is in neo-scholasticism, traditionalism, and neo-Thomism.[17] Knight stated, "The perennialists, therefore, advocate a return to the absolutes and focus on the time-honored ideas of human culture—those ideas that have proven their validity and usefulness by having withstood the tests of time."[18] Among the best-known advocates of perennialism were the University of Chicago's Robert Maynard Hutchinson and Mortimer J. Adler.

---

15. Ibid., 84.
16. Kneller, *Introduction to the Philosophy of Education*, 55.
17. Anthony and Benson, *Exploring the History*, 397.
18. Knight, *Philosophy and Education*, 108

Perennialists hold that truth is rational, revealed, and knowable and that by wrestling with the ideas presented in literary classics, students will become both more educated and increasingly moral as well. Perennialist education focuses on the traditional three Rs of reading, writing, and arithmetic. Along with the great books of the culture (particularly Western culture), perennialists emphasize writing in response to the ideas presented in literature and mathematics. Anthony and Benson stated that for perennialists, "Mathematics is held as a primary venue of instruction because it employs pure reasoning and is not influenced by the transcendent affairs of life."[19]

Vocational education is not a high value of perennialists. Instead, educators influenced by perennialism want to exercise and stretch students' intellect and, thereby, shape their minds. The teacher is the mediator and repository of the truth that he or she communicates to students, primarily by lecture. While other teaching methods may appear occasionally, perennialist teachers are committed to communicating the truth to students by very traditional educational methods. Lecture, rote memorization, and analysis of ideas by writing are valued teaching methods. In the perennialist classroom, there is little emphasis on democracy in learning as the teacher and other educational experts are much better suited to make educational choices than are students.

Christian educators influenced by perennialism will especially emphasize content. They will drill students regarding their denomination's customs, beliefs, and practices. At their best, perennialist educators consciously look backwards and recognize that they stand on the shoulders of church leaders who have gone before them. Generally, perennialist teachers are much more concerned with communicating the great truths of the past than they are with experimenting with new methodologies. Some who espouse perennialism are reluctant to acknowledge that the world has changed and claim this philosophy as validation for their "we've always done it this way" rationalizations.

Essentialism

Essentialism was another educational philosophy that arose in reaction to progressivism. Philosophically, essentialism grew from the merging of idealism and realism.[20] William C. Bagley may have been the first to articulate the essentialist approach. Bagley and other essentialist educators were concerned that progressive educational practices were too soft. Those advocating essentialism tended to believe that education had lost its way. Their remedy was to reincorporate more discipline into the classroom and return to a focus on the basics of education.[21]

---

19. Anthony and Benson, *Exploring the History*, 398

20. Ibid., 393.

21. Knight, *Philosophy and Education*, 113.

While essentialism and perennialism can appear similar, there are some significant differences. Essentialism lacked the focused philosophic base from which perennialism grew.[22] Kneller contrasted essentialism with perennialism this way:

> First, it [essentialism] advocates a less totally "intellectual" education, for it is concerned not so much with certain supposedly eternal truths as with the adjustment of the individual to his physical and social environment. Second, it is more willing to absorb the positive contributions that progressivism has made to educational methods. Finally, where perennialism reveres the great creative achievements of the past as timeless expressions of man's universal insights, essentialism uses them as sources of knowledge for dealing with problems of the present.[23]

Essentialism focuses on a classical curriculum and tends to treat learners as cognitive receptacles, vessels just waiting to be filled with knowledge. Lecture is the preferred teaching method, and essentialist teachers make use of few, if any, other methods. Classrooms of essentialist teachers tend to be very formal.[24] According to essentialist educators, "learning is hard work and requires discipline."[25] The learning task is so vitally important that it must be aggressively pursued within very clear parameters. Knight stated that for essentialists, "the school's first task is to teach basic knowledge...[and] the teacher is the locus of classroom authority."[26] Therefore, the teacher or administrators who know what is best for students will make curricular decisions rather than building on student interests. Those things deemed essential, that are "the tried-and-true heritage of skills, facts, and laws of knowledge acquisition," should constitute curriculum, according to Anthony and Benson.[27]

Warren Benson described the following as the central tenets of essentialist approaches to education:

1. Learning, by its very nature demands the discipline and diligence of the student.

2. The major initiative in the teaching/learning process is with the teacher.

3. The focus of the teaching/learning act is the acquiring of the stated curriculum by the student.

---

22. Ibid.

23. Kneller, *Introduction to the Philosophy of Education*, 60–61.

24. Anthony & Benson, *Exploring the History*, 395.

25. Knight, *Philosophy and Education*, 117.

26. Ibid., 116f.

27. Anthony and Benson, *Exploring the History*, 394–95.

4.   The teacher is to identify and employ the finest teaching methods which call for mental response and discipline of the child. The school must support the teacher in the endeavor.[28]

In the early part of the twenty-first century, according to Knight, "essentialism forms the main stream of popular education thought in most countries, including the United States. It is a conservative position and, as a result, is more concerned with the school's function of transmitting tested facts and truth than it is with innovation and educational frills."[29] Essentialism began to gain momentum in the United States with the Soviets' launching of Sputnik. During the Cold War, trailing enemies technologically created deep fears. This became a rallying point for essentialists with the perception that American students were behind.[30] Recently, the fear that American students are behind has fueled a fear that the United States would lose economically as other countries move ahead in technology. The early twenty-first-century focus on testing and educational accountability that is integral in the No Child Left Behind legislation illustrates essentialism on a nationwide scale. The underlying belief is that with more rigor and discipline (now typically described as "accountability" for kids, teachers, and administrators), students will be better educated and the country will be more successful. So, in the midst of great social upheavals, testing mandates have forced educators to focus on the transmission of content, at times, with little regard for the development of the whole learner.

Behaviorism

Behaviorism also arose in response to progressivism and is a powerful approach to shaping the lives and learning of students. Educators frequently employ behaviorist approaches because they are effective in bringing about desired outcomes. From the sticker reward chart in the schoolroom to the child who takes home the shiny bicycle for memorizing the most Scripture verses in vacation Bible school, behaviorist approaches are ubiquitous in schooling as well as in the children's ministries in churches.

Perry Downs described these reasons for the popularity of behaviorism:

First, it is highly "scientific," being guided by the rules of empirical inquiry. It yields nicely to statistical analysis and is easily reduced to hard data... Second, it provides a wonderful escape from responsibility. If it is true that human behavior is wholly determined by environment, then everything we do is a result of factors outside of ourselves and we can in no way be held responsible... Third, in many instances behaviorism works. For certain

28. Benson, "Essentialism," 258.

29. Knight, *Philosophy and Education*, 113.

30. Ibid., 114.

kinds of learning in which behaviors need to be acquired, behaviorism can be highly effective.[31]

Knight said, "Behaviorism is in one sense a psychological theory, but in another sense it has burst the bounds of traditional psychological concerns and has developed into a full-blown educational theory."[32] The roots of behaviorism are in the psychological works of theorists like B. F. Skinner, Ivan Pavlov, Edward Thorndike, and John Watson. These theorists alleged that controlling the environment of subjects allowed others to shape them in powerful ways. Skinner critiqued the traditional view that humans are self-directed and not products of their environments this way: "Autonomous man is a device used to explain what we cannot explain away in any other way. He has been constructed from our ignorance and as our understanding increases, the very stuff of which he is composed vanishes."[33] Knight identified these as foundational assumptions in behaviorism: "Human beings are highly developed animals who learn the same way that other animals learn...Education is a process of behavioral engineering...The teacher's role is to create an effective learning environment... Efficiency, economy, precision, and objectivity are central value considerations in education."[34]

Educational leaders in the church should be wary of uncritically adopting behaviorist methods. Behaviorism makes some assumptions that are incongruous with both Christian faith and sound educational practice. First, it is important to note that the word *educate* literally means "to lead out." Therefore, education at its best implies helping learners, created in the *imago dei*, to discover and live out their God-given potential. Behaviorist approaches do not maintain this level of dignity for humans. In response to objections that behaviorism tended to treat humans as animals, Skinner wrote, "'Animal is a pejorative term, but only because 'man' has been made spuriously honorific."[35] Skinner's words should cause concern for Christians considering behaviorism as their principal educational philosophy.

Second, behaviorism's use of rewards and punishment manipulates learners toward outcomes that are generally external to the learner. Education that is Christian should assist learners to develop their potential in cooperation with the Holy Spirit, who is at work in their lives. One of the measures of personal and spiritual maturity is the level to which learners become intrinsically motivated. Because behavioristic approaches view people primarily as being acted upon and

---

31. Downs, *Teaching for Spiritual Growth*, 72.
32. Knight, *Philosophy and Education*, 126.
33. Skinner, *Beyond Freedom and Dignity*, 200.
34. Knight, *Philosophy and Education*, 128–130.
35. Skinner, *Beyond Freedom and Dignity*, 201.

only responding to external stimuli, learners remain more passive than active and will not become intrinsically motivated.

Third, Perry Downs stated that behaviorism "assumes that the person doing the 'modifying' knows best how the other person should behave."[36] This assumption displaces both God and the learners from their rightful places in the formation of learners and puts teachers and educational technocrats in their place.

There are a few exceptional times in the lives of learners when behaviorist approaches may be appropriate. Utilizing behavior modification in interventions to influence persons away from destructive and anti-social behaviors makes sense in order to protect the learner and others. However, the use of behaviorist approaches should be reserved for those needed interventions.

Educational Humanism

Humanistic education, not to be confused with secular humanism, has built on the work of psychologists Abraham Maslow and Carl Rogers. Their work focused on the needs of persons and the ability of persons to make meaningful choices in their own best interests. Humanistic psychologies assert that humans continually mature. John Dettoni and James Wilhoit observed, "We view human beings as active participants in their own development rather than as persons who are merely unfolding according to a predetermined genetic pattern, or are merely living out the scripts imposed on them by a prior generation or contemporary society or are merely a bundle of conditioned reflexes."[37]

Humanistic psychologies appreciate people's genetic makeups, hopes, and desires. At the same time, educational humanism recognizes that people live in and interact with contexts that to some extent influence who they are becoming. William Yount stated, "Humanistic teaching methods focus on learner experiences, emotions, values, and choices, and are better suited to situations where appreciation of subjects is the primary goal."[38] The church's educational ministry is certainly a place where valuing the subject is imperative.

Anthony and Benson outlined these principles that define the approach of humanistic education: (1) a learning environment that is free from fear and manipulative methods, (2) teachers' relationships with students marked by trust and concern, (3) attention given to the affective domain of learning, (4) respect and dialog characterize interactions between teachers and learners, (5) a wide variety of instructional methodologies employed, and (6) instructional methodologies valued as a means of facilitating students' self-discovery.[39]

Developmentalism grows naturally from a humanistic understanding of learners. The works of Jean Piaget, Lawrence Kohlberg, and James Fowler,

---

36. Downs, *Teaching for Spiritual Growth*, 72.

37. Dettoni and Wilhoit, *Nurture That Is Christian*, 27–28.

38. Yount, *Created to Learn*, 238.

39. Anthony and Benson, *Exploring the History*, 175–76.

among many others, provide helpful insights into the internal structures that change over time and influence how people think and grow. According to Downs, "Developmentalism is an approach that is highly compatible with a Christian perspective and offers helpful insights for the educational ministry of the church.[40] For the Christian developmentalist, these structures are part of the way that God has created human beings. According to James Wilhoit, "The developmentalist seeks to help Christians gain a more useful knowledge of the faith and encourage them to work out an understanding of their beliefs that fits the world as they see it."[41]

Summing Up the Philosophies

There are certainly more philosophies of education than the few discussed here. However, beyond these, the differences are subtle and there is much overlapping, making it difficult to distinguish between them. Some have suggested postmodernism as an educational philosophy. While postmodernism has a strong influence on learners, especially related to how people understand truth, it lacks the coherence of an educational philosophy. John Wesley was involved in and wrote about education. However, he did not articulate an educational philosophy, and there was not anything particularly new in what he said about education. It seems that Wesley's childhood experiences with his mother, Susannah, had strongly influenced his views on education.

So, which of these educational philosophies is the right one? Which is the most Christian? Hardly any person, local church, or denomination will operate entirely within only one of these five educational philosophies. In fact, an examination of most any church's approach to education would likely reveal at least some elements of all these philosophies. The issue is not so much a matter of which approach is right, because there are elements of truth in all of them. The critical issue is which philosophy ought to be foundational in ministry for understanding people and helping them to become the mature disciples that God intends. At the heart of the Christian faith is the message of the gospel of Jesus Christ that one generation has been communicating to the next for two thousand years. Therefore, some have inferred that perennialism is the most appropriate. Others have suggested that essentialist approaches are most appropriate, based on the desire to communicate the gospel message efficiently to large numbers of people and get them to understand the content and respond affirmatively. And some are so passionately convinced that Christian teachers should do whatever they can to get everyone they can to pray the "sinner's prayer" that they have adopted behaviorist methods. Yet for a variety of reasons, each of these philosophies is inadequate.

---

40. Downs, *Teaching for Spiritual Growth*, 78; for an excellent description of developmental assumptions, see pp 73–78.

41. Wilhoit, *Christian Education*, 94.

	Progressivism	Perennialism	Essentialism	Behaviorism	Educational Humanism
What are the purposes for educating?	The classroom becomes a microcosm for democracy in the larger society	Communicate significant truths from past generations	Build foundations for vocational success	Train people for appropriate roles	Draw learners toward higher levels of thought based on life structures
What is the nature of truth?	Pragmatic	Discovered and passed from one generation to following generations	Not a central concern	Not a central concern	Knowable at increasingly deeper levels as learners develop
What is the nature of learners?	Active and inquisitive	Learn best by rote memory	Cognitive receptacles to be filled	Passive, to be acted upon	Full of potential based on human genetics
Where should the locus of authority be in education?	Learners, as they possess an innate desire to learn	Teachers and tradition are mediators of truth	Teachers and other educational authorities	Teachers as technicians shaping the environments	Learners and teachers working cooperatively
Which approaches and methods are appropriate given foundational beliefs?	Promote discovery by connecting to students' interests and problem solving	Lecture, reading, and writing in response to classic literature	Lecture and other methods that will help learners acquire basic knowledge	Conditioning learners by controlling environments through reward and punishment	Builds on relationships between teachers and learners to facilitate discovery through a wide variety of methods

Table 1. Educational Philosophies Compared

Because Christians (especially Wesleyans) hold to the dignity of humans and the God-given right of persons to determine their courses in life as they search for meaning, educational humanism informed by some elements of progressivism provides the most appropriate foundation for Christian education. Educational humanism best fits Christian understandings of people, provides the most insights regarding how people learn, and informs discipling practices for assisting people to shape their lives in response to the gospel of Jesus Christ.

What Constitutes Christian Education?

So what is it that makes education Christian? For too long church leaders have equated learning and discipleship with mastery of biblical content or their denomination's doctrine, as if just knowing was of ultimate importance. As a result, the church's teaching ministry has often focused on transmission (or dumping) of content and manipulating environments through behaviorist methods.

An approach to education is distinctively Christian if it has these characteristics: mature discipleship as the goal, Bible and church's teachings as important content, biblically and theologically informed view of persons, the Holy Spirit as teacher, and methods that are compatible with a high view of persons. In contemporary culture, mature discipleship will not emerge in the lives of believers if the church continues only to employ the tired approaches of the past. It is essential that educators create new approaches building on biblically informed views of persons and embrace methods that welcome the Holy Spirit as teacher.

Groome's Shared Praxis

Thomas Groome's shared praxis approach to teaching is an excellent example of a teaching style that helps learners integrate faith into their lives while drawing them toward mature discipleship. Groome describes praxis simply as "Learning from what we are doing or from what is going on in life around us."[42] Groome's approach builds on theologically and developmentally appropriate understandings of people and employs intentional processes to help them toward mature discipleship. According to Groome, "Shared praxis is really an attitude and style of teaching, which the teacher must develop and grow into from using it."[43] He outlined the shared praxis process this way, "Christian religious education by shared praxis can be described *as a group of Christians sharing in dialogue their critical reflection on present action in light of the Christian Story and its Vision toward the end of lived Christian faith.*[44]

---

42. Groome, "Using Praxis in Your Classroom," 20.

43. Groome, *Christian Religious Education*, 224.

44. Ibid., 184.

Groome's five steps of Christian education by shared praxis are these:

1. The participants are invited to name their own activity concerning the topic for attention (present action).
2. They are invited to reflect on why they do what they do, and what the likely or intended consequences of their actions are (critical reflection).
3. The educator makes present to the group the Christian community Story concerning the topic at hand and the faith response it invites (Story and Vision).
4. The participants are invited to appropriate the Story to their lives in a dialectic with their own stories (dialectic between Story and stories).
5. There is an opportunity to choose a personal faith response for the future (dialectic between Vision and visions). [45]

One of the most important characteristics of Groome's approach is that he intentionally involves learners in theological reflection on their lives. Groome stated, "Praxis invites people to learn from their own lives in the world; it is the conviction that people's own praxis is a present source of God's self-disclosure to them."[46] Praxis, says Groome, is not learning only from reflection; that would be theory. It is not just learning from action, which would be practice. It is the convergence of those two.[47] An important caveat for understanding and employing praxis is to move away from artificially separating theory and practice. Educators, according to Groome, need to view theory and practice as "twin movements of the same activity that are united dialectically."[48]

Groome has based his commitment to shared praxis on his belief that this approach is capable of promoting "knowing" in the biblical sense, that the connection between theory and practice is more likely to promote lives of integrity, and that it promotes emancipation and human freedom.[49] As the educator connects the group's reflection on life to the story of the gospel, the experience helps learners toward a more complete understanding both of the gospel and how to live their lives.

From Schooling to Discipling

Behaviorism, perennialism, and essentialism all suggest schooling approaches to educational ministry. The church has been eager to pick up on schooling approaches. One of the big innovations of the eighteenth century was the

---

45. Ibid., 207–8.
46. Groome, "Using Praxis in Your Classroom," 21.
47. Ibid., 20.
48. Groome, *Christian Religious Education*, 152.
49. Ibid., 177.

Sunday school. It is not that Sunday school was a bad idea. When it emerged, it was a very good idea and continued to be for a long time. Sunday school is by no means the only Christian education program built on the schooling model. At this point, the schooling approach has been tried again and again with the same results; it generally comes up short when it comes to life transformation.

Church leaders are often eager for the next program-in-a-box that is going to revolutionize their Christian educational ministry. The church is not so much in need of better programs and methods, though those may need improvement. The primary need is for a better foundation for educational ministries. What Groome and others have suggested is a kind of multidimensional educational model that has the potential to engage learners and teachers in processes that will be messy and inefficient. Yet in these relationships and in the journey together through the church's ministry, the Holy Spirit can work to transform people into maturing, world-changing disciples of Jesus Christ.

Becoming an effective church educator requires more than just methods. The church teaches to make disciples. Disciple-making through transforming lives requires that educators not only know the content of Christian education, but just as importantly, ministry leaders must create a culture that values and operates from a consistent and compatible philosophy of education in order to cooperate with the transforming work of the Holy Spirit toward the mission of the church in the world.

Bibliography

Anthony, Michael J. and Warren S. Benson. *Exploring the History and Philosophy of Christian Education: Principles for the 21st Century.* Grand Rapids, MI: Kregel, 2003.

Aristotle. *Politics,* Vol.VIII:2.

Benson, Warren. "Essentialism." In *Evangelical Dictionary of Christian Education,* edited by Michael Anthony, 257–59. Grand Rapids, MI: Baker Book House, 2001.

Burgess, Harold W. *Models of Religious Education: Theory and Practice in Historical and Contemporary Perspective,* rev. ed. Nappanee, IN: Evangel Publishing House, 2001.

Dettoni, John and James Wilhoit. *Nurture That Is Christian: Developmental Perspectives on Christian Education.* Grand Rapids, MI: BridgePoint Books, 1998.

Downs, Perry. *Teaching for Spiritual Growth: An Introduction to Christian Education.* Grand Rapids, MI: Zondervan, 1994.

Groome, Thomas H. *Christian Religious Education: Sharing Our Story and Vision.* San Francisco, CA: Harper and Row, 1980.

Groome, Thomas. "Using Praxis in Your Classroom." *YouthWorker,* Summer 1990.

Kneller, George F. *Introduction to the Philosophy of Education,* 2nd ed. New York: John Wiley and Sons, 1971.

Knight, George R. *Philosophy and Education: An Introduction in Christian Perspective,* 3rd ed. Berrien Springs, MI: Andrews University Press, 1998.

Ornstein, Allan C. and Daniel U. Levine. *Foundations of Education,* 9th ed. Boston: Houghton Mifflin, 2006.

Skinner, B. F. *Beyond Freedom and Dignity.* New York: Alfred A. Knopf, 1972.

Ward, Ted. "Facing Foundational Issues." In *Reader in Christian Education: Foundations and Basic Perspectives,* edited by Eugene Gibbs, 331–48. Grand Rapids: Baker, 1992.

Wilhoit, James. *Christian Education and the Search for Meaning,* 2nd ed. Grand Rapids, MI: Baker Books, 1991.

Yount, William R. *Created to Learn: A Christian Teacher's Introduction to Educational Psychology.* Nashville, TN: Broadman and Holman, 1996.

CHAPTER SEVEN

Premodern, Modern, and Postmodern Modes of Thinking and Being

DAWN MEADOWS

> And the Scriptures were written to teach and encourage us by giving us hope.
>
> —Romans 15:4

In his popular comic strip *Calvin and Hobbes*, cartoonist Bill Watterson often illustrated the complex relationship between the main character, school-age Calvin, and his father, referred to simply as Dad. In one particularly poignant Sunday morning strip, Watterson offered a departure from his typical style of illustrating this world and instead used a cubist, Picasso-esque style in the first few blocks of the day's story. The reader views the world through Calvin's eyes as he bemoans, "It all started when Calvin engaged his Dad in a minor debate! Soon Calvin could see both sides of the issue! Then poor Calvin began to see both sides of everything!" He continues, "The traditional single viewpoint has been abandoned!...The multiple views provide too much information!...Calvin quickly tries to eliminate all but one perspective!" The strip ends with Calvin's successfully regaining the view of the world that he is accustomed to and in his addressing his father saying, "You're still wrong, Dad."

In this particular strip, Watterson addresses an experience common to humanity. When exposed to a different way of viewing reality, there is a choice to be made about how to process the new perspective being offered. Some, like Calvin, will deny that the information exists, some will acknowledge the information and consider its implications, and still others will abandon all previous perceptions to accept the new outlook fully and live within its boundaries.

No matter the response to differing points of view, the reality remains: people do not always view the world around them as others do. It does not matter if there is distance determined by living on different streets, in different countries, or in different centuries, human autonomy allows for the ability to perceive reality as individuals. As the world has progressed through the years in self-awareness, cultural development and technology, the overall worldview of humanity has also developed and changed.

The term *worldview* is central to the content of this chapter. The term, of course, has nothing to do with a person's eyesight or with pictures of earth taken from space. Worldview has to do with a person's perception of reality. In this regard, James W. Sire offers a helpful definition of worldview:

> A world view is a commitment, a fundamental orientation of the heart, that can be expressed as a story or in a set of presuppositions (assumptions which may be true, partially true or false) which we hold (consciously or subconsciously, consistently or inconsistently) about the basic constitution of reality, and that provides the foundation on which we live and more and have our being."[1]

Every human being has a worldview. It comes from a lifetime of information gathered from influences, experiences, and teachings. As it is true that an individual has a worldview, so too does a people in any given period in history. In this respect, "worldview suggests how everything looks to a people, 'the designation of the existent as a whole.'"[2]

It is not surprising that the learning program of an average church would not think to consider the implications of the changing modes of thinking throughout history. It is admittedly a seemingly dry and academic topic; how a Peruvian farmer thought and learned five hundred years ago might seem to have little relevance to what happens in today's Sunday school classroom full of five-year-olds. How much frustration might be spared a church educator, paid or volunteer, if a clearer understanding of how learners think were part of his or her teaching toolbox? Part of the intent and hope of this chapter is to offer insight into the history of thought and to encourage the reader to consider the worldview of those in his or her care so that maximum learning can be achieved.

---

1. Sire, *Universe Next Door*, 17.
2. Redfield, *Primitive World*, 86.

Three broad divisions of the development of human thought are generally accepted: premodern, modern and postmodern. Each is characterized by a particular understanding of the world and how humans have interacted with it.

Premodernity is most readily identified as including all of human history up to around the sixteenth century AD. Within this expanse of time, many subdivisions have been made to reflect the rich and varied cultures found within it. However, for purposes of this chapter, a broader perspective of this division of human history will be taken as time before what is commonly defined as "modern." The ancient civilizations, such as Mesopotamia, Greece, Rome, Egypt, India, China, and Native America, were all premodern in thought and practice. During this time the Pyramids, the Great Wall of China, and the Parthenon were all constructed. Great strides in civilization were taken as thinkers considered religious and philosophic questions, military leaders conquered lands, and new continents were discovered and mapped. The texts of the most-followed religions of the world were authored during this time, including the Torah of the Jews, the Islamic Koran, and, of course, the Christian Bible. Yet, for all of its achievement during this period, the foundational worldview of humanity changed very little. There was no concept of a germ, a virus, a force called gravity, a standard measurement for time, or a solar system. For premodern humans, what was seen in the world was all that there was, and the basic understanding about any given object was accepted by people as truth. This was a world of myth, magic, and cult. Social scientist Earl Babbie offers this explanation:

> No cavemom said to her cavekid, "Our tribe makes an assumption that evil spirits reside in the Old Twisted Tree." No, she said, "STAY OUT OF THAT TREE OR YOU'LL TURN INTO A TOAD!" As humans evolved and became aware of their diversity, they came to recognize that others did not always share their views of things. Thus, they may have discovered that another tribe didn't buy the wicked tree thing; in fact, the second tribe felt the spirits in the tree were holy and beneficial. The discovery of this diversity led members of the first tribe to conclude that "some tribes I could name are pretty stupid."[3]

This premodern perspective was shared by the Israelites as they developed an understanding of the personal being whom they worshiped, known to them as "I AM," a process that is recorded in Old Testament scripture. The linguistic style, structure of writing, and imagery used in the Hebrew Scripture reflects the cultural worldview of its people. And yet, as Redfield emphasizes, "the radical achievement of the Hebrews in putting God entirely outside of the physical universe and attaching all value to God is recognized as an immense and unique

---

3. Babbie, *Practice of Social Research*, 21.

achievement."[4] While other cultures held to a worldview that was trapped inside the understanding of the known world, the Hebrews understood that Yahweh existed independently of their reality and had broken into it to make himself known.[5]

And it was also into the premodern world that the Christian church was born. The illnesses that Jesus cured were not understood the way they would be today. When Paul was celebrated as a god in Lystra, it was not a surprise or a stretch considering the pantheon of gods already being worshiped by his hearers. As the centuries passed and the church spread throughout the known world and came into influence and power, a sense of tradition developed that served as a foundation of the faith. The questions addressed by the early church fathers had found answers that believers put trust in, and since so few could actually read Scripture due to the high rate of illiteracy and lack of large numbers of copies, church tradition offered a consistency of thought and practice that changed little for many centuries.

During the early years of the Christian Church, people learned about and understood the world largely in a religious context. By the Middle Ages, Europe had established itself as the center of the Western church, practiced as Roman Catholicism. Within this culture, two sources of education found support and favor:

> Scholars in urban universities, beginning from traditionally authoritative texts, interpreted them using techniques of rational argument, with the aim of greater knowledge. Monks and nuns in the mostly rural monasteries and convents relied on slow, repetitive, devotional rumination over Bible passages—a process called *lectio divina*, or 'divine reading'—to purify the soul and draw the reader into deeper spirituality. These different attitudes toward education shared a fundamental confidence that what was needed for both knowledge and virtue could be found in the resources of tradition.[6]

Rather than simply a long-held habit, "tradition in this sense of the term, offers some clear advantage to human inquiry. By accepting what everybody knows, you are spared the overwhelming task of starting from scratch...We often speak of 'standing on the shoulders of giants,' that is, of previous generations,"[7] and it was on the shoulders of the church fathers that believers stood without need to question why they believed as they did. However, as the medieval age began to wane, the days of premodern acceptance of tradition gave way to a

---

4. Redfield, *Primitive World*, 102.

5. The practice of good biblical studies at an academic level can help in the understanding of the world from which Hebrew and Christian Scripture developed. Placing modern perspective onto these premodern works is dangerous for understanding the intent of Scripture.

6. White, *Postmodernism 101*, 25.

7. Babbie, *Practice of Social Research*, 19.

new way of thinking and learning that would usher in a time of rapid change that would impact the entire world.

Crane Brinton writes, *"Modern* derives from a late Latin adverb meaning *just now*, and in English is found in its current sense, contrasted with *ancient*, as early as the 16th century."[8] There is no one event or date that marks the transition from premodernity to the modern period; the shift was instead initiated by a series of occurrences, not all related, that offered a completely new worldview based largely on the human capacity to reason. Sociologist Immanuel Wallerstein, however, offers an historical comparative perspective on the meaning of *modern*:

> Some 50 years ago, "modern" had two clear connotations. One was positive and forward-looking...The term was situated in a conceptual framework of the presumed endlessness of technological progress, and therefore of constant innovation...[There was] a second major connotation to the concept of modern, one that was more oppositional than affirmative. To be modern signified to be anti-medieval, in the antinomy in which the concept "medieval" incarnated narrow-mindedness, dogmatism, and above all constraints on authority...but it was not a triumph of humanity over nature; it was rather a triumph of humanity over itself.[9]

By the mid-sixteenth century, the tradition of the Christian church had been tainted by unethical practices discovered among its leaders. Warring popes, swindling bishops, and immoral priests had begun to draw fire for their actions. With the hope for a refocus on the purity and purpose of the church, a young monk named Martin Luther became the reluctant instigator and leader of what is now known as the Protestant Reformation. What began as a questioning of the authority and governance of the church developed into a movement of also questioning the authoritative sources of long-held church tradition. The invention of the printing press put the Holy Bible into the hands of the average person, allowing for personal study, reflection and interpretation. Questions could be asked about why any particular teaching was offered. The claims of Nicolas Copernicus and Galileo Galilei challenged the long-standing view (staunchly defended by the Christian church) that the earth was the center of the universe with the idea that the sun instead was the central body around which others orbited.[10] These events, along with many others, initiated the movement toward a modern view of reality, which invited questioning and observation and became the seedbed of scientific study. The unquestioning trust in tradition, particularly religious tradition, which had been the foundation for the thought and func-

---

8. Brinton, *Shaping of Modern Thought*, 22.

9. Wallerstein, "End to What Modernity?," 471–88.

10. White, *Postmodernism 101*, 29.

tion of the Western world, gave way to the possibilities that science and reason could offer.

In these years, invention and progress became the motivating factor for human development. Mary E. Lee addresses the shift in thinking toward the potential for a better world: "The characterization of the Modern era is rooted in Western society's widespread adoption of this concept of social progress as arising from advances in human knowledge and reason."[11] The study of science blossomed out of the religious idea that God the creator had given humans minds that could think, consider, discover, invent, and problem-solve. Difficulties that had plagued humanity, such as disease, injustice, social unrest, and war, could be addressed and possibly solved through the active pursuit of discovery.

A new height was reached by this new worldview with the arrival of a period known simply as the Enlightenment. Eighteenth-century Europe became the center for the fine-tuning of the significance of the shift toward modern thinking. The premodern form of learning through university-style scholarship transformed into a culture that embraced critical thought, experimentation, and the sharing of ideas in societies of learning that focused on the discovery of natural law rather than the memorization of the traditional church teaching.[12] The fundamental idea of this movement was to free the human mind from "religious dogma, superstition, and over-adherence to historical precedent and irrelevant tradition that the way to escape from this, to move forward, was to seek for true knowledge in every sphere of life, to establish the truth and build on it."[13] As a more educated society developed, the masses had opportunity to share and participate in the discussion of ideas. The basic right to an education was born out of the desire for the forward progress of humanity and the belief that each individual can contribute toward it. The value of learning came from the transference of knowledge gained through study and discovery; a human could "know" because something had been "proven."

The Enlightenment also brought to the forefront the challenge of addressing the relationship between faith and science—a crisis of faith for some, a point of dissention for others. The ultimate stance of the proponent for naturalism, a view firmly planted in Enlightenment thought, leaves no room for miracle or the interaction between humanity and deity. Orthodox Christian doctrine holds firmly to the reality of a personal, Creator-God working among his creation and interacting with it.

Albert Outler points out that John Wesley, one of the great Christian theologians to have lived and taught during the Enlightenment era, was forced to face head on the issue of reaching out to an increasingly secular society. Outler likens Wesley to the first Christian theologian, Origen, who spoke of "plun-

---

11. Lee, "Modernity and Progress," 2.

12. Kaufman and Slettedahl Macpherson, *Britain and the Americas*, s.v. "Enlightenment."

13. *Bloomsbury Guide to Human Thought*, s.v. "Enlightenment."

dering the Egyptians" when thinking on the Old Testament account of the Israelites' release from their captors. "'Plundering the Egyptians,' he explained, is a metaphor pointing to the freedom that Christians have (by divine allowance) to explore, appraise, and appropriate all the insights and resources of any and all secular culture."[14]

In other words, Wesley led the way in encouraging those of the Christian faith to explore and consider all the wealth of knowledge made available to them. Wesley valued the opportunity to read, to study, to converse, and so to engage the secular culture rather than turning from it. Outler continues, Wesley's "preaching and teaching offered both the gospel *and* a liberal education, as an integrated experience to the common people who heard him gladly."[15]

Technology and industry fueled the continuation of modern thought throughout the nineteenth and twentieth centuries. Yet for all of its enthusiasm and optimism, the modern age seemed to revisit the very issues it desired to leave behind. The hope for an end to war came to a discouraging halt as governments continued to wrestle for power, most notably in the fighting of two world wars. The technology and industry that made life easier also dislocated families as extended members chose or were forced to move to find work and income. Many diseases were found to be preventable, but others eluded the ability of science and research for finding cures. The world that had once seemed to be on the road toward a utopian existence did not seem to be getting any better at all, and confidence in the human ability to usher in true progress began to fade.

This disillusionment led to the rise of what is referred to as *postmodernity*, an era that found its beginnings in the 1950s and is still in its infancy. It is a worldview strongly characterized by its reaction against the modern perspective of reality, as more emphasis is placed on personal experience. Postmodern thought "involves a radical questioning of the grounds upon which knowledge claims are made."[16] Where modernity had offered an assurance that truth could be known, postmodernity suggests that nothing can be known with certainty. Take for instance the study of the history of the United States, which has undergone significant changes in recent years. Thomas Jefferson was studied in public schools for decades as the author of the Declaration of Independence, third president of the United States, inventor, farmer, and architect. Research, styled after the modern ethos, has found that Jefferson also owned slaves and fathered numerous children through affairs with a servant girl. Postmodern thinking takes such a dissonance between what students are taught to know and what actually is as reason for mistrust and skepticism. While some may praise Thomas Jefferson for his statesmanship and service to country, others criticize his seem-

---

14. Outler, *Theology in the Wesleyan Spirit*, 4.

15. Ibid., 6.

16. Barsky, *Encyclopedia of Postmodernism*, s.v. "postmodernity."

ingly inconsistent lifestyle. Earl Babbie tackles this dilemma within the specific area of social science:

> The postmodern view represents a critical dilemma for scientists. While their task is to observe and understand what is "really" happening, they are all human and, as such bring along personal orientations that will color what they observe and how they explain it. There is ultimately no way people can totally step outside their humanness to see and understand the world as it "really" is.
>
> Whereas the modern view acknowledges the inevitability of human subjectivity, the postmodern view suggests there is actually no "objective" reality to be observed in the first place. There are only our several subjective views.[17]

There is a popular illustration that makes the point more profoundly:

The premodern umpire says, "I call 'em as they are!"
The modern umpire says, "I call 'em as I see 'em!"
The postmodern umpire says, "They ain't nothin' 'til I call 'em!"

This simple illustration based on a widely understood situation within baseball helps to clarify the progression of thought toward postmodern. The premodern thinker views the world, makes conclusions about it, and understands it as it is. The modern thinker examines the world, studies its make-up, and bases understanding on knowledge gained through reasoned consideration. The postmodern thinker experiences the world, allows for multiple and disparate experiences among humans, and accepts that nothing actual may ever be known about anything.

The impact on learning brought on by the shift to acknowledging postmodern thought is substantial. In an effort to affirm the unique learning experience of the individual, the acknowledgement of each person's learning style is encouraged. In a family with three children, each may best receive and integrate information differently; either as an auditory, a visual, or a kinesthetic learner. "Rather than hierarchical relationships, contemporary schools tend toward egalitarianism and collaborations in which teachers and students alike voice their input in small group settings."[18] The premodern and modern idea of an expert who delivers knowledge to a student is set aside for a group dynamic in which everyone plays a part in imparting information. David Elkind explains:

---

17. Babbie, *Practice of Social Research*, 25.
18. Vejar, "Social Institutions in Postmodern Society," 1–9.

Like modernism, postmodernism is largely a Western phenomenon. And, as happened with the rise of modernism, the rise of postmodernism is occurring not all at once but at different times, in different places, and in a variety of social institutions. Nonetheless, it has its own basic model and correlated themes. Modernity celebrated reason and paid homage to the ideal of liberty and freedom for all individuals. Postmodernism venerates language, rather than thought, and honors human diversity as much as it does human individuality.[19]

Postmodern thought has not yet reached maturity. It is not easily defined, and it is difficult to assign a structure to its processes. However, the impact of postmodern thought is readily felt in all areas of life. For decades to come, social structures, global economies, governmental systems, and religious institutions will all be working through the ramifications of leading a global community whose worldview is in flux.

There is one thing that the three views of reality discussed in this chapter have in common. Premodern, modern, and postmodern thought all find foundation in wrestling with the basic question, What is truth? The study of Christian theology also considers truth and its basis.

Wesley balanced his work on an informal underpinning that was later formalized by Outler and titled the Wesleyan Quadrilateral. He noted that Wesley emphasized four elements used by believers in considering the revelation of God as truth: Scripture, tradition, reason, and experience. In the words of Don Thorsen, "Although Christians make decisions in a variety of ways, the Wesleyan quadrilateral represents a helpful model for conceptualizing the way they make decisions in relationship to scripture along with other factors that affect their decision making process, including church tradition, critical thinking, and relevant experience."[20]

An interesting correspondence can be found between the progression of human thought, as overviewed within this chapter, and Wesley's approach to Christian thought and life. For centuries, premodern confidence in church **tradition** was foundational for Christians who needed to be told what to believe. Wesley affirms that Christian thought should measure itself against the years of thought that went into the development of orthodox teaching. Those who live in the twenty-first century are not the first to encounter difficulty and questions regarding the spiritual journey. Those who have gone before can and do have something to say that is relevant and informative to a contemporary believer.

Modern thinking freed the believer to allow himself or herself to question and consider the why of faith. As Origen's "plundering the Egyptians" model has shown, there is much to be gained by engaging culture and learning from

---

19. Elkind, "School and Family in the Postmodern World," 8.
20. Don Thorsen, "What Is the Wesleyan Quadrilateral."

the best thinkers of the day. Wesley saw no need for believers to "check their brains at the door" to be sincere in faith. The use of Scripture, the consideration of tradition, and the interpretation of experience all benefit from sound **reason** and good thinking that honors that One who created the mind.

The **experience** of the individual will be central to the postmodern lifestyle. As he reflected on his own life, most especially his salvation at a prayer meeting in London, Wesley encouraged the recognition of experience as vital to spirituality. The Christian worldview holds fast to the belief that there is an experience, or leap of faith, that marks a believer. The God of Christianity desires to interact with humanity and to be experienced through the work of the Holy Spirit.

That said, it must be remembered that none of these three are infallible. Tradition can be manipulated and skewed to serve those in power. Reason can lead to a denial of the miraculous and the loss of wonder in a creator God. Experience is contrary and can change from one moment to the next. On those grounds, the Wesleyan Quadrilateral must not be viewed as an equality of four parts. **Scripture**, God's revelation and his reaching out to humanity, holds sway over the other three. It has been the normative authority from the days of the Old Testament until today upon which and from which truth is established. We know because God has chosen to reveal something of himself through his revelation. Neither tradition, reason, nor experience should be given foothold to overshadow the truth of revelation.

Within any single church community, all three views of reality discussed here can be present. It could be possible for an individual to hold a premodern view of the biblical teaching of creation, a modern view of church governance, and a postmodern view of worship styles. There are no clear boundaries set by age, gender, class, ethnicity, or length of spiritual walk. The challenge for the church educator is not only to acknowledge the presence of multiple worldviews but to navigate among them (or perhaps in spite of them) and to develop a system of learning that holds the truth of Christianity as central to educational structure. God's gift of Christian community calls for all to come together for fellowship, worship, and learning; seeking his design for structure is always a good place to start.

Bibliography

Arthur, Mikaila Mariel Lemonik. "Modernity and the Individual," EBSCO Research Starters. EBSCO Publishing Inc., 2009.

Babbie, Earl. *The Practice of Social Research*, 8th ed. Belmont, CA: Wadsworth Publishing Company, 1998.

Barsky, Robert. *Encyclopedia of Postmodernism*. London: Routledge, 2001, s.v. "postmodernity."

Bloomsbury Guide to Human Thought. London: Bloomsbury Publishing Ltd, 1993, s.v. "Enlightenment."

Bratcher, Dennis. "Genesis Bible Study: Lesson Two: The Cultural Context of Israel." CRI/Voice Institute, 2010, http://www.crivoice.org/biblestudy/bbgen2.html (accessed November 14, 2010).

———. "Speaking the Language of Canaan: The Old Testament and the Israelite Perception of the Physical World." CRI/Voice Institute, 2010, http://www.crivoice.org/langcaan.html (accessed November 14, 2010).

Brinton, Crane. *The Shaping of Modern Thought*. Englewood Cliffs, NJ: Prentice Hall, 1963.

Dawson, Lorne L. "Antimodernism, Modernism, and Postmodernism: Struggling with the Cultural Significance of New Religious Movements." Sociology of Religion 59, no. 2 (Summer 1998): 131–56.

Elkind, David. "School and Family in the Postmodern World." *Phi Delta Kappan* 77, no. 1 (September 1995): 8.

Freeman, Charles. "Threefold Mystery." *History Today* 58, no. 2 (February 1, 2008): 22–24.

Kaufman, Will and Heidi Slettedahl Macpherson, eds. *Britain and the Americas: Culture, Politics, and History*. Santa Barbara: ABC-CLIO, 2005, s.v. "Enlightenment."

Knight, Hal. "John Wesley and the Emerging Church." *Preacher's Magazine*, Advent/Christmas 2007–2008.

Lee, Mary E. "Modernity and Progress." In Research Starters: Sociology. EBSCO Publishing Inc., 2009.

Outler, Albert C. *Evangelism and the Wesleyan Spirit*. Nashville, TN: Discipleship Resources, 1996.

———. *Theology in the Wesleyan Spirit*. Nashville, TN: Discipleship Resources, 1975.

Redfield, Robert. *The Primitive World and Its Transformations*. Ithaca, NY: Cornell University Press, 1953.

Sire, James W. *The Universe Next Door: A Basic Worldview Catalog*, 4th ed. Downer's Grove, IL: InterVarsity Press, 2004.

Taylor, Mark. "Postmodern Pedagogy: Teaching and Learning with Generation Next," *mcli Forum* 9 (Spring 2005). http://www.mcli.dist.maricopa.edu/forum.

Thorsen, Don. "What Is the Wesleyan Quadrilateral." http://www.wesley-anquadrilateral.com/?p=30 (posted April 3, 2009; accessed November 14, 2010).

Vejar, Cynthia. "Social Institutions in Postmodern Society." In Research Starters: Sociology. EBSCO Publishing Inc., 2009.

Wallerstein, Immanuel. "The End to What Modernity?" *Theory and Society* 24, no. 4 (August 1995): 471–88.

White, Heath. *Postmodernism 101: A First Course for the Curious Christian*. Grand Rapids, MI: Brazos Press, 2006.

CHAPTER EIGHT

Human Development

JOHN H. AUKERMAN

> Jesus became wise, and he grew strong.
> God was pleased with him and so
> were the people.
>
> —Luke 2:52

The concept of human development was formed by the modern academic disciplines of psychology and sociology, which speak of intellectual, psychological, and social development. These concepts are not found in the Bible. About the closest one might come is Luke 2:52, written by a physician, noting that the boy Jesus grew in four ways: intellectually, physically, spiritually, and socially. Taking that as a cue, Wesleyan Holiness Christian educators can improve their teaching by taking into account the contributions of scientific study concerning human development. This chapter presents only the highlights of a few developmental systems and is not adequate for full understanding; the interested reader will want to consult the resources listed at the end.

Intellectual Development

The most prominent theory of intellectual development in the second half of the twentieth century was proposed by Swiss developmental psychologist Jean Piaget (1896–1980). He suggested that all individuals progress through four periods of intellectual development, culminating sometime during adolescence in the ability to perform what he called Formal Operations.

According to Piaget, intellectual development begins in the Sensorimotor Period, from birth through approximately age two. A newborn baby is a bundle of reflexes; for example, when an object comes in contact with the lips of an infant, those lips begin to suck. As time goes by, the reflexes recede and the young child begins to manipulate objects in an ever-growing search for novelty. Piaget identified those processes as the beginning of thought. Somewhere in this period, the child begins to recognize words, which are abstract symbols that mean something; this child also begins to speak a few words.

Somewhere around age two, the child enters the Preoperational Period of intellectual development, which lasts approximately until age seven. It is important to understand that there are no hard-and-fast boundaries between any of these periods; each one begins prior to the end of its predecessor. In the Preoperational Period, the toddler develops language; words become extremely useful abstractions that stand for absent objects and events. In this process, the child begins to develop concepts, but they are always pre-concepts, not true concepts. For example, the Preoperational child will learn that a dog is a four-legged creature and might overgeneralize the concept to identify all four-legged creatures as dogs (e.g., cats, horses, elephants).

At around age seven, the Concrete Operational Period begins; it lasts roughly through eleven years of age. The Concrete Operational child is capable of developing true concepts and is able to think, but the thinking is always concrete; the child is not yet capable of dealing with abstractions.

Piaget's theory holds that the Formal Operational Period begins at age eleven or older and lasts throughout adulthood. Thinking is flexible and effective, and the adolescent is capable of imagining many possibilities, including hypothetical reasoning (if A, then B). He says that adult intelligence is characterized by stability.

It seems reasonable to the writer of this chapter that Piaget might have missed something important about adult intelligence. After the storm and stress of adolescence, with the accumulation of a growing reservoir of knowledge, it seems as if something new emerges in adulthood: wisdom. Wisdom goes beyond Formal Operations, is capable of considering many truths at once, can hold seeming contradictions together, and transcends the normal logic of Formal Operations. The wise Christian educator would do well to teach adults differently than teens.

Psychosocial Development

Erik Erikson (1902-1994) was a Danish-German-American developmental psychologist and psychoanalyst who proposed eight stages of human development. He said that there is a psychosocial conflict in each stage, that is, the individual's needs are pitted against society's demands. The successful resolution of conflict in each stage produces certain basic human qualities, resulting in a mature, mentally and socially healthy adult.

Key to this theory is the concept of Developmental Task: an activity that arises in the life of an individual, the successful completion of which leads to happiness and to success with later tasks. Failure leads to unhappiness, societal disapproval, and difficulty with later tasks. The good news is that earlier crises and failures can be corrected by success in present and future stages, which brings to mind 2 Corinthians 5:17, "Anyone who belongs to Christ is a new person. The past is forgotten, and everything is new."

Another key to understanding Erikson's theory is that all eight of these conflicts are thought to be present in one's life every day. Erikson proposes only that one of the eight conflicts is primary during a particular stage of life.

The most effective way to read Table 1 on the next page is, Conflict 1, Trust vs. Mistrust, is worked out in relationship with the mother and other primary caregivers. By successfully performing these (and other) developmental tasks, the person will achieve the human quality of hope. Even though Erikson was not Christian (he was born to a Jewish family), it is fascinating to note the number of commonalities his theory has with Christian theology.

Development of Moral Reasoning

Lawrence Kohlberg (1927–87) was an American psychologist at Harvard University. He was interested in moral reasoning—not moral behavior, but the reasons why people make moral decisions. For example, two individuals each believe that cheating is wrong, but for completely different reasons: one person says, "It's wrong because I might get caught," while the other says, "It's wrong because it undermines the trust necessary to preserve society."

Kohlberg concluded that all people pass through an invariant sequence of predictable stages of moral reasoning, which relate directly to Piaget's Periods of Intellectual Development and actually depend on intellectual development. He said that cognitive awareness of moral principles develops in adolescence and that it is the level of intellectual development that makes the difference; someone who is thinking at the level of Concrete Operations is not capable of advanced moral reasoning.

In Kohlberg's First Level, Pre-Conventional Moral Reasoning, there are two distinct stages. In Stage 1, the Punishment and Obedience Orientation, "might makes right;" the pleasure-pain principle determines morality. This person learns to avoid punishment at all costs and never questions authority for any reason whatsoever. In Stage 2, the Instrumental Relativist Orientation, the watchword is "Look out for Number One!" Moral choices are made on the basis of whatever satisfies "my" needs; people in this stage of moral reason see nothing wrong with stealing if it meets their needs.

Table 1. Erikson's Eight Stages of Human Development

Conflict	Relationships	Selected Developmental Tasks	Human Quality
1. Trust vs. Mistrust	Mother and other Primary Caregivers	Feed easily; Sleep deeply; Relax bowels; Let mother out of sight	Hope
2. Autonomy vs. Shame and Doubt	Parents or Parent Substitutes	Gain realistic view of competencies; Express choices; Learn own pace of doing things; Learn how to get assistance; Gain significant degree of control over self and environment	Will
3. Initiative vs. Guilt	Family	Play creatively; Explore with vigor, curiosity, and eagerness	Purpose
4. Industry vs. Inferiority	Neighbors and Schools	Make friends; Develop social skills; Succeed in school (academically and socially); Learn how things work; Psychologically break away from parents	Competence
5. Identity vs. Identity Confusion	Peer Groups and Adult Role Models	Put together accrued experiences of life; Know "who I am"; Find stability in a changing world; Meet requirements of significant people and society; Prepare to leave parents' home	Stability
6. Intimacy vs. Isolation	Male and Female Friends, Spouse	Choose and begin a career; Manage a home; Assume social responsibility; Form a philosophy of life; Adapt to a new social life (For some: Choose a spouse, Start a family, Raise children)	Love
7. Generativity vs. Stagnation	Family, Job, Community	Maintain previously close relationships; Expand circle of friends; Adjust to physiological changes; Attain satisfactory level of productivity; Develop leisure activities (For some: Assist children to independence)	Care
8. Integrity vs. Despair	All of Humanity	Adjust to aging process; Adjust to invalidism (own and spouse's); Adjust to retirement; Adjust to reduced income; Prepare for death (For some: Adjust to death of spouse)	Wisdom

Kohlberg's Second Level is called Conventional Moral Reasoning. This is when societal standards become important, so he entitled Stage 3 the Good Boy/Nice Girl Orientation. For a Stage 3 person, winning the approval of others by being "nice" is of utmost importance; this is what determines right and wrong; it often results in the so-called herd mentality of adolescent behavior. Moral reasoning then progresses to Stage 4, the Law and Order Orientation; here "right behavior" consists of blind obedience to fixed rules and regulations and maintenance of the social order at all costs. This person's motto might be "Do your duty!" or "Respect authority!" and they believe that it is never good to break any rule for any reason whatsoever. The law is everyone's ultimate guarantee of freedom and safety, and it must be obeyed at all costs.

Years after Kohlberg published his original research, he added a necessary transition between Stages 4 and 5. And rather than renumbering the stages, he inserted Stage 4½, Criticism and Questioning. Before an individual can develop Post-Conventional Moral Reasoning, he needs to work through these issues, asking questions such as "What *should* our laws be?" and "What *should* society do to be moral?"

Only after dealing with the tough issues of Stage 4½ do people move ahead to Kohlberg's Third Level, Post-Conventional Moral Reasoning. At this level, society is no longer an end in itself. There are some broader, universal standards of right and wrong to which the individual subscribes. In Stage 5, the Social Contract Orientation, individual rights must be considered, but only within the broader standards determined by society. Consensus is valued, and "right and wrong" are a matter of personal value and opinion, but only after considering the values and opinions of everyone else. The concept of law is still important, but the law may be changed for the good of individuals. This is the official position of the United States Constitution, and it has influenced the moral reasoning of virtually every adult in Wesleyan Holiness churches in America. A small minority of folks enter Stage 6 moral reasoning, the Universal Ethical Principle Orientation, where there is respect for individual dignity within the framework of self-chosen, universal ideals. An example from the teaching of Jesus would be the Golden Rule, "Treat others as you want them to treat you. This is what the Law and the Prophets are all about" (Matthew 7:12). This person realizes that "my set of values is only one set among many that are valid."

The flaw in Kohlberg's theory is that he built it on longitudinal studies of men and boys, completely overlooking the development of moral reasoning in women and girls. Whenever females were evaluated for moral reasoning, they showed a level of development inferior to that of men. Carol Gilligan, one of Kohlberg's students, has been one of the most outspoken critics of his work.[1] She contends that Kohlberg's approach failed to take into account the major concerns and perspectives of women.

---

1. Gilligan, *In a Different Voice.*

Society seems to demand that men be assertive and use independent judgment, but it seem to expect women to be concerned with the well-being of others and to sacrifice themselves to ensure that well-being. According to Gilligan's research, women tend to see morality in terms of selfishness versus responsibility. To be moral, for a woman, is to exercise care and to avoid harm. Gilligan concluded that men tend to make moral decisions on the basis of justice and fairness, while women tend to think more about specific people and their responsibilities to them. Men seem to care about individual rights; women seem to care about relationships and a decision's effect on the wider circle.

Faith Development

James Fowler, raised in old-style Methodism and converted in a tent meeting, studied human development at Harvard under Kohlberg. As a born-again Christian, his lifelong work was to blend Christian theology with human development theories; the result was the first major theory of faith development. Fowler's theory of faith stages is not universally accepted, but it offers a well-grounded structure to understand what faith is and how it might grow in the individual.

The theological foundation for Fowler's Faith Development Theory was informed by Paul Tillich and H. Richard Niebuhr. Fowler's dissertation, "To See the Kingdom," centers on Niebuhr's conviction of the sovereignty of God: the priority of God in existence, in value (whatever *is*, is good, because God made it), and in power. Fowler assumes that all human beings have a vocation (a calling) to partnership with God. He defines conversion as a gradual or sudden change in a person's center of values, images of and relation to power, and master story (e.g., What's my life really all about?).

Fowler's research led him to three major conclusions: (1) faith is a universal (all humans are people of faith), (2) faith is a verb (it is not something to be possessed; it is something to be done), and (3) there is a sequence of stage-like ways of being in faith. His stages try to describe uniform and predictable ways of being in faith, not the content of faith. According to Fowler, no one is purely in any one stage; about half of one's faith is in a given stage, with the other half in at least the two surrounding stages.

Stage 1, Primal Faith, emerges in the first two years of life as a prelanguage disposition of trust that forms with parents and others. Its main effect is to offset the anxiety that arises whenever mom or dad is out of sight.

At about age two, a revolution happens in a child. Language emerges to mediate relationships with others in new and exciting ways. Words become powerful conveyors of wants, desires, ideas, and stories. The young child intuits faith and projects the faith of powerful adults onto her own life. Therefore Fowler called Stage 2 Intuitive-Projective Faith. This stage is filled with fantasy, strong taboos, and powerful images; it imitates adults and fuses fact, fantasy, and feeling.

Around the time a child starts elementary school, a new stage begins. Because the child can build concrete categories of space, time, and causality, he starts thinking about right and wrong, good and evil, with a strong sense of moral reciprocity. Faith becomes a matter of reliance on stories; hence Fowler called Stage 3 Mythic-Literal Faith. It rises during the school years and beyond; some adolescents, and even a few adults, find themselves primarily in this stage. *Myth* here is used in the technical sense: a "traditional story of ostensibly historical events that serves to unfold part of the world view of a people or explain a practice, belief, or natural phenomenon."[2] *Literal* means that the Stage 3 individual accepts the myth in a literal, concrete sense. This is a stable, linear, predictable faith; it provides comfort and security. The person takes on the stories of the community they belong to, for stories give unity and value to life. Beliefs are literal, symbols are one-dimensional, and there are strict rules of right and wrong. A sense of fairness and reciprocity reigns. Affiliation is important. Stage 3 faith is largely unaware of self, is anthropomorphic, and conforms to authority and tradition. From this stage on, all stages describe ways of being in faith that can typify adults as well as the age groups where they usually begin.

Somewhere around eleven years of age, some people begin to experience the breakdown of the moral principle of reciprocity: they find that bad things happen to good people and that good things happen to bad people. Their image of God becomes tarnished; by observation and experience, they find that either God is powerless, asleep, or taking a vacation. The God who is constructed on the basis of moral reciprocity dies, therefore, and must be replaced. The transition between stages 3 and 4 can often be a time of intense anguish, struggle, grief, and guilt.

Stage 4, Synthetic-Conventional Faith, typically begins in adolescence and beyond. *Synthetic* does not mean artificial; rather, it means pulling together the accumulated experiences of life into a unity, a synthesis. The Stage 4 person draws together her stories, values, and beliefs into a supportive and orienting unity. She struggles with composing a story of my stories, a sense of the meaning of life in general, and my life in particular. The research indicates that this happens best, during adolescence, through the individual's relationships with peers and significant adults. It is a nonanalytical synthesis, with no critical reflection. The conventional is seen as normative, "Everybody everywhere believes just like we do." This faith is dependent, conformist, and not self aware. Authority figures shape faith, belief, and practice.

The transition into Stage 5 is brought about by a variety of life experiences that make it necessary to objectify, examine, and make critical choices about the defining elements of identity and faith. This is often a time of spiri-

---

2. *Webster's Ninth New Collegiate Dictionary*, s.v. "myth."

tual danger: when the conventional faith is discarded, often faith itself is abandoned. Previously unexamined beliefs are critically reflected upon, and those that survive become "mine;" they are personally owned by this person. Stage 5, Individuative-Reflective Faith, typically rises in young adulthood and beyond. There is an internal source of authority, a self-fulfillment, a personal taking of responsibility, and self-actualization. This person demythologizes, or discards, mythological forms in order to uncover their underlying meaning. Fowler contends that there is a substantial presence of Individuative-Reflective Faith in a typical congregation; these folks see the church as existing to meet their needs. Often they have either an overinflated or underinflated self image, each of which needs to be submitted to God in sanctifying surrender of self. Stage 5 people need Christian community and spiritual direction.

For a small minority (7% of the general population), there seems to be a transition to a new stage of faith that Fowler called Stage 6, Conjunctive Faith. This is usually possible only in midlife and beyond, although a tiny fraction of unusually mature younger people can find themselves in this stage. Fowler named it Conjunctive Faith because it is the conjunction, or coming together, of opposites, the idea that God is the being in whom all opposites and contradictions meet and are reconciled. Most adults cannot even understand this stage of faith, let alone attain it. These people can maintain emotional detachment and appreciate both sides of an issue. They practice dialectical knowing and see truth as multidimensional. They are reclaiming and reworking their past. They seek to unify opposites and find it possible by entering a second naiveté. Their thinking is postcritical, well past what they did in Individuative-Reflective Faith.

Fowler identified four hallmarks of the transition to Conjunctive Faith: (1) Awareness of the need to face and hold together several unmistakable polar tensions in one's life. (2) A felt sense that truth is more complex than most of the crystal-clear, either-or categories that used to work. In its richness, truth must be approached from at least two angles simultaneously. This kind of faith cherishes paradox and the apparent contradictions of life in its quest for ultimate truth. (3) A move beyond demythologization and the critical translation of the mythic and the symbolic: a second naiveté, a postcritical receptivity and readiness for participation in the reality that is expressed by myth and symbol. (4) A genuine openness to the truths of traditions and communities other than one's own. This is not relativism; it is a disciplined openness to the truths of those who are different—other. And it is based on a deep commitment to one's own tradition coupled with the realization that ultimate truth is bigger than any single tradition can surround.

For an extremely small portion of the human family (0.3% of the general population), there comes a transition to the last stage Fowler identified. Stage 7, Universalizing Faith, is characterized by an emptying of self—a God-grounded selfhood in which self is no longer the primary reference point of reality. These individuals, often called mystics, have somehow been drawn beyond the finite centers of human value and power. They are heedless of self-preservation and have a sense of oneness with God. They focus on truth, justice, and goodness. Life is both loved and loosely held. Stage 7 people are ready to die for others, ready to spend and be spent in making the kingdom actual. Jesus himself is an example of Universalizing Faith; the Greek of Philippians 1:7 says that "he emptied himself," and he certainly had a sense of oneness with the Father and paid no heed to self-preservation.

The writer of this chapter heard Fowler say that a person's faith is like a bale of hay: the baling wire holds the hay together, representing the faith that holds a person's life together. At all stages of faith, the wire that holds the bale (i.e., life) together is a good thing. It is therefore always appropriate for Christian educators to respect and honor every individual's current faith stage, and it is never appropriate to denigrate someone who is at a perceived "lesser" stage of faith. To snip the baling wire is to commit an act of spiritual violence.

This writer also heard Fowler say that this is a spiral theory. He said it is not a stairstep approach to understanding faith, that nobody ever completely leaves a stage. Each faith stage contains within itself the full repertoire of responses of all the previous stages. And much like a coiled spring, when it is compressed, it gets stronger until it reaches a point where it is strong enough to resist any further compression. The application is that when life gets tough, believers find it easy, normal, and natural to use old, well-learned, well-known faith responses, finding within themselves the strength to push back.

Upon further reflection, this writer gained another insight into the spiral theory. It is that, when a spring is pulled and stretched beyond its capacity, it is ruined. It will never be good for its intended purpose. And if a Christian educator tries to push a person to a "higher" stage of faith, that person may be stretched too far and damaged. Teachers cannot force a person to move to a new stage of faith; it is much better to nurture them at their current stage and leave the faith development to the Holy Spirit.

Bibliography

Erikson, Erik H. *Childhood and Society*. New York: W.W. Norton, 1985.

———— *Identity, Youth, and Crisis*. New York: W.W. Norton, 1968.

Fowler, James W. *Faith Development and Pastoral Care*. Philadelphia: Fortress Press, 1986.

———— *Stages of Faith: The Psychology of Human Development and the Quest for Meaning*. San Francisco, CA: Harper & Row, 1981.

Gilligan, Carol. *In a Different Voice: Psychological Theory and Women's Development*. Cambridge, MA: Harvard University Press, 1982.

Kitchener, Richard F. *Piaget's Theory of Knowledge: Genetic Epistemology & Scientific Reason.* New Haven, CT: Yale University Press, 1986.

Kohlberg, Lawrence. *The Psychology of Moral Development: The Nature and Validity of Moral Stages.* San Francisco, CA: Harper & Row, 1984.

Singer, Dorothy G. *A Piaget Primer: How a Child Thinks.* Madison, CT: International Universities Press, 1997.

CHAPTER NINE

The Power of Story

JOHN M. JOHNSON

> Jesus used stories when he spoke to the people. In fact, he did not tell them anything without using stories.
>
> —Matthew 13:34

Christian education is discipleship all dressed up for church. "Discipleship is the process of learning to follow Christ. It is primarily a commitment to Christ, obedience to his lordship, and a willingness to be transformed into his likeness. This growth involves inward spiritual maturity and outward obedience, discipline, witness, and service. It is best facilitated in a one-on-one relationship between teacher and student, discipler and disciple."[1]

Christian education is spiritual formation, that is, the process of transforming us into the image of Jesus. Richard Foster says that the church is at its best in doing this when it focuses on Jesus Christ, the Christian Scriptures, and spiritual disciplines.[2] Often spiritual formation is spoken of as "the process by which believers become more fully conformed and united to Christ."[3]

Christian education (discipleship/formation) then is that process of learning to follow Jesus, wherever he leads. It is about being experientially transformed into his likeness or, as Dallas Willard says, "learning to do the deeds of Christ in the power of Christ."[4] In this view Christian education is much more

1. Johnson, "Enhancing the Quality," 4.
2. Foster, "Spiritual Formation: A Pastoral Letter."
3. Howard, "On Spiritual Formation."
4. Willard, "How Does the Disciple Live."

than learning content or exposure to religious practices, although it includes them.[5] It is about becoming mature, whole, and Christlike. It is, after all, Jesus who sets the goal of discipleship: "When a disciple is fully trained, he or she will look like his master" (Luke 6:40, author's paraphrase).

Christian educators have a range of activities, modes of instruction, and directed experiences at their disposal to foster such life change. Of these instructional tools, perhaps the most useful is the story. The focus of this chapter is on the use of narrative as a key component in the transformational process toward Christlikeness.

Jeffery Arthurs provides the following definition of biblical narrative: "A historically accurate, artistically sophisticated account of persons and actions in a setting designed to reveal God and edify the reader."[6] The Bible is full of stories; narrative, far and away, is the single largest genre in Scripture. Scholars estimate that 60–75 percent of the biblical record is made up of narrative.

When I first started to teach and preach, I gravitated to stories. They seemed easier, friendlier, and more accessible. Other genres of Scripture, like Law, Epistle, and Apocalypse, seemed colder, aloof, less inviting.

My grandmother Leona Johnson loved her grandchildren, baking, and stories. After baking a fresh batch of cookies, or perhaps while they were still in the oven, she loved to gather her grandchildren around her in order to read them a story. Grandmothers instinctively know the power of stories. I remember snuggling close to her, smelling her special grandmother scent, feeling the warmth of her baker's hands on my leg, no doubt placed there to keep me from squirming, and listening to her read stories.

I realize this will quickly reveal my age, but I remember sitting "Indian style" on the floor in Mrs. Herrington's Sunday school classroom. A skilled practitioner of the flannel graph, she regularly, faithfully, and intentionally displayed the stories of Jesus to her charges.[7] I have a particular recollection of the Palm Sunday story told with practiced ease, the scenes unfolding almost like a film strip, which was, at the time, the epitome of high tech.[8] I also remember acting out the stories; the good Samaritan was a particular favorite of mine because

---

5. "Christian education is the whole enterprise of shaping that new life in Christ, telling stories of the people of God that shape the faith by which the babe in Christ believes. Christian education is not merely informative or catechetical; it shapes our characters as disciples of the Master. As such, it is the ministry not of some segment of the church, but the whole church" (Strege, *Tell Me Another Tale*, 41).

6. Arthurs, *Preaching with Variety*, 64.

7. Flannel graphs may have gone the way of the dinosaur. However, their power of retelling the story is not totally lost. A recent Warner Pacific colleague, Andy Magel, used to entertain, equip, inspire, edify, and even rebuke Millennials of this campus in chapels through the use of a digital version of the flannel graph. He calls it flannel vision. I call it effective.

8. High tech today includes all manner of things. A simple search on the web will reveal a great variety of storytelling and presenting options: software, videos, online resources, and more.

we boys could actually pretend to beat up our unfortunate classmate who was selected to play the role of the man on the road from Jerusalem to Jericho.[9]

And what about the sermons I remember? My father once preached a sermon on the story of the prophet Jonah. He used a story of a young girl whose family was moving from the East Coast of the United States to the gold fields of Bodi, California. He quoted what this girl wrote in her diary upon learning that she and her family were moving to a town that was noted for its saloons and brothels: "Good-bye, God. I'm going to Bodi," wrote the girl. That phrase has become almost legendary in our family. It is an apt illustration, to be sure, that highlights the dangers of a good illustrative story: people will remember the story and forget the message. Why is that? It is that stories, like catchy jingles, are mentally sticky. They clearly have staying power long after propositional truth has vanished like dew in the noonday sun, even as they continue to intrigue and incite the imagination.

The Bible consists of a vast array of stories: Old Testament narratives, Acts, the Gospels, parables, and enacted parables used by both the Old Testament prophets and Jesus himself.[10] Although each of these genres is different in that they require some rather specific guidelines for uncovering their message and meaning, the biblical record clearly indicates that God and his people dearly "love a good story."[11]

Stories have power among other things to

- teach without being preachy.
- sneak up on the listener.
- organize content.
- stir the imagination.
- communicate across cultures.
- create community.
- depict godliness.
- inspire hope.
- instill joy.
- stir up longing.
- extend perseverance.
- reignite passion.

9. Enacted drama is still popular for children, youth, and adults. Another variation of this is telling a story through the "Godly Play" model, which uses simple wooden figures to meaningfully retell the biblical story (Berryman, *Godly Play*).

10. "Most of the Bible consists of stories. Why? Partly because God knows that people like and remember stories better than lists of abstract propositions. And even more important, the stories remind us that life is a story, and that God is not an abstract doctrine, but a Person" (Lee-Thorp, *Story of Stories*, 7).

11. Fee and Stuart, *How to Read*.

- call forth new understandings.
- call into question long-held assumptions.

The good story cannot be held at arm's length. It makes its way past personal defenses, past intellectual or cultural barriers, and makes itself known to the listener. Aptly appreciated and effectively told, the story becomes the guest, sometimes uninvited, that knocks persistently at the door of one's heart. Shared with skill and sensitivity, the story becomes entertainment, instruction, and vehicle of transformation.

> Storytelling, therefore, is an essential element in order to ignite and engender the process of transformation into Christlikeness. The educator must facilitate a move into the story. Where does my story intersect God's Story? How is my story enhanced by, explained by, or enriched by The Story? In other words, since the Christian educator is concerned with the formation of Christian disciples, the Christian educator asks questions like, 'The story of the Good Samaritan; the prodigal child, the older brother, and the silly father; the lost lamb; Jesus' crucifixion—how are these not only stories I read, learn, and tell, but how are these my stories as well? Where am I in all this?'[12]

I have had the opportunity to travel, speak, and teach in numerous places among numerous peoples. One afternoon in rural Bangladesh, the national leader, Tapan Borman, leaned over and told me that in just a few minutes he was going to ask me to share yet again, this time with a group of about seventy-five children. It had been a long day of traveling and speaking. I had already spoken in various contexts to different audiences. I was tired, dirty, and mentally ready to "pack it up." I suppose I could have shared one of the devotions I had shared previously, but I did not feel satisfied to do so. Mentally, I went into overdrive. What would I share? What story would I tell? I have had this happen on numerous occasions: In Myanmar, I told the story of Jesus' telling his disciples to let the children come to him. In Korea, I acted out the story of the faith-filled tightrope walker. In Egypt, I shared the story of Daniel in the lion's den (with appropriate sound effects). But what would I share with these Muslim, Hindu, and Christian children (and their parents listening intently through open windows and between bamboo-slat walls) in rural Bangladesh? Then I remembered a story of Peter's walking on the water. I read the story (Matt 14:22–33) and then invited some eager children forward and asked them to act out the story. What energy! What passion! What fun! And then I asked a few questions about Jesus, and Peter, and what the story meant to them. I finished with verses 32 and 33:

---

12. Arthur Kelly, e-mail to author, August 17, 2009.

"When Jesus and Peter got into the boat, the wind died down. The men in the boat worshiped Jesus and said, "You really are the Son of God!'"

Those children (and parents and villagers) learned a story about Jesus. They found out it was okay to put themselves in the story. They heard about faith and they saw worship in action. Through this story, the message that Jesus is the Son of God was affirmed. On that hot day in rural Bangladesh, Muslim, Hindu, and Christian children heard and then acted a story and enjoyed the whole experience. Through this simple story, enacted by Bengali-speaking children, a whole village learned a powerful truth: the ultimate God who controls the created order is intimately connected with those who have chosen to journey with him.[13]

Telling stories is one of the marks of being truly human.[14] Stanley Hauerwas would certainly affirm this and then move beyond it to speak about the church. He argues cogently that the church is a "story-formed community."[15] By this Hauerwas means that the stories of Israel and Jesus provide convictions about how to live, alternatives to deceptive philosophies and practices outside the community of faith, a way of living with integrity and skill, the desire and ability to endure amid the paradoxical tensions of life, social significance and purpose for the community of faith, and a common commitment to life lived in faithful relationship with both God and neighbor. These stories of Israel and Jesus become the central narratives for the Christian educator.

What follows are six examples of a narrative approach to Bible study:

1. The Story Elements: Setting, Characters, and Plot
2. Brainstorming: Exposing Content, Exploring Convergence
3. Inductive Bible Study: The Move from Observation through Interpretation to Application
4. Story-in-a-Sentence: Synthesizing and Re-telling
5. *Lectio Divina*: "Let's read it one more time."
6. Paraphrase: An Imaginative Retelling

1. The Story Elements: Setting, Characters, and Plot

Every narrative is made up of three basic elements: setting, characters, and plot. The wise Christian educator is able to recognize and utilize these elements to

---

13. In his wonderful chapter titled "When God Was a Tailor," Zahniser explores this theme (Zahniser, *Symbol and Ceremony*, 32–43). He writes: "Cross-cultural discipling involves helping all believers see that the ultimate Creator wants to be their Companion—wants to be involved in their intimate issues of their individual and communal lives. In the Bible God plays both roles" (33).

14. Wright, *Simply Christian*, 49.

15. Hauerwas, *Community of Character*, 51.

assist his or her students in discovering and applying the meaning of the narrative in today's context.

Setting

Students of biblical narrative must pay particular attention to the setting. The setting provides the stage where the story is played out. The setting exposes physical and sequential time, culture and worldview, mood, and the glue that holds a story together. Think of the setting for a diamond ring: if the setting is defective, the beauty and power of the story will be lost. If, then, the biblical storyteller spends time developing the setting, we slow down and explore what is being said.[16]

Places have particular names in Scripture. Often those places described in the story reveal helpful clues to unpacking the meaning of a story. Slow down when reading biblical stories when encountering names. Do this not just because they are hard to pronounce but because they have hidden meaning. Ask yourself, Is the storyteller flashing me a clue about this story through the place names?[17]

Characters

The characters of a story are more than "those with a speaking part." Dialogue is important, to be sure. Who is speaking and to whom? Often the dialogue reveals the heart, passion, and purpose of the character. What is he or she after? The setting of the story may reveal a stressful moment or a joyful reunion. The dialogue will reveal the quality and character of the person in the scene. Sometimes biblical narratives are designed to show that one character is righteous and the other is not. Through dialogue, the storyteller can get his readers "leaning" in one direction or another, either for or against the character. It should be noted again the biblical narratives are written to teach us about God (or to reveal God). Therefore, particular attention should be given to dialogue that takes place between God and his people or leader and/or Jesus and the crowds, his disciples, or a particular individual.

Like biblical places, biblical characters have names, and those names also help uncover the powerful truths of the story. Abraham, Jacob, Elijah, Malachi, Emmanuel, Jesus, and Peter are all major characters in the biblical story. Each name aids in the telling and hearing of the story.

---

16. In his chapter titled "The Stories of the Bible," Ryken speaks insightfully about how the narrative works in Scripture (Ryken, *How to Read*, 33–73).

17. As an example, Beer-Sheba is more than the southernmost boundry lines of Israel, e.g. "from Dan to Beer-Sheba" (1 Sam 3:20). Beer-Sheba is the name of a place, and that place has a meaning. It means the "well of the oath," and it is the place where Abraham called on El Olam, "the God that is everlastingly able to fulfill his promise" (Gen 21:33). Is it any wonder then that the troublesome story of the sacrifice of Isaac in Genesis is bookended by reference to Beer-Sheba? (Gen 21:33 and 22:19).

Plot

Ask any second grader and they can tell a story's plot. Every story has one. Plots speak of movement. The power of the story is revealed through plot. A plot provides background, conflict, rising action, climax, and (sometimes) resolution.[18] The background gets the story moving. At some point, fairly early in the narrative, a problem arises. And this problem intensifies to the point of a climax. At this point the story shifts toward a resolution. The resolution provides some sort of settlement to the conflict and may provide an affirmation of truth, at times in a mini speech by one of the main characters. Of course, some stories are open-ended. No one knows how the prodigal narrative ends (Luke 15:11–32), nor does anyone really know whether or not the rich young ruler ever returned to Christ (Matt 19:16–30).[19]

Setting, dialogue, and plot have been intentionally arranged (sometimes the story arranges itself) by the storyteller to entertain, moralize, and/or teach.[20] When studying a biblical narrative, also listen for literary features: personification, hyperbole, satire, and irony. These are clues to the important meaning of the story.

A word is in order about the particular gospel narrative that appears below. Matthew, Mark, and Luke (the Synoptic Gospels) often give us the same story, the same incident, and the same teaching. At times there are slight differences in word order. Sometimes the stories themselves are placed in a different sequential context. From time to time, a story or teaching is unique to one Gospel writer or another, depending on his sources, his audience, intent, or style of writing.

In the story below, the healing of the centurion's servant appears in both Matthew and Luke. Luke's account will be read first followed by Matthew's. Although much of the narrative is the same, there are clearly some differences as well.

The Narrative: Luke 7:1–10 and Matthew 8:5–13
Summary of the Narrative

Once Jesus had completed some of his most important teaching, the Sermon on the Plain (Luke) and the Sermon on the Mount (Matthew), he entered an impor-

---

18. Arthurs, *Preaching with Variety*, 70.

19. Koyama asks the question, "Is our relationship with Jesus so easily severed or broken? Is it so fragile? Is such a going away sorrowful the end of the possibility of the community of grace in the name of Jesus Christ who is called 'Emmanuel (God with us)' (Matt. 1:23)?" (Koyama, *No Handle on the Cross*, 65).

20. "Stories engage the reader by being allusive, suggestive, and evocative. There is something about a plot, characters, dramatic intensity, tension, and resolution that absorbs readers on several levels. Biblical stories engage their readers in assessing their religious motivations, understanding, and responses. One can come back to a familiar story and find new meaning and value in it. Each rereading can be an enriching experience that leads to new insight and new motivation. This is one reason the liturgy reads and rereads the biblical story" (Hoppe, *New Light from Old Stories*, viii).

tant regional town. A Roman centurion (or some of his appointees, depending on the account) approached Jesus with a request to heal his slave. The Roman centurion displayed remarkable faith and Jesus publicly praised him

Approach: "Foreign Faith"

Luke's telling:

Setting:

- Capernaum, which is on the northern shore of the Sea of Galilee.
- Jesus has just given a major sermon on the life of faith. He has covered several big practical issues: spiritual rewards and blessings, loving your enemies, blessing those who curse you, praying for those who abuse you, forgiving, giving to those who ask, not judging, doing and speaking good from the inside out, and so on. (See Luke 6. Called the Sermon on the Plain; especially v 17). (*Background*)

Characters:

- Jesus (and his disciples?)
- An occupying Roman centurion and his "highly valued slave"
- Jewish elders
- Crowds of people

Plot and Dialogue:

- The centurion's "highly valued" slave is ill (high money value or high relationship value?). (*conflict*—also called initiating moment or point of attack)
- The centurion sends his committee of influence, Jewish elders from the city, to Jesus. They say, "He is worthy of having you do this for him. He loves our people. He even built us a synagogue." (*rising action*)
- Jesus goes with the elders in the direction of the centurion's home. (*rising action*)
- The centurion sends out his friends with a message, "I am not worthy." It is interesting that the first group declares that the man is worthy but the centurion himself declares he is not worthy. Then the centurion says through his friends to Jesus, "Just speak the words. I understand how authority works. I recognize your authority." (*rising action*)
- Jesus is amazed and turns to the crowds and says, "I have not found faith like this anywhere in Israel." (*climax*—Sometimes this is called the intellectual or the decision climax, which leads to the next bullet, which is called the dramatic conflict. Sometimes these are nearly simultaneous,

and sometimes separated by quite a bit. The intellectual climax is the point of no return.)

- Then the slave is healed. (*resolution*)

Message in a sentence: This foreigner has exhibited great faith not found among Jesus' own people.

Matthew's telling:

Setting:

- Capernaum.
- Jesus has just spoken the Sermon on the Mount (ch 5–7). (*background*)

Characters:

- Jesus (and his disciples?)
- An occupying Roman centurion and his "highly valued slave"
- Crowds of people

Plot and Dialogue:

- Jesus enters the city and the centurion himself comes to Jesus. He himself makes the request that Jesus heal his servant. (*conflict*)
- Jesus agrees to "come and heal" the servant. (*rising action*)
- Centurion says that he is not worthy for Jesus to enter his home and, therefore, appeals to Jesus to just speak a word of healing. He understands how authority works and recognizes that Jesus has the necessary authority. (*rising action*)
- Jesus is amazed and says to the people: "I have never found such faith in Israel. Many are going to come, like this centurion to enter into a relationship with God, but you on the inside are going to be booted out." (*climax*)
- Jesus heals the servant. (*resolution*)

What is this story about?

1. It is obviously about faith, foreign faith. Such faith is often foreign to the audience of Jesus and to contemporary readers as well. People today must have faith in Jesus in the midst of all the struggles, temptations, and difficulties of life.

2. This story is about authority. Jesus has authority over this world and human lives within this world. The listener must go to him (Matthew).

3. This is a story about intercession. There are times that folks approach Jesus on behalf of another (Luke and Matthew). This is not to impress Jesus but to intercede.

4. This story is about being worthy. In the presence of Jesus, all find themselves unworthy. Imagine: Jesus considers our struggles worthy of his time.

5. This is also a story of rebuke. Just because people have the right credentials (born and raised in some particular Holiness church) doesn't mean that the requirement for life within the family of God is anything less. Faith is the key for entry into the family of God, and faith is the permission to remain within the family of God.

Concluding Comments on Narrative and Story Elements

The biblical record is literature. Scripture consists of stories that have been told and retold—campfire and dinner time stories. At some point these oral stories were gathered, edited, and written. Once presented in a literary format, they have been published, translated, and republished numerous times. The Bible is holy, inspired, human-divine literature, but it is literature nonetheless. When the Christian educator studies and presents a story according to some of the basic strategies of other great literature, great content, understandable and valuable, is laid bare and the obedient reader can faithfully apply it to his or her life.

2. Brainstorming: Exposing Content, Exploring Convergence

Brainstorming is the process of engaging a gathering of learners with a few well-chosen questions. No answer is wrong. All responses are recorded on butcher paper, whiteboards, or digitally-projected computer screens. What is important is to capture the essence of what has been said. Brainstorming is based on the belief that there is power in community. One person's comment will trigger another's. Each individual comment has value. Yet when combined, the whole is greater than the sum of the parts. Once the comments are gathered, then the skillful educator will lead the group in exploring the convergence of Scripture with community, the Word with reality, the Message with experience. When the process of brainstorming is applied to the telling of a story, the results can far exceed what the educator envisioned.

The Narrative: Genesis 17:1–17; 18:1–15; and 21:1–8
Summary of the Narrative

Abraham receives a remarkable promise. Even though Sarah is well beyond the normal child-bearing age, the Lord declares that they are going to have a child, an heir. The Lord announces that through this child, he is going to bless the nations. When Abraham and Sarah hear this promise, they both laugh. But it is the Lord who gets the last laugh. In response to the birth of this promised child, Abraham and Sarah name the boy Isaac, a name that means "laughter."

Approach: "God gets the last laugh."

The Abraham story is full of remarkable promises, power, pain, and pathos. It is about calling, obedience, and faith. Equally so, it is a story about debilitating disobedience, dissolving faith, and distressing consequences of disloyalty. This story has the miraculous, the mysterious, and the mirthful. This is one of those "something-for-everyone" kind of stories. At the center of the story are promise and fulfillment. Some would say that this story speaks of the eventual faithfulness of Abraham. Rather, this is a story about the eternal faithfulness of Yahweh.

But to use this story as an illustration for a topical teaching on faithfulness is to miss the point. This story teaches that God is faithful and that the only correct response to God's faithfulness is obedience without using those words.

The Lord called Abram to get up and leave everything to follow him. The Lord said that he would bless Abram, and through his family, he would bless the nations. Without many more details than that, Abram left his homeland and ventured off with the Lord. In the course of following the Lord, Abram's father died and they came into a land that was experiencing famine. He and Sarai wandered to Egypt for protection. At the border, Abram realized this might not have been such a good idea. He became fearful that his beautiful wife would be taken and that he would be killed. So he cooked up a lie. When the lie was uncovered, Pharaoh booted them out of his country, surprisingly with all kinds of gifts.

Abram became a wealthy man. But his wealth only brought him hardship and pain. He and his nephew Lot parted company because they had so much stuff. The Lord began to promise Abram that he was going to have a big family: "Look at the stars of the sky. Look at the sand on the seashore. Can you count the stars? Can you count the grains of sand?" A smile broke out on Abraham's face. "No," he said. "Well, neither will you be able to count your descendents," the Lord affirmed.

At first that promise was enough. As time passed and nothing happened, Abram's faith in the promise began to waver. Sarah also got tired of waiting and she gave Abraham her slave girl so he could have a baby by her. But that was not what the Lord intended; a baby was born named Ishmael ("God hears"), but this was not the promised child.

Finally the Lord came and spoke to Abraham. The Lord made an agreement with Abram and changed his name to Abraham. "Your wife Sarah will have a child. It is through this child that I will bless the world," God said. And Abraham doubled over in laughter and fell on his face before God (17:17). Not too long after that, the Lord came to Abraham and Sarah's campsite for a visit. He again reiterated that Sarah was going to have a baby. Sarah laughed to herself, "Now that I am worn out and my husband is old, will I really know such happiness?" The Lord knew instantly that Sarah had laughed at his words. When confronted, Sarah denied that she had laughed. "The Lord said, "I'll be back this time next year, and when I do, Sarah will already have a baby" (18:10). And that is exactly what happened: God was good to Sarah and gave her a son. "Who would have ever imagined it?" Sarah wondered out loud. And they named the boy Isaac, which means laughter, for God had indeed gotten the last laugh.

In story form, students learn a great deal about God, his way, and also about the life of faithfulness. Perhaps in a time of brainstorming after telling this story, students might come up with the following insights:

- God is a superintending God. He can take the best and worst of our lives and weave them into something meaningful for us and for others.
- God calls us beyond ourselves to places that we cannot see.
- Nothing is impossible with God.
- God fulfills his promises.
- God is with us on the journey.
- God does not abandon dysfunctional families.
- Wealth is not always a blessing. It can sometimes be a curse.
- We too are called to be obedient. God is faithful; we are to be obedient.

Concluding Comments on Narrative and Brainstorming:

As the educator facilitates this discussion, more than summative comments are sought. This becomes the time when the group, and the individuals within the group, begin to process the import of the narrative. The observations that have been brainstormed become wonderful springboards for further discussion and reflection.

- What questions do you have for this story?
- Where did you see yourself in this story?
- What questions does this story ask of you?
- How will you live differently as a result of 'rightly hearing' this story?
- What kind of community would we be if we took the insights of this story and faithfully applied them?

The danger with employing this brainstorming activity is that the facilitator does not persist with the narrative and the group long enough to explore these very real questions of application.

3. Inductive Bible Study: The Move from Observation Through Interpretation to Application

Inductive Bible Study is the process of exploring the biblical text from three very specific and logically sequential points of view: observation, interpretation, and application. The framework for an inductive study might look like this:

I. Observation

    a. Genre (the type of literature)?

    b. Literary context (immediate passages around this one)?

    c. Historical context (when)?

    d. Physical context (where)? Place information? Geographical information?

    e. Who is speaking and to whom?

    f. Who is the main character?

    g. Key words?

    h. Lists of things?

    i. Repeated words?

    j. Teaching or doctrine expressed?

    k. Grammatical ideas: contrasts, comparisons, expressions?

    l. Overarching theme or themes?

II. Interpretation

    a. Main idea?

    b. What issue or theme does the passage speak to? What statements does it make about that subject?

    c. Questions for the passage?

    d. Cross referencing the passage?

    e. How will a concordance help?

    f. What additional help would be in a commentary?

    g. Write a personal paraphrase of the passage.

III. Application

    a. What questions does the passage ask of me?

    b. How do I live into the insights of the passage?

    c. What specific things do I need to change in my life as a result of reading and studying this passage?

d. What does this passage say to me regarding my church, my world, my context?

e. Identify a particular verse (or section) within the passage that you will memorize.[21]

The process of inductive Bible study can be accomplished either individually or as a group. When dealing with a biblical narrative, this tool is particularly powerful.

The Narrative: 2 Samuel 11–12
Summary of the Narrative

David was an excellent ruler. He slew giants and gave glory to God. He accepted help and gave friendship. He didn't take the opportunity to kill Saul, his enemy, even when he could have. He praised God and his companions. He trusted God and, for the most part, lived a life that pleased his people and his God. But the story of David would not be complete without the record of his mighty failures. He failed God and he failed his family.

The story of David and Bathsheba is one of the most familiar stories in the Hebrew Bible. The story of David and his sons, Amnon and Absalom, is not so widely known (2 Samuel 13–15 and beyond).

In chapter 11 of 2 Samuel we read, "It was now spring, the time when kings go to war...." David calls for and takes Bathsheba; they "hook up" some might say, and Bathsheba gets pregnant. In an attempt to cover up his sin, David commits another sin, this time killing Uriah. (By the way, Uriah the Hittite is not just any soldier in David's army. Although he was a foreigner, he lives next door to the king. He is also listed in 2 Samuel 23:39 as one of the men that David wanted to praise.) God confronts David through the prophet Nathan and doles out a heavy punishment.

The Approach: "Everybody Needs a Nathan"
Observations

- Genre: Old Testament Narrative, yet buried within it is a parable.
- David does not go out to war with his army.
- David took what was not his. Was Bathsheba a willing participant?
- David and Uriah are set in startling contrast with each other:
    * King vs. Soldier
    * Not at war vs. At war

---

21. This model of inductive study has been compiled and developed by the author over more than three decades of teaching. There are certainly no novel or unique questions in this list.

- * Disobedient vs. Obedient
- * Insider (Israelite) vs. Outsider (Hittite)
- * Unrighteous vs. Righteous
- Nathan and Joab are set in contrast with each other:
  - * Prophet vs. General
  - * Advisor to king vs. Under command of king
  - * Willing to say the hard things vs. Willing to turn a blind eye
  - * Concerned for righteousness vs. Concerned for political outcomes
- Literary context: Rise of David and decline of family
- Historical Context: Davidic monarchy
- Physical Context: Jerusalem, Zion, the city of YHWH
- YHWH: Stories within Scripture are designed to teach us primarily about YHWH. Certainly, this is a story with other major and minor characters: David, Nathan, Joab, Bathsheba, Uriah, guards at the gate, soldiers in the field, and the child that dies.
- Key words: "You are the man!"
- Themes: Sinfulness and holiness, repentance, there is no such thing as a private sin
- This scripture ends with one of those troubling sections that speak of God "making David's young son very sick." In fact, if we read on further, we will find that David's son dies.

Interpretations

- Main ideas: Sin has consequences. God sees. God will not tolerate sin.
- God has "models of righteousness" and "spokespersons for righteousness" in this world.
- Questions: What was Bathsheba's role in this story? Was she complicit? Joab was indeed part of the cover-up. Why did he not speak up? Political reasons, friendship reasons, kings have rights-and-privileges reasons, or military chain-of-command reasons. Was David bored, lustful, or seduced?
- Certainly the power of this story resides in the small declarative sentence: "You are the man!" Was this said in anger, disgust, sadness, or fear?
- Cross-References: Psalm 51, 2 Samuel 23:39.

Application

- Questions the passage asks of me:
    * How do I define sinfulness according to this story?
    * What am I doing with my sinfulness? Covering it or revealing it?
    * In the midst of my sinfulness, which do we need most: a Joab or a Nathan?
    * Who is my Nathan?

Who was Nathan? He was an advisor to the king, a friend, and, we are told, a prophet. He was a person that King David turned to for advice, counsel, friendship, clarification, direction—a spokesperson of God.

What is a prophet? Someone who foretells the future? In some cases, yes, but in this case, Nathan is one who speaks God's words of power, intention, and correction into the life of the king.

It is enviable to be in Nathan's position when things are going well. "A friend of the king," now that is a great title. Think about it. It would be like going into Nathan's office and seeing his picture with the king and all the important people of the kingdom. However, when things are going bad, when you have to speak truth into the life of a sinful leader, a leader who is publicly recognized as being a good and godly man, being the friend of the king isn't such a hot thing. In fact, it can be down right dangerous. Throughout history, Nathans have been excommunicated, kicked out of office, experienced broken friendships, and often killed.

Yet, in our story, God speaks his message of confrontation and condemnation to David through Nathan. Now I am not sure how it worked on that day that Nathan confronted David. We really are not told. But somehow, Nathan finds out about David's indiscretion. And Nathan courageously goes to the king. He has the king's ear, so to speak. When he speaks, the king listens. He has a proven track record with the king.

Nathan confronts the king. Was he afraid to come right out and confront the king? We certainly know the power of a story, and if we don't, we can see it here. Nathan tells a story, a parable. David reacts or, we might say, "gets hooked by the story," and makes a pronouncement about what should happen to this rich man. "This man deserves to die!" David pronounces. It is at this point that Nathan says rather directly, "You are the man!"

Here is the deal. Everyone needs a Nathan—someone in whom we have confidence, someone who can speak truth into our lives, someone who can stand, if necessary, against our self-denials and self-justifications. We need someone like Nathan that can talk us out of our best laid plans of cover-up, misinformation, and sin.

Too often we look for a Joab—a general, a person of power, a person with authority—to carry out our worst ideas with little or no moral integrity. The Joabs are concerned more about the end result than truth in general or our spiritual lives in particular. **The Nathans are concerned about truth and our spiritual lives.**

Finding a Nathan
- Develop friendships.
- Discern trust.
- Invite the Nathan in.
- Invest yourself in your Nathan.
- Allow your Nathan to speak truth into you life.
- Remember that most of the time your Nathan will add joy, companionship, and friendship to your life. At other times, as your Nathan discerns your error, he or she will apply truth to your life. This may well cut you deeply.
- Respond with grace and humility.
- Evaluate your Nathan's words.
- Confess and make restitution, if necessary.
- Move on in the company of your Nathan.

Concluding Comments on Narrative and Inductive Bible Study:

Inductive Bible Study is a valuable tool in the Christian educator's tool kit. This approach allows the educator to explore Scripture methodically. As the educator moves naturally from observation to interpretation and on to application, the truth and power of the narrative is exposed, unpacked, and applied.

4. Story-in-a-Sentence: Synthesizing and Retelling

Someone has said that it takes more work to be brief than verbose. Summarizing and synthesizing is the process of distilling a narrative down to its most salient point. In order to do this, exegesis is required. The goal of exegesis is "to reach an informed understanding of the text ... that is a cogent, informed interpretation...based on one's encounter with and investigation of a text at a given period of time."[22] To uncover the meaning of the text, careful exegetical methods must be applied.[23] The basic two-step exegetical exercise is designed to answer the following two questions:

---

22. Hayes and Holladay, *Biblical Exegesis*, 23.

23. Kaiser and Silva lay out a discovery process of the meaning of the text (exegesis). Issues of the original language, historical setting, meaning in original context, historicity, literary setting, canonical

- What did this text mean to the original audience in its original context?
- What does this text mean in today's context?

First steps might include:
- Who is the main character of the story?[24]
- What did this story mean in its original context or community?
- What can be learned in the humor, satire, or pathos of the story?
- What idioms are employed within the story?
- Why might this story have been shared; e.g., to establish identity, challenge orthodox opinion, open the community to the alien, determine judgment, and so forth.

Only after these and other questions have been explored can the student begin to ask the second step questions:

- What does this story mean today?
- How might the truth of this story be summarized, so that it still faithfully conveys the import in a form that is easy to memorize?
- Now that the story has been summarized into one sentence, has the power of the story dissipated?

Once an intense study of the text is completed and the student of Scripture has attempted to establish the meaning of the text, then the work of synthesis begins. It is here that the synthesizer works to "shrink" the meaning of the text or narrative into one cogent sentence. Stories are relayed in Scripture for a purpose: expose that purpose and condense it into one sentence. It should be noted, however, that anyone and everyone who summarizes and synthesizes the same story will not necessarily expose the same single interpretation or application of that purpose. It is possible, depending on the reader and the reader's context, that a differing "voice" may emerge and call the reader to account.[25]

---

setting, history of interpretation, and finally present significance are addressed. Note that issues of present significance is the very last step in this detailed process (Kaiser and Silva, *Introduction to Biblical Hermeneutics*, 19–22).

24. Fee and Stuart, *How to Read*, 91. It is helpful to remember that stories have three levels. Level One is where God's plan is worked out. Level Two is the story of God's people at work. Level Three is the individual narrative at hand. Ultimately the narrative at hand has been included in Scripture to tell us about the main character, and that main actor is God.

25 Nouwen explores the story from different perspectives according to his personal journey. At first he understood the story through the "eyes" of the rebellious younger brother, the self-righteous elder brother and finally through the extravagant father (Nouwen, *Return of the Prodigal Son*).

And once the story has been synthesized, then, from that most basic element of truthful content, the story can be faithfully "rebuilt" so as to speak to a new contemporary context.

The Narrative: Jeremiah 1:1–10
Summary of the Narrative

The Lord calls Jeremiah to speak prophetically to the people of Judah during the waning days of the kingdom. Jeremiah is not at all interested in the task. In fact, he is fearful. He begs out because he is young and inexperienced. But the Lord will not let him off the hook. The Lord acknowledges that the task is not an easy one but then declares that he will be with Jeremiah and will keep him safe. The Lord then touches Jeremiah's mouth and says that he has not only given Jeremiah the words to speak but the authority with which to speak them.

The Approach: "On Mission with Yahweh"

This story might be summarized in one sentence like this: "Ministry is living and speaking the word of God in our own context and with our own words."

This is a story that has a

- Context.
- Conviction.
- Co-mission.
- Commission.

Context:
- The Lord came to speak to Jeremiah at a particular historical time, circumstance, and situation. The Lord's word came at a particular time. The word came in the days of Josiah, a time of hopeful renewal, and ends with a time of exile. Clearly the story does not end well (vv 1–3).

Conviction:
- The Lord is, in fact, YHWH, the God who is active and present in every situation to bring about my / our deliverance (v 4).
- The Lord creates, comes, speaks, equips, appoints, rebukes, commissions, and sends. Jeremiah cannot seem to get around the conviction that he was created for this day, this task, this purpose (v 5).

Co-Mission:
- This is a co-mission of a young, insecure prophet (Jeremiah) and an awesome, promise-keeping God (YHWH) (v 2).

- The Lord says to Jeremiah that he and the prophet are on this journey, on task, together. YHWH allows no excuses (I can't speak, I'm too young). The Lord is committed not only to be with Jeremiah but also to protect him. As if that were not enough, YHWH says that he will speak through Jeremiah. That is an amazing thing. And—get this—Jeremiah will speak to the nations! A message of judgment and hope, destruction and rebuilding (vv 7–8).

Commission:

- The Lord calls, commands, and commissions his prophet to stand and be counted. "Do not be afraid. Do not be dismayed. Know that you will be delivered. **Your delivery will come in the midst of your obedience.** My power will make you strong…like a wall of bronze. They will fight against you but they will not win" (vv 17–18).
- The Lord gives his message to Jeremiah and then sends him out with authority. Jeremiah gets the whole deal: words and authority (appointed over nations and kingdoms). "The Lord reached out his hand, and then he touched my mouth and said, 'I am giving you the words to say, and I am sending you with authority to speak to the nations for me. You will tell them of doom and destruction and of rising and rebuilding again" (vv 9–10).

In the same way that God created, called, and commissioned Jeremiah, he is creating, calling, and commissioning you. Perhaps you are able with Jeremiah to articulate that YHWH is in the midst of creating you "for such a time as this" (Est 4:14). Or perhaps you are not there at all.

At times you may feel like crying out, "You have got to be kidding! I don't know enough Bible. I am so young and inexperienced that no one will take me seriously." But the amazing thing is this: YHWH wants to speak through you. It actually involves YHWH speaking and you speaking, YHWH acting and you acting, you, even you!

YHWH says rather bluntly, "Get over yourself and get on with it!" Your prophetic task is to speak the truth and to stand steady. You can do this because YHWH is with you. Your deliverance will come in the midst of your obedience!

You have been created for ministry; you may not yet know the specific form of ministry. Listen to your Creator. Lean on him, lean into him.

YHWH is calling you to speak for him, to stand with him in this world—at this time. YHWH is touching your mouth, giving you his words, sending you with his authority—to the nations. Tell them of doom and hope, of destruction and rebuilding. Be completely consumed by God's thoughts and words. Be about his agenda. Boldly speak the truth. Intentionally model the gospel.

As was said earlier, this story might be summarized in one sentence like this: "Ministry is living and speaking the word of God in our own context and with our own words." What might happen if that story, once summarized, was retold in a contemporary way?

- In the days when President Obama was newly in office…
- In the days of postmodernism, wars raging in Iraq and Afghanistan, gas prices rising, HIV-AIDS, climate change, poverty, homelessness, earthquakes and cyclones, recession and attempted recovery, globalization…
- In the days of a church with "laryngitis" of voice and half-hearted holiness of hands…
- In the days when the words "Love God and love your neighbor" were gaining some traction among a few…

The Word of the Lord came to me, a young servant,

And the Lord spoke to me: "You will speak for me in this context and contexts not your own. Don't even give the excuse that you are too young or ill-equipped. I will be with you. We will speak, and live, and act together." And I had this growing conviction that I had been created for such a time as this. When YHWH spoke, I listened. And what YHWH spoke, I spoke, wherever I went regardless of the consequences. And YHWH was good to his promises.

Concluding Comments of Narrative and Story-in-a-Sentence and Retelling:

The act of summarizing, synthesizing, and condensing is both a demanding and delightful task. It is demanding in that one does not want to "squeeze out" important truth in a narrative. It is demanding because this task of synthesizing a narrative requires utmost exegetical diligence and rigor. The narrative form, content, and context of the story must be explored. However, once this has been accomplished and the story has been condensed (not in a moralistic way), then the student can begin the delightful task of retelling the story in a manner that contemporary listeners may access. The narrative gains its "voice" again in a new setting.

5. *Lectio Divina*: "Let's read it one more time."

Lectio Divina is an historic practice of reading Scripture devotionally. *Lectio Divina* is designed so a person may encounter the sacred text and thereby facilitate spiritual transformation. The classic practice involves four steps: reading (*lectio*), meditating (*meditatio*), responding (*oratio*), and contemplating (*contemplatio*). Someone has compared this practice to eating an apple: taking a bite (*lectio*), chewing (*meditatio*), savoring (*oratio*), and digesting (*contemplatio*).[26] Robert Mulholland helpfully presents the process of *Lectio Divina* in the following way:

Silencio	Preparation for spiritual reading
	Inner shift from control to receptivity
	From information to formation
	From observation to obedience
Lectio	Reading/receiving
	Nurtures "sensing" dynamic
Meditatio	Processing
	Nurtures "thinking" dynamic
Oratio	Responses to God from the heart
	Nurtures "feeling" dynamic
Contemplatio	Yielding and waiting upon God
	Nurtures "intuitive" dynamic
Incarnatio	Living out the text[27]

Lectio Divina involves engaging the text, questioning the narrative again and again. After choosing a text or narrative, a classic version of *Lectio Divina* would involve the following questions:

- What word or phrase stands out to me?
- What is this passage saying to me?
- What is this passage calling me to do?

So *Lectio Divina* allows us to sit at the feet of the storyteller and listen to the narrative from various angles and perspectives. It seeks to employ our imagination. We are called upon to place ourselves squarely within the text. It calls to us, invites us, implores us, chastises us, comforts us, welcomes us. Certain words

---

26. Smith, Maria. "Lectio Divina Prayer Method." Christian Classics Ethereal Library. http://www.ccel.org/node/5086 (accessed March 2, 2010).

27. Taken from *Invitation to a Journey: A Road Map for Spiritual Formation* by M. Robert Mulholland, Jr, p. 113. Copyright © 1993 M. Robert Mulholland, Jr. Used by permission of InterVarsity Press, PO Box 1400, Downers Grove, IL 60515. www.ivpress.com.

or phrases demand our attention. The text is read again. Words are savored, pondered, rolled over in the mind, and explored. Yet again the text is read.

Lectio Divina is a process through which we ask questions of Scripture, but in the end, it is Sripture asking questions of us. In the end, *Lectio Divina* is a practice of surrender: "Lord, speak. Your servant is listening. I am content to be in your presence."

As you begin to practice *Lectio Divina* with the passage below, you might want to find a comfortable place. Center your thoughts on Jesus. Breathe deeply. Read through this story several different times, perhaps focusing on different elements and the questions above.

The Narrative: Luke 4:1–15
Summary of the Narrative

After Jesus was baptized by John and was blessed by his Father, the Spirit "drove" him into the wilderness. It was there that he was tested. It was there that he encountered the devil. It was there that Jesus won out in a series of temptations. And the devil was forced to retreat until another time. After these temptations, Jesus returned to Galilee and began his ministry in the power of the Spirit. And people took notice of his words and actions.

The Approach: Questions to Be Asked of This Story

Jesus has been baptized and has heard his Father in heaven pronounce a blessing on him. What did it feel like for Jesus to be led out—or even thrust out—by the Spirit into the wilderness?

Jesus was famished and then the temptations began. What was that like?

What did the scorching sun and burning sand feel like?

The devil was a liar, for he did not have the power or influence that he claimed. Yet how much those words—"If you are the Son of God…"—must have stung a famished Jesus. What did it feel like for Jesus to be slapped with those words?

Jesus used God's Word to deflect the devil's temptations. How did it feel when the devil turned the tables on Jesus and threw God's Word in his face in his third temptation?

When Jesus was victorious over the devil, we are told that "he (the devil) departed from him until an opportune time." How did Jesus feel?

Could Jesus have given in to these temptations? What might have been the result?

Are these temptations the basics of life, politics, and religion temptations—or are they temptations that address what kind of messiah Jesus will be?

Was this a Jesus like us, who was tempted in every way but did not sin (Heb 4:14)? Or was this a victorious Jesus, Son of God, who went out into the devil's territory and defeated him?

Is it possible that the devil's first "opportune time" was when Jesus was "praised by everyone" in verse 15?

Questions This Story Asks of Us

Have I heard with assurance that I am God's child and that he is well-pleased with me?

- Am I surprised and caught off guard when I find myself in the deserts of life, famished and tempted?
- Where are the deserts of my life? Label them.
- Am I conversant enough in God's Word that I can employ it faithfully in the face of temptation?
- At this moment in my life, do I need an intimate Jesus, one who suffers like me and does not sin? Or do I need an ultimate victorious Jesus, one who strides out into the devil's space and takes him on, on my behalf?
- How does this story challenge me to be faithful?
- How do I do when God and everyone else seems to speak well of me?

Process of Surrender

"Lord Jesus Christ, Son of God, I surrender to you. I choose not to surrender to the devil. In the face of my temptations this day, I choose to follow your example. I believe that to be a faithful disciple I must follow your example. I commit myself to the study, meditation, and memorization of your word. I will intentionally attune my ear to your voice rather than the voice of the liar. I believe today that God is my Father. He has claimed me as his child. He has provided for me a means of escape from every turmoil, test, and temptation. Lord Jesus, I am thankful for your victory on this day and throughout your earthly life. I am thankful that you reign victoriously even today. In you I find my method of faithfulness, in you I find my escape, in you I find my victory—today and forever."

Concluding Comments on Narrative and Lectio Divina:

Lectio Divina, the process of holy reading, allows the educator as an individual, or as a facilitator of a group of learners, to listen intently and intentionally to the narrative. It is all right, in fact, it is expected, to employ the imagination. Imagination is viewed as a holy attribute of humanity: "What did it smell like? How did Jesus feel when …? What was it like to feel pressed by God into an uncomfortable place?" And the amazing thing is this: in time the scripture begins to question the reader: "How would you respond if you were in a similar situation? If this is what faithfulness looks like in Jesus, what might it look like in me? Am I comforted by this passage or confronted by this passage?" *Lectio Divina* is a wonderful conductor of the power of a narrative.

6. Paraphrase: An Imaginative Retelling

Paraphrasing Scripture is a spiritual discipline. It has been made most famous recently by Eugene Peterson in his retelling of Scripture in *The Message*. Peterson writes in the introduction:

> This version of the New Testament in a contemporary idiom keeps the language of the Message current and fresh and understandable in the same language in which we do our shopping, talk with friends, worry about world affairs, and teach our children table manners. The goal is not to render a word-for-word conversation of Greek into English, but rather to convert the tone, the rhythm, the events, the ideas, into the way we actually think and speak.[28]

To paraphrase a story requires an application of previous disciplines: brainstorming, inductive study, synthesizing, and *Lectio Divina*. Once those have been accomplished, the educator can begin the work of paraphrasing and recasting the story in a faithful manner to a new audience in a new context.

The Narrative: John 13:1-32
Summary of the narrative

Jesus gathered with his disciples to celebrate Passover. He knew that his ministry on earth was coming to an end. He knew he would be leaving his disciples. He knew that none of his disciples were fully committed. He also knew that the disciples where not ready to face the reality of his bloody death or their temptation to flee, hide, or deny. Jesus chose this moment to model humility and reinterpret the Passover celebration. Jesus also looked Satan in the eye and did not blink.

The Approach: "The New Moses and the Strongman"

In the days of Moses, God wrenched his people from the hand of the most powerful man on earth. God sent forth an angel of death silently by night. Death was like an incoming tide that rose higher and higher, claiming the firstborn of every house, from the poorest clapboard hovel to the strongman's massive stone palace. Yet as the awful tide of death rolled on, whenever it came to the home of one of God's people, it would froth and foam just inches from the door and

---

28. Peterson, *The Message*, 7.

then recede, daring not to enter, as if it were obeying orders from the Almighty himself. And indeed it was.

Moses and God's people had been spared the breakers of death that rolled into Egypt on that fateful night because they had marked their homes in the exact manner that God had instructed. Blood from a spotless lamb was applied to the doorpost of each Hebrew home with a hyssop branch. The blood-sprinkled doorpost was more than a sign of obedience to God, more than a sign of membership and solidarity within the community of faith. The lamb's blood was a sign of command to the waves of deathly destruction: "Do not enter this home! Do not harm the people who dwell here!" The brownish flecks on the doorframe cried out, "Stop short! Stop short!" Every home not so marked experienced death. The high tide of doom swept away the most prized and cherished ones of each household. As a result, a painful, heart-rending cry arose in the land of the Egyptian strongman. He was forced to let God's people go.

Centuries later, a small group gathered to remember and celebrate this act of holy history. On this night, a new Moses gathered with a handful of his followers to rejoice that God had once very decisively entered in on the side of his people and provided their rescue from bondage. Their rejoicing was tempered by their doubts, fears, and questions. Only the leader, the new Moses himself, knew that the time had come for him to leave his followers and return to the Father, the very same God who sent the wave of death, established the sign of the bloody door post, and ultimately freed his people from the tightly clinched grip of the Egyptian strongman. Only the leader, a new and greater Moses, knew the extent to which God was, at that very moment, entering in on the side of his people once again. A far more decisive battle was about to be fought against the strongman from hell itself.

The strongman had been at work to cripple and disenfranchise God's people. He had played on the people's prejudices, doubts, and fears. He also used the people's own nationalistic longings. The strongman had won over a great many who sat in the seats of power. But the key to his plan against the new Moses was to nourish the frustration and impatience of one from among the new deliverer's very own group. The strongman needed a willing volunteer. The strongman had decided that either of the followers, Simon or Judas, would be perfect. If he were able to win over both, it would be that much better.

On this night of celebration and remembrance, the new Moses and the strongman entered a duel to the death. The new Moses knew that he came from God and would return to God. He knew of the strongman's deception. He knew of the treachery. He knew about the opposition's payoff. He knew that those closest to him would fall away under the pressure of the moment.

He knew the cost he would be required to pay in order to defeat the strongman forever. He knew! This new Moses also knew that he had all of heaven's power at his disposal.

Outside in the darkened alleyway, the strongman waited. He was already prepared for battle. He was armed to the teeth with all the wicked tools of deception and death that hell could offer. Peering through a knothole in the door, he longed to enter into the room to sow discord among the followers, but he dared not, for he knew that he could never stand in the presence of the new Moses unless one of the deliverer's followers would invite him in.

As the strongman watched, the new Moses made a move as if he were now ready to equip himself for battle. The strongman tensed at the door, and as he did he issued an order that put all of his vast demonic army on the highest state of alert.

"I wonder what weapons of war this so-called deliverer will employ?" he hissed silently to himself.

The strongman was thrown off guard when the new Moses removed his garment and reached, not for sword and armor, but for a towel and basin.

When the new Moses bent to wash his followers' feet, the strongman began to laugh. It was not a silent snicker. It was a boisterous kind of drunken-sailor laugh. It was a derisive laugh. It was a laugh that bellowed forth from the prince of darkness. The strongman could not have laughed harder if the new Moses had picked up Legos and begun to fashion a weapon.

The deliverer began with those followers nearest him. As he washed the feet of each follower, the new Moses shared an intimate conversation with each. The strongman strained his ears to hear what was being said, but he could not. Finally the new Moses reached the far end of the U-shaped table. The place was normally reserved for the slave. The follower named Simon was in that place. It was the slave, not the master, who was to be washing the feet of those present.

A smile began to spread across the face of the strongman. He put his mouth near the knothole and whispered, "Don't you dare let him wash your feet!"

Simon had sat speechless as the new Moses had stooped to wash the feet of his followers. As the deliverer now knelt before him, a mixture of offense, surprise, and indignation crashed over him. Masters don't wash feet. Slaves do. It was offensive to Simon that the one he respected and followed would do such a menial and dirty task. It surprised him that the new Moses was doing the assignment that for whatever reason was to be his by virtue of his position at the table. The indignation was directed toward the others who had allowed their master to degrade himself. "I value our master too much. He will never wash my feet!" he stormed inwardly. The inward storm burst forth with great fury and frustration.

"Lord, are you going to wash my feet?" It wasn't a question at all. It was a declaration that announced, "There is no way that I am going to let you wash my feet! Never!"

The strongman prepared to enter the room. All he waited for was a word of invitation from Simon. The strongman knew that Simon was about to unbolt the door and let him in. But the long awaited invitation didn't come.

"If I don't wash you," the deliverer said, "you really don't belong to me."

After an awkward pause Simon bowed his head and replied, "Lord, don't just wash my feet. Wash my hands and head as well."

The strongman shook with rage. "Leave Simon! Now!" he thundered. Turning to the assembly of evil around him, he commanded, "Leave him! I'll return to him later. I still have my eye on the other one."

The strongman again focused on the conversation in the room. It was as if the new Moses were eavesdropping on the strongman and not the other way around. "...And you, my followers, are clean, except one of you."

The deliverer already knew who would betray him. The words were like music in the ears of the strongman. Although he didn't know who, he now knew for certain that his plan would work. He had never felt a greater thrill. He was closing in on an eternal checkmate, the ultimate victory that even the new Moses couldn't stop. Delay, maybe, but not stop. A once-and-for-all victory was about to be handed him on a silver, no, gold platter.

A question bubbled up briefly in the brackish backwaters of his mind: "If defeat was certain for this self-proclaimed deliverer, why did he exude such an air of confidence?" Quickly he flushed the troubling thought from his mind.

"Who? I want to know who my new teammate is," with sarcastic emphasis on "teammate."

The new Moses again put on his garment and assumed the role of teacher. "Do you understand what I have done?" he asked. "You call me teacher and Lord, and you should, because that is who I am."

The strongman turned to the demon at his right hand and replied, "Please! I think I'm going to be sick." He pretended to vomit. The strongman and the demon rolled with laughter.

"If I, your teacher and Lord, have washed your feet, you should do the same for each other...I tell you for certain that servants are not greater than their master, and messengers are not greater than the one who sent them."

The evil strongman spun and faced his troops and spoke. All the humor was gone from his voice. He sounded a warning, "Almost all of what this do-gooder says is hogwash. But take to heart what he says about servants and their master." He paused for effect. Then with the veins bulging on the side of his neck he screamed, "I am your only master! You work for me! I demand total allegiance and instant obedience!" Flecks of spittle collected on the edge of his unkempt beard. Fire burned in his eyes. Undisguisable fear emanated from his legions.

As the strongman ranted, the teacher continued, "The man who ate with me has turned against me." The new Moses was quoting Scripture. This was the strongman's favorite memory verse. He snapped his attention back to the room where the small group had gathered. He fastened his eye again to the chink in the door.

"I am telling you this before it all happens. Then when it does happen, you will believe who I am."

"A two-bit Savior," the strongman laughed. "A Savior who promises heaven and can't even save himself from his own piddly band of buddies isn't worth much."

The confidence that had troubled the strongman earlier began to fade as the new Moses spoke. In direct proportion, the strongman began to puff up and strut around like a peacock. "I tell you for certain that one of you will betray me."

Confusion descended on the small band like a cold, damp mist. The followers were speechless. They stared at each other, unable to comprehend.

The new Moses had one or two among the twelve who were like Joshua of old, loyal and fully able to carry on after he had gone. One was named John. "When this battle is over and I have disposed of the new Moses, I'll take care of the rest, one by one," the strongman thought to himself. Snapping his fingers, instantly his aide de camp appeared at his shoulder. "Make a note," he commanded. "That one sitting next to the pretender," he said, pointing a boney finger directly at the follower named John, "when this is all over I want to arrange to send him off to some God-forsaken spot on this globe of mine. He's too influential. We must banish him!"

The aide dutifully recorded every word. It was obvious that the aide enjoyed his work very much, for he could not keep from smiling as he recorded the memo.

The one who sat closest to the new Moses leaned his head back on the chest of his master and asked, "Lord, which one of us are you talking about?"

This was the million-dollar question! With growing delight, the strongman let his hungry gaze fall first on Simon and then on Judas. All heaven and hell stood silent as the new Moses spoke.

"I will dip this piece of bread in the sauce and give it to the one I am talking about," the deliverer said. Then the new Moses dipped a broken piece of unleavened bread into the sop and gave it to Judas. As Judas's fingers closed on the piece of bread, the invitation to the strongman was offered. The strongman whisked into the room and took control of Judas in the same instant.

With the strongman in control of Judas, the deliverer spoke, "Go quickly and do what you have to do." Both Judas and the strongman-deceiver understood the command. The followers did not. Some among them thought perhaps that Judas was going to buy some additional items for the feast. Others thought that

Judas was going out to make an offering on their behalf to the poor. Whatever the others thought really made little difference. With the strongman firmly in control, Judas left the gathering. It was not surprising that as he left, the room was enveloped by an inky, evil blackness. None of the followers present could see what took place outside the room. Of course the new Moses knew. The strongman-deceiver handed Judas over to his number two demons and then returned to his place by the now open door. He still had hopes that he could win over Simon as well. "A little insurance is what I'm looking for," he crooned.

The new Moses now spoke again. "I will not take evasive action. I will be glorified, that is, I will suffer and die. But God will glorify me, and through all of this God will receive much praise and honor. All of this will happen very soon." The words were like a rubber ball striking a hard surface; they simply bounced away before the followers had a chance to grasp their meaning.

"Gobbledy-goop," the strongman-deceiver whispered.

The deliverer continued, "I won't be with you much longer. You will look for me but won't be able to find me. As I told others, I now tell you, 'You cannot go where I am going.' But I am giving you a new command. You must love one another in the same way that I have loved you. If you do this, everyone will know that you are truly my followers."

"Ask him where he is going," the strongman-deceiver hissed.

It was Simon who spoke up. "Where are you going, Lord?"

The new Moses answered, "You can't go with me now, but later on you will."

"Ha!" the strongman blurted out. "You won't want to go where I plan to send this pretender!"

Simon immediately responded, "Lord, why can't I go with you now. I would die for you!"

"Simon, me boy," the strongman said in a fake Irish accent, "you have just sealed your fate. You will forever be known as the one who denied the pretender.

"Not a bad night's work," the strongman said, verbally patting himself on the back. "I set a trap for two and I caught two—one betrayer and one denier!" The strongman was so proud of himself that he no longer cared what the deliverer had to say to his followers. The strongman joined his legions in a Mardi Gras-like parade. The parade began a raucous celebration that spread throughout the globe. Evil was celebrating the apparent victory over God's anointed.

Even if the strongman had wanted to, it would not have been possible for him to hear as the deliverer spoke words of comfort to his followers. "Don't worry. Have faith in God and in me. There are many rooms in my Father's house. I wouldn't tell you this unless it was true. I am going to prepare a place for each of you."

Later on he said, "I won't leave you like orphans. I will come back to you. The time will come and is already here when all of you will be scattered. Each of you will go back home and leave me by myself. But the Father will be with me, and I won't be alone. I have told you this so you might have peace in your hearts. While you are in the world, you will have to suffer. But cheer up! I have defeated the world."

His meaning was clear. He had already defeated the strongman.

In the days of the new Moses, God wrenched his people from the hand of the evil strongman once and for all. God did not send an *angel of death* to sweep over the land. This time he sent the *Son of Life*.

The offer of life was for all: rich and poor, strong and weak, good and the agents of evil themselves. All could find new life, hope and deliverance through the new Moses. It is true that in order to grant all life, hope, and deliverance, the new Moses had to die a cruel death on a cross. But then he knew the price all along and he willingly paid it in full.

The new Moses became our spotless lamb, and by faith we have marked the doorposts of our lives with his blood. The good news is this: the strongman's grip on our lives has been broken forever. Hallelujah!

Concluding Comments on Narrative and Paraphrase:

When the imagination is faithful and intentionally engaged, the paraphrase has an opportunity to speak powerfully again to a new community of learners. We are often afraid to allow our imaginations to take flight: "This is God's Word. Isn't there some sort of curse in Revelation that prohibits us from adding to or deleting from his Word?" Be not encumbered.

When we paraphrase, we have the opportunity to bring stories from their original culture and context into ours. The paraphrase above is an attempt to tell the story that embeds John's Gospel within our culture that talks much about spirits and demons. It is an attempt to place John's story within our Mardi Gras culture. It is hoped that the power and victory of Jesus comes across with its original power, simply retold in such a way that a new generation will sit down to listen and rise up to live more faithfully in our day.

Conclusion: Tapping Into the Power of a Story

When my children were young, every evening as I put them to bed, I would create and tell them a story. Jonni, our daughter, had her stories about "The Too-Tired Turtle." This turtle had one adventure or another. At the most thrilling points in the story the little girl would discover that the turtle had fallen asleep.

Our son, Will, had his stories, too. His stories were about "Frisbee the Frog." Frisbee the Frog always got into mischief, yet on a nightly basis, he made it home, safe and sound, in some remarkable way.

As our family traveled from church to church on itineration in the United States, or in Korea or Egypt as missionaries, I told my children (and my wife, Gwen) the story of the Snikledorffers. We went through several generations with this family. They were German, of course, and had immigrated to the United States. We followed the parents, Herman and Sarah, and their three boys, as they adjusted to life in the United States. Probably what my children will remember most about these stories is that Herman was bald except for one long hair in the center of his head. He never cut that hair and he would carefully coil it on his head so it looked like he had hair after all. It was the ultimate comb-over; however, on windy days it would blow off his head and cause all sorts of mayhem. As the storyteller, I intentionally wove in stories of language and culture clashes. When we would receive joyful or troubling news from home, that news would find its way into the stories. I spoke about loneliness, hope, laughter, patience, death, discipline, and a whole host of topics. Now it is true that I could have gathered my children on my knee and taught them propositional truth about those issues. But Jonni and Will would have never sat still long enough to get through my first point, no matter how wonderfully well-arranged my outline. But if I told a Snikledorffer story, a Too-Tired Turtle story, or a Frisbee the Frog story, I had their full attention.

Those who wrote, edited, and published the Bible certainly knew the power of stories. We have prehistory stories, patriarch stories, captivity and deliverance stories, conquest stories, monarchy stories, exile-and-return stories, Jesus stories, early church stories, and even apocalyptic stories. When Jesus was trying to teach the people of his day important kingdom topics, he too employed the use of narrative. That is why Matthew writes, "Jesus used stories when he spoke to the people. In fact, he did not tell them anything without using stories" (13:34).

The wise Christian educator will tap into the power of a story. To do so, he or she must clearly understand the literary structure of a story and experiment with different methods of delivering a story. A wealth of information about the value of story and the techniques of employing a story are found within disciplines we call Christian education, discipleship, and spiritual formation.

In our postmodern world, perhaps, Christian educators and parents alike need to rediscover the power of story. The world around us is not looking for polished theological truth or three-point sermons. But if we are listening carefully we will hear what I heard so often when my children were young, "Daddy, tell us a story."

Bibliography

Arthurs, Jeffrey D. *Preaching with Variety*. Grand Rapids, MI: Kregel, 2007.

Berryman, Jerome W. *Godly Play*. San Francisco, CA: Augsburg Fortress, 1995.

Fee, Gordon D. and Douglas Stuart. *How to Read the Bible for All Its Worth*. Grand Rapids, MI: Zondervan, 2003.

Foster, Richard. "Spiritual Formation: A Pastoral Letter." *Heart to Heart*, November 1996: 1–3. http://www.theooze.com/articles/article.cfm?id=744&page=1 (accessed August 8, 2009).

Hauerwas, Stanley. *A Community of Character*. Norte Dame, IN: University of Norte Dame Press, 1981.

Hayes, John H. and Carl R. Holladay. *Biblical Exegesis: A Beginner's Handbook*. Atlanta, GA: John Knox Press, 1987.

Hoppe, Leslie J. *New Light from Old Stories*. New York: Paulist Press, 2005.

Howard, Evan B. "On Spiritual Formation." Spirituality Shoppe Newsletter 4, no. 2 (September 1999). http://www.livingwatercoaching.com/article-spiritual-formation.htm.

Johnson, John M. "Enhancing the Quality of Christian Leaders Through Discipleship." DMin diss., Ashland Theological Seminary, 1999.

Kaiser, Walter C. and Moisés Silva. *An Introduction to Biblical Hermeneutics*. Grand Rapids, MI: Zondervan, 1994.

Koyama, Kosuke. *No Handle on the Cross*. Maryknoll, NY: Orbis Books, 1973.

Lee-Thorp, Karen. *The Story of Stories*. Colorado Springs, CO: NavPress, 1991.

Mulholland, M. Robert. *Invitation to a Journey*. Downers Grove: InterVarsity Press, 1993.

Nouwen, Henri J. M. *The Return of the Prodigal Son*. New York: Doubleday, 1992.

Peterson, Eugene H.. *The Message: The New Testament in Contemporary English*. Colorado Springs, CO: NavPress, 1993.

Ryken, Lyland. *How to Read the Bible as Literature*. Grand Rapids, MI: Zondervan, 1984.

Strege, Merle D. *Tell Me Another Tale*. Anderson, IN: Warner Press, 1993.

Willard, Dallas. "How Does the Disciple Live?" *Radix* 34, no 3 (Spring 2009). http://www.dwillard.org/articles/artview.asp?artID=103 (accessed November 14, 2010).

Wright, N. T. *Simply Christian*. New York: Harper Collins, 2005.

Zahniser, A. H. Mathias. *Symbol and Ceremony: Making Disciples Across Cultures*. Monrovia, CA: MARC, 1997.

CHAPTER TEN

Reaching Out and Bringing in Education, Evangelism, and the Nurture of Christian Faith

SARAH BLAKE

> Anyone who belongs to Christ is a new person. The past is forgotten, and everything is new.
>
> —2 Corinthians 5:17

For all of her life, Anne held a definite position concerning Jesus: she was a Jew, and Jesus was not the Messiah.[1] However, experiences during recent years created great emotional turmoil for her. She labeled herself a mystic and began to open herself to learning from other spiritual traditions in her quest to find peace. Her explorations eventually led her into contact with several Christians.

At first, discussions were focused solely on Anne's desire to learn more about how her new friends practiced their faith. She maintained her position that belief in Jesus was not congruent with her Jewish heritage; but she was intrigued by stories about why her Christian friends accepted him as Messiah.

Anne's friends did not press her concerning her beliefs. They provided explanations and information when she asked for them and provided suggestions for

---

1 Anne (name has been changed), telephone interview by author, April 2, 2010.

further reading when she seemed open. At times, Anne approached discussions academically. At other times, she struggled openly with her emotional turmoil.

After several years of dialogue, Anne took a step that surprised her friends. She began to attend a church, identifying herself as "a Jew among Christians." She explained, "I wanted to find a group of people who lived like Jesus." In her ongoing discussions with her friends, she began to explore questions about how to handle the impact of her decision upon her relationships in the Jewish community.

Anne's attitude about Jesus changed dramatically. She said, "If Jesus is not the Messiah, then I really can't deal with that anymore. I need to have a teacher that would match Jesus." Her voice was passionate. However, she could not bring herself to be baptized. "I am not a Christian," she said. "I am still a Jew. I won't join the church, even if I do worship there."

Defining Christianity

While Anne could not put her thoughts completely into words, her response concerning baptism reveals something about the message often communicated to unchurched people by churchgoers. Many people often associate "being a Christian" with particular expectations that they do not necessarily associate with following Jesus. According to George Hunter, churches often unconsciously communicate various expectations about what it means to be a Christian. These expectations may fall into ten areas: (1) be religious, (2) believe like us, (3) behave like us, (4) experience like us, (5) become like us (culturally), (6) be good citizens, (7) share our politics, (8) support the institutional church, (9) prepare people for heaven, and (10) be like us in sacraments or devotions.[2] Sometimes church members or leaders communicate that several of these criteria must be met in order to be considered "Christian," even while preaching a message of grace.

These conflicting messages can cause confusion for people in the early stages of belief about the desirability of community in the process of faith formation. Tim, who is still in the seeker stage, explained this confusion, "I want a place to ask questions; but my questions offend people. I need to be able to question what it means for the Bible to be the Word of God. But you don't do that in the church. I believe in God, and at some point I think I would like to find a church to attend; but I don't know that it is necessary for me to attend church in order to practice my faith."[3] Where Anne finds the church to be a place where her growing faith is nurtured, Tim experiences it as a place where his exploration may be stifled before he can reach a place of faith. As a person who desires to pursue faith, he is very cautious about the ways in which he nurtures his growth process; and he avoids further stifling experiences.

---

2. Hunter, *Church for the Unchurched*, 37–41.

3. Tim (name has been changed), telephone interview by author, April 15, 2010.

When participating in conversations with seekers, it is important that Christians understand stages of discipleship and be able to relate in a way that facilitates exploration and growth. It is also important to understand things that hinder discipleship, and to be able to alter one's methods in order to meet the needs of a given situation.

This chapter explores stages of discipleship, the importance of evangelism in the discipleship process, how to educate people for evangelism, the evangelism process, concerns about nominal Christians, special concerns for the evangelism of children and youth, and the role of holiness. Finally, recommendations are provided for creating an atmosphere that is safe, one in which discipleship can take place and new Christians can receive help in managing their relationships with the church and with people who may be opposed to their newfound faith.

A Model for Discipleship

Hunter proposed a model of discipleship in response to the seeker's lack of knowledge of what it means to be Christian. His model identified ten stages of discipleship, comparing them to bowling pins.

> Each of the ten pins is named, and each row of pins is also named. The one pin in the first row deals with what most modern secular people need to Discover before they can effectively begin the Christian pilgrimage. The second row, with two pins, features what God wants all people to Experience. The third row, with three pins, identifies the essential features of the New Life in Christ. The fourth row, with four pins, focuses on the New Lifestyle to which Christ calls us.[4]

Hunter's ten pins are:

1. Recognition of the fact that the seeker matters to God (in this stage they may experiment with prayer)
2. New relationship with God
3. New relationship with the people of God
4. Doing the will of God
5. Love for people and creatures
6. Freedom in Christ
7. Attention to godly things
8. Lifestyle of service and ministry
9. Lifestyle of witness and mission
10. New identity in Christ[5]

4. Hunter, *Church for the Unchurched*, 44–45.

5. Ibid, 45–54.

The Importance of Evangelism in the Discipleship Process

Anne's journey into the church was an intentional one, made to take her into contact with Jesus. According to Norma Cook Everest, this kind of journey is less common than the kind of conversion that occurred because a church member shared the gospel outside the church community. Everest wrote, "Once in a while, someone will simply be passing by the church on a Sunday morning and walk in. Once in a while, the quoting of a random Bible passage will bring a person to faith. But only once in a while. Most of the time, we need to reach out and intentionally meet people where they are."[6] The activities that provide the vehicle for outreach are often labeled as "evangelism." Ben Campbell Johnson defined evangelism as the process by which a connection between God and a human is facilitated.[7] He explained that many things can serve to facilitate this connection, including but not limited to the worshiping community, the Bible, and nature. Encounters may emphasize God's love, God's presence, God's forgiveness, or God's providence.[8]

Church groups or individuals may engage in several kinds of activities in an effort to connect with people and help them connect with God. These include activities to meet needs, healing services, special presentations, concerts, revivals, and door-to-door evangelism. Hunter explained that evangelism has two prongs. One relates to lifestyle: the person becomes a follower of Jesus, living according to his power and will and following his teachings. The other prong relates to community: the person becomes devoted to the community of God, participating in worship and service.[9] Accounts of evangelistic work found in the Acts of the Apostles feature this two-pronged approach.

Educating the Church for Evangelism

Evangelism that is based on relationship can have a powerful impact, even when other methods have affected a person negatively. Christians have often been taught and encouraged to approach strangers and share scripture-heavy messages, leading to an encouragement to pray a prayer of decision. Tim's reaction to these door-to-door evangelists illustrates the futility of this approach: "People quote Bible verses to me, thinking that will make me believe. These little quotations don't mean anything to me. I haven't even decided if I believe this stuff yet."

Tim's journey toward faith has occurred over a period of years through dialogue with trusted individuals. These friends have assisted him in responding to events that Tim has come to understand represent God's pursuit of him.

---

6. Norma Cook Everest, "Learn to Share Christ in the Languages of People's Daily Lives," in Everest, *Christian Education as Evangelism*, 122.

7. Johnson, *Speaking of God*, 23.

8. Ibid., 22.

9. Hunter, *Contagious Congregation*, 23.

He believes that some of those events can only be explained in terms of God's intervention.

According to Ravi Zacharias, people are often drawn to Christ because of a supernatural event or because of the love or life example of a friend.[10] This initial encounter makes way for the sharing of the gospel through discussion. Hunter explained that many secular people have little understanding of Christian culture or experience of church.[11] Evangelistic discussions must often be ongoing in order to help the person develop a framework needed to understand the gospel when it is shared.

Language can create openness, or it can place barriers between the Christian and the unchurched person. Johnson contrasted the ideas of "God-talk," the overuse of language referring to God in conversation, and "God-speech," which is honest discussion about God.[12] God-talk can overwhelm people and inoculate them against hearing the gospel. God-speech, on the other hand, is appropriate to the situation and may be received well. It is important that Christians learn how to speak with unchurched individuals in natural ways, using "God-speech" where appropriate, so that people hear authentic stories of God's action in the lives of their friends.

Natural relationship-building is also important. One common complaint of unchurched individuals is that they feel their relationships with Christians are always about the Christians' desire to convert them. Tim explained that he avoids Christians if he perceives they are motivated in this way.

Everest proposed relating to secular people in terms of vocation (what one does every day), location (where one spends time most often), relationships, and outlook.[13] In order to do this, Christians need to be acquainted with "the secular world." However, Christians often lose contact with the secular world in the attempt to maintain holy lives. Laura, who became a Christian in her teens, stopped reading literature or listening to music that was not overtly Christian. After several years, Laura realized that her staunch stance on holiness made it difficult for her to relate to unchurched people. She now struggles to find a balance between holiness and relationship.[14] According to Hunter, many Christians are not acquainted with unchurched people and are hesitant to share their faith despite encouragement and the availability of evangelism training.[15] The fact that many Christians cannot identify unchurched people in their circles of influence is problematic. Secular culture is as unfamiliar to the church as church culture is to secular people.

---

10. Ravi Zacharias, "The Touch of Truth," in Carson, *Telling the Truth*, 37.

11. Hunter, *Church for the Unchurched*, 20.

12. Johnson, *Speaking of God*, 11.

13. Norma Cook Everest, "Learn to Share Christ in the Languages of People's Daily Lives," in Everest, *Christian Education as Evangelism*, 122.

14. Laura (name has been changed), telephone interview by author, April 25, 2010.

15. Hunter, *Church for the Unchurched*, 23–24.

How can Christians maintain an acquaintance with the secular world? When one Holiness group, the Church of God (Anderson, Indiana), was still a fledgling movement, Russell Byrum, one of its leaders, encouraged ministers to be well read in history, biography, science, philosophy, other religions, and literature, noting that preachers may come into contact with people from a variety of backgrounds.[16] Byrum's advice is wise for laypeople as well. In today's mobile society, Christians may come into contact with people from a variety of ethnic, educational, and socioeconomic backgrounds. Christians should not limit their reading material to what is Christian; and they should not limit their socializing to groups of Christians. Being well-read and well-socialized will prepare them for relationships that serve as natural conduits of God's love.

Jesus' journey with his disciples was a journey of intensive training in disciple making, beginning with the call of Peter (Matt 4:19). His interactions enabled his disciples to learn to make disciples within the cultural milieu, learning by observing and asking questions of him and interacting with each other.

The church must similarly train people for disciple making. Its educational program must include training in how to build relationships with people from a variety of backgrounds, how to listen actively to their stories, how and when to share one's own testimony, and how to ask questions that will encourage exploration of the Christian faith. These things can be modeled in all types of educational groups. Icebreakers and discussion starters might include gathering information about group members' families, occupations, hobbies, recent activities, and so on. These pieces of information provide the framework for relating in fellowship or, when appropriate, in evangelism. At other times during the group discussion process, different questions can encourage the sharing of personal stories, discussion of elements of Christian experience, and responses to scripture. Role playing can also be a useful tool to assist people in building skills in initiating conversations.

The Evangelism Process

Since the evangelism process seeks the conversion of the unsaved person, the church's education program must also help people to identify levels of receptivity, tailor their efforts at evangelism accordingly, and enable Christians to recognize signs of conversion in seekers.

Hunter explained that a person's receptivity may fluctuate during his or her lifetime.[17] He classified undiscipled people into five categories: receptive, interested, indifferent, resistant, and hostile, proposing a visitation schedule based on the level of a person's receptivity.[18] He stressed that achieving a ministry of presence is necessary before the gospel can be proclaimed and may help to move

---

16. Russell R. Byrum, "The Preacher Among His Books," *Our Ministerial Letter*, April 1917, 9.

17. Hunter, *Contagious Congregation*, 107.

18. Ibid, 128.

a person from resistance to receptivity.[19] As Tim's journey demonstrates, this process can take months or even years. Johnson proposed that the most effective process is spiritual guidance rather than proclamation or manipulation.[20]

For some people, the evangelistic process does not end in conversion at all. Carrie attended a seeker-friendly church for several years and joined a small group, searching for answers to her questions and something that would lead to a connection with God. She never found answers to her deepest questions. "Finally," she explained, "I realized that I didn't need to know. I didn't need to use God as an answer." Today, Carrie is an atheist. She relates respectfully to her Christian friends and teaches her children about the way that Christians practice their faith; but she does not believe in God and does not anticipate that she will ever become open to changing her beliefs.[21]

Hunter's proposed visitation schedule has some weaknesses. It may reinforce in the minds of less receptive persons the idea that Christians are only interested in proselytizing them. An ongoing presence can allow for the development of receptivity, whereas seasonal visits can sometimes breed further hostility. When planning visits with persons who are receptive, it is important to account for the impact of stressful events in their lives, which may place strain on their time. A person who is weighed down by the responsibility of caring for a family member with a terminal illness may be deeply touched by an offer of assistance with practical tasks. On the other hand, too many visits may further stress the person. Sensitivity to the direction of the Holy Spirit is needed when relating to the unchurched.

Door-to-door evangelists and revivalists often rely on prayers of confession as signs of conversion. The weakness of this practice is that the new convert is often left to search for sources of further spiritual guidance and may fail to maintain steady growth in faith. Kristin's experience demonstrates this problem. Kristin responded to an altar call at a Christian concert when she was a teenager.[22] "I didn't really know what I was doing," she said. "Someone asked me if I was saved, and I said I didn't think so. Then she took me back to a room and talked to me about salvation." Kristin did not find a church to attend for another year.

Hunter encouraged a new paradigm for thinking about conversion: "Evangelizing happens when the RECEIVER (receptor, respondent) turns (1) to Christ, (2) to the Christian message and ethic, (3) to a Christian congregation, and (4) to the world, in love and mission—in any order."[23] Recognizing the signs that a person is approaching one of these turns, a person who serves as a

---

19. Ibid, 135.

20. Johnson, *Speaking of God*, 15.

21. Carrie (name has been changed), telephone interview by author, April 17, 2010.

22. Kristin (name has been changed), telephone interview by author, April 17, 2010.

23. Hunter, *Contagious Congregation*, 27.

spiritual guide can point out God's action or discuss the application of scriptural principles to a given situation, thus providing the connection needed to enable the person to make another step on the spiritual journey. This practice is similar to the strategy that Bill Hybels uses to expose seekers to Scripture during worship services. G. A. Pritchard explained, "In order to provide meaningful engagement with scripture, Bill Hybels begins by engaging seekers concerning a topic of importance in their daily lives and refers to the common message that Scripture brings to people's needs."[24]

The Importance of Nurturing Nominal Christians

The number of people who have made initial decisions to follow Christ and have not experienced vibrancy in their faith is alarming. Hunter noted that a great amount of time is spent on attempts to evangelize these "nominal Christians," who have often become immunized to the gospel, instead of reaching out to people outside the church who are receptive. However, he also noted that many nominal Christians have not taken all of the turns in the conversion process, and therefore, the church cannot abandon them in evangelism efforts.[25]

The problem of nominality illustrates what happens when the two prongs of evangelism have failed to work together. Eddie Gibbs explained:

> There are those who continue to belong while they no longer believe; on the other hand, there are those who believe even though they cease to belong.
>
> The Lausanne task group which studied nominality identified five types of nominal Christian which it categorized as follows:
>
> 1. Attends church regularly and worships devoutly, but who has no personal relationship with Jesus Christ.
> 2. Attends church regularly but for cultural reasons only.
> 3. Attends church only for major church festivals (Christmas, Easter, etc.) and ceremonies (weddings, baptisms, funerals).
> 4. Hardly ever attends church but maintains a church relationship for reasons of security, emotional or family ties, or tradition.
> 5. Has no relationship to any specific church and never attends but yet considers himself a believer in God (in a traditional Christian sense).[26]

Johnson suggested that those who believe but do not belong may return to the church at some point with numerous questions and that those who have remained in the church without experiencing dynamic faith pose a special chal-

---

24. Pritchard, *Willow Creek Seeker Services*, 145.

25. Hunter, *Contagious Congregation*, 27.

26. Gibbs, *In Name Only*, 23.

lenge to the church, suggesting that both groups can benefit from spiritual guidance.[27] Nurture of nominal Christians benefits the whole community.

Special Considerations for the Nurture of Children and Youth

Kristin shared not only about the lag between her initial salvation experience but about other experiences that highlight the need for attention to particular concerns in the evangelism of children and youth. She explained that her mother expressed confusion about her conversion, saying, "I thought you did that when you were little." Her mother's confusion indicates that perhaps her mother was a nominal Christian who did not attend church, and thus Kristin's faith was never nurtured. This illustrates the link between the importance of nurturing the faith of nominal Christians and the evangelism of children and youth.

Kristin's experiences also illustrate the challenges of guiding children and youth from a basic understanding of biblical stories to deeper levels of faith. She explained, "I knew about Jesus' death and resurrection; but to me they were facts, like Columbus discovered America. I didn't know what they meant." Much like the seeker, youth need to explore the meaning of stories for their lives.

John Westerhoff highlighted important theological foundations for Christian education that are found in liberation theology.[28] First, God sets captives free. God's liberation is something with which people who experience conversion as adults identify with in some manner; but children often do not identify with this concept because they do not understand sin as captivity. Instead, they understand sin as an act of disobedience that deserves punishment. April, who became a believer at age twelve, explained,

> I grew up in the church, and my early experiences are of trying to be good and failing, always feeling that I was a bad girl. By the time I was ready to give my life to Christ, I had begun hitting myself every time I did something wrong and was even starting to use hateful self-talk under my breath, thinking that if I just got it in my head how bad I had been, I would remember how bad it felt to punish myself and I would stop doing whatever I had done. It never worked, and I was allured by the idea that Jesus took all this upon him and loved me even though I was so bad.[29]

As April's experience demonstrates, children can be led into a saving faith through learning about Jesus' act of atonement; but in the discipleship process, they must develop an appreciation for the work of Christ in freeing people who are in oppressive situations. Memory-making and the social nature of salvation

---

27. Johnson, *Speaking of God*, 21.

28. Westerhoff, *Will Our Children Have Faith?*, 32–33.

29. April (name has been changed), interview by author, April 15, 2010.

play an important role in this learning process.[30] Children and youth must learn to connect the concepts from biblical stories with concepts about how God acts in the world today and concepts about how people live as Christians in the world today.

Society has become individualistic, and Christians have come to treat salvation as an individual process. Jim Wallace said that conversion "is always personal, but it is never private."[31] Wallace's initial conversion experience occurred early in his life; and he remembers it as "private and abstract, focused primarily on a few personal habits and practices." His later experiences led him to a conversion which connected his faith with historical experience; and he associates this with his "deeper conversion."[32] Both of Wallace's experiences were legitimate aspects of the impact of salvation on a person's life. However, he did not perceive that the two experiences were connected. Instead, the later experience superseded the first and gave a deeper meaning to how one should live as a Christian. If the experiences had been connected, they would have been two aspects of the Christian life working in tandem to shape the holy life. Personal habits change because of the growth of godly character. Godly character also builds concern for the poor and oppressed populations that results in appropriate actions that impact the world.

Discipling children and youth requires connecting knowledge and experience so that faith has opportunity to mature. Children, like seekers, must have safe spaces to ask questions that may seem offensive, outlandish, or silly. Because children's emotional development is still immature, leaders and parents must give special attention to the impact that children's explorations have on each other.

The Role of Holiness

The relationship between holiness expectations and the gospel message can affect discipleship in powerful ways. When messages about morality and the gospel are out of balance, discipleship can be hindered. Tim explained that during his childhood, church members worshiped and then went home and drank heavily, lived in abusive relationships, and so forth. This inconsistency contributed to his departure from the church while he was still only a child. The failure of the people to live consistently communicated to Tim that there was no power in the message that was preached for real life change.

Zacharias warned of a different problem: that of having morality without a consistent gospel message. He said,

---

30. Westerhoff, *Will Our Children Have Faith?*, 32–33.

31. Wallace, *Call to Conversion*, 6.

32. Ibid, xvii.

All around us we hear thundering forth the word morality. Yes, we must be a moral people. But morality is a fruit, not a tree. The tree is rooted in Christ's righteousness from whom the nourishment comes to produce the fruit of moral purity. I challenge you: when you are preaching righteousness, when you are calling a people to goodness, do not stop with morality alone, because a nation can be morally lost just as easily as immorally lost. What you have to point to ultimately is the centerpiece of righteousness, our Lord Jesus Christ.[33]

As Anne's experience demonstrates, a blend of holiness with a strong gospel message communicates that the gospel has the power to change lives and leads to conversion. Anne explained, "Holiness is when I feel and act in a way that builds light…It's got a lot to do with purity and being like Jesus." She went on, "And yet there are places where it's holy but also cluttered. There are people who come in, street people who don't conduct themselves with respect. There's also darkness in the same moment."

The process of guiding people into holiness is a great challenge. At times it requires Christians to alter their own standards in order to communicate openness to newcomers who are unaccustomed, for example, to unfamiliar standards of dress. Laura explained, "Sometimes a person isn't failing to dress up to church standards because of disrespect. Once, a church member confronted me privately about my failure to wear dresses to church. If she had asked instead of informing me about church standards, I would have told her that my one dress needed dry cleaning and I didn't have the money."

Laura's dilemma illustrates the importance of most important aspects of the evangelism and nurture process. Above all, the discipleship process is a process of guidance. The spiritual journey is perhaps the most intimate journey of a person's life other than marriage. The journey into the holy life must also be a journey in which people can confront strongholds from their past in an atmosphere of safety.

Creating a Safe Atmosphere for Discipleship

Through small groups and classes, the church provides opportunities for people to receive the faith, question it, and adapt it to new situations and contexts.[34] Diane Hymans explained: "Education in the church serves both to initiate persons into the tradition and to help persons adapt that tradition to changing social and historical contexts. Initiation may apply especially to children and to newcomers to the faith, perhaps even to those who are not yet ready to commit

---

33. Zacharias, "The Touch of Truth," in Carson, *Telling the Truth*, 37.

34. Diane J. Hymans, "Education and Evangelism: Is the Connection Essential?" in Everest, *Christian Education as Evangelism*, 19.

to it."[35] Some groups can give special attention to members who have questions about theological concepts that are uncomfortable, such as Tim's question about what it means for the Bible to be the Word of God. Discussion of such questions would allow Tim to be "initiated" into the Christian faith and explore it, taking time to make a decision about his readiness to make a commitment.

The small group space provides safety for the sharing of personal stories, which are an important part of the faith development process. Johnson wrote, "Conversion in a personal life means the alteration of their story. If the story carries both their meaning and their identity, change requires an enormous risk."[36] Small group settings or Sunday school classes with an environment of vulnerability and safety provide space where personal stories can be shared and the possibility of change can be explored. When change occurs, it can be celebrated in the small group community. Discipleship can also continue in that same community.

It is important to note that when seekers do not have an existing relationship with a church member, they may test the personality of the church before getting involved with a small group. In the beginning of this chapter, Anne's search for "people who lived like Jesus" was emphasized. Other seekers share this search. Tim could not explain what he would look for in a church, but he explained that he would approach a church cautiously and would expect it to be a place where people could be vulnerable. Dan, a young Christian who is exploring new churches, explained that he prefers to get a general feel for the personality of the church and gradually get involved over a period of time.[37] If people don't speak to him, he tends to feel unwelcome and is less likely to involve himself in small groups.

Juggling Identities

When seekers begin to attend church, they may feel as though they have entered a new culture, especially if the church uses unfamiliar songs and educational processes that are not especially designed to meet the needs of seekers. Through relationships built with members of the church, they will begin to learn about the forms of worship and expected behaviors for various settings (educational groups, worship services, etc.). Howard Culbertson refers to this process of adjustment to a new cultural setting as "acculturation." In time, if persons adapt to the degree that their behavior becomes natural, they are considered "assimilated."[38]

Like Anne, many people live between two worlds. They struggle to grow in their newfound faith while also maintaining relationships with unbelieving

---

35. Ibid.

36. Johnson, *Speaking of God*, 57.

37. Dan (name has been changed), telephone interview by author, April 28, 2010.

38. Culbertson, "Enculturation and Acculturation."

family members. Their needs regarding this struggle are many. As Kristin's experience demonstrates, these needs include a need for shared celebration. When she shared with her father that she had become a Christian, he said, "Oh, you'll get over it." Having not found a church yet, she experienced a significant letdown. A church family would have been able to assist Kristin in celebrating her transition, and though there is nothing like sharing such an event with a family member, this would have eased the feeling of letdown.

Jesus' imperatives to share the good news included new converts. For example, the testimony of a new female convert was responsible for the evangelization of many Samaritan people (John 4:39). New believers need training in how to share their faith effectively. Their training should include the importance of continuing to grow in maturity and how to become sensitive to the Holy Spirit's direction. In this way, the whole church participates in the task of evangelism.

Bibliography

Arn, Win and Charles Arn. *Catch the Age Wave: A Handbook for Ministry with Senior Adults*. Kansas City, MO: Beacon Hill, 1999.

Carson, D. A., ed. *Telling the Truth: Evangelizing Postmoderns*. Grand Rapids, MI: Zondervan, 2007.

Culbertson, Howard. "Enculturation and Acculturation: A Reading for Cultural Anthropology." http://home.snu.edu/~HCULBERT/encultur.htm (accessed July 20, 2010). Adapted from Stephen A. Grunlan and Marvin K. Mayers. *Cultural Anthropology: A Christian Perspective*. Grand Rapids, MI: Zondervan, 1979.

Everest, Norma Cook, ed. *Christian Education as Evangelism*. Minneapolis, MN: Fortress, 2007.

Gibbs, Eddie. *In Name Only*. Pasadena, CA: Fuller Seminary Press, 1994.

Green, Michael. *Evangelism in the Early Church*. Grand Rapids, MI: Eerdmans, 1970.

Hunter, George. *Church for the Unchurched*. Nashville, TN: Abingdon, 1996.

_____. *The Contagious Congregation*. Nashville, TN: Abingdon, 1979.

Hybels, Bill. *Just Walk Across the Room: Simple Steps Pointing People to Faith*. Grand Rapids, MI: Zondervan, 2006.

Jacks, Bob and Matthew Jacks. *Divine Appointments*. Colorado Springs, CO: NavPress, 2002.

Johnson, Ben Campbell. *Speaking of God: Evangelism as Initial Spiritual Guidance*. Louisville, KY: Westminster/John Knox, 1991.

Keller, Timothy. *The Reason for God: Belief in an Age of Skepticism*. New York: Dutton Adult, 2008.

Pritchard, G. A. *Willow Creek Seeker Services: Evaluating a New Way of Doing Church*. Grand Rapids, MI: Baker Books, 1996.

Sider, Ronald J. *Good News and Good Works*. Grand Rapids, MI: Baker Books, 1993.

Wallace, Jim. *The Call to Conversion: Why Faith Is Always Personal but Never Private*. New York: HarperSanFrancisco, 1981.

Westerhoff, John H. *Will Our Children Have Faith?* New York: Harper and Row, 1976.

PART TWO

PLANNING

CHAPTER ELEVEN

Administering Christian Education

ROGER MCKENZIE

> My friends, choose seven men who are respected and wise and filled with God's Spirit. We will put them in charge of these things.
>
> —Acts 6:3

Administering Christian education is vitally important because in these administrative processes the philosophy of education begins to be lived out in the context of the local church. Educational ministry planning should reflect and support the church's vision as well as provide a framework for moving the church toward its goals for educational ministries for persons of all ages.

The Christian Education Pastor

As Christian education ministries have become increasingly specialized, many churches have chosen to call ministry specialists, such as a children's pastor, youth pastor, and small groups pastor, in lieu of the generalist Christian education pastor. However, the role of the Christian education generalist, though sometimes missing, remains very important in administering Christian education in the local church. While assembling a staff of specialists has some merit, it is difficult for all but megachurches to have large enough educational ministry staffs to avoid creating significant gaps in their educational ministry leadership. Therefore, for most churches it is still preferable to have one Christian education generalist to oversee the breadth of educational ministries and to work with both lay and clergy ministry specialists to see the big picture for Christian education in the local church.

One of the essential functions of the Christian education pastor is to articulate and communicate a vision for the educational ministries of the local church. This vision should be consistent with the biblical purposes for the church, inspired by God for the local setting, consistent with the overall vision for ministry for the local church, shaped by key educational ministry leaders, and affirmed by the senior pastor and other pastoral staff colleagues. This vision for educational ministry then should be the foundation of the Christian education pastor's work and for all he or she attempts to accomplish with the Christian education committee. Because educational ministries can be quite broad, there will be many opportunities (temptations) to go in a variety of directions. However, the Christian education pastor can help keep ministries focused by only pursuing those opportunities that build directly on the agreed upon vision.

There are a number of other vital roles for the Christian education pastor. Shaping the work of the Christian education committee is a central concern. When the Christian education committee functions well, it not only makes decisions but also takes the steps to begin implementation of those plans. Personnel decisions are crucial, not only to the success of programs, but also to the well-being of participants, especially children and youth. Equipping people for ministry is among the most basic of the tasks of the minister of Christian education. Because educational ministry involves many persons and roles, Christian education pastors must put systems in place that will equip people for a wide variety of ministry roles. Evaluation of personnel and programs is often left incomplete or undone, but it is an important function for the minister of education. Short of engaging in evaluation, there is little basis on which to know if ministries are succeeding and contributing to the fulfillment of the vision for educational ministries.

The Christian Education Committee

A Christian education pastor working with a team, often a Christian education committee, typically provides leadership for educational ministries. The team concept is vitally important in educational ministry. There is far too much for one person to do, or even to oversee all aspects of educational ministry, even in a small church. Furthermore, building a team of leaders is theologically consistent with spiritual gifts theology as well as the body metaphor that is so prevalent in the New Testament. An Old Testament basis for team leadership goes all the way back to Moses in Exodus 18. Jethro's advice, when Moses was trying to do all the leading himself, was this, "That isn't the best way to do it. You and the people who come to you will soon be worn out. The job is too much for one person; you can't do it alone. God will help you if you follow my advice. You should be the one to speak to God for the people"(Ex 18:17–19). Moses took his father-in-law's advice (as difficult as it may have been for a son-in-law) and established a shared leadership environment that met the needs of the people, equipped new leaders, and made Moses' workload manageable.

Deciding the makeup of the Christian education committee is a key concern. It is important to have team members with a variety of experiences and perspectives on educational ministry. There is need for a mixture of spiritual and personality gifts on this team. For example, every team needs a visionary or two, but a team full of visionaries would never accomplish the nuts-and-bolts details that are so important to administering Christian education ministries. There are just a couple of options for calling together the Christian education committee. The first, and frequently used option, is to determine the Christian education committee by voting. Some North American denominations and congregations take pride in how democratic their practices are. While allowing the church's membership to have a voice in selecting its leadership can be important, voting may not be the best way to assemble a task-oriented group. Voting tends to create popularity contests, often keeps the same people in the same roles even after their passion for that ministry has waned, and unnecessarily eliminates very qualified people. A second option is to appoint members to the Christian education committee. With this option, the Christian education pastor or other educational ministry leader(s), sometimes in conjunction with the church board, will invite those of their choosing to serve on the Christian education committee. This option has the strongest potential for gathering a team that has an appropriate range of leadership strengths. A third option essentially combines the first two options by allowing Christian education pastors to assemble the team, which is subject to ratification by the congregation.

It is essential, when gathering the Christian education committee, to clarify the responsibilities for serving. Unfortunately, too many church people have become accustomed to board and committee roles that require little beyond going and sitting in meetings to make decisions, doing little outside that board-room context. An effective Christian education committee should include those who are actively involved in educational ministry leadership in the church. One way of making certain that the Christian education committee is actively involved in ministry is to make up the team from representatives of various constituent ministry groups. For example, the Christian education committee might include representatives from children's ministry, youth ministry, young adult ministry, senior adult ministry, and small group ministries. However, it is important, that in the context of this committee, that team members not just represent (or protect) their particular areas; they have the responsibility for shaping educational ministry for the spiritual growth of the entire congregation.

For this reason, it is desirable to have some at-large members of the committee as well.

One of the areas where Christian education committees (and churches) often struggle is planning strategically rather than merely reacting to situations. Too often, churches have not wrestled with why they are doing educational ministry or how educational ministries fit into the overall ministry plan of the church, so it can be difficult to decide on strategies. Frequently, the result has been the multiplication of programs without clearly defined goals. A well-meaning parishioner suggests adopting a program that appears to be producing good results in a nearby church, and the Christian education committee reacts to the idea rather than asking how or if it fits into to the long-range ministry plan for the church. Another risk when churches are not strategic in planning is that educational ministries may only be tangentially connected to the life of the entire church. In 1989, Stuart Cummings-Bond critiqued the practice of youth ministry operating outside the life of the larger church, thereby creating what he called the "one-eared Mickey Mouse" model.[1]

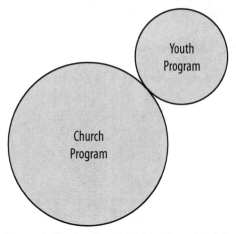

Figure 1. The One-Eared Mickey Mouse Model

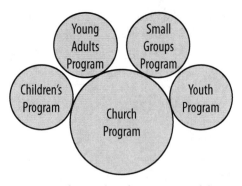

Figure 2. Multi-eared Mickey Mouse Model

Since then, it seems that other educational ministries have followed the pattern of operating on the edge of the church community, producing what might be called a multi-eared Mickey Mouse model. The result has often been a fragmented approach to educational ministry and diminishing of the unity of the church.

One of the vitally important jobs of the Christian education committee is to create a holistic educational ministry culture that brings educational ministries within the life and strategic planning of the entire church.

---

1. Cummings-Bond, "The One-Eared Mickey Mouse," 76.

Key Considerations in Christian Education Planning

In *The Purpose Driven Church*, Rick Warren suggested that ministry leaders carefully examine their contexts to see where God is already at work and ride those waves rather than trying to create new waves.[2] This is an important reminder to educational ministry leaders that God's Holy Spirit is already at work in their communities, churches, and people. The job of leaders in planning is to be sensitive to his guidance and to follow his direction. Educational ministry leadership is as much or more about being spiritually in tune as it is about having good leadership skills and mastery of administrative techniques.

Figure 3. Considerations in Educational Ministry Planning

A second consideration in educational ministry planning relates to needs. Some needs are obvious; for example, the need to disciple believers should always be a concern for Christian education planning. Other needs that Christian education ministries ought to address may not be nearly so obvious. For example, a community may have a need for a particular Christian education ministry because it is near a university, there are many recent immigrants, or the area has some other distinctive characteristic. Each of these needs represents an opportunity for the church to respond and make a difference in the lives of people and draw them toward a (deeper) relationship with Jesus. Robert Raikes was responding to just such a community need when he founded the Sunday school on the behalf of working children in Gloucester, England, in 1780.

A third consideration for Christian education planning is calling. Most affirm that God calls individual Christians to particular areas of ministry. Therefore, it seems logical that if God calls individuals he may also call churches to engage in particular ministries within the community. Those administering Christian education in local churches cannot ignore the God-given dreams and aspirations of those whom God has placed in their churches. God's call not only relates to calling and placing of personnel, but also to direction for the church's ministries. In some ways, administering educational ministry is like putting together

---

2. Warren, *Purpose Driven Church*, 14.

a puzzle. God has provided the goal and the pieces, but it may not be clear what the final picture will be until those God has called to be overseers have assembled the pieces.

A fourth consideration for planning in educational ministry is spiritual gifts. In each local church God has given spiritual gifts to people and provided important resources that he intends for use in ministry. Spiritual gifts are Holy Spirit–given and –empowered abilities used by his people in service to church and world. The primary spiritual gifts passages are Romans 12, 1 Corinthians 12, and Ephesians 4. These scriptures, along with a few other passages, suggest that there are more than twenty gifts that God gives to his people to empower them and their churches for ministry. In the past, some suggested placing people in ministry positions based almost exclusively on their spiritual gift(s). Giftedness is an important factor; however, it in itself is not sufficient to determine direction or ministry calling. However, when leaders consider spiritual gifts in conjunction with God's call, community needs, and evidence of where the Holy Spirit is already at work, planning educational ministry becomes much clearer. Not taking into consideration all four of these considerations is like the basketball coach who decides whether to play a man-to-man or zone defense before she meets her team.

There are certainly many other influencers of educational ministry planning. Local church traditions, church size and location, budget, and facilities all exert pressures related to planning. Even the church building will influence planning. While the building is not the church, decisions regarding facilities shape approaches to ministry, sometimes for decades to come. While all these will influence Christian education planning, educational ministry leaders must be intentional that a Spirit-inspired vision drive the ministry and not a hodgepodge of trivial factors.

Personnel for Christian Education

Personnel issues are of critical importance for educational ministries. To a great degree, those entrusted with leading educational ministries will determine the success or failure of those ministries and have tremendous influence in people's lives. Mark Senter described calling personnel as "perhaps the most unglamorous part of the education ministry of the local church—and yet one of the most essential."[3] All too often, important goals have gone unmet and good plans have gone awry because of poor personnel decisions, or those in place were not appropriately equipped to lead. Christian education is too important to allow just any warm-bodied person of dubious spiritual maturity to fill a ministry position. Ministers of Christian education have the responsibility for the spiritual growth of those served by Christian education ministries as well as a responsibility for those they call to shape and lead those ministries. The Wesleyan Holiness

---

3. Senter, *Recruiting Volunteers in the Church*, 11.

message is instructive in practical ways when it comes to educational ministry staffing. The call to holiness is not only a call to a more moral lifestyle; it is also a call to vocation. Maturing disciples, as they are becoming more like Christ, ought to be actively engaged in ministry as a part of their response to Christ's call to follow and serve him. Those serving in leadership in Christian education have the privilege and responsibility to help people respond to God's calling on their lives.

Those who have served in local church ministry leadership know the relief of getting that last key person in place for the upcoming church year. The temptation then is to relax and not be concerned about personnel issues for a while. However, staffing must to be a year-round concern for the minister of Christian education as well as those giving leadership to specific ministry areas. Not paying attention to calling people into ministry is shortsighted and suggests that expectations for the ministry are low and that the ministry will not grow and need additional staff. Over time as people grow, change, and relocate, there is constantly a need for calling and equipping others to serve in educational ministry. The job of calling and equipping is never done!

Healthy approaches to identifying and calling volunteers into educational ministry can involve a wide range of persons. Current volunteers and participants can help identify those who may be well-suited to involvement in those educational ministries. Through prayer, networking, ministry fairs, and referrals from those leading other ministries, Christian educators can develop a working list of those they should consider and nurture toward educational ministry leadership.

It is easy for educational ministry staffing to become just another task among many that the Christian education pastor or ministry leader needs to accomplish. When leaders approach staffing as just another chore on the checklist, it may easily degenerate to recruiting warm bodies to open jobs. On the other hand, calling, equipping, and placing people in ministry can become a powerful and meaningful process when it emerges out of the leader's practice of spiritual disciplines. Educational ministry staffing changes dramatically when, after prayer and fasting, and in response to the leading of the Holy Spirit, the leader approaches potential volunteers with opportunities to serve. Then instead of just looking to fill slots, the minister of Christian education is looking to place maturing disciples into venues of service and leadership where they can utilize their gifts in ministry to others as they continue to grow on their own spiritual journeys.

While there are many appropriate ways to go about calling people to ministry involvement, there are a few that leaders should avoid. In almost all cases, public pleas for ministry volunteers are inappropriate and counterproductive. Advertising the need for educational ministry volunteers in an announcement during worship, a newsletter, or, worse yet, on a Web site demeans the importance of that role by implying that almost anyone could fill that position. These public pleas are also open invitations to those who should not be in those roles. These kinds of invitations may solicit responses from those lacking spiritual or personal maturity, those who would be seeking positions primarily to feed their own ego needs rather than to serve, or those who have a history of abuse that is unknown to the church.

Calling persons to ministry requires that leaders know whom they are placing in those service roles. No longer is it acceptable to get to know people as they serve.

Figure 4. Volunteer Ministry Cycle

Because people have become so mobile, references are vitally important, and leaders must check those references. Further, for those who want to work with youth, children, or vulnerable adults, background checks (including criminal history searches) should now be standard in the application and deployment process. Conducting those background checks will help to protect kids and teens as well as help to shield the church from an accusation of negligence should an adult be accused of an inappropriate action.

God has called clergy to equip his people for serving in ministry. Peter Drucker, in *Managing the Non-Profit Organization*, suggested viewing volunteers as unpaid staff "so you don't treat them as 'volunteers' but as staff members. The only difference is that they are part time and they are not being paid. But when it comes to performance, performance is performance."[4] This attitude will diminish the distinction between clergy and laity and will focus the attention on growing volunteers and accomplishing the ministry.

Launching Volunteers into Ministry

Volunteers should become engaged in their ministries soon after accepting their calls. If too much time lapses between accepting the position, initial equipping, and beginning that role, volunteers may have second thoughts or become distracted by other things. Therefore, following an orientation and as soon as it is practical, volunteers should get to work in their ministries.[5]

The ministry description is a vitally important tool both in calling persons to ministries and in helping to shape their work in those roles. Frequently, leaders have assumed that position titles were sufficient in explaining ministry roles,

---

4. Drucker, *Managing the Non-Profit Organization*, 165.

5. Ratcliff and Neff, *Complete Guide to Religious Education Volunteers*, 119.

but often that is far from true. Detailed ministry descriptions should be in place before calling persons to those roles. Ministry descriptions should include a position title, brief overview of the role, qualifications, specific responsibilities, relationships, and expectations for participation in equipping and growth experiences. As ministry positions evolve over time, leaders should review and update ministry descriptions. Reviewing ministry descriptions every couple of years will ensure that the description still fits the role. From the ministry descriptions, leaders should develop covenants for each of the educational ministry roles. Covenants are a natural extension of the position description that further describes expectations and relationships between ministry volunteers and those served by the ministry, the church, and, ultimately, God. Because educational ministry volunteers are influential persons in the lives of those to whom they minister, the covenant should call them to a high standard of ministry and to exemplary living.

Performance evaluations are scary to many volunteers. However, with the right attitude and approach, leaders can make performance reviews less intimidating and more affirming. Some volunteers incorrectly believe that whatever they offer to the Lord and to the church should just be accepted as good enough. Because the stakes are so high for educational ministry, leaders must take evaluations very seriously in order to be good stewards of resources and opportunities. Perceptive Christian education leaders know that in every volunteer there is room for improvement, and they work in nonthreatening and creative ways to help their volunteers identify areas where they most need to grow. Ultimately, the purpose of evaluation is not to embarrass or remove volunteers from ministry but to help them to grow in their ability to serve God and his church and to confirm that volunteers are serving in the most appropriate places. On the other hand, performance evaluations are very intimidating and even unfair if leaders have not carefully communicated the criteria for evaluation in the ministry description and the covenant. Utilizing forms that allow volunteers to assess their own performance in relationship to the ministry description and covenant can provide a less intimidating starting point for evaluation.

Often Christian education pastors and other ministry leaders avoid performance reviews of personnel as the process can create some uncomfortable conversations. Conducting evaluation interviews can be very time consuming as well; a common mistake in evaluation is that leaders often put it off too long. Having an initial evaluation conversation within the first couple of months can help to get volunteers off to a good start. Formative evaluation has as its goal providing feedback to volunteers so that they can understand and improve along the way. When leaders delay evaluation and then try to address several issues with volunteers at one time, they are more likely to create a negative experience.

Out of those evaluation conversations, ministry leaders should get a sense of their volunteers' effectiveness in their current roles. In order to enhance volunteers' effectiveness, the need for specific kinds of equipping may become apparent. Further, the Christian education pastor should get a sense of the level of satisfaction that the volunteers have experienced in their ministries. Appropriately placed volunteers who have been aptly equipped for their ministries should be growing in confidence and fulfillment. When volunteers are doing good jobs and are effective, they are likely to want to continue in their ministry roles. If they are not finding satisfaction, it is important for ministry leaders to work with those volunteers to clarify their callings and help them find more suitable venues for service.

Leadership Development

As educational ministries grow and volunteers mature, leadership development becomes imperative. Educational ministry leaders must make opportunities available for volunteers to grow. A good beginning point is with the Christian education committee and others in leadership. The Christian education pastor should help these key leaders grow in their understanding of the biblical and theological foundations, philosophy, and administration of educational ministry. Inclusion of an equipping time for leaders in Christian education committee meetings is a place to start. In addition, the minister of Christian education can personally invest in key leaders through mentoring.

Educational ministry leaders need to talk consistently about and model leadership growth and development. Participation in and reflection on leadership development activities needs to be included as part of the evaluation of ministry volunteers. One of the most familiar forms of leadership development has been the Sunday school teachers' meeting. Teachers' meetings can be valuable for sharing information. Departmental meetings that cluster volunteers based on the ages and characteristics of those served in their ministries can help volunteers to understand better the needs of those to whom they minister. In recent years as educational ministries have multiplied so has the need for equipping. While there will still be a place for teachers' meetings, there are many more approaches that can be employed.

Taking ministry volunteers to workshops and conferences is a valuable investment in their lives. In many regions there are a variety of workshop opportunities for those serving in Christian education ministries. Curriculum publishers have been good providers of traveling workshops that can be quite helpful, especially for those using their curriculum. There are regional Christian education organizations that hold conventions or workshops at regular intervals that can be formative for volunteers and to which Christian education pastors can contribute. For example, the Christian Ministries Training Association sponsors the Greater Los Angeles Sunday School Convention[6]; on the Atlantic coast,

---

6. http://www.cmtaconvention.org

there are the Mid-Atlantic Christian Education Association[7] and the Greater Washington Christian Education Association[8] in the Washington D.C. area. Many denominations provide opportunities for equipping for Christian education at conferences and conventions or in other venues. The Church of God (Anderson) holds numerous workshops during its annual North American Convention[9] in Indiana and the Church of the Nazarene has its Barefoot Ministries events in various cities for those engaged in youth ministry.[10] The Spiritual Formation Department of the Wesleyan Church does an annual equipping tour for educational ministry leaders and volunteers.[11] Nondenominational publishers Group and Youth Specialties are well known for their big events. Youth Specialties has held its National Youth Workers Conference for many years now.[12] Group is also well known for its Life Serve and Simply Youth Ministry conferences.[13]

Technology has expanded offerings for equipping those serving in educational ministry. First there were videotape series, then DVDs. Now Webinars are increasing in numbers and expanding the availability of equipping experiences for those involved serving in Christian education. Cokesbury's Web site has links to several Webinars.[14] The LOGOS Ministry provides both Webinars and holds children's ministry workshops regionally.[15] Webinars and other online equipping opportunities are likely to multiply in the near future.

The leadership development approaches discussed above are good for inspiration and sharing information. Apprenticeships help volunteers to develop confidence and skills through on the job experiences. Apprenticeships are a good way to help orient new volunteers to the important roles and tasks related to the ministries in which they serve. An apprentice is a novice who works alongside and under the supervision of someone more experienced in order to learn how to do the job. Sunday school and other small group ministries have utilized apprenticeships effectively by pairing a new teacher, often in an assistant role, with a more experienced teacher who instructs the new teacher on how to accomplish the work. Over time the apprentice takes on increasing leadership functions. Eventually, apprentices graduate into roles where they function more independently. Apprentice roles can be effective ways of helping teenagers become involved in educational ministry as well.

Mentoring is a powerful approach to facilitate growth in younger leaders. While many talk about mentoring, oftentimes only a few do a good job

7. http://www.macea.org

8. http://www.gwcea.com

9. http://www.chog.org

10. http://barefootministries.com

11. http://headhearthand.com

12. http://www.youthspecialties.com

13. http://www.group.com/workshops

14. http://www.cokesbury.com/forms/DynamicContent.aspx?id=120&pageid=599

15. http://www.thelogosministry.org

of helping to make possible life-changing mentoring relationships. Mentoring relationships are typically one-on-one and connect a mentor with a protégé (or mentee). Mentors are more experienced in life, service to God, and their own spiritual development. The relationship between the protégé and the mentor focuses on the spiritual and personal growth of the protégé. Mentoring differs from an apprenticeship in that apprenticeship helps the person grow into a particular job; on the other hand, mentoring focuses on the development of the protégé's full potential. Mentoring is not a quick way to multiply the pool of volunteers. However, a good mentoring relationship can cultivate persons who may become well-grounded leaders of educational ministries. It is good practice for Christian education pastors as well as key lay leaders in educational ministries to be actively involved in mentoring. As part of their overall leadership development focus, Christian education pastors can help to set up mentoring dyads within the church.

Ministry Evaluation

The objective for Christian education states the destination toward which educational ministries should be going. The Ministry Action Plan (MAP) is the route toward the destination chosen by educational ministry leaders. Evaluation assesses the progress toward that destination. Those who have traveled with children know that there is one urgent question that recurs over and over. That question, of course, is, "Are we there yet?" Christian education leaders need to be asking the same question regarding progress toward their objective. Several related questions are important as well:

- Where are we now in relation to where we started?
- What are the evidences of progress (growth and change in people)?
- Where are we in relation to where we want to be? (or to where God wants us to be?)
- Is the original destination still where we ought to be going?
- Does it make sense to continue on this route now? Could another route get us to the same destination sooner or with fewer bumps in the road? Do we need to detour to somewhere else along the way?

Evaluation of systems and ministries is an essential part of administering Christian education. At regular intervals, it is important to step back and take a look at the whole of educational ministries in the local church to make sure they are moving toward the established goals.

Chapter 12 presents the need for local churches to establish a Ministry Action Plan (MAP) that grows from their implementation of the objective of Christian education in their ministry context. However, maps are of little use to those who do not know where they are now. One day a phone call came in from a family member saying, "I'm lost. How do I get home?" The response was "Where are you now?" The caller replied, "I don't know." Now that is a problem, because it is almost impossible to give directions to someone who knows where he would like to be but does not know where he is now. Evaluation in educational ministry is in some ways like a GPS (global positioning system), which can pinpoint the lost traveler's location. Once the traveler knows where she is, then the map becomes a useful tool for plotting a course toward the destination.

So how can churches determine the effects of their educational ministries? First, they can measure those things that lend themselves to being easily measurable. While attendance numbers only tell part of the story, they are one concrete indicator of the reach of educational ministries. Do ministries generate enthusiasm among those who regularly attend that causes them to bring friends and relatives? Do new persons come back subsequent times?

Second, churches can look a little deeper to observe who is participating as well as who is not participating. The old saying that "people vote with their feet" is largely true. Previous generations would do something because it was expected of them, sometimes regardless of the quality. Current generations are attracted to quality experiences that connect to a desire or need in their lives; short of making that connection, it is difficult to get people to participate. Are there trends based on age, longevity at the church, or other factors? Has the ministry actually reached those whom leaders expected that it would reach? What about strategies for advertising ministries? To what extent are people in the church and community aware of the ministry?

Third, churches should look deeply at what is happening in the lives of participants in those ministries. In what ways are these educational ministries contributing to the overall health of the church? Do participants testify to changed lives? In conversations with family and friends of participants, do they tell stories of change in the lives of participants? Once leaders have had these conversations, it can be helpful to use surveys to obtain more data regarding the strength of ministry programs. Not only should participants complete surveys, but those who are not currently participating should complete surveys in order to gain a better understanding of why they have chosen not to participate. Perhaps those who do not participate should even be invited to help construct and administer the survey; their insights will be extremely valuable.

Administering Christian education is a multifaceted, team-oriented venture. Administering well requires both good organizational skills and careful attention to communication. The local church's vision for living out its own contextualized objective for Christian education should be the foundation on which every educational ministry is built.

Bibliography

Cummings-Bond, Stuart. "The One-Eared Mickey Mouse." *Youthworker*, Fall 1989, 76.

Drucker, Peter F. *Managing the Non-Profit Organization: Principles and Practices.* San Francisco, CA: HarperCollins, 1990.

Senter, Mark H., III. *Recruiting Volunteers in the Church.* Wheaton, IL: Victor Books, 1990.

Ratcliff, Donald, and Blake J. Neff. *The Complete Guide to Religious Education Volunteers.* Birmingham, AL: Religious Education Press, 1993.

Warren, Rick. *The Purpose Driven Church.* Grand Rapids, MI: Zondervan, 1995.

Sample Ministry Description

Ministry position title: Small group leader for adults

Qualifications

- Growing Christian
- Upholds church membership commitments
- Exemplary Christian lifestyle
- Completed initial small group leader equipping and/or served as an assistant group leader

Responsibilities

- Prepare for and facilitate a Bible lesson for your small group.
- Work with the assistant group leader to help him/her learn group leadership responsibilities.
- Contact group members by phone or face to face outside the group at least once per month.
- Participate in at least one leadership development experience during the year.

Time commitments:

- Commitment is to serve as group leader for one year.
- Leaders can expect to spend two to three hours per week in preparation to facilitate the small group session.
- One to two hours per week will be required to keep in contact with group members, address pastoral care needs, and follow up on those absent.

Accountability: Reports to the director of small group ministries for adults

Sample Ministry Leadership Covenant

As a small group leader, I covenant with my church and leaders to do the following during the upcoming year:

1. Pursue a growing relationship with Christ.
2. Participate in our church's worship experiences every week unless prohibited by illness or travel.
3. Uphold the membership commitments of our church.
4. Speak positively regarding our church.
5. Seek to live an exemplary Christian lifestyle.
6. Prepare well for small group Bible studies by spending two to three hours per week in study.
7. Build and maintain good relationships with small group participants to provide encouragement and pastoral care.
8. Follow-up with phone calls or visits to those who are absent from group or who have pastoral care needs.
9. Continue to grow as a small group leader through participating in at least one leadership development experience.
10. Receive guidance from and cooperate with the director of small group ministries for adults.

_____

Signature, Small Group Leader

_____

Signature, Director of Small Group Ministries for Adults

Sample Self-Evaluation Form

Respond to the following based on your experiences over the past year while you were serving as a small group leader in preparation for a conversation with the director of small group ministries for adults.

SD=Strongly Disagree, D=Disagree, U=Undecided, A=Agree, SA=Strongly Agree

                                    SD D U A SA

1. **I have pursued a growing relationship with Christ.**

   What are your areas of growth?

   Any areas where are you struggling?

2. **I have participated in our church's worship**   SD D U A SA
   experiences every week unless prohibited by illness or travel.

   How has God spoken to you in worship?

3. **I have upheld the membership commitments of** SD D U A SA
   our church faithfully.

   Do you have any objections to or concerns with membership commitments?

4. **I have spoken positively regarding our church**   SD D U A SA
   and leaders.

   Are there issues of strong disagreement for you with the direction of our church?

5. **I have sought to live an exemplary Christian**   SD D U A SA
   lifestyle.

   How has the Holy Spirit helped you to live this Christian life?

6. **I have prepared well for small group Bible**   SD   D   U   A   SA
    studies by spending two to three hours per
    week in study.

    Do you find preparation for your group study
    satisfying?

7. **I have worked to build and maintain good**   SD   D   U   A   SA
    relationships with small group participants to
    provide encouragement and pastoral care.

    Give an example of someone whom you were
    able to help.

8. **I have followed up with phone calls or visits to**   SD   D   U   A   SA
    those who are absent from group or who had
    pastoral care needs.

9. **I participated in a leadership development**   SD   D   U   A   SA
    experience recommended for small group
    leaders.

    In which leadership development event did you
    participate?

10. **I have cheerfully accepted guidance from and**   SD   D   U   A   SA
    cooperated with the director of small group
    ministries for adults.

In what ways have you found serving as a small group leader to be fulfilling?

If invited, would you be willing to continue serving as a small group leader?

Based on your self-evaluation, to which of the above areas should you give special attention over the coming year?

CHAPTER TWELVE

Goals and Objectives in Christian Education

ROGER MCKENZIE

> 200 leaders from Issachar, along with troops under their command—these leaders knew the right time to do what needed to be done.
>
> —1 Chronicles 12:32

In the local church, knowing what to do and how to do it in Christian education ministries is at times an almost overwhelming challenge. The field of Christian education is in the midst of dramatic change. Christian education practices are significantly different today than they were just a generation ago. The demise of the Sunday school in many churches has created a void in educational ministry practice that leaders have yet to fill, especially related to the systematic study of the Bible. Curriculum has changed with the movement away from the quarterly toward topical study approaches, children's church has expanded to include a wider age range, and there has been an increased use of small groups for all age levels.

Another of those areas of change has been the dramatic move from Christian education generalists in local churches toward specialists. Specialists are likely to bring much needed focus to their particular areas of expertise, such as children's ministry, youth ministry, or senior adult ministry. Yet Kevin Lawson has suggested that if the trend toward specialization continues, local churches who live out a broad vision for educational ministry might be lost along with consistency for ministry philosophy.[1] In order to avoid becoming like "the man who threw himself on his horse and rode off in all directions" in the twenty-first century, it is important to consider anew what the field of Christian education is all about.

The Objective of Christian Education

Many have sought to define an overall objective for Christian education at various times. One of the more significant attempts was the framing of "The Objective of Christian Education" (referred to hereafter as "the Objective") in 1966 by The Cooperative Curriculum Project of the Division of Christian Education of the National Council of Churches. Here is the statement:

> The objective for Christian education is that all persons be aware of God through his self-disclosure, especially his redeeming love as revealed in Jesus Christ, and that they respond in faith and love—to the end that they may know who they are and what their human situation means, grow as sons of God rooted in the Christian community, live in the Spirit of God in every relationship, fulfill their common discipleship in the world, and abide in the Christian hope.[2]

Strengths of the Objective

There are a number of strengths to this statement of the Objective. First, the description of the field as *Christian* education as opposed to *religious* education is preferable terminology. While the differences in these terms can be subtle and nuanced, the term *Christian education* generally refers to a distinctively Christian and typically more biblical approach to processes and content related to spiritual formation.

Second, in the Objective, Christian education is described as being for all persons, with the desire that they become aware of God and respond in faith and love to his self-revelation. "The phrase 'all persons,' implies the outreach and evangelistic thrust of the church's teaching ministry."[3] This position fits well with the Wesleyan theological position that Jesus' sacrifice makes salvation available for all persons.

Third, the Objective focuses on the centrality of God's initiative and self-disclosure. The Christian life is only available because God has taken the initiative and has chosen to reveal himself to humanity. Human response is required,

---

1. Lawson, "Marginalization and Renewal," 450.

2. Division of Christian Education of the National Council of Churches of Christ, *Church's Educational Ministry*, 8.

3. Ibid., 11.

but God is the initiator, and without his work for salvation, humans are without hope.

Fourth, the Christ-centric emphasis of the Objective is vitally important. The focus on the redemptive work of Jesus Christ is central to Christian theology and, therefore, foundational to Christian education.

Fifth, the Objective's emphasis on identity is a reminder that one of the important dimensions of faith is about finding and making meaning. In fact, James Fowler described the construction of meaning as a significant component of what it means to have faith.[4] Helping people to know who they are in relationship to God is at the heart of what educational ministry is about.

Sixth, transformation is an important emphasis in the Objective. The Objective suggests that "response in faith and love" are early steps toward transformed living. This emphasis on transformation is certainly in keeping with Wesleyan emphases regarding the life of salvation.

Seventh, the Objective stressed growth in the context of the Christian community, which implies a strong role for the church. Wesley emphasized the importance of the community in many ways but especially in his class meetings and the accountability they encouraged. Thomas Groome has suggested, "Community is the primary context for 'being saved' and 'becoming human.'"[5]

And finally eighth, the Objective's emphasis on "discipleship in the world" while living hopefully is appropriate. Authentic Christian faith must result in disciples whose lifestyles are different because they belong to Christ.

Weaknesses of the Objective

The strengths discussed make the Objective a valuable tool for educational ministry leaders. However, there are also some important weaknesses in the statement as articulated by the participants with the Cooperative Curriculum Project.

First, by far the most problematic issue with the Objective is the omission of any reference to Christian Scripture. Without a clear grounding in Scripture, educational ministry is without an authority base, and therefore, those who base their understanding and practice of Christian education on the Objective may wander aimlessly. It is the careful grounding of educational ministry in Scripture that helps to make it distinctively Christian.

Second, as worded, the Objective appears to delimit the Holy Spirit's role to relationships. A distinctly Wesleyan approach to Christian education will acknowledge a much larger function for the Holy Spirit, both in the lives of individuals and in the community of faith.

Third, the framers of the Objective wrote in the mid-1960s and assumed Christendom's continuing dominance, which has since eroded in many cultures,

---

4. Fowler, *Stages of Faith*, 40.

5. Groome, *Educating for Life*, 175.

particularly in the United States and Western Europe. For educational ministry to be effective, leaders must be aware of the ministry context within the culture.

Toward a Revised Objective

Given these strengths and weaknesses in the Objective, an updated objective from a distinctively Wesleyan perspective could be helpful for Christian education leaders in a new century. A first step toward an updated Objective is to review other statements of objective (purpose) for Christian education.

Here is Dennis Williams' definition:

The purpose of Christian education is to bring people to a saving faith in Jesus Christ, to train them in a life of discipleship, and to equip them for Christian service in the world today. It is to develop in believers a biblical worldview that will assist them in making significant decisions from a Christian perspective. It is helping believers to "think Christianly" about all areas of life so that they can impact society with the message of the gospel. In essence, it is the development of a Christian worldview.[6]

Robert Pazmiño has stated that Christian education is the

deliberate, systematic, and sustained divine and human effort to share or appropriate the knowledge, values, attitudes, skills, sensitivities, and behaviors that comprise or are consistent with the Christian faith. It fosters the change, renewal, and reformation of persons, groups and structures by the power of the Holy Spirit to conform to the revealed will of God as expressed in the Old and New Testaments and preeminently in the person of Jesus Christ, as well as any outcomes of that effort.[7]

Kevin Lawson described evangelical Christian education as follows:

Evangelical Christian education then is characterized by a strong emphasis on the study and application of Scripture to life, the presentation of the gospel of Jesus Christ and encouragement of conversion, and the prayerful partnership of teachers with the Holy Spirit in nurturing a growing faith toward faithfulness in character and life in the image of Jesus Christ.[8]

The Church of God (Anderson, Indiana) adopted the following revision of the 1966 objective:

---

6. Williams, "Christian Education," 133.

7. Pazmiño, *Foundational Issues in Christian Education*, 87.

8. Lawson, "Marginalization and Renewal," 438.

The objective of the church's educational ministry is that all persons be aware of God through all the ways he makes himself known, especially through his redeeming love as revealed in Jesus Christ, and that they respond in faith and love—to the end that as new persons in Christ they may know who they are and what their human situation means, grow as sons of God rooted in the Christian community, yield themselves to the Holy Spirit, live in obedience to the will of God in every relationship, fulfill their common discipleship and mission in the world, and abide in the Christian hope.[9]

A. Elwood Sanner and A. F. Harper in conjunction with other authors consulted with about forty Nazarene Christian educators in shaping the following objective statement for Christian education:

> To confront developing persons with biblical truth and secular thought, including the church's history, polity, and doctrine...
> > in order that they may respond fully to God's love as revealed in Jesus Christ, though the experiences of conversion and entire sanctification,
> > and may progressively develop mature, Christlike, integrated characters, guided by consistent, practical Christian ethics, and be strongly motivated in churchmanship,
> > and be constantly sensitive to the Holy Spirit's leadership in all their social relationships and vocational pursuits,
> > and work redemptively in a changing society as witness for Christ.[10]

Perry Downs stated: "Christian education, simply defined, is the ministry of bringing the believer to maturity in Jesus Christ."[11]

There are several similar themes in these objective statements. First, almost all these objective statements include an emphasis on the Bible. A couple are quite forthright in emphasizing Bible teaching. Others discuss helping learners develop a biblical worldview or learn to think as Christians. Second, several statements emphasize salvation. Christian education must be concerned with helping all persons come to faith in Christ. While Downs is correct to suggest helping believers come to maturity in Christ as an appropriate goal, Christian education must be concerned for both believers and nonbelievers. Third, most of these objective statements point out the need for believers to continue to mature as

---

9. Typewritten and glued inside the front cover of Lottie Franklin's personal copy of Division of Christian Education of the National Council of Churches of Christ, Church's Educational Ministry. Lottie Franklin was one of six Church of God (Anderson) members of the Cooperative Curriculum Project.

10. Sanner and Harper, *Exploring Christian Education*, 27.

11. Downs, *Teaching for Spiritual Growth*, 16.

disciples. Lawson's definition is helpful in placing growth in Christlikeness as of primary importance. Sanner and Harper describe the progressive development of Christian character. Fourth, these statements of objective almost all emphasize vocation in some way. Christian faith not only changes people's status in relationship to God, it also changes their life calling. Educational ministry must help God's people to become engaged in God's work through lives of service.

While there are many similarities among these statements, some contain unique features that made them invaluable. Pazmiño's suggestion that Christian education is both a "divine and human" effort is important. The psalmist wrote, "Unless the LORD builds the house, the builders labor in vain" (Ps 127:1 NIV). Christian educators labor in vain as well unless the Lord is at work in them and through them. Further, Pazmiño's focus on transformation through the power of the Holy Spirit toward conformity to the will of God is a much needed one. The Church of God (Anderson), following the Objective, emphasized understanding self and life as critical to Christian education. Its focus on yielding to the Holy Spirit is helpful as well. The Nazarene statement articulated by Sanner and Harper is helpful in placing educational ministries in the contexts of the participants' social relationships as well as broader society.

With these statements in mind, here is a revised objective for Christian education for the twenty-first century that builds on the strengths of Wesleyan theology:

> The objective of the church's teaching ministry is that all persons would encounter God through his love as revealed in Jesus Christ, the Bible, and other forms of God's self-disclosure; experience the transforming power of full salvation; become mature disciples who live as Kingdom citizens who, as they become more like Jesus, serve God and others; and abide in the Christian hope.

This revised objective includes several loaded phrases; therefore, a phrase-by-phrase analysis may be helpful.

First, this revised objective follows the Objective by emphasizing encounter with God. Central to Christian education is that "all persons would encounter God through his love as revealed in Jesus Christ, the Bible, and other forms of God's self-disclosure." This revised objective statement, in contrast to the Objective, emphasizes the importance of Scripture as God's self-revelation. (Given the make-up of the participating denominations, it is surprising that

Scripture was absent from the statement of the Objective.[12]) A distinctively Wesleyan approach to Christian education must include Scripture. John Wesley said of himself in the preface to his published sermons, "Let me be *homo unius libri*," a man of one book.[13] In understanding Wesley's so-called quadrilateral of Scripture, tradition, reason, and experience, Scripture must be the senior partner. The Bible is essential in educational ministry, yet Wesleyan Christian education will be built on a distinctive hermeneutic. Donald Dayton wrote of Wesley, "At many points Wesley sounds like a son of the Reformation in his emphasis on the finality of biblical authority and in his desire to be, in the much quoted phrase, a *homo unius libri* (a 'man of one book). But Wesley's conjunctive way of thinking puts Scripture in a larger context of authority quite different from that produced by the *'solas'* of the Reformation."[14] Therefore, Wesleyan Christian education must place a high value on Scripture while at the same time approaching the biblical text with an appropriate hermeneutic that will distinguish Wesleyan educational ministry somewhat from broader evangelicalism.

Second, the revised objective has as its aim that persons will "experience the transforming power of full salvation." While the Objective implied transformation, the revised objective is more overt in making that transformation central. Further, this transformation is toward full salvation, which in Wesleyan theology includes much more than mere justification. The term "full salvation" in some ways may seem archaic, but it is a good descriptor of what Christian life yielded to the Holy Spirit really means. In the words of Charles Foster,

> Historically, the goals of Christian religious education have emphasized, in John Wesley's words, salvation and sanctification...Despite the familiarity of these ideas in church conversations about educating for faith, I am increasingly convinced that most North American churches—conservative or liberal, orthodox or non-traditional—actually sponsor an education more dependent on popular understandings of psychology, therapy, and marketing.[15]

---

12. Participating denominations were as follows: Advent Christian Church, African Methodist Episcopal Church, American Baptist Convention, Christian Church (Disciples of Christ), Church of the Brethren, Church of God (Anderson), Church of the Nazarene, Cumberland Presbyterian Church, The Evangelical United Brethren Church, Mennonite Church, The Methodist Church, Presbyterian Church in Canada, Presbyterian Church in the U.S., The Protestant Episcopal Church, Southern Baptist Convention, United Church of Canada.

13. John Wesley, "A Farther Appeal to Men of Reason and Religion," in Wesley, *Works of John Wesley*, 11:105.

14. Dayton, "Use of Scripture," 129.

15. Foster, *Educating Christians*, 27.

Wesley explained full salvation this way,

> By salvation I mean, not barely (according to the vulgar notion) deliverance from hell, or going to heaven, but a present deliverance from sin, a restoration of the soul to its primitive health, its original purity; a recovery of the divine nature; the renewal of our souls after the image of God in righteousness and true holiness, in justice, mercy, and truth. This implies all holy and heavenly tempers, and by consequence all holiness of conversation.[16]

Third, the revised objective calls for believers to "become mature disciples who live as Kingdom citizens who, as they become more like Jesus, serve God and others." Mature discipleship in the lives of believers and the community of faith is the end goal for the church's teaching ministry. In the church, there are many conversations about discipleship, along with discipleship programs and materials. However, in many church contexts, it remains unclear what it means to be a Christian disciple. As long as the church is unclear about what discipleship means, helping to form people spiritually toward discipleship will be an elusive task. Educational ministry has frequently focused too much on the cognitive learning domain and thereby placed too much emphasis on the acquisition of knowledge as the primary indicator of spirituality. The result has been the reduction of Christian education to communicating factual content. Parishioners have responded by developing one of two common attitudes. The first attitude, which church leaders often view as quite pious, is the "feed me, feed me" attitude. These have equated Christian growth with feeding on spiritual content. Apathy is the second attitude, which grows from the realization that there has to be more to living as Christian than just knowledge and a frustration that they cannot seem to find "the more."

While knowing is important, it is not the most important mark of Christian maturity. Jesus pointed to obedience as a primary indicator of mature discipleship when he said, "If anyone loves me, they will obey me" (John 14:23). The obedience to which Christ calls his followers is to more than just a list of dos and don'ts. The Christian education that is needed for the twenty-first century will teach kingdom living empowered by the presence of the Holy Spirit. The kingdom of God was a central emphasis in Jesus' teaching ministry. While the kingdom can be somewhat difficult to define, Jesus outlined the values of his kingdom when he announced his ministry as recorded in Luke 4:18–19, "The Lord's Spirit has come to me, because he has chosen me to tell the good news to the poor. The Lord has sent me to announce freedom for prisoners, to give sight to the blind, to free everyone who suffers, and to say, 'This is the year the Lord has chosen.'" His focus on the gospel as good news to the poor, prisoners,

---

16. Wesley, "Farther Appeal to Men of Reason and Religion," in Wesley, *Works of John Wesley*, 11:106.

blind, and the suffering calls for educational ministry not only to teach about these issues but to equip, and then mobilize the church in reaching out in the name of Christ as through the power of the Spirit his kingdom is present now.

Finally, the revised objective follows the Objective in calling for followers of Christ to "abide in the Christian hope." A significant part of the church's teaching ministry is to help people lean forward into the future with eschatological hope toward the return of Christ. Christ followers ought to look forward to the return of Jesus. Many church teachers know by experience that it has been easier to get Christian disciples to *say* that their hope is in the return of Christ than to actually see that lifestyle as an outcome of their ministries. Maturing disciples recognize that until Christ's coming, they live with both the already and the not yet in terms of the kingdom in this present world. Therefore, one of the important tasks is to teach disciples to live in faithful anticipation and hope. Those who live toward the return of Christ are much more likely to become like Jesus. Wesleyans should be optimistic that real transformation can take place in believers' lives, in churches, and in the world so that mature disciples will abide in this Christian hope.

Far too many Christian educators simply go through the motions of doing what has always been done or following the latest trend as they lead local church educational ministries. Neither the latest trends nor uncritically repeated traditions can provide appropriate theological and philosophical foundations for Christian education as a discipline or for its expression in local church practice. The revised statement of objective suggests important aims for educational ministry along with grounding in Wesleyan theology. Its potential for helping shape positive educational ministry practice is not in how catchy it is (or is not) but in where it can point leaders as they shape the teaching ministry of the churches they serve.

Local Church Educational Goals and Objectives

Occasionally, some people enjoy heading out on an adventure not knowing the final destination. Such impulsive outings can provide a break from routines that may feel too closely scripted. However, in the local church's ministry, it is more likely that too little planning has gone into determining the overall direction of the educational ministries and that leaders have not scripted strategies closely enough. One of the dangers of shaping a statement of objective (purpose or mission statement) is that once leaders have polished the language and gotten the wording just right, it is tempting to set the statement aside and then move on to the next item on the agenda. However, their entire agenda of educational ministry ought to be shaped by their stated objective. Frequently, educational ministry leaders in local churches have not carefully considered the ultimate purpose(s) of Christian education (the why) before beginning to focus on methods (the how). As Christian educators go back to consider purpose, methods often need to be updated or changed in order to achieve the desired objective.

Chapter 6 suggests mature discipleship as the ultimate goal for Christian education. Every ministry within the church needs clearly defined goals in order to chart an intentional path that is likely to bring about desired outcomes. When ministry goals are clear, it is easier to move as a team in the same direction, recruit volunteers, equip teachers and leaders, and conduct evaluation. Christian education leaders carefully planning goals, objectives, and then action steps will have a ministry action plan (MAP) that will help them move from big general ideas toward implementation. When it comes to creating the MAP for educational

Figure 1. Ministry Action Plan Filters

ministry, it can be helpful to imagine a series of filters that help leaders sift out what is less important so that the church's Christian education ministry can focus on the more important.

1. The biblical mission for the church is the first filter. In scripture, God has given the church its mission. Leaders should jettison those things that do not help the church toward living out its mission in the world.

2. The local church's vision provides a second filter. Congregations must determine how they will live out the God-given mission in their particular context. Things that do not lead toward living out the vision are probably little more than unnecessary distractions.

3. Educational ministry goals make up the third filter. These goals describe how educational ministries will help equip individuals and the church community to live out the church's vision as disciples.

4. Statements of objectives shape the fourth filter. Objectives articulate what needs to happen in the lives of people in regard to achieving the educational ministry goals.

5. Learning activities are the fifth step. These activities should engage learners in experiences that will help them to realize the objectives and ultimately to become more like Jesus.

Though each church's MAP will necessarily differ, the following educational ministry goals stated in the revised objective for Christian education should be reflected in the MAP:

- Learners will encounter God through his love as revealed in Jesus Christ, the Bible, and other forms of God's self-disclosure.
- Learners will experience the transforming power of full salvation.
- Learners will become mature disciples who live as kingdom citizens who, as they become more like Jesus, serve God and others.
- Learners will abide in the Christian hope.

The goals in the revised objective are necessarily broad to address the purposes of the church's educational ministry; therefore, it will be helpful for local church educators to make them a bit more precise by creating a series of specific goals for each of the broad goal areas. For example, the first goal in the revised objective is about encountering God through his many forms of self-revelation. A more specific goal would be that "learners will encounter God through the Bible." While this goal is more clearly defined, it is not yet so clear-cut as to suggest specific actions. This is where objectives enter. Some characteristics of objectives are as follows:

1. Objectives should be important.
2. Objectives should be measurable.
3. Objectives should place the priority on the learners, not the teacher.
4. Objectives should be achievable as leaders and ministries are empowered by the Spirit.

Educators typically articulate objectives in relationship to learning domains. Those domains are cognitive, affective, and psychomotor. An oversimplified but helpful way of describing these domains relates to what educators want learners to know, feel, and do. One of the difficulties in shaping objectives is that frequently educators have shaped objectives for one domain independent from consideration of the other domains. Therefore, objectives may focus too much on one domain or another, resulting in an unbalanced educational plan that does not address the needs of the whole learner across the domains.

Norman Steinaker and M. Robert Bell devised a schema for addressing educational objectives to all three domains in the lives of learners at the same time that is particularly useful for Christian education. This can provide a helpful corrective to the tendency to focus too much on the cognitive domain (what learners know). Effective Christian educators do want learners to know, but also to have an emotive reaction to what they know and then live their lives in response

Table 1. Steinaker and Bell's Experiential Taxonomy	
Taxonomic Levels	Steps
1.0 Exposure	
1.1 Sensory	I hear the song.
1.2 Response	I enjoy it.
1.3 Readiness	I want to hear the song again.
2.0 Participation	
2.1 Representation	I attempt to reproduce the melody.
2.2 Modification	I add my own emphasis or style.
3.0 Identification	
3.1 Reinforcement	I repeat the song and the style often.
3.2 Emotion	It is now one of "my" songs.
3.3 Personal	I prefer "my" version or as "I" feel I first heard it to others.
3.4 Sharing	
4.0 Internalization	
4.1 Expansion	Based on previous reactions, it is not just one of my songs, it's "me" and I find opportunities to use it.
4.2 Intrinsic	The words and music now have a special meaning to me that they may not have for others.
5.0 Dissemination	
5.1 Informational	I provide opportunities for others to use and experience "my" version.
5.2 Homiletic	I feel and act as though others must feel as "I" do about "my" version.

to the learning they have embraced. Steinaker and Bell's way of approaching objectives allows educators to take learners on a journey that begins in exposure to a subject and finally leads them to care so deeply about what they have learned that they want to tell it to others and have them respond as they have. In Table 1, Steinaker and Bell have illustrated the level of objectives as students might relate to a song. As Christian educators it is easy to see how these levels can relate to the story of the gospel as well.

---

17 This table was published in Norman Steinaker and M. Robert Bell, *The Experiential Taxonomy: A New Approach to Teaching and Learning*, Educational Psychology (New York: Academic Press, 1979). Copyright Academic Press. Used by permission.

Building on the goal that "learners will encounter God through the Bible" might lead to learning objectives like these following Steinaker and Bell's taxonomy:

1. Learners will hear and respond with joy to Bible stories about God's love.
2. Learners will retell Bible stories in their own words.
3. Learners will grow in their love for Bible stories so that those stories become their stories.
4. Learners will dig deep into Bible stories and shape their lives in response to those stories.
5. Learners will share their Bible stories with others and want others to respond to those stories as they have.

With specific and measurable objectives in place, educators can complete their MAP by designing learning activities that will help learners to accomplish the objectives and mature as disciples. One of the benefits of a well-designed MAP is that it not only charts a course, but it provides criteria for evaluation. Evaluation done based on predetermined criteria provides objective data for course correction and decision making for future planning.

Bibliography

Dayton, Donald W. "The Use of Scripture in the Wesleyan Tradition." In *The Use of the Bible in Theology: Evangelical Options*, edited by Robert K. Johnston, 121–36. Atlanta, GA: John Knox, 1985.

Division of Christian Education of the National Council of Churches of Christ in the United States of America, Cooperative Curriculum Project. *The Church's Education Ministry: A Curriculum Plan*. St. Louis, MO: The Bethany Press, 1966.

Downs, Perry. *Teaching for Spiritual Growth: An Introduction to Christian Education*. Grand Rapids, MI: Zondervan, 1994.

Foster, Charles R. *Educating Christians: The Future of Christian Education*. Nashville, TN: Abingdon Press, 1994.

Fowler, James N. *Stages of Faith: The Psychology of Human Development and the Quest for Meaning*. San Francisco, CA: Harper and Row, 1981.

Groome, Thomas H. *Educating for Life: A Spiritual Vision for Every Teacher and Parent*. Allen, TX: Thomas More, 1998.

Lawson, Kevin E. "Marginalization and Renewal: Evangelical Christian Education in the Twentieth Century." *Religious Education* 98, no. 4 (Fall 2003): 437–53.

Pazmiño, Robert W. *Foundational Issues in Christian Education: An Introduction in Evangelical Perspective,* 2nd ed. Grand Rapids, MI: Baker Books, 1997.

Sanner, Elwood A. and A.F. Harper, eds. *Exploring Christian Education*. Kansas City, MO: Beacon Hill Press, 1978.

Steinaker, Norman and M. Robert Bell. *The Experiential Taxonomy: A New Approach to Teaching and Learning*. New York: Academic Press, 1979.

Wesley, John. *The Works of John Wesley*. Vol. 11, *The Appeals to Men of Reason and Religion and Certain Related Open Letters*. Edited by Gerald R. Cragg. Nashville, TN: Abingdon Press, 1989.

Williams, Dennis E. "Christian Education." In *Evangelical Dictionary of Christian Education*, edited by Michael Anthony, 132–34. Grand Rapids, MI: Baker Book House, 2001.

CHAPTER THIRTEEN

How to Study the Bible

JERRY HICKSON

> Do your best to win God's approval as a
> worker who doesn't need to be ashamed
> and who teaches only the true message.
>
> —2 Timothy 2:15

The Bible provides an objective foundation that keeps spirituality Christian. Those who aspire to be teachers in Christian education must themselves be disciplined students of God's Word. This requires more than simply studying the lesson plan or listening to the pastor's sermon. A variety of methods can be used to develop a strategy for studying the Bible.

Prayer in Bible Study

Whatever method is used, Bible reading should always be a matter of prayer. The Bible is approached as something more than mere literature. Each session should begin with a prayer for the illumination of the Holy Spirit. A time of quiet will be helpful to prepare mind and spirit. A prayerful mindset should continue throughout the reading of the passage, allowing God to speak. After reading the passage, prayer continues as the message found there becomes a matter for conversation with God. At times, the reader will want to "pray the Scriptures," paraphrasing the text itself into a personalized prayer from the reader to God (more below). At other times, the reader will be stimulated into discussion with God as the truth of the Word is applied to personal circumstances.

Reading Through the Whole Bible

One method for personal Bible study is to read the entire Bible over a period of time. Comprehensive Bible reading provides an unsurpassed method for absorbing the breadth of the richness of the Bible.

> The popular devotional practice of a brief Bible reading each morning is a little like trying to take a shower one drop at a time. Just as we simply cannot get a shower that way, we simply cannot become a biblically saturated person that way.[1]

> To take a book of the Bible, to immerse one's self in it and to be grasped by it, is to have one's life literally revolutionized. This requires study and the training of the attention. The student stays with it through barren day after barren day, until at last the meaning is clear, and transformation happens in his life.[2]

Several options are available to the Bible student who wants to study Scripture comprehensively. Starting at Genesis and reading through to Revelation is probably the least effective method of comprehensive Bible reading. Many have set out on this route only to lose heart, perhaps midway through Leviticus. Readers who use this method are more likely to be successful if they are familiar with the different types of literature found in the Bible, the historical background, and the process used in assembling the books into the format we now have.

Use of a resource like *The One Year Bible*[3] is more effective as a daily dose of New Testament is added to the Old Testament readings, which include a psalm and some of Proverbs. This offers a little more variety and the promise of a little spice to help as less colorful passages are being read.[4]

A daily lectionary provides a resource for comprehensive reading of the Bible, usually over more than one year.[5] Lectionaries usually include readings from the Gospels, the Epistles, an Old Testament passage, and one or more

---

1. Foster, *Streams of Living Water*, 232.

2. Elizabeth O'Conner, cited in Foster and Yanni, *Celebrating the Disciplines: A Journal Workbook*, 110.

3. This resource is available in several translations. The NIV, KJV, Living, and NLT are published by Tyndale House Publishers. The ESV Bible is from Crossway Bibles. Nelson Bibles provides a version in NKJV. An online version can be found at http://www.oneyearbibleonline.com/.

4. The author has been using a study guide he prepared in 1990 that selects readings from each of six different types of biblical literature. Each week, the reading includes a passage from the Gospels (or Acts), the Epistles (or Revelation), the Old Testament narratives, the prophetic writings, the Psalms, and the wisdom literature (Job, Proverbs, Ecclesiastes, Song of Solomon).

5. An online resource based on the Common Revised Lectionary is found at http://www.crivoice.com.

psalms. Lectionaries usually follow the church calendar so that the texts read have some relation to the season.

Reading the entire Bible, whether over a year or over two or three years, is an ambitious goal. While no other method offers the depth of insight into the commonly overlooked parts of the Bible, few readers have the time or discipline to achieve this objective. Further, the amount of reading required encourages speed-reading instead of reflective reading. This method should probably be reserved for the more mature Bible student.

Instead of attempting to read the entire Bible, the Bible student can engage whole books of the Bible. This can be accomplished in one reading for shorter books or over a period of days or weeks for longer books. Besides simply reading the text, the reader will do well to study background material on this book (see below). The reader might choose to study a longer passage within a book, like the Sermon on the Mount in Matthew 5–7.

Use of Bible Background Information

Bible reading is greatly enhanced by an understanding of context and the cultural background associated with the passage. The reader should be familiar with the various genres (see below) used in biblical literature in order to interpret appropriately.

Before beginning the study of any book of the Bible, the reader should have an understanding of the background of that book. Who wrote this? To whom was it written? What time period did this book come from? What was the purpose for which this book was written? Some biblical books give this information more readily than others. In some cases, mystery remains in spite of the efforts of scholarship.

Commentaries and Bible dictionaries are helpful when studying the background of a biblical book or passage. At a minimum, a good study Bible offers an introduction to each book and notes to explain the relevant background. The Internet is providing an ever-growing resource for biblical study, but the reader should browse these with caution.

The Bible student should always use Bible resources as supplements, keeping the Bible passage itself as the prime source of learning. Besides using reference materials for introductory background, the reader may want to consult Bible dictionaries or concordances when a difficult word or passage requires further investigation.

Reflective Devotional Reading of Short Passages

Rather than comprehensive Bible reading, many are better advised to read short passages of Scripture, taking time to reflect on the meaning. Reading more verses does not always lead to better Bible study. Using as little as a single verse, the emphasis here is on contemplation and prayer. Many use devotional guides like *Daily Bread*[6] or *The Upper Room*.[7] Others use a more independent process of inductive Bible study and/or the ancient practice of *lectio divina* (see below) to study a short passage of Scripture. In devotional reading, study aids and exegetical analysis are avoided in favor of personal application. The objective is to hear a personal message from God through his Word. The reader will still benefit from an understanding of the context and the background of the biblical passage. Best results come with choosing passages that encompass a full unit—whether a story, poem, or topic.

Inductive Bible Study

Maximum benefit from Bible reading comes from a more intense method than simply glossing over a passage of Scripture. Inductive Bible study is an intentional process of unlocking the power of a Scripture text through careful analysis. A core idea is letting the Bible speak for itself rather than using Scriptures to prove some predetermined point. One outline for inductive Bible study is repetition, concentration, comprehension, and reflection.[8] The message of the Bible often begins to become clear after the first reading as the passage is reviewed several times. Concentration entails careful analysis of what is found. The five Ws of journalism provide a tool, as the reader discerns the who, what, when, where, and why of the passage. This step may require use of study helps to explore these items, although readers may recognize things from past study. Outlining a text, giving each passage a title, and identifying the key themes is another approach. As readers engage in the process, the key truths and intent of the passage are revealed. As these steps raise issues, readers must consider how the principles apply to their own lives. This personalization of the message is what makes inductive Bible study so beneficial.

Lectio Divina

Some have found help in practices of spiritual formation used by Christians for centuries, including *lectio divina*. This process is similar to the inductive Bible study method used by many modern evangelicals. The four steps are titled *Lectio*, *Meditatio*, *Oratio*, and *Contemplatio*. The reader begins with *Lectio*, reading the text several times, preferably reading out loud. *Meditatio* is a time of focus on the passage, perhaps using visualization to make the story come to life. *Oratio* is a time of prayer as the issues presented by the passage become a matter for conversation with God. Readers might here "pray the Scriptures" as they para-

---

6. *Our Daily Bread* is published by Radio Bible Class. http://www.rbc.org/index.aspx.
7. *The Upper Room* (Nashville, TN). http://www.upperroom.org/devotional/.
8. More extensive discussion is found in Foster, *Celebration of Discipline*, 64–66.

phrase and personalize the words of the Bible passage. *Contemplatio* is a time of quiet meditation as the student remains in the presence of God and listens for his voice. The shortest portion of Scripture can be developed into quite a lengthy time of rich interaction with God and His Word.[9]

Use of Study Bibles

A number of study Bibles are available from different publishers. Some of these offer useful helps including footnotes and reference material at the back of the book. The Bible student should be mindful of the theological bias presented by the writers of the helps. At all times, the Bible should be given first priority, with the study helps providing a supportive role. Study Bibles may be available in one or more versions. The student who has been using a particular study Bible exclusively might be well served to switch to another study Bible or a Bible without the helps.[10]

Which Translation Is Best?

Few Bible students have mastered the original languages of the Bible (Greek, Hebrew, and a little Aramaic) to read the Bible in its original form. So we have to read a Bible translation in a language we can understand. A large number of versions are available in the English language. These can be categorized by their approach to translation. Readers may choose the translation they prefer, guided by an understanding of the nature of that version. Some translations attempt the most direct (word for word) translation possible, while others work to translate concepts (dynamic equivalence) without being bound by the syntax of Greek or Hebrew. Others take a looser approach, offering a paraphrase. For scholarly study, a translation by a committee of scholars is preferable to a translation by an individual. For careful study, the reader is advised to use more than one translation, balancing different approaches: perhaps comparing a direct translation with a dynamic equivalence version or contrasting the translation of a committee of scholars with the paraphrase of a gifted writer.

The reader who wants a very direct translation, preferring the most literal translation, would be well advised to try the New American Standard Bible. Because the translators chose to use a word-for-word translation approach, this version tends to sound awkward or unnatural. This is because English syntax sometimes works differently than the biblical languages. For this reason, the NASB is better suited for use in the study than in public worship. Other versions that tend to be more direct include the King James Version, the New King

---

9. A number of books and Web sites are available detailing this process, including Keith Drury's *Listening for God Through Romans*.

10. A personal favorite for this writer is the *Thompson Chain Reference Bible* in the New International Version.

James, the Revised Standard (or the New Revised Standard), and the English Standard Version.

The reader who wants a version that uses more readable English while maintaining a high level of accuracy in translation would be well advised to try the New International Version (or the Today's NIV). These translators used the dynamic equivalence method, where whole phrases and sentences are rendered for a similar meaning rather than insisting on a word-to-word equivalence. At times, this approach introduces a looseness that might create difficulty for theological or textual analysis, but the overall effect results in easier reading and may be better for public reading in worship. Other versions using dynamic equivalence include the New Living Version, God's Word, and the Good News Translation (also known as Today's English Version).

The reader may also choose to use a paraphrase. These versions take a more lax approach to translation than the dynamic equivalence versions, trying to produce a more readable product. Paraphrases are increasingly vulnerable to theological bias, especially since they are usually done by an individual instead of a committee of scholars. A paraphrase may be based on an English translation rather than on careful translation directly from the ancient texts. Paraphrases from recent decades include *The Message* and the Living Bible. The New Living Translation presents a significant improvement as a committee of scholars worked to refine the paraphrase first presented by Kenneth Taylor.

As stated before, translations prepared by a committee of scholars tend to be more reliable that those prepared by an individual. Most of the direct translation and dynamic equivalence versions were prepared by qualified committees of biblical scholars. Paraphrases tend to be written by individuals. Notable examples of committee translations include the King James Version, New King James, Revised Standard, New Revised Standard, New International Version, and the New Living Version. Notable examples of translations by an individual include the Living Bible, J. B. Phillips, and *The Message*. Either approach can be useful, but the presence of multiple scholars makes the committee translations more reliable.

Some versions are rendered with limited vocabulary to make them accessible to readers with less education or those whose primary language is other than English. One example is the Contemporary English Version, which was written at a grade school level.

Some versions are available that were written for some special effect. The Amplified Bible offers multiple English alternatives for words that may have a richer nuance than one word will carry. Some versions tend to be more amusing than valuable for study. The Cottonpatch version was written with a distinct southern drawl. Another version uses the street urban language commonly known as ebonics.

A word is in order about the King James (or Authorized) Version. This version is cherished by some to the exclusion of all others. An obvious issue is the use of Shakespearean English that is not familiar to most readers. A less obvious issue is the manuscripts on which the translation was based. In the years since 1611, many manuscripts of the Bible have been discovered, some of which are significantly older (and therefore more accurate) than those used by the translators of the Authorized Version. The New King James is an attempt to update the archaic language, but it did not resolve the reliance on the old *Textus Receptus*. Those who have learned to love the sound of the King James may well continue to use it, although it would be wise to compare the results found in a more recent version. Those not familiar with this old version should feel free to explore more contemporary alternatives.

Reading Different Types of Biblical Literature (Genre)

One way to enrich Bible reading is to vary the types of biblical literature studied. Readings from the New Testament letters are very popular, as are readings from the Gospels. The Epistles offer direct teaching in little more than a verse, while the Gospels offer much of the same or easy-to-digest stories from the life of Jesus. The Bible reader is advised to attempt reading of other narratives such as those found in the Old Testament, along with the poetic writings of the Psalms and Wisdom literature, or to venture into the prophetic writings.

The novice student is needs to learn the differences between the different types of biblical literature. The reader who does not understand the differences between narrative, didactic, poetry, prophetic oracles, and apocalyptic is prone to misinterpret the meaning of a Bible text.

When reading *narrative* passages, the reader should be watching for elements like character, setting, and plot. Narrative passages are common in the Gospels, Acts of the Apostles, and the first seventeen books of the Old Testament. When reading narratives, the reader often will need to cover more verses to get a full story. Often, the reader must work to discern the implications of the story.

When reading *didactic* passages, the reader should keep in mind who is writing or speaking, what topic is being presented, and how the thoughts are developed. Didactic passages are common in the Epistles but can be found among the Gospels, especially in the "red letter" parts where Jesus is teaching.

When reading *poetic* passages, the reader should be aware of stylistic issues, such as parallelism, and should consider the type of poetry (e.g. praise psalm or lament) this passage represents. Poetry is found throughout the Psalms, Proverbs, Ecclesiastes, and Song of Solomon. Most of the book of Job is poetic, with the exception of the first two chapters and the final several chapters. Poetry is common in the prophetic writings and is found throughout the rest of the Bible.

Prophetic books present their own challenges as do apocalyptic books like Revelation. Readers should prepare themselves with study of the difference between prophetic and apocalyptic and should study the backgrounds of these types of literature. Care should be taken to let the text speak for itself rather than bringing expectations shaped by popular understanding of prophetic predictions of future events.

While the entire Bible is the inspired Word of God, it contains a diverse library of books written by different authors using very different styles. Understanding these factors will increase the proper understanding of the Scriptures.[11]

Alternative Methods for Bible Study

Several alternative methods are available to the Bible student. These include memorization, theme or character studies, paraphrase, praying the Scripture, singing the Scripture, and visualization.

Bible memorization is committing to memory verses or longer passages of Scripture. This practice may be more difficult for adults than children, but it is still beneficial. Through memorization, the Word of God is hidden in the heart (Ps 119:11), where it is available for the Spirit to use in spiritual formation and for fighting temptation. Resources are available that provide tips on verses to memorize. Readers may well choose memory verses based on their own discovery. When choosing a verse or passage to memorize, chapter and verse divisions are not as important as natural breaks in thought. When selecting which parts of a verse to memorize, care should be taken to avoid twisting the passage to mean something other than the context would indicate. Popular choices for shorter verses to memorize would include 2 Chronicles 7:14; Proverbs 3:5–6; Ezekiel 11:19; John 8:36; Romans 12:1–2; 1 Corinthians 6:19–20; Galatians 2:20; Ephesians 2:8–10; and James 1:27.[12] Longer passages that might be memorized include Psalm 23; 1 Corinthians 13; Philippians 4:4–8; James 1:22–25; and 1 John 2:15–17.[13]

---

11. One resource for exploring biblical genre is Fee and Stuart, *How to Read the Bible for All Its Worth*.

12. Others include Ps 17:8; 20:7; 27:1, 4:63:1, 3–4; 119:9–11; Prov 1:7; 4:23; 9:10; Isa 26:3–4; 30:21; 40:31; 52:7; 53:6; Jer 17:7; 24:7; 29:13; Micah 6:8; Hab 2:20; Zech 4:6; Matt 5:13–14, 44, 48; 6:24; 7:7–8, 13–14; 9:37–38; 10:38–39, 42; Mark 9:23, 35; 10:43, 45; 11:24; John 3:16–18; 6:47; 10:10; 11:25; 13:34–35; 14:6, 21; 15:5, 17; Acts 1:8; 2:21; 4:12; Rom 1:16–17; 5:8; 6:18; 8:28; 10:8, 13; 13:4; 1 Cor 1:27–29; 10:13; 2 Cor 5:16, 20; 7:1; 9:6, 7; Gal 5:1; 6:2; Eph 2:19–20; 5:18; Col 4:5–6; 1 Thess 4:7–8; 1 Tim 6:6, 12, 17; 2 Tim 1:7; 2:2, 15, 22; 3:16–17; Titus 3:5; Heb 4:12; 13:9; James 1:19–20, 21, 26; 4:7, 10, 17; 1 Peter 1:15; 2:24–25; 3:15; 4:10; 5:7, 8–9; 2 Peter 1:20–21; 1 John 2:6; 4:10, 19; 5:18; Rev 3:20.

13. Others include Deut 6:4–9; Ps 19:7–11; 24:7–10; 100; 103:1–5; 139; Eccl 3:1–8; Isa 1:10–19; 55:6–12; Matt 5:3–12; 6:19–21, 25–34; 7:1–5, 24–27; 22:37–40; 28:18–20; Mark 8:34–38; John 1:1–5, 10–14; Rom 8:28–30; 1 Cor 15:50–54; Eph 3:14–21; 4:1–6; Phil 3:7–16; Col 1:15–23; 3:1–5, 12–18; 1 Thess 5:16–24; Titus 2:11–14; Heb 4:14–16; James 1:2–8, 13–17; 2 Peter 1:3–11; 1 John 1:8–2:3; 3:1–3, 9–10, 16–18, 23–24; 5:11–13.

Theme studies and *character studies* involve the reading of selective passages to follow an individual or concept across the Bible. Perhaps the reader wants to search the passages that use the word *holiness*. Or perhaps the reader wants to study the life of Peter. Resources like a topical Bible or concordance are useful for identifying relevant passages. Computer Bibles and Bible Web sites offer another technique for combing through the Scriptures for word studies or tracking specific names. Theme studies might be developed on holiness or obedience. Popular choices for character studies include the lives of Deborah, Moses, David, Mary, and Peter. While these studies can be personally constructed, a number of published studies are available.

Paraphrase is the rewriting of a verse or passage in one's own words. This process helps to digest the meaning of the Scripture. Some published paraphrases are available, including the *Living Bible* and *The Message*. Bible readers can rework their understanding of a Bible translation into their own words. Most likely, the words used will be those of the reader's own vocabulary. The paraphrase might make specific application that fits the needs of the reader.

Praying the Scripture is a process of personalizing the message of a passage in conversation with God. The simplest approach is to insert your own name wherever possible. For example, while reading John 3:16, the reader might say, "For God so loved (enter own name) that he gave his only Son, that if (enter own name) might believe in him, (enter own name) might not perish but have eternal life." At times, the student may diverge from the words of the Bible to illustrate or elaborate as moved by the Scripture. Sometimes, the text will be used unaltered as the words are found to be meaningful without alteration. Many of the psalms can be used this way, including 61:4 (NIV), "I long to dwell in your tent forever and take refuge in the shelter of your wings," or 102:1–2 (NIV), "Hear my prayer, O LORD; let my cry for help come to you. Do not hide your face from me when I am in distress. Turn your ear to me when I call, answer me quickly." From here, the prayer can continue the train of thought with a more personalized prayer.

Singing the Scripture is setting biblical text to a tune. Many texts have already been set to music. For those so inclined, the use of music can help to interact with the messages of the Bible. The reader might compose original songs, setting a verse or passage to a familiar tune or one composed for the text. Much of the Bible is written poetically and is easily set to music. Even more didactic prose can be used for lyrical expression.

Visualization is using the mental camera to animate the stories told in narrative passages. This method is especially helpful given the importance of imagery in our culture. When using visualization, readers should try to notice details they have previously overlooked. When studying Acts 16:25–28, the reader should see the darkness, hear the tunes being sung, feel the rumbling, and absorb the terror of the jailer. The point of perspective can be shifted, viewing the story again in the shoes of a different character. When reading the parable of the prodigal (Luke 15:11–31), perhaps the reader should take the viewpoint of the elder brother after considering the perspective of the younger son.

Application

The reader must guard against falling into a ritual of mindless reading or reading only for academic purpose. The Bible is more than a novel or a textbook. At all times, the reader must read with an ear open to hear what God might be saying. At times, this message might be different from what anyone else would find in the same text. Having understood the meaning of a passage, readers are well advised to dwell a little longer to consider how this is relevant to their own lives and what they will do about it in the days to come. For the serious Bible student, the reflection involved in application can easily take more time than the reading of the Bible passage itself.

Journaling

Many Bible students have found benefit in recording their thoughts in writing. These might include first impressions, paraphrases, prayers, questions, and practical applications. If the reader chooses to jump from one part of the Bible to another, the journal can provide a log to record the path taken. Referring back to the journal months or years later provides its own grist for spiritual development.

Time Schedule

Each Bible student will have to determine what schedule proves most productive and workable. For some, the best approach is to rise a little earlier than normal each morning for a time of concentrated study. Others will do well with a designated time at the end of the day. Some will be able to make an appointment in the middle of the day that they set aside for biblical study. Some will find best results with a more flexible approach, although not having a daily regimen increases the possibility that Bible study will not happen. The more the reader follows a daily pattern of study, the more benefits he or she is likely to experience. Perhaps a blended approach could be constructed with a daily regimen of a few minutes of devotional study combined with a session of an hour or more once a week for more academic study. Rather than conforming to someone else's pattern, the reader must determine what approach best fits his or her own temperament and lifestyle.

Conclusion

The Bible is simple enough that any Christian can understand its truth, yet it is so deep and complex that the most mature and informed reader is at times astounded with the mystery of its meaning. Christian educators must devote themselves to careful study of God's Word. For some, use of a published guide and a daily appointment provides the best structure for disciplined personal Bible study. Others will find more satisfaction with a personalized approach combining various techniques that might change from time to time. To be a teacher of the Bible, one must first be a diligent student.

Bibliography

Drury, Keith. *Listening for God Through Romans*. Lectio Divina Series. Indianapolis, IN: Wesleyan Publishing House, 2006.

Fee, Gordon D. and Douglas Stuart. *How to Read the Bible for All Its Worth*. Grand Rapids, MI: Zondervan, 2003.

Foster, Richard J. *Celebration of Discipline*. San Francisco, CA: HarperSanFrancisco, 1998.

———. *Streams of Living Water*. San Francisco, CA: HarperSanFrancisco, 1998.

Foster, Richard J. and Kathryn A. Yanni. *Celebrating the Disciplines: A Journal Workbook*. San Francisco, CA: HarperOne, 1992.

CHAPTER FOURTEEN

Choosing and Evaluating Curriculum

KEITH DRURY

> And we must be determined to run the
> race that is ahead of us.
>
> —Hebrews 12:1b

What Is Curriculum?

The word *curriculum* comes from a Latin term meaning "to run," which implies a predetermined route. A footrace is designed to run along a pre-established route or course. While the author of Hebrews did not have in mind the printed curriculum materials when calling his readers to "run the race ahead of us" (Heb 12:1), the notion that there is a certain sequence or route set before a Christian is certainly implied. Curriculum is a planned route of learning and change. In Christian education the term *curriculum* is more commonly used to refer to actual materials that are built on the curriculum plan.[1]

There is, however, a larger way to see curriculum. It can be seen as this: everything that happens in church life—referring to all the activities and experiences the church uses to accomplish its mission—evangelism, discipleship, fellowship, worship, and service is curriculum in the larger sense. Chapter 18 outlines this broader approach to curriculum. This chapter focuses on the more

---

1. D. Campbell Wyckoff has an excellent overview of this concept in his foreword to Howard P. Colson and Raymond M. Rigdon, *Understanding Your Church's Curriculum* (Nashville, TN: Broadman Press, 1981).

popular understanding of curriculum as the printed materials (as well as audio and visual resources) used in Christian education classes as a plan of study.

What Makes Curriculum *Curriculum?*

Just because a book is printed or a video series is produced does not make it curriculum. Curriculum is *a planned sequence of learning experiences that organizes learning and change in an orderly manner to accomplish the spiritual development of people.*

- Curriculum is *planned*. It has a learning plan, sometimes over ten years or more, asking the question, "What learning should happen by the end of this period?"

- It is *sequential* and thus asks the question, "What should be learned first before other learning follows?"

- Curriculum is *organized* and asks, "How should this learning be placed in relationship with other learning?"

- Christian education curriculum focuses on both *learning and change* by asking, "What do students need to know and how do they need to change?"

- It is *orderly* by asking, "What is the best way to put all these experiences together in a single comprehensive package?"

- Finally, the curriculum of Christian education seeks to accomplish *spiritual development* of Christians, so it asks, "What learning and experiences will contribute to the spiritual development of people?"

Curriculum Through History

The people of God have always given care to teaching each other and the next generation, even before there were written materials. During the time of the patriarchs, the family was the primary vehicle through which to pass on the faith. The curriculum then was the story of God's dealings with his people in the past. Retelling "our story" communicated who God's people were and implied how they should live. Thus the first curriculum was a narrative one, a story passed from generation to generation long before anything was written down.

After several thousand years, this oral curriculum was eventually written down and the books of Moses and the prophets emerged as a written point of reference. However, the teaching of the time continued to be mostly narrative and largely kept in the hands of parents. Experiential learning was merged with formal storytelling as rituals emerged, such as the annual Passover celebration, in which symbolic elements, such as eating unleavened bread or bitter herbs, prompted questions to which the telling became the teaching explanation.

It was probably during the Babylonian exile when a new approach to curriculum arose as the synagogue emerged. Here the Law and Prophets were studied, read, memorized, and merged with worship and prayers; parents had a new ally in religious education—a believing community organized for study.

During the first century, the early church faced the challenge of discipling a large number of Gentile converts who had little knowledge of the Law or even of there being only one God. These early Christian leaders developed a comprehensive curriculum leading to baptism.[2] The process often lasted up to two years and appears to have used a personal mentor who taught the candidate using the curriculum of the "Two Ways" found in *The Didache,* an early church discipleship and worship manual, some contents dating to the late first century.[3]

By the Middle Ages, catechism became the initial curriculum leading to confirmation; it focused on children or adult converts. But in one sense, the church year of the Middle Ages was the core experiential curriculum of sorts for celebrating the essentials of Christianity in an annual cycle, along with the visual curriculum of painting and stained glass.

The Reformation brought a revival of both the catechism and increased teaching and instruction from the pulpit. John Wesley launched class meetings, which used a curriculum of accountability for small group discipleship. The explosive growth of the Sunday school movement in the United States and Canada brought a great demand for a more formal long-term curriculum. In 1869 the National Sunday School Convention started preparing Uniform Lessons based on one passage of Scripture for all ages and all denominations. This movement lasted almost one hundred years, and in most cities and towns across America, every Sunday school class of all ages in virtually all denominations studied a common passage of Scripture. By 1908 graded lessons emerged that more carefully considered the needs at each age level and offered different stories for different ages. Through the twentieth century, curriculum publishing became an elaborate and careful discipline leading to a dozen or more full lines of curriculum materials for all ages.

Important Curriculum Terms

Like any sophisticated endeavor, the discipline of curriculum development has some unique terms. Knowing these terms enables a Christian educator better to understand and evaluate the curricular resources available. While there are additional terms besides the following, this list provides a basic vocabulary for evaluating and selecting curricular materials, which will be the major focus of this chapter.

Goals and objectives. A curriculum has *goals* it plans to accomplish long term (over months and years) and *objectives* that it hopes to accomplish short term

2. Milavec, *Didache.*

3. For more information, see Holmes, *Apostolic Fathers.*

(in a unit or single lesson). The use of these two terms is reversed in education from their popular use in business and leadership. If a Christian educator works with a church that has done strategic planning that was influenced by business vocabulary, these terms are often used with the exact opposite meaning; for example in business, objectives may be long term or strategic, and goals are often considered short term or tactical. While the business use of the terms has gained popularity, education (and thus curriculum) tends to insist on using the terms the other way around: objectives are short term—as in "lesson objectives"—and goals are long term. Either way, goals and objectives are the curriculum's stated intentions—what it is trying to accomplish.

Outcomes. Some curricular materials prefer to use the term *outcomes.* To some the term *objective* sounds like the teacher (or curriculum) is trying to "do" something to the student. Wording of an outcome tends to describe the desired effect from the student's perspective rather than from the teacher's or curriculum's point of view. An outcome might read, "That the student will feel grateful for God's care and love" or "That the student will thank God for his care and love."

Cognitive-affective-behavioral. When Christian educators write goals or outcomes, they often organize them into three domains. Statements that describe knowledge are *cognitive outcomes*, those which describe feelings and attitudes are *affective outcomes*, and those describing actions are *behavioral outcomes*. Sometimes these three domains are described by using simpler terms such as "know-feel-do," or "head-heart-hands."

Educational mission. Most curriculum plans have somewhere a statement of what the entire multiyear curriculum plan is trying to accomplish over a decade or longer. This educational mission statement usually does not appear in the individual products but is used in planning the entire line of curriculum. It may appear in a general advertising piece for a line of curriculum, and it may be titled variously as "Educational Objective" or "Comprehensive Goal" or another such term describing the purpose of the comprehensive curriculum. An educational objective is like a mission statement for the curriculum. It might read something like this: *To help individuals recognize God as revealed in Scripture, respond in personal faith, seek to follow him as fully devoted Christians, be incorporated into Christ's church and become actively involved in God's mission in the world, as they live in the full power of the Holy Spirit growing to Christian maturity.*

Scope and sequence. The scope is the range of the subject matter to be covered. A curriculum cannot cover everything in the Bible for all ages, so the *scope* narrows and defines the subject matter to be covered. When this subject matter is put in the order it is to be studied, this is called the *sequence.* Thus, these two combined are referred to as *scope and sequence,* which includes the content that will be covered by the curriculum and the order in which it will be covered. An entire curriculum line has a scope and sequence, as well as each age level having its own scope and sequence. Many publishers provide these in a colorful folder so the individual teacher can see the part he or she plays in the comprehensive curriculum plan.

Area or theme. Sometimes a curriculum's scope and sequence is broken down into areas or themes, which are often theological or thematic emphases of the curriculum. An example of areas might be: revelation, redemption, salvation, vocation, the church, and mission. That is, a curriculum using these areas or themes would select scriptures and learning activities that focus on these themes in a regular revisited cycle for all ages.

Teaching strategy. Most curriculum materials have a teaching strategy, which is a design or outline for moving through a lesson in a way that will initiate learning and spiritual life change. This teaching strategy is the carefully constructed plan for each lesson, built on an understanding of how people grow and change at that age level. It considers factors like *age level readiness* and *attention span* of the students. Some typical teaching strategy outlines are:

- Explore the Bible (read, study, compare, hear, discuss, meditate, talk)
- Discover truth (discover underlying significance and meaning and coming to an "Aha! moment" or "Eureka!")
- Appropriate (own the truth as a student, buy in, accept, respond)
- Apply (put into practice the learning, implement, live out in life based on the truth)

A change-oriented adult teaching strategy plan might look like this:

1. Engage interest
2. Explore the Bible
3. Apply to life
4. Challenge
5. Response

Rhyming is a clever way to remember teaching strategies:

Hook (capture interest)
Book (study the Bible)
Look (examine life—apply)
Took (enact into life)

A teaching strategy outline should be adapted to the age level and might include interest centers, prayer time, worship and singing, snacks, or crafts. It is usually repeated every week like an order of service for worship. The teaching strategy is a common template of sequential learning activities arranged as the usual outline for the lesson.

Grab-Bag Resourcing

Having studied the characteristics of curriculum, many Christian educators admit their local church has none—at least no *comprehensive* curriculum. In many churches the individual classes have resources, but the church has no over-all curriculum plan. In such "grab-bag resourcing" the teachers (sometimes even Christian educators!) simply reach into the bag of resources available and select whichever one is most appealing at the time. Thus, the second grade class might use resources from one publisher's curriculum while the third grade uses another and the fourth grade students still a third—all based on different plans of study. This sort of grab-bag resourcing fills up the class time and may entertain the students and "keep them busy," but it lacks an over-all comprehensive plan for learning. It is why sometimes for three years straight, students repeat the story of the woman at the well but they never hear the story of Zacchaeus.

Curriculum publishers develop materials on a larger plan so that there is an orderly coverage of the content over three, six, or ten (or more) years in an orderly sequence. Curriculum is planned, intentional, sequenced, and comprehensive. Anything less is just random resourcing. A good curriculum plan is carefully designed to achieve objectives from cradle to grave. Thus, choosing a curriculum is not an activity for each class or teacher but a comprehensive decision of the whole church; it is a major responsibility of a Christian education board and the director or minister of Christian education.

Selecting Curriculum

Examining and selecting curriculum material is a major task of a Christian educator and the local church sponsoring spiritual formation. It should not be a casual decision decided on a frivolous basis, like how colorful the booklets are or how cute the pictures appear. Color and attractiveness are certainly important factors, but they are not the primary factors. Generally, a new Christian educator on staff at a church does not set out during the first year to tackle changing curriculum or eliminating all the grab-bag resourcing. However, after a year or two, most professional Christian educators recognize that if they are going to do more than randomized entertainment, tackling the decision to unify a comprehensive curriculum will have to occur. The following is a six-step process for making that decision. Each Christian educator will develop his or her own plan, but basically this choice usually involves a process including something like these steps.

1. Organize the decision-makers.

Who decides what curriculum a church will use? In a church using the grab-bag resourcing model, anyone can decide, including each new teacher of a class. In a church with a more professional approach to spiritual formation, a group usually decides, often chaired by the professional Christian educator. A church's polity and organizational chart might name this decision-making body and a Christian educator will call this decision-making group to meet. It may be a Christian education board or committee, or in some churches it could include other ministerial staff along with the Christian education director or minister. The process is a demanding one and cannot be done in one or two meetings but is accomplished over several months or even a full year.

The first meeting of this group usually begins with a review of the recent history of curriculum selection in the church and the problems and challenges of grab-bag resourcing. Then the meeting moves on to equipping the group in curricular theory, which will likely include some of the information covered above, along with a review of the local church's mission statement and strategic planning document, if it is available.

The first decision-making item on the agenda is usually the question of whether the church will establish a unified curriculum policy or stay with a randomized process of selection. The notion of every age level selecting its own curriculum is especially popular in America, where some like the idea of this individual rights approach. But even if the idea of a unified choice fails and the church decides to permit various publishers to support various age levels, the policy of who approves curriculum at each age level is still a matter of group decision. Few churches would be satisfied with a teacher's selecting theologically false materials or some cult's curriculum for their age level. Most churches expect some approval process for even mix-and-match patchwork curriculum.

At the end of this first meeting, assignments are usually made to prepare the members to undertake the longest and perhaps the most important task ahead—establishing the criteria for curriculum selection. Members are asked to bring to the next meeting several criteria they believe should be a part of the final standards for curriculum choices—what they think a good curriculum should offer: criteria like theological stance, ease of use, or options and alternative activities.

2. Establish the evaluation criteria.

This stage is the longest step in the process of curriculum selection, but it is the most rewarding since everyone involved grows and learns through the process. The process itself is an educational endeavor and can be a wonderful means of teacher education. Rather than adopting one of the many readily available evaluation forms offered by curriculum publishers, a church that makes its own form will make wiser decisions. That does not mean the group will not consult the forms available from publishers to get ideas, but the making of standards for a local church yields such marvelous educational outcomes for those involved that taking the shortcut should be avoided wherever possible. Following are the kinds of criteria that such a group often develops, but again, it is best for the group to construct these in the process rather than adopting this or any other list. It is best to make a list as a group and then consult other lists to see if anything is missing.

Goals and Objectives. Does each lesson include appropriate learning objectives and do the activities accomplish the objectives? Do these objectives support the educational goals of this church—that is, do they accomplish its specific stated discipleship mission? Is the over-all goal of this curriculum consistent with this church's own mission statement?

Theological Emphasis. What is the theological stance of this curriculum publisher? Is it in harmony with this church's stance or where does it stand at odds? Does this curriculum come from a specific denominational or doctrinal stance that fits this church? Does this curriculum claim to avoid doctrine altogether, and if so, is this church willing to sacrifice specific doctrinal teaching or find another way to emphasize specific doctrines or special emphases? What is missing in this curriculum that this church holds dear? What is present that is out of harmony with this church's doctrines?

Bible. Is this curriculum biblically sound? Does the hermeneutic behind the use of Scripture fit this church's hermeneutic? Does it include the right balance of Bible and other activities, or does it downplay one or the other too much? Is the biblical content faithful to Scripture? What authority does it give to the Bible and to other sources of authority? Do lessons appropriately interpret the Bible? Is there the desired balance between the Old and the New Testaments and between the Gospels and the Epistles? Does it adequately cover the portions of Scripture that this church considers critical to know? What role does Bible memorization play in it, and does that match this church's values?

Application. Does this curriculum teach toward life change, or is it primarily a cognitive curriculum? Does it give relevant and practical examples of life application for learners? Do the lessons make practical application to life?

Special Values. Does this curriculum adequately represent special emphases and values of this congregation? How does it approach the unity of the body of Christ? How does it deal with racial matters in lessons and art? How does it represent the clergy—as all male or also including female ministers? Does it adequately represent in art and content multicultural and multiethnic emphases? How does it treat gender, disabilities, economic status, and race? How does it approach eternal security, sanctification, holiness, tongues, salvation, and other doctrinal issues that this church cares about?

Parental Involvement. For children's and teen's curriculum, how does it get parents involved? How will parents be encouraged to get involved with their children's spiritual growth by using this curriculum? Does it include take-home materials for students to show to parents so that the lesson can be applied outside of church?

Methodology. Do the student's manuals correlate well to the teacher's manual? Are the activities age-appropriate, safe, creative, and varied? Is there too little or too much repetition? Does it rely on too few constantly repeated teaching methods? Are the teaching methods realistic for an average teacher to prepare? Does it require too much time to prepare? What is the balance between content-transmission and relationship-building, and does that match this church's own values?

Flexibility. Is this curriculum adaptable to various group sizes? Do the lessons fit into this church's time frame? Are there enough ideas and activities so teachers don't run out of activities? Are there options and choices when a particular activity does not fit this church's situation or the required supplies are not available?

Age-Level Appropriateness. Over the period of a dozen weeks, are the activities of this curriculum age appropriate, or are some activities too advanced or too juvenile for students? Does it expect too much or too little of this church's students considering the average student's development?

Preparation. Does this curriculum equip teachers as they prepare so that over a year or more teachers are developed by using the curriculum weekly? Does it aid the spiritual formation of the teacher? How long does it take to prepare an average lesson? Does it provide too little help or too much? Does it provide teacher tips on a regular basis? Does it lead the teacher step by step? Does it provide a supplies list, and are the materials listed easy to find? Are supplies reasonable to purchase, or does it expect teachers to purchase hard-to-find items or expensive supplies?

Attractiveness. Is this curriculum visually attractive for the teacher? Is it attractive for the students? Is the layout and design easy to follow? What do the art and pictures communicate to the students? How does it present the face and figure of Jesus? Are biblical illustrations and artwork appropriate, accurate, up-to-date, and appropriate for students of this age? Does it have a table of contents and easy-to-read outline of the quarter or month?

Cost and Value. What is the average cost per teacher? Cost per student? Is it a good value compared to other curriculum products? Can it be re-used? What hidden costs, such as supplies and photocopying, does it have? How much would this curriculum line affect the budget, and how does that compare to other lines?

The above list is by no means exhaustive, but it is given as an example of the kinds of criteria that a board or committee might develop in their own thinking. When the group comes together with their ideas, the Christian educator (or other chair) can lead the group to "merge and purge" the list—combining the work of the group and purging duplications. Only after this work is done should the group consult other evaluation devices or the above list to see what is missing from their own list. It is important at this stage not to debate the comparative value of the items on the list—that happens in the next step.

3. Weight the criteria.

Once all the criteria are listed, the group can begin to weigh each criterion compared to the others. Usually matters of doctrine will receive a heavier weighting than color or ease of use. One way to weight the various criteria is with a one-to-ten scale and then compile and average all the votes. In smaller groups or boards, a similar result can be had through a discussion and consent. A group might select two meta-categories—one for nonnegotiable items like theology and the rest that are just weighted scores. For example, in some churches, a curriculum that espouses eternal security or rejects women's ordination would be automatically eliminated even if it had attractive color and was easy to use. Some things are nonnegotiable and having a committee decide on matters like this is an educative process (and why the ministerial staff is often interested in participating in this process).

When this step is completed, the board or committee will have produced a questionnaire with a list of the criteria they believe to be most important in selecting their curriculum. The process to this stage is so rewarding and instructive that even if a church were not selecting curriculum, it would still be a worthy undertaking. The committee then saves their weighting numbers and creates a questionnaire without the weighting—including just the numbers one to ten for each item. The weighting data are saved for use in step six.

4. Send for samples and documentation.

Now is the time to send for samples of curriculum. With investigation the committee can usually eliminate some curriculum publishers before this stage using the nonnegotiable criteria. Among those remaining, the Christian education board usually selects three or four to examine. Of course a church would include its own denomination's publisher in this process, along with other like-minded publishers. Most publishers are happy to send free curriculum samples for such an evaluation. Indeed some publishers will ask to send a sales representative to your board or committee, but most Christian educators are wary of these "sell-job" presentations and politely decline these offers. It may take several weeks to a month (and sometimes longer depending on printing inventory) before a church receives these samples, and the project can be left to marinate until the samples arrive.

5. Evaluate the curriculum materials.

When all the curriculum samples arrive, the committee gathers again to begin the evaluation. The danger at this stage is to forget the work already done and start making shallow choices based on color or nifty appurtenances included with the curriculum materials. It is the leader's job at this stage to keep the group on track to make a high-quality professional decision using the questionnaire produced over the last few months. Usually curriculum samples are given to several teachers of that grade level for them to examine (or even try out teaching a few weeks); then they complete the evaluation questionnaire. Some of the criteria can be answered by looking at curriculum materials, but many require actual teaching to make an informed judgment. Generally having more than one teacher per age level is wise so that one person's bias does not throw the entire process off kilter. This step can take up to a month or more before the teachers have made their evaluation and returned them to the Christian education board or committee.

6. Make a decision.

Once all the questionnaires (and the returned curricular materials) are in hand, the board is now ready to tabulate the results and make a decision. However, this sort of decision is more than adding up the numbers from the teachers' one-to-ten evaluations. At this stage the committee returns to its weighting of the criteria, where they considered some criteria more important than others. In fact, the board or committee might revisit their former weighting and revise it based on new information. Active discussion ensues, and the decision-making process might extend for several meetings.

Eventually, the group can come to a decision and make a choice of one or another of the curriculum lines they examined and tested. Ideally the choice would be for a whole line of curriculum and not the mix-and-match patchwork of using one publisher for one age group and a different for another. While some churches take this approach, it flies in the face of curriculum theory, which attempts to build the learning and experiences of one age group on that of the prior age group. But in one or two meetings, the group usually makes a firm decision. Having put in all the effort to this stage, such a decision will be fairly firm—few will want to start all over again.

Of course, many denominational publishing houses would say of this entire process, "Why not just use your own denomination's curriculum materials, because this work has already been done for you." And they would be right! Denominational curriculum publishers have already made a list of the important doctrines, values, and emphases of their church and produce curriculum materials in harmony with these. However, still some denominational churches will choose other curriculum materials usually based on things like ease of use, attractive colors, pricing, or less preparation time.

7. Plan periodic assessments.

After all this work to make a solid professional decision on curriculum materials, most churches will not want to be constantly revisiting the decision. However, assessing curriculum materials should be an ongoing, or at least periodic, process. Publishers and editors are keen to hear from grassroots teachers about how a particular lesson or activity worked out in a classroom. Curriculum materials are usually published on a cycle, and thus every lesson is revised and repeated in the future, so input from teachers can improve the lesson the next time around. The board or committee that worked for months to make the initial choice of a curriculum line should at least gather once a year for cake and coffee just to celebrate the hard effort they put into making such a professional and unifying decision!

Everybody Ought to Know

The task of Christian education is enormous. When leaving for Jerusalem, the apostle Paul said, "I have told you everything God wants you to know" (Acts 20:27). Jesus instructed his followers to make disciples as they went to the people of all nations. He then elaborated, "teach them to do everything I have told you" (Matt 28:20). This is the massive task of Christian education—teaching people to know everything God wants them to know and teaching them to incorporate into a holy lifestyle everything Christ taught. The curriculum of Christian education is the *planned sequence of learning experiences that organizes learning and change in an orderly manner to accomplish the spiritual development of people.* A carefully planned and taught curriculum is one of the most powerful tools to fashion a holy people of God.

Bibliography

Colson, Howard P. and Raymond M. Rigdon, *Understanding Your Church's Curriculum.* Nashville, TN: Broadman Press, 1981.

Holmes, Michael W., trans. *Apostolic Fathers: Greek Texts and English Translations.* Grand Rapids, MI: Baker, 1999.

Milavec, Aaron. *The Didache: Text, Translation, Analysis and Commentary.* Collegeville, MN: Michael Glazier/Liturgical Press, 2004.

CHAPTER FIFTEEN

The Teaching-Learning Transaction

JANE KENNARD

> Keep on being faithful to what you were
> taught and to what you believed. After all,
> you know who taught you these things.
> Since childhood, you have known the
> Holy Scriptures that are able to make you
> wise enough to have faith in Christ Jesus
> and be saved.
>
> 2 Timothy 3:14–15

Like the proverbial youngster answering a parent's after school inquiry, "What did you learn today?" with a shrug and half-hearted "Oh, nothing much," persons may perceive that not much entered their learning radar on any particular day. Actually, the chances are pretty high that any ordinary human being learns or relearns something during the course of any ordinary day. So what is there to learn? Some are figuring out how to download iPod tunes while others tinker with a new video game. College students may be exploring how to study more profitably for an upcoming test. The business person on the bus is trying to make sense out of a sudoku puzzle. This chapter explores dimensions of the learning process, what learning is and how it happens.

What Is Learning?

Assuming learning is an inherent human capacity and occurs with or without our intentional awareness, consider another question. How does anyone know when he or she has learned something? Do they just know that they know? Are feelings involved?

For example, Nate's laptop computer purchased three years ago with hard-earned cash is getting slower and slower, seriously hampering his social networking routine and, of course, research for this semester's twelve-page term paper. Disappointing? Irritating? For sure. What to think? What to do? Odds are he will talk to the nearest tech wizard, vent his frustration, listen, and digest as much as possible about computer processors and memory upgrades, all the while contemplating sources of funding for this inevitable expenditure. A week later he is contentedly web surfing, chatting online with friends, and engaged in a "copy and paste" research strategy for his term paper. Benjamin Bloom, a renowned educational theorist at the University of Chicago for thirty years, suggests that, in situations like this and hundreds of others individuals' experience daily, learning occurs within three domains or categories.[1]

First, learning takes place in the **cognitive** or intellectual domain. Acquiring specific facts, understanding concepts, and recalling procedures or patterns make up this category of learning. All things intellectual and knowledge-based form the cognitive learning type. It is, perhaps, the new vocabulary and understanding of gigabytes, RAM, and dual processors Nate attained while assimilating the computer geek's wisdom.

The **affective** or attitudinal domain is the second way learning happens. The feelings, values and motivations typically inherent in a variety of experiences form part of the learning matrix. Willingness to pay attention to and use the information explicated about computers indicates the merit or value one places in obtaining pertinent knowledge in making decisions. Feelings of frustration with slow-running machines point to the assumed worth of keeping up with online relationships and making productive use of perhaps limited time to investigate a research topic.

The third domain of learning is the **behavioral** or psychomotor type of learning. Developing particular motor skills or muscle coordination through practice fits this arena of learning. Maneuvering a car into a parallel parking spot requires learning in this domain. Similarly, gaining proficiency in operating an updated version of computer software necessitates adjusting or relearning eye-hand coordinated movements.

A component common to each of these domains of learning is the concept of *change*. Simply put, learning **equals** change.[2] Learning involves intellectual, affective, and behavioral change. For instance, Leslie, an aspiring piano player,

---

1. Bloom, *Taxonomy of Educational Objectives*, 7.
2. Galindo, *Craft of Christian Teaching*, 24.

must understand how to interpret musical notes printed on paper and recognize those notes on a keyboard. That is cognitive learning. It also involves behavioral learning since each printed note translates into positioning and moving hands and fingers at the right place and in the correct sequence along the piano keys. Over time, feelings of satisfaction and accomplishment emerge as practice renders the pianist proficient in producing pleasurable melodies: affective learning has occurred. Thus, learning can be described as changes in thinking, feeling, and doing. This definition implies, as Bloom reiterated, that "the purpose of education is to change the thoughts, feelings, and actions of students."[3]

This means that natural processes of growth or maturation, such as physical development, cannot be classified as learning. A three-year old learns to fit puzzle pieces into a wooden frame, but no intellectual or behavioral changes are involved in the child's growing into a larger set of clothes.

From a Christian perspective, learning incorporates both natural and supernatural dimensions. Theologically, we affirm the capacity to learn as an innate feature of the Creator's design for human beings. The Holy Spirit's work prompts and enables cognitive, affective, and behavioral transformations beyond the scope of any educational endeavor. The Gospel writer Luke speaks to these aspects of learning when he says that "Jesus became wise, and he grew strong. God was please with him and so were the people." (2:52).

How Does Learning Occur?

Learning happens. It happens every day, every hour, every minute. It is so natural that most of the time persons are oblivious to its occurrence. As noted earlier, learning is a necessity, a requirement for problem solving, skill advancement, personal well-being, and indeed survival. Stroke victims, for instance, endure months of physical and emotional recovery exercises to regain intellectual capacities, such as language skills, and bodily dexterity involving both large and small motor skills. Their return to the normalcy of daily life depends on cognitive, affective and behavioral learning. So it is with all individuals in every aspect of life.

So, how does learning happen? Good question! No easy or quick answer. Why? Because "learning is largely a mystery."[4] While there is no debate about its occurrence, the question of how learning happens continues to stimulate numerous queries. What follows is a brief look at theories about how learning occurs within the three domains of learning. It is helpful and convenient to separate the domains for study, but in reality learning is a holistic and inter-related function.

Unraveling the mystery of learning is, of course, no small affair since it has much to do with what we call gray matter, the human brain. So how do

---

3. Bloom, *All Our Children Learning*, 180.
4. Issler and Habermass, *Teaching for Reconciliation*, 23.

brains learn? Complex and multifaceted processes involving about one hundred billion nerve cells called neurons facilitate the brain's performance. Each neuron consists of dendrites, a cell body, and an axon covered by an insulating myelin sheath. Electrical impulses dispensed by thousands of neurons enter the cell body of a single neuron through its dendrites. When a critical intensity of input is reached, the cell body discharges an electrical impulse that navigates down the axon. Chemicals called neurotransmitters, which are released by axon endings and cling to dendrite receptors, facilitate the jump or synapse to neighboring neurons. In

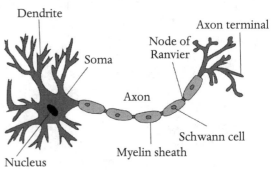

Courtesy of Quasar Jarosz at en.wikpedia.org. Used by permission.

Figure 1. Structure of a Neuron

this way, each neuron connects to other neurons through an average of fifty thousand synapses. The rapid, repeated, and parallel neural firing of electrical impulses produces a labyrinth, or network, of information processing systems throughout the brain's gray matter. Learning is linked with the frequency and intensity of neural connections and subsequent patterned connections. Linkages found useful by the brain endure, while less useful connections are purged as the brain prunes and reinforces connections based on experience. Thus, the more frequently linkages occur, the stronger the connection. This then is the basis for memory and, therefore, learning; it also explains why practicing a skill or reinforcing information facilitates prompt recall.[5]

Clearly the brain learns more than facts and figures, the stuff of the cognitive domain. It is also the crucible of feelings and attitudes. The limbic system, sometimes called the emotional brain, consists of a group of interconnected brain structures that transfer informa-

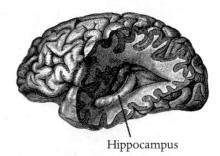

Hippocampus

Figure 2. The Hippocampus

tion into memory, a key component of learning processes. One of these structures, the hippocampus, located deep within the temporal lobe, functions as a processing center for producing, sorting, and storing memories. To illustrate, recall the first day of college or a first date. Spilling spaghetti on the floor at a

---

5. Sprenger, *Learning and Memory*, 1–14.

restaurant or getting lost looking for the campus bookstore is remembered since such events carry an emotional impact. Through its work of making memories and associations, the hippocampus also ensures that you remember the physical surroundings, sounds, and perhaps smells of the occasion. Because the hippocampus is essential in forming new memories, persons suffering from Alzheimer's disease, which erodes hippocampus tissue, are stuck in memories of the past. Hence, memory and emotion are intimately related to the process of learning.[6]

Advocates of brain-based learning propose that matching teaching strategies with inherent brain functions significantly enhances learning potential. Based on cognitive neuroscience research, this approach highlights findings regarding the brain's plasticity and pattern-making capacities. Educators Caine and Caine, provide the following twelve principles foundational to understanding and applying insights resulting from neuro-imaging:

1. Learning is physiological.
2. The brain-mind is social.
3. The search for meaning is innate.
4. The search for meaning occurs through patterning.
5. Emotions are critical to patterning.
6. The brain-mind processes parts and wholes simultaneously.
7. Learning involves both focused attention and peripheral perception.
8. Learning always involves conscious and unconscious processes.
9. There are at least two approaches to memory: archiving individual facts and skills or making sense of experience.
10. Learning is developmental.
11. Complex learning is enhanced by challenge and inhibited by threat associated with helplessness.
12. Each brain is uniquely organized.[7]

In addition, the brain's dependency on experience is particularly noteworthy with regard to the notion that there are optimal periods of brain development for particular kinds of learning. These intervals, called sensitive periods, refer to times "when the effect of experience on the brain is particularly strong during a limited period in development."[8] This suggests, for example, that learning to read during a sensitive period changes brain circuitry in basic ways, causing

---

6. Ibid., 46, 50–54.

7. Caine and Caine, "Understanding a Brain Based Approach," 66–70.

8. Knudsen, "Sensitive Periods," 1412–27.

specific patterns of connectivity among neurons to be stabilized and preferred, that is, to be learned.[9]

Hemispheric dominance, or left brain/right brain theory, has also influenced educators' notions about how learning occurs by suggesting that each side of the brain processes information differently. Sperry's split-brain research proposed that specific cognitive functions flow from the "two minds" of the brain. The left hemisphere is the logical, analytical, and rational mind, while the right hemisphere is the intuitive, random, and creative mind. Individuals with left-brain dominance prefer structured, highly verbal, and sequential instructional activities.[10] Multiple choice test questions on this chapter's content or outlining its main points are favored assignments. On the other hand, producing a poster or short video to illustrate chapter highlights would delight the student with right brain dominance. Here the creative process is more satisfying than the resulting art work. In contrast, achieving a perfect test score rewards the left brain thinker.

At What Levels Does Learning Occur in the Three Domains?

Levels of Learning in the Cognitive Domain

Connecting brains with learning is a familiar idea. Typically brain function is associated with a particular kind of learning, namely, the acquisition of knowledge or, in terms described earlier, cognitive learning. Storing new information, however, is not all there is to the brain's capacity to process experience. Bloom and his associates identified six levels or degrees of *cognitive functioning*, each level involving greater complexity than the previous.[11] The progressive nature of the intellectual skills involved in each category of Bloom's hierarchy or taxonomy provides a framework for developing instructional methods to facilitate level-appropriate learning. Here is a sequence of planning discussion questions for a four-week unit focusing on the Beatitudes (Matt 5:1–11) with teens as the participants:

> *Knowledge*: How often does the phrase "Blessed are you…" occur in these verses? Where and to whom is Jesus speaking? Recognizing, naming, describing, and recalling information is the task of the first level of the taxonomy. Thinking is straightforward and typically easy to assess. Persons either know the answer or they don't.

> *Comprehension*: Now the focus is on understanding, explaining or interpreting knowledge. Paraphrasing "Blessed are the poor in spirit, for theirs is

---

9. Ibid.

10. Sperry, "Consciousness, Personal Identity and the Divided Brain," 666–67.

11. Bloom, *Taxonomy of Educational Objectives*, 18.

the kingdom of heaven," encourages teens to grapple with Jesus' intended meaning. Grasping the concept of being "poor in spirit" requires a more complex thought process than simply remembering the statement itself.

Application: Extending one's understanding of what "poor in spirit" means in order to describe its implications for daily life at school illustrates a sixteen-year-old's capacity to apply knowledge and meaning. Application is about using facts and principles to solve problems or complete tasks.

Analysis: Nudging teens toward this level of thinking could mean asking them to ponder what Jesus meant by "Blessed are the meek" as compared to "Blessed are the poor in spirit." What is the difference between being meek and being poor in spirit? The critical thinking required for analysis entails mental activities such as breaking something down into its component parts, identifying underlying relationships among various elements, and recognizing hidden meanings.

Synthesis: Creating something new out of prior knowledge and understanding is the task at this level. What new insights might emerge if the values inherent in the Ten Commandments are considered in conjunction with the viewpoint of the Beatitudes? Constructing, inventing and rearranging ideas or patterns calls for upper-level intellectual abilities. From a developmental perspective, most youth will be stretched by this kind of cognitive challenge.

Evaluation: Which of the Beatitudes do you think is particularly important for Christian teens to live by in today's culture? Why? Responding to these questions necessitates making judgments, hypothesizing, and justifying a decision. Proposing and defending a thoughtful answer will take time and mental effort.

A revision of the taxonomy by a team of Bloom's followers reverses the order of the last two levels. Synthesizing, it is offered, presupposes an evaluative process. In reference to the example cited above, coming to some conclusion about viable points of convergence between the Ten Commandments and the Beatitudes would require making judgments about any suggested responses. In the revised taxonomy, verbs replaced nouns as follows: remembering (knowledge), understanding (comprehension), applying, analyzing, evaluating, and creating (synthesis).[12]

---

12. Anderson and Krathwohl, *Taxonomy for Learning*, 67–68.

Levels of Learning in the Affective Domain

It is one thing to know, understand, apply, and analyze the Beatitudes, and quite another to value the kind of living they promote. Believing the truth of "Blessed are the merciful, for they will be shown mercy" (Matt 5:7 NIV) calls for an openness to consider the authenticity of Christ's words as recorded in Scripture. Without a positive inclination or attitude toward considering the potential importance of the Beatitudes, the information will likely go in one ear and out the other. Feelings about the subject matter, the teacher, classmates, and the classroom are inherently connected to learning. Krathwohl, Bloom, and Masis developed a taxonomy for the affective domain of learning, the five levels progressing in increased complexity[13]:

Receiving or Attending: As mentioned earlier, a willingness to pay attention to a particular idea or viewpoint is the first step in the valuing process. Despite growing up with an "every man for himself" perspective, a young male might read with care an article about biblical perspectives on helping the homeless and oppressed.

Responding: Intrigued by the words of Jesus, "Whenever you did it for any of my people, no matter how unimportant they seemed, you did it for me" (Matt 25:40), a young adult meets with a campus ministry leader to discuss this passage in more depth. A willingness to listen to a particular viewpoint turns into exploring it with a sustained appreciation and consideration for the issues.

Valuing: Convinced of the spiritual significance of caring for the poor and oppressed, the student participates in a weeklong mission trip to paint and repair several Appalachian homes. Commitment to a particular belief or perspective over other points of view characterizes this level. Thinking and pondering moves toward taking action.

Organizing: At this stage priorities change, resulting in a reorganization or rearrangement of life to accommodate the internalized value. The young adult sponsors an underprivileged child in Uganda through monthly donations and takes an active leadership role in Mission Club projects.

Characterizing: Over time, the student's life so characterizes a spirit of compassion and service that he or she receives the "Service above Self" award granted annually by the campus community. Life becomes all about living out the espoused value system.

---

13. Krathwohl, Bloom, and Masia, *Taxonomy of Educational Objectives*, 35.

Perhaps it goes without saying that feelings (positive and negative) influence learning. What often does not get as much attention, however, is how feelings affect motivation and engagement. Content to which there is a "ho-hum" or ambivalent attitude is difficult not only to teach but to learn. When the emotional components of any subject are taken into account, learning becomes more meaningful.

The extent to which a person values something is difficult to measure. While it is relatively easy to evaluate whether a twelve-year old can recite the Ten Commandments (cognitive domain), determining his or her attitude about the Ten Commandments is quite another matter. Is it possible to discern the degree to which someone internalizes values related to stealing, lying, or honoring his or her parents? Paying attention to sixth graders' interactions with their parents in the church lobby, at home, or during a family campout provides strong clues to the strength of conviction tied to the fifth commandment. A youngster's daily obedience to a parent's request to collect household trash, for instance, cultivates good emotional and bodily habits that contribute to the development of Christian character. Behavior mirrors a person's value system.

Levels of Learning in the Behavioral Domain

Whether playing checkers or the piano, driving a motorcycle, praying, or journaling, everyone learns a variety of behavioral competencies throughout life. How did this type of learning occur? The taxonomy below is a combination of several different taxonomies describing the process of advancing from watching to mastering a physical skill; habits connected to spiritual and emotional life develop in similar fashion[14]:

Observing: Watching grandmother combine ingredients for a chocolate cake and then sinking teeth into the mouth-watering product is the first step toward making the delicacy oneself. Observing a more experienced person perform an activity initiates the process of learning a behavior. It involves using sensory cues as well to grasp meanings and skills. Giving active mental attention to a friend's explanation about the stress-relieving benefits of journaling prompts a young mother to browse through Internet articles on the subject.

Imitating: Trying out the behavior under the observant eye of an experienced person is the second step. Grandmother observes carefully as the aspiring cook ponders the recipe, measures and dumps flour, salt, cocoa and eggs into the bowl. Accurate direction and feedback enable the learner

---

14. Brett Bixler, "Psychomotor Domain Taxonomy," http://www.personal.psu.edu/bxb11/Objectives/psychomotor.htm (accessed November 17, 2010).

to pull a good replica of grandmother's cake out of the oven. Although not a seasoned bakery chef, the attempt to copy behavior produced satisfying results.

Practicing: Repeating a skill sequence from start to finish many times produces performances of increased competence. Writing daily journal entries and establishing a weekly routine of cake-making greatly enhances confidence and ability over time. The behavior is becoming automatic or habitual.

Adapting: Watching, imitating, and practicing result in perfected skill. Fine-tuning occurs by making minor adjustments to fit one's particular aptitudes or push for improvement. Gooey cakes and runny frosting are things of the past, but input from a cooking show mentor or coach is sought occasionally. After months of using prescribed writing exercises, the young mother now speaks about herself as a journal keeper who freely modifies others' suggestions and creates her own writing prompts.

The three taxonomies provide a framework for evaluating the extent to which learning occurs in the cognitive, affective, and behavioral domains. Facilitating movement in each domain is the goal of teaching. This is the journey toward wholeness and holiness, toward personal and spiritual maturity.[15] Called to foster growth in persons of all ages, Christian teachers affirm the apostle Paul's encouragement to seek "the knowledge of the Son of God and become mature, attaining to the whole measure of the fullness of Christ" (Eph 4:13 NIV).

What Facilitates Learning?

Here are some teens lounging on sofas, sprawled on the floor, and perched on stools. Lively chatter fills the room. Stacy, the group's drama queen, details the latest hit movie for those clustered around her. Brad, the football jock, challenges Tim, a straight-A student, to an arm-wrestling match while Jeremy, the tech wizard, clocks their efforts with precision and flair. How can movement through the levels of cognitive, affective, and behavioral learning be achieved to any extent in this group? How can teachers facilitate learning among a variety of individuals?

This section explores three approaches to understanding how persons learn. Identifying learning preferences and styles is a critical step toward planning lessons that engage students in meaningful learning. Kolb's four learning styles come first. The modalities or senses most used in learning will be explored next. Finally, Dunn and Dunn's 21 elements of learning will be presented in summary form.

---

15. Steele, *On the Way*, 105–6.

Learning Styles

David Kolb's model of learning styles is based on the notion that learning occurs along two dimensions, the first related to how experience is perceived and the second to how experience is processed. In the *perceiving dimension*, people have a preference along a continuum between looking at things in raw or concrete form (Concrete Experience) and looking at things through concepts and ideas (Abstract Conceptualization). In the *processing dimension*, persons have a preference along a continuum between trying things out (Active Experimentation) and watching to see what happens when others try things out (Reflective Observation).[16] Kolb places these continuums along horizontal and vertical axes as illustrated in Figure 3.

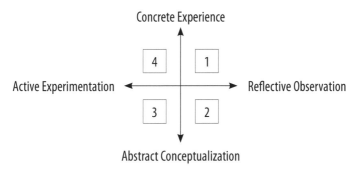

Figure 3. Kolb's Model of Learning Styles

Learning styles are defined in terms of a person's preferred continuum combinations. This results in four approaches to learning[17]:

1. *The Diverger or Imaginative Learner*: Combining an interest in concrete experience and reflective observation, imaginative learners think deeply about their experiences. This equips them to engender numerous ideas or possibilities from a single experience. Concerned about personal meaning, these students want an answer to the question, "Why do I need to know this?" They thrive on relationships and often do their best thinking in dialogue with others.

2. *The Assimilator or Analytic Learner*: These students ponder information carefully. They readily tune in to experts who provide answers to the question, "What do I need to know?" Assimilators are good at inductive reasoning and appreciate predictable, simple learning environments. Content to work alone or in groups, these analytic types function well

---

16. Kolb, "Experience Based Learning Systems," 5.

17. Ibid., 8–9.

in traditional classrooms where well-organized lectures and discussions are instructional norms.

3. *The Converger or Commonsense Learner:* The commonsense learner is primarily interested in finding out how things work. These hands-on learners strive to make practical application of learning. Convergers mull things over and then use their ideas to solve problems. They are fixers and doers, always testing theories in the real world.

4. *The Accommodator or Dynamic Learner:* These students have a strong preference for action instead of thinking. Learning is all about "What if?" and "Why not?" Creative and spontaneous, dynamic learners deplore routine and enjoy situations calling for flexibility and doing something new.

No learning style fits a student perfectly. Jeremy, the tech wizard, shows characteristics of both the Commonsense and Dynamic learner, while Suzanne, the "brain," primarily fits the Analytic Learner profile with tendencies toward the Imaginative Learner too. According to Kolb, incorporating elements of all four learning styles makes for the best learning situation. McCarthy suggests that understanding the four learning styles as sequential steps (imaginative—analytic—commonsense—dynamic) of a learning cycle allows teachers to plan for each student's learning preferences.[18] Students participate in all steps of the learning cycle but are assured of one or two parts of the lesson matching the way they learn best.

Modalities

Experiencing the world comes primarily through human senses or modalities. All learners receive and learn information through auditory, visual, and tactile/kinesthetic sense channels but often prefer one over the others. Repeating a phone number after hearing it once or twice comes naturally for the auditory learner. Retention is enhanced for visual learners when items such as pictures, movie clips, charts and posters are used plentifully. Physical movement helps tactile/kinesthetic learners maintain focus and learn. Taking seriously the question, "What will students see, hear, and do during this lesson?" gives teachers strong clues about ways to improve teaching and learning.

21 Elements of Learning

Another path to understanding learner preferences emerges from the work of Kenneth and Rita Dunn. Based on the premise that individuals have a unique set of biological and developmental characteristics, they identified twenty-one learning preferences within five categories or strands of stimuli.[19]

---

18. Bernice McCarthy, "A Cycle of Instruction," http://www.aboutlearning.com.

19 Dunn, "Understanding the Dunn and Dunn Learning Styles."

1. *Environmental stimuli*: This category includes sound, light, temperature, and room design preferences. One person may study best in a cool, bright room, while another may need background music and a comfortable sofa to promote learning.

2. *Emotional stimuli*: Some students want precise details about an assignment and get it done before going on to other tasks. Other students thrive on doing a project their own way and juggle several jobs at the same time. These are preferences related to motivation, persistence, responsibility, and structure.

3. *Sociological stimuli*: Here the focus is on how people prefer to learn in association with others. A student may favor learning alone or with one other person, with a teacher or a nonthreatening colleague, as part of a team or in a variety of groupings.

4. *Physiological stimuli*: Some people experience greater energy and alertness in the morning, while others function best at night. Other individuals study better with a beverage and snack at hand and take frequent breaks to move around. Modality (auditory, visual, tactile/kinesthetic) preferences along with time of day, intake and mobility preferences are included in this category.

5. *Psychological stimuli*: Included in this grouping are left brain/right brain (hemispheric) preferences and the extent to which persons respond impulsively (acting before thinking) or reflectively (thinking before acting). Global thinkers who first process the big picture before moving to the details versus analytic thinkers who see details first and then broad concepts are also included in this category of psychological preferences.

Observant teachers who support students' preferences and assist them in identifying specific ways to boost learning are honoring Jesus' invitation to make disciples, "teaching them to obey everything I have commanded you" (Matt 28:20 NIV).

Conclusion

This chapter began with the idea that learning is about cognitive, affective, and behavioral change. Educators who want to bring about these types of change in students for the cause of Christ wisely consider twenty-first century realities. Consider the cultural shifts from valuing community instead of the individual, from prizing the relational versus the rational, and from esteeming experience over knowledge: what difference do these make in how learning occurs? If effective and valuable learning toward Christlikeness is the goal, then the process of learning must be understood in the context of today's world. This is what it means to be competent Christian educators, teachers who understand and appreciate the nature of learning while simultaneously trusting the Holy Spirit to accomplish spiritual results.

Bibliography

Anderson, L. W. and D. R. Krathwohl, eds. *A Taxonomy for Learning, Teaching, and Assessing: A Revision of Bloom's Taxonomy of Educational Objectives*. New York: Longman, 2001.

Bloom, Benjamin. *All Our Children Learning*. New York: McGraw-Hill, 1982.

Bloom, Benjamin, ed. *Taxonomy of Educational Objectives: The Classification of Educational Goals by a Committee of College and University Examiners. Handbook 1: Cognitive Domain*. New York, NY: David McKay, 1956.

Caine, Renate N. and Geoffrey Caine. "Understanding a Brain Based Approach to Learning and Teaching." *Educational Leadership* 48, no. 6 (1990): 66–70.

Dunn, Rita. "Understanding the Dunn and Dunn Learning Styles Model and the Need for Individual Diagnosis and Prescription." *Journal of Reading, Writing, and Learning Disabilities International*, 6, no. 3 (1990): 223–47.

Galindo, Israel. *The Craft of Christian Teaching*. Valley Forge, PA: Judson Press, 1998.

Issler, Klaus and Ronald T. Habermass. *Teaching for Reconciliation: Foundations and Practice of Christian Educational Ministry*. Grand Rapids, MI: Baker Books, 1997.

Knudsen, Eric I. "Sensitive Periods in the Development of the Brain and Behavior." *Journal of Cognitive Neuroscience* 16, no. 8 (2004): 1412–27.

Kolb, David A. "Experience Based Learning Systems." In *Kolb Learning Style Inventory*. Philadelphia, PA: Hay Group, 2007.

Krathwohl, D. R., B. S. Bloom, and B. B. Masia. *Taxonomy of Educational Objectives: The Classification of Educational Goals. Handbook II: Affective Domain*. New York: David McKay, 1964.

Sperry, Roger. "Consciousness, Personal Identity and the Divided Brain," *Neuropsychology* 22, no. 6 (1984): 666–67.

Sprenger, Marilee. *Learning and Memory*. Alexandria, VA: Association of Supervision and Curriculum Development, 1999.

Steele, Les L. *On the Way: A Practical Theology of Christian Formation*. Eugene, OR: Wipf and Stock, 2001.

CHAPTER SIXTEEN

Planning to Teach

JANE KENNARD

> My friends, we should not all try to
> become teachers. In fact, teachers will be
> judged more strictly than others.
>
> —James 3:1

For any future ministry leader or someone already functioning in that capacity, this chapter contains "bread and butter" or "PB & J" material. This chapter is about basic, use-it-almost-every-day stuff. More often than not, functioning effectively in leadership involves teaching at some point. Whatever the ministry leadership role, teaching will be an expectation. Regardless of one's level of comfort with the idea, the ability to teach is a fundamental skill generally assumed to be part of any leadership package. This assumption carries well beyond the obvious need for directors of youth and children's ministries to teach youngsters and train adult volunteers. Leaders of mission and outreach endeavors, musicians, worship leaders, senior ministers, and executive pastors must be prepared to instruct, coach, and equip congregants of all ages.

Becoming an effective teacher requires, at minimum, attending to the fundamental matters described in this chapter such as the teaching role, lesson planning, and choosing learning strategies. Building on the elements of learning theory explained in the previous chapter, this chapter provides a basic path toward designing an instructional session.

Teaching Has Eternal Significance

Why does the New Testament writer James (3:1) caution his Christian brothers and sisters about putting on the mantle of teacher? How is it that those who teach are held to a higher standard than other Christ followers? Teaching has eternal significance. Jesus' ministry is the quintessential illustration of this truth. He was, after all, commonly addressed as rabbi, meaning teacher in Hebrew. When the Samaritan woman came to draw well water at noon (John 4), little did she know how transformative a few teaching moments with Jesus would be. Two seconds, twenty-minutes, or two hours with a prepared and perceptive teacher may impact a child's or teen's life for eternity.

Donald Griggs offers several metaphors for the teaching role with potential for nurturing learners in spiritual growth. Above all, Christian teachers are God's messengers.[1] Are pastors the only ones called by God to be his spokespersons? There is no wiggle room here. Scripture is poignant and clear: "And God has placed in the church first of all apostles, second prophets, third teachers..." (1 Cor 12:28 NIV).

Embracing the teaching role places one in a long lineup of educators spanning generations since the time of creation, whose mission it was to communicate God's truth. "In the beginning God created" (Gen 1:1). The Creator reveals and teaches about who he is through his creative work, the glory and majesty of his created order (Ps 19). Faithful Hebrew parents followed Moses's admonition (Deut 6:4–9) to tell the stories of Yahweh's provision and deliverance. Ezra, the scribe, facilitated the reading and application of the Law (Neh 8:1–8), moving the wayward Israelites toward repentance and renewal. Today's Christian teachers are partners with God in his long-standing, continuing educative efforts in the world. Teaching is truly a sacred honor!

Accepting the responsibility to teach also means a commitment to nurturing relationships with students, to exhibit the care, encouragement, and acceptance of a friend.[2] Again, Trinitarian theology enriches an understanding of this key role of an educator as companion and friend. Father, Son, and Holy Spirit share an association characterized by rapport, mutuality, love, and respect.[3] The teaching-learning process bursts with potential when teachers and learners esteem and care for one another in warm and considerate ways. Insights, emotions, and actions of eternal import take shape within open, warm relationships engendering trust and respect.

---

1. Griggs, *Teaching Today's Teachers to Teach*, 38.

2. Ibid., 37.

3. Cladis, *Leading the Team-Based Church*, 4–6.

Approaches to Teaching

If the teaching-learning process embodies enormous potential of eternal consequence, careful consideration of the process itself is imperative. How, then, can the teaching-learning process be envisioned or handled to best advantage? Several responses to this question are important to keep in mind. First, however, reflect on the following classroom scenarios.

Scenario A. Ted, a senior-high Sunday school teacher, has just finished reviewing his lecture notes as class members begin arriving. He moves easily among the teens, greeting each with a smile, handshake, or arm around a shoulder. Ted's preparation is easy to spot. Paper, pencils, and Bibles are readily available on a small table at the back of the room. Upfront, several words are printed clearly on a dry erase board. Chairs form a half circle facing a small lectern. About twelve youth chat freely as Ted calls for the group's attention. "I'm going to lay a historical and contextual foundation for our study of Philippians," he explains, "as we begin exploring how to live vibrant, joyful Christian lives at school and in our families." For the next twenty minutes Ted shares enthusiastically from his notes, pausing two or three times to invite questions and respond to comments. A few students seem to be taking notes while most locate the verses in their Bibles Ted is referencing. Occasionally, several teens carry on brief whispered conversations.

Scenario B. Jennifer, one of the fourth-grade Wednesday evening Bible Club teachers, has carefully prepared five learning stations for about sixteen children. The theme for tonight is "Joy in the Lord," and each station is equipped with the materials and instructions for a learning activity focused on verses from Philippians. As Jennifer welcomes children at the door, she directs each child to a different learning station, where adult helpers wait to assist as needed. Within ten minutes small groups of children are busy at each of the stations. One team practices a skit. Another group focuses on a contemporary paraphrase of the hymn "Joyful, Joyful, We Adore Thee." Jennifer wanders from group to group answering questions and commenting on students' work. She enjoys the lively, purposeful hum that fills the room.

As different as they are, the potential for learning is evident in each scenario. Why then, does Ted teach one way and Jennifer another? What accounts for the differences? Two approaches to teaching are illustrated in these classroom scenarios: the transmissive or traditional approach and the dialogical or discovery approach. Think about these educational approaches as opposite ends of a continuum. While some educators seem to espouse one approach to the exclusion of the other, most use each approach in varying degrees depending on learners' developmental stage, the physical setting, subject matter, and available resources. Both approaches are valid and frequently employed. However, it is important to understand that each is based on different assumptions.

Transmissive/Traditional   Dialogical/Discovery

Figure 1. The Continuum of Approaches to Teaching

Griggs contrasts the role of a transmitter and a translator as a way of exploring the underlying differences between the transmissive and dialogical frameworks. "A transmitter sends messages in one direction, from the source (teacher) to the receiver (learner)."[4] From this perspective, the goal of a well-prepared, knowledgeable expert is to convey information to an attentive audience. Of course, the degree to which students tune in is up to them. They control the volume and may, in fact, choose to change channels. Interaction tends to be teacher-controlled, resulting in more formal relationships with students. Lecture, tests, memorization, and note-taking are commonly employed as teaching methods.

According to Ausubel, the transmitter model can be effectively and appropriately used to promote "meaningful learning." In contrast to "rote learning," which, he suggests, is unrelated to experience and soon forgotten, "meaningful learning" involves assimilating new concepts into existing cognitive structures and is more likely to be remembered long term.[5] Ausubel devised an instructional strategy called an advance organizer to facilitate linkages between old and new information. Functioning as a bridge, an advance organizer provides a connection between what the learner already knows and new material. More than simply offering a summary of previous material, teachers use strategies such as concept mapping or cross-referencing to help learners make the connective leap. Comparative advance organizers introduce new information by drawing analogies with familiar ideas. In highly verbal, content-heavy lessons, Ausubel concludes that the transmitter or "telling" stance is an efficient and valuable approach to consider.[6]

While transmitters focus on one-way, teacher-to-student communication, Griggs notes that translators concern themselves with two-way, student-to-student and student-to-teacher communication. "A translator is someone who helps facilitate communication between persons who are otherwise unable to communicate with each other."[7] Here the educator concentrates on understanding the world of the student through focused listening and observation in order to devise pertinent learning strategies. Thus, the goal of a well-prepared, knowledgeable teacher is to design learning strategies that involve learners in a process of communication between the content and their experience. Teaching methods in which learners are directly involved in talking and doing take priority.

---

4. Griggs, *Teaching Today's Teachers to Teach*, 39.

5. Ausubel, Novak, and Hanesian, *Educational Psychology*, 46–50.

6. Ibid., 170–73.

7. Griggs, *Teaching Today's Teachers to Teach*, 39.

Active engagement with others and the subject matter results in lively, bustling classrooms. Teachers serve as planners and guides while taking the posture of companions-in-learning. An atmosphere of cooperation and friendship supports the process of exploration and hands-on discovery.

The translator model fits well with Jerome Bruner's notion that "knowing is a process, not a product."[8] This means that the learning journey, or how learning occurs, becomes the focal point. Not that the content or what is learned becomes unimportant, but that the learning process itself holds significant instructional value. Relying on persons' natural curiosity, intuition, and innate ability to construct new ideas based on current or past knowledge, teachers see students as capable of learning on their own with support and encouragement. Direct or vicarious experiences bear significant learning potential. Nonthreatening and stimulating classroom environments create a climate of openness and exploration. For Bruner, education is a process of discovery driven by an individual's intrinsic motives for learning.[9]

As noted earlier, both the transmissive and dialogical approaches hold instructional value. It is important to observe, however, that educators often tend to embrace one or the other based on their own learning styles and preferences. Since students have a similar propensity, it is desirable that instructional plans account for a variety of learning preferences. Teaching children, of course, requires a preponderance of dialogical or discovery components given the nature of their physical, cognitive, and social development. Perhaps the common assumption that adults prefer transmissive or traditional teaching method merits reexamination. Howard Hendricks asserts that "maximum learning is always the result of maximum involvement."[10]

Hendricks and other lay and professional educators refer to Edgar Dale's Cone of Experience for guidance about the idea that direct experience, as compared to verbal explanations, heightens learning potential. Figure 2 on the next page illustrates Dale's original concept of a continuum of learning events. While not based on concrete research, Dale's proposal makes sense intuitively. The more senses are engaged in the learning process, or the more "whole person" involvement transpires, the greater the likelihood of recall and change occurring. When memory and understanding are enhanced through doing, the potential for change and transformation multiplies.

Simply doing, however, is not enough. Hendricks advises that activity must be meaningful. "Activity is never an end in itself; it's always a means to an end."[11] What makes activity meaningful? According to Hendricks, meaningful activity encourages students to make immediate application of what is being taught.

---

8. Bruner, *Toward a Theory of Instruction*, 72.

9. Ibid., 114.

10. Hendricks, *Teaching to Change Lives*, 56.

11. Ibid.

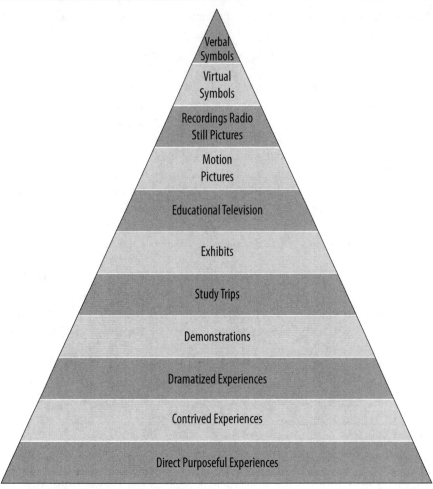

Figure 2. Dale's Cone of Experience[12]

A teacher should ask "So what?" often. Providing freedom within an appropriate amount of structure invites students to make choices, learn from mistakes, and own the process. Activities with a clear purpose stimulate involvement in contrast to easily identifiable busywork. Purposeful learning engages true issues of human existence and reflects authentically on the real lives of biblical characters.[13] Participatory activities for learners of all ages will aid in addressing Hendricks's claim that "Christian Education today is entirely too passive."[14]

---

12. Dale, *Audio-Visual Methods in Teaching*, 6.
13. Ibid., 61–65.
14. Ibid., 55.

Designing a Lesson Plan

Perhaps it is obvious by now that influencing persons for eternity through teaching requires intentionality. Planning is not optional. This means that educators are curriculum writers whether they design lessons from scratch or use published curriculum materials.[15] Every session plan needs the adjustments and alterations made by teachers who are well acquainted with the learning preferences and life experiences of a particular group of learners. Tailor-made lessons, shaped by the Holy Spirit's guidance, are powerful.

This section presents basic guidelines for developing Bible lesson plans. Here is an outline for designing a session from scratch. This kind of project requires an imaginative, almost playful mindset as well as a logical step-by-step process. Much of what follows can be applied to revising published curriculum lessons too. This is the work of the teacher as curriculum writer.

Pray: Planning to teach is a profound responsibility and privilege. It is an endeavor whose life-transforming goals cannot be reached without the empowerment of the Holy Spirit. It is through prayer that the work of the Spirit to enlighten, convict, encourage, and multiply human efforts is embraced. Inviting God's presence at the outset puts the entire process in perspective. This is about placing oneself at the feet of the Educator, ready to listen and learn.

Choose and Clarify a Scripture Focus: Familiarity with a particular group of students is clearly a plus in determining a scriptural focal point. What themes pertinent to the life stages, interests, and concerns of the group come to mind, and how does the Bible speak to those needs? Perhaps ideas emerging from a previous session provide clues for this one. Working with published curriculum entails determining whether the proposed passage is a good fit for a group's journey toward discovery and understanding.

The number and length of Scripture passages to be addressed in one session will vary according to learners' developmental level and thematic components. Perhaps specific sections of long narratives or an array of related passages will suffice. Handling ten to fifteen verses or less at a time is advisable.

Study and Write: It is imperative that the process of choosing and clarifying a focal biblical passage fuses with immersing oneself in a study of the proposed section of Scripture. There is no substitute for focused examination of the biblical passage from which a lesson will be developed. The teacher needs to dig deep and gather input from several commentaries, relevant books,

---

15. Griggs, *Teaching Today's Teachers to Teach*, 40.

Bible dictionaries, and reliable Web sites, such as www.biblestudytools.com and www.biblegateway.com. The process of comprehending and connecting meaningfully with Scripture requires intentionality and patience. In a spirit of openness, the teacher continues the quest for the theme or main idea most relevant for the group and pinpoints a key verse that captures the heart of the subject.

Discernment is often enhanced by jotting down the stream of ideas and insights emerging throughout the study process. Prayerfully mulling over a list of seemingly random thoughts recorded on paper is part of the creative process of capturing the most fitting focus. While seasoned teachers may solidify a focus rather quickly, most benefit from allowing ideas to percolate over a period of several days. There is a sense in which content options are inspired and revealed. Christian teachers "must not dismiss the presence of inspiration in the ordinary process of…developing lesson plans that systematically guide students into new territory."[16]

State the Main Idea: A reasonably succinct statement of one or two sentences should be the culminating step of studying the selected scripture. Stating the big idea or theme provides direction for the next step of writing learning objectives and developing lesson steps.

Write Learning Objectives: Learning objectives are about expectations. What does the teacher expect learners to accomplish during a lesson? What are the hoped for results? Objectives provide a helpful way to elaborate on the main idea using the three domains of learning (see Chapter 15): cognitive, affective, and behavioral. Essentially, learning objectives spell out answers to the following questions (examples are based on the story of blind Bartimaeus in Mark 10:46–52):

1. What do I want learners to *know?*
   By the end of the session, students will be able to *retell* the conversation between Jesus and Bartimaeus.
2. What do I want learners to *feel?*
   During the session, learners will *recognize* and *express gratitude* for Jesus' compassion toward Bartimaeus and themselves.
3. What do I want learners to *do?*
   At the end of the session, students will *decide* on a blind spot in their own lives and *ask* for Jesus' healing touch.

---

16. Pazmiño, *Basics of Teaching for Christians*, 33.

Objectives convey learning expectations best when a verb is used to express an action to be undertaken. While not all participants will accomplish each action, stated objectives serve as benchmarks for planning and evaluation.[17] Notice that each statement is directed toward what learners, not teachers, will accomplish. Lesson plans support student learning through the various instructional methods designed by the teacher. It is important to write one or more objectives directly related to the main idea of the lesson for the "know-feel-do" categories of learning.

Develop the Lesson Outline: The session outline identifies and describes the proposed learning activities and how they are related to each other. Using a sequence of lesson steps and then selecting appropriate learning activities for each step brings clarity to the process. While many lesson patterns are possible, two are offered here.

Lesson Pattern A
<u>A</u>wareness: sparking interest and introducing the main thrust of the lesson.
<u>B</u>ible Exploration: investigating the Scripture passage in ways that draw out pertinent information and meanings.
<u>C</u>rossing Point: exploring ways in which biblical understandings have implications for daily life; discovering how God's truth intersects with learners' experience.
<u>D</u>ecide to Act: choosing to take action in ways that live out God's truth in daily life.

Lesson Pattern B
Hook: grab attention and arouse curiosity in the main focus of the lesson.
Book: introduce and explore the biblical passage to discover information and meanings.
Look: examine and illustrate life applications of biblical meanings.
Took: challenge and inspire toward personal action; bring closure to the session.[18]

After choosing a lesson pattern, the task becomes one of identifying learning strategies or activities that match the purpose of each step and the lesson objectives. This is a matter of asking, for instance, What learning activities have the potential to arouse students' interest in the topic and invite their engagement in it? As options come to mind, one or two

17. Griggs, *Teaching Today's Teachers to Teach*, 82.
18. Richards, *Creative Bible Teaching*, 108–10.

good possibilities will rise to the surface. The process of brainstorming and selecting teaching methods for each step continues, keeping in mind the movement or flow of the lesson. Is there a logical transition from one activity to another? How well do the "puzzle pieces" fit together to create a lesson that communicates the main idea and facilitates the accomplishment of the learning objectives?

Every lesson has boundaries that come into play throughout the design process. Considering questions such as the following is always vital since the responses influence the potential effectiveness of a lesson that when "taught," carries the promise of spiritual significance for the people of God.

1. How does each learning activity fit the time parameters of the teaching period?
2. Are the necessary materials available and affordable?
3. How closely do the planned activities match the developmental capabilities of the students?
4. How does the classroom space itself suggest or limit what can be done?
5. What influence does the size of the anticipated group have on what can happen?
6. How much weight are individual and group likes and dislikes being given?
7. How well are students' learning preferences taken into consideration? For example, what will persons see (visual), hear (auditory), and do (kinesthetic)? How will the four learning styles be addressed? (imaginative, analytical, common sense, and dynamic; note chapter 15 content)
8. Is there variety in the types of learning activities? Are learners working alone and in pairs or groups? Are some activities fast-paced, while others are reflective?
9. Does everything support the learning objectives? Is there busywork that adds very little, if anything, to the purposes of the lesson?

Making adjustments in response to these nine questions goes a long way toward developing an engaging, evocative lesson. Above all, student participation throughout the session is a key ingredient. Learning, as Pazmiño states, "is dependent on the active participation of persons and their ownership of the instructional content."[19] This means that teaching requires familiarity with a range of age-appropriate learning activities. No effort to increase one's repertoire of student-focused learning activities through observation, reading,

---

19. Pazmiño, *Basics of Teaching for Christians*, 73.

and experimentation will likely go unrewarded. All through the planning and teaching process the intention is that students learn; that change occurs in their thoughts, feelings, and behavior.

Asking Questions

Asking questions is integral to the teaching-learning endeavor. Unfortunately, preparing questions as part of the planning process is often overlooked. The strategic placement of questions may facilitate transitions from one lesson step to another, encourage critical thinking, and serve to evaluate the extent to which learning has occurred. Most of all, posing questions is an important route to student involvement.

Questions come in various styles. Not all questions are appropriate for all parts of a lesson. Griggs delineates three categories of questions: informational, analytical, and personal.[20] Informational questions call for facts and details. They have right and wrong answers. "Where was blind Bartimaeus when he called out to Jesus?" is an example of this type of question. While they are among the easiest to create, the usefulness of informational questions is limited beyond the knowledge level of Bloom's taxonomy of cognitive functioning (see chapter 15). Clearly, questions of this type are beneficial for determining the degree of factual recall but need to be consistently followed by analytical questions if thinking is to be expanded.

Inquiries of an analytical nature provide an opportunity for an assortment of responses. Answers are not clear-cut since these questions trigger the imagination and prompt reflection. Thus, they invite learners to experiment with concepts, formulate new ideas, and think deeply. Discussion is a likely result. Sections of a lesson that explore the meaning and application of biblical truths are especially suitable spots for analytical questions. Asking, "Why do you suppose Jesus asked Bartimaeus what he wanted him to do for him instead of attending to the obvious fact that Bartimaeus was blind?" opens up a conversation in which many perspectives are welcome and suitable.

"How would you reply if Jesus asked you, 'What do you want me to do for you?'" is an illustration of what Griggs calls personal questions. Direct appeal to "personal experiences, beliefs, feelings, and values" is offered through these questions.[21] Learners are invited to connect God's Word with their own journey. This is where eternal truth meets human reality. Such questions may need to be answered in private but can also kindle meaningful conversations when students feel safe with each other. Understandably, personal questions call for openness and acceptance to a greater extent than analytical questions.

Questions that can be answered by a simple "Yes" or "No" should be avoided. Was Bartimaeus excited when Jesus stopped to talk to him? Yes! The question is

---

20. Griggs, *Teaching Today's Teachers to Teach*, 114–16.
21. Ibid., 116.

answered. Further comment is not required. Keeping questions open-ended even when they are informational strengthens participation and thinking. Extending closed questions by adding "Why?" or "How?" turns them into analytical questions with stronger potential for further reflection.

It is worth noticing that the question about Bartimaeus in the previous paragraph could be understood to imply a desired answer: "Bartimaeus was excited when Jesus stopped to talk to him, wasn't he?" Again, these types of questions circumvent meaningful dialogue and thought.

Conclusion

This chapter has explained the bare essentials of designing a teaching plan. While biblical content provided a framework for outlining the process, the same guidelines apply to creating a plan for teaching any topic. Whatever the subject, the Christian teacher does well to seek the blessing and leadership of the Holy Spirit. It is imperative to recognize also, that who the teacher is, is as important or perhaps more important than the best lesson plan. As the apostle Paul puts it, "But you are our letter, and you are in our hearts for everyone to read and understand. You are like a letter written by Christ and delivered by us. But you are not written with pen and ink or on tablets made of stone. You are written in our hearts by the Spirit of the living God" (2 Cor 3:2–3).

Bibliography

Ausubel, David P., Joseph D. Novak, and Helen Hanesian. *Educational Psychology: A Cognitive View*. New York: Holt, Rinehart and Winston, 1978.

Bruner, Jerome S. *Toward a Theory of Instruction*. Cambridge, MA: Harvard University Press, 1966.

Cladis, George. *Leading the Team-Based Church*. San Francisco, CA: Jossey-Bass, 1999.

Dale, Edgar. *Audio-Visual Methods in Teaching*. New York: Dryden Press, 1948.

Griggs, Donald L. *Teaching Today's Teachers to Teach*. Nashville, TN: Abingdon Press, 2003.

Hendricks, Howard. *Teaching to Change Lives*. Sisters, OR: Multnomah, 1987.

Pazmiño, Robert W. *Basics of Teaching for Christians*. Grand Rapids, MI: Baker Books, 1998.

Richards, Lawrence O. *Creative Bible Teaching*. Chicago, IL: Moody Press, 1970.

CHAPTER SEVENTEEN

A Place to Teach: Educational Facilities

KRISTIN D. LONGENECKER BULLOCK

> Jesus went all over Galilee, teaching in the
> Jewish meeting places and preaching the
> good news about God's kingdom.
>
> —Matthew 4:23a

When working with an educational ministry of the church, it is obvious to plan for curriculum, snacks or refreshments, volunteers, and supplies. But many educators do not plan well for the space they will use and the resources that would make it much easier to build relationships and communicate. What all educators need to take into account is that the way they do ministry is as important as what they teach.[1]

Much research has been done on the ideal environments for student learning. Varieties of teaching methods have developed over time to increase the productivity of lesson plans. Whether it is Montessori-style, learning center, or large-lecture format, the lesson can be enhanced or inhibited by the surroundings.

Many facilities are aging or were built for a time when classrooms were constructed for different needs. Some congregations rent or own facilities that

---

1. May, Poterski, Stonehouse, and Cannell, *Children Matter*.

were once offices, malls, or schools. In some church traditions there is little or no educational space outside of the sanctuary.

This chapter will examine the historical and cultural values that have influenced education in the church, facility utilization, concepts for creating new spaces, developmental needs, and trends in church and education.

Historical Roots

One of the first models of education in the church began among the early Jewish people. The temple was not just a place for worshiping God but also a place to learn and hear teaching on the Holy Scriptures. Jesus grew up going to temple and synagogue. As a young boy, Jesus was taken to Jerusalem for the Passover. But instead of returning home with the family, Jesus was found in the temple learning and asking questions and giving amazing answers (Luke 2:41–49).

The early Christian fellowship did not meet in dedicated "Christian" space, nor was there any specific guidance from Jesus or the apostles to create any kind of physical structure. For the first century, Christians gathered in the same place they had always gathered—in Jerusalem with the Jews in the temple and synagogue.[2] The early Messianic group was so successful in spreading their teaching that they were repeatedly asked to leave but continued to come to the temple.[3]

Relations with the Jewish people decayed to the point where a believer named Stephen was stoned.[4] To avoid persecution, the believers moved away from Jerusalem and into Judea and Samaria, spreading the news of Jesus Christ.[5] As the Christian church moved out of the temple and synagogue, they found other space, like the houses of wealthy patrons.[6] Even by the first century after Christ's death, the early meeting records of the *Didache*, a teaching and worship order document in the early church, do not include specifications or recommendations for the place where the word and table of God would be celebrated.[7]

In the fourth century, the ruler Constantine had a vision of the cross as a sign of victory. Until this time, Christians were widely persecuted. But with the royal recognition of Christianity, it was not just elevated to the status of an official religion but also viewed as a royal sign.[8] In a great reversal, what was once a domestic movement became popular and widespread. People from around Constantine's kingdom joined the church and brought with them a cosmopolitan understanding of religious practice. Buildings were built to commemorate holy places, and meeting places were fashioned after the Roman government

---

2. Acts 2:46.

3. Acts 5:42.

4. Acts 6:8–7:60, the story of Stephen's arrest, trial, and stoning.

5. Acts 8:1–4.

6. Johnson, *Among the Gentiles*, 138.

7. John Chapman, "Didache," Catholic Answers, http://oce.catholic.com/index.php?title=Didache (accessed May 30, 2010).

8. Johnson, 258.

buildings of the day.[9] Now the church was established and would expand freely in number of converts, definition of structure and authority, and influence of politics and daily life.

In the medieval church, biblical education was done primarily for those who would become church specialists or were educated and wealthy, while those who could not read or afford the Bible used tools like devotional books or *Biblia Pauperum* that were like comic strips.[10] Monastic traditions like the Dominican and Franciscan studied the Bible in the scholastic tradition and used it for personal meditation and devotion.[11] There was great devotion to the Scriptures, but for the majority of people, it was an admiration from a distance.

Change came as many independent elements converged. First, there were many religious reformers like Martin Luther who had experienced the power of personal Scripture study. At the same time, copies of the Scriptures in the common vernacular were being circulated. But real change came as a growing class in Europe with expendable money was able to act as finanical patrons to scholars and translators of Scripture.[12] Finally, the emergence of the printing press solidified the new availability of the Bible to all people.[13] As the Reformation emerged, Bible studies for common people grew, and without the church's traditional cannonical interpretations, a diversity of views emerged.[14]

With direct access to the Bible, what was once an elite activity among a few specialists and privileged people became a staple of the middle, working class. Groups like the Quakers in Wales began to create schools outside of universities to teach literacy along with Bible study.[15] In Gloucester, England, the earliest form of Sunday school was established. It was championed by Robert Raikes for the children of chimney sweeps.[16] What is significant of these early models of education in the church was that these forms established a new liturgy for many churches that included Bible study. But it also established the concept that education could be evangelism and community service.

In the next hundred years, the institution of Sunday school became a part of most denominations and congregations. With more innovative uses of buses to transport people to church, improved curriculum, and strengthening of effective teaching practices, Sunday schools grew and so did the need for separate,

9. Couchenour, *Churches...Before You Build*, 19.

10. Fernandez-Armesto and Wilson, *Reformations*, 33.

11. Ibid., 15.

12. The system of patronage was wide spread in Europe during this time period. What is significant about the increased patronage by middle class sponsors was that it allowed for a larger variety of ideas to be shared in the marketplace.

13. Ibid., 35

14. Ibid., 36–38.

15. Mark K. Smith, "Quakers and Adult Schools," August 7, 1997, http://www.infed.org/walking/wa-quak.htm (accessed May 30, 2010).

16. Mark K. Smith, "Robert Raikes and Sunday Schools," August 30, 2000, http://www.infed.org/walking/wa-raikes.htm (accessed May 30, 2010).

dedicated space for classrooms. Because of these modern developments, it is now considered normal to have educational space alongside worship space.

Educational space in a congregation should not just be a series of white walls with tables and chairs. It needs to meet the needs of the congregation now and in the future. It should take into account the developmental needs of the ages that will use the space, and it should say something about how the church views relationships with God, other Christians, and the community.

Facility Utilization

Because each facility is unique, it will be important to begin with a survey of facility utilization. Leaders should begin by creating a map of the facility with lists of square footage for each space. Square footage is the product of the width of the room multiplied by the length of the room. The location of permanent fixtures should be included, such as pews, benches, sinks, cabinets, closets, and electrical outlets. Including storage spaces is also necessary, because sometimes with a little paint, storage spaces could be repurposed for meeting space for education.

To complete a facility utilization study, a list of all the groups that meet in the church should be completed. It is important to include the average size of each gathering and where and when they usually meet. If any groups meet off campus, they should be included in the study to better understand the complete needs of the congregation.

This information can help a congregation determine the need for rearranging meeting space, using alternate space outside of the building, or renovating existing space (e.g., tearing down walls, adding plumbing). The best planning not only takes into account the current needs but also considers how to meet needs creatively in the future.

According to a study of congregations across the country, funded by the Lilly Endowment and coordinated by the Hartford Institute for Religion Research at the Hartford Seminary, 76 percent of respondents believe that their worship space is about right or more than what they need, regardless of where they are in the country and what denomination or

Table 1. Church Gathering Educational Needs[17]	
	Sq. Feet Per person
Children[18]	25
Youth	12
Adults	12
Multi-purpose use	18-22

---

17. Couchenour, *Churches...Before You Build*, 166–68.

18. To best serve educational needs, there should not be more than twenty-four children in a single room.

faith group they are affiliated with.[19] But 59 percent felt that they did not have adequate space for the educational needs of the congregation, and 43 percent did not have a large enough space for fellowship and parking. [20] These are considerable deficiencies, considering that over 90 percent of Protestant congregations have a weekend Sunday school program.[21]

How Does a Facility Meet the Needs?

Using the facility map and the list of groups, arrangements may be made for optimum utilization. If several groups meet at the same time, some assignment of priority may need to be given. An educator should be cautious not to categorize one group as more important than others. Groups may be willing to consider alternate times that could maximize meeting space availability.

If lack of space is the major concern, some of the groups may be willing to meet at different times, especially if childcare is not an issue. Many churches maximize space by hosting groups at less busy times. Still other options are local coffee shops, restaurants or homes, or even sharing space with another congregation or social group.

If there is a good amount of space but not adequate room for larger events and changing needs, the church may need to consider reconfiguring current rooms and storage space. Are there rooms that could be connected and a wall removed? Are there storage rooms that could be reclaimed and cleaned? Does a door need to be moved or widened to accommodate a wheelchair? Could the church partner with another church or facility to host major events?

Finally, a fresh coat of paint, well applied, is a must. Plain white walls can feel fresh, but having a few accent walls helps define space and feel more inviting. Windows, furniture, and carpet should be clean, fresh, and inviting. Bathrooms and hallways need special attention. Just like having a visitor in someone's house, attention to detail and frequent cleaning and maintenance welcome those who come into a space.

Creating New Space

Whether it is a part of a larger building plan or an independent building dedicated primarily to education, the earliest consideration needs to be made to provide adequate, long-term, flexible space. In order to facilitate a long-range perspective, a team of teachers, adults, youth, children, and parents can help to shed light on the current needs and trends. An historical review of the individual

19. Hartford Institute of Religion Research at the Hartford Seminary, *Faith Communities Today (FACT) 2000, Combined Results*, WORSHSIZ (Weighted by WEIGHT), 2000, http://www.thearda.com/Archive/Files/Analysis/FACTAG/FACTAG_Var63_1.asp (accessed May 4, 2010).

20. Ibid., Codebook, http://www.thearda.com/Archive/Files/Codebooks/FACTAG_CB.asp (accessed May 4, 2010), questions 64–66.

21. Ibid., HAVESS (Weighted by WEIGHT), http://www.thearda.com/Archive/Files/Analysis/FACTAG/FACTAG_Var69_1.asp (accessed May 4, 2010).

church tradition and a tour of a few local churches of the same tradition and of different traditions will guide the group in considering the options. It also may be helpful to consider the local educational facilities of the majority of the congregation. Finally, the vision of the church should help determine the direction of the growth of the educational facilities. All of these elements will help guide the initial conversations with potential consultants, architects, and contractors.

Universal Access

All facilities need to take initiative to provide universal access (for those with physical limitations) in the building stage. There are a wide variety of standards and recommendations for universal access. In many states, only minimal modifications are regulated.

It may be a helpful exercise for educators to imagine someone in a wheelchair. How easy would it be to find a place to park, get into the church, and find a reserved place for the wheelchair with a seat for a helper? Could someone find a restroom large enough for a wheelchair and an assistant? Is it easy to sit in the pews or chairs with a leg brace or crutches? It may be surprising to many that the same needs are applicable for parents with young children in strollers.

Nursery and Weekday Schools

Additionally, in new facilities thought should be given to future plans for a nursery school or other educational institution. In Protestant churches, 30 to 40 percent directly provide childcare for daycare, preschool, or after/before school programs.[22] Potential outreach and significant witness to the community can start with establishing a preschool at the church.

Before building begins, the state should be contacted about the regulations for nurseries and preschools. The building codes are often much more strict than churches imagine, and spaces that are not planned correctly will not be allowed to start a childcare ministry. Codes do change continuously, but if a church starts with a state-of-the-art facility, it may only need minor retrofitting later.

Safe Spaces

Churches should make every effort to provide spaces that are free from physical, sexual, and emotional abuse. All classrooms should have windows in interior doors or window panels next to doors that are not covered by blinds or curtains. When at all possible, children who are the same age level should be the only ones using bathrooms while in class. Children are vulnerable to sexual abuse when bathrooms are shared with older children and adults.

---

22. Ibid., DAYC_Y1 (Weighted by WEIGHT), http://www.thearda.com/Archive/Files/Analysis/FACTAG/FACTAG_Var165_1.asp (accessed May 5, 2010).

Are there clear escape plans to safety and emergency plans from each classroom? In every room, there should be a clear emergency escape plan, and well-stocked first-aid kits with universal precaution procedures should be prominently displayed. Regular training for the staff and volunteers in the latest life-saving techniques should be provided and paid for by the church. It is helpful to plan fire drills with the leaders of programs and have plans as appropriate for earthquakes and tornadoes and other natural disasters.

Safe outdoor play areas and structures are welcoming to families, care providers, volunteers, and children alike. Play equipment needs to be free of splinters and breaks. Weight limits of equipment and number of children at a time on a structure should be posted. The safest surfaces tend to be soft, such as grass, several inches of wood chips, or a composite foam surface. Hard surfaces, such as concrete or gravel, may be more durable but can cause unnecessary injuries on a playground. There should be no holes in the ground and the area should be clear of debris, such as glass and trash.

When they moved from Texas, Beverly Jane immediately began looking for a church. She fondly remembered her years as a child and youth at the church and wanted the same for her five children. So her first week she went to the church down the street. It was relatively large with kids playing everywhere and lots of educational programs. But what meant the most to her was that her children could freely and safely explore and play on the playground equipment. She loved to take her shoes off and walk in the grass with her one-year-old. While she stayed at the church because of the people, it was the care that the church took to create space for her children that brought her to the church.

Hospitality

Educators need to make sure that visitors and guests can find rooms or events. Signs need to be clear and should be easily found throughout common areas. Church leaders can get ideas from malls and stores, because they do this very well. To get an outside perspective, it might be helpful to invite someone who has never been to a church to find the rooms and events, especially when no one else is around to help.

Inevitably every church needs space to prepare food and drink. Most classes need a place to store supplies and to prepare refreshments. Creating a usable space near classrooms is a good way to prepare for the hospitality needs of the congregation and others who might use the facility.

Media-Equipped Rooms

While technology continues to change, the need for it as a tool does not. Availability of basic media, such as sound systems and Internet access, for example, can aid teachers. If a church cannot afford to have media for each room, it is possible to create a few media carts that can be used and returned to a secure location. Plain white walls provide an inexpensive place to project images.

Creating Policies for Facilities

A facility needs clear policies about who can use the space and equipment and how it can be used. Having outside groups use the church is a way to create goodwill or generate income, as long as they are welcomed and understand what is expected of them. Is there a place for them to smoke and dispose of their cigarettes? Can they freely walk in the building, even if they are in the youth area during an event? For weddings, can the group use a toddler room for childcare? Can people drink on campus? Is it a peanut-free campus? There are many policies that are helpful in relation to how the facility is used and when well designed help speak to the faith and traditions of the church.

Many congregations do not consider the importance of offering peanut-free spaces. While children often outgrow this deadly allergy, the church's snacks, events, and play structures can be covered with peanut dust from the hands and mouths of unsuspecting children and adults. And often allergies are not discussed with teachers or at special events, and children can have life-threatening attacks.

Providing peanut-free environments begins with a campus policy that is followed by children and adults. First, ingredient labels should be checked for nuts. Many brands list the allergens in the ingredients: M&M's contain peanuts whether they are peanut or plain, for example. But a food must also be uncontaminated. If it is produced on shared equipment with products that include peanuts, it is not safe. If a product is produced in a facility where peanuts or other nuts are present, it is generally still safe.

With all allergies, a good educator includes parents in the process of creating snacks. It can sometimes mean the difference between life and death.

Developmental Needs

Newborns and Toddlers

Possibly the most demanding of all age groups, the littlest members of the congregation and their parents need the same kind of facilities and supplies they have at home. This includes a place to change diapers and clothes, space for private nursing, either child-sized toilets or larger stalls for parent and child, spaces to prepare bottles, comfortable places to sit, and places to roam when little bodies get restless.

Many churches may not provide for this age since there is so much equipment and space that is needed to minister to families with children under five. However, a church that is committed to expressing the love of Christ and building relationships with families must pay close attention to this age group. When parents know their children are loved, they feel loved too.

Every church should install and maintain changing stations in at least two restrooms near the sanctuary. Since men and women share parenting responsibilities, it is important to provide space in both the women's and men's restrooms for a changing table. Stocking these tables with helpful emergency supplies—extra diapers in different sizes, wipes, and cleaning supplies for inevitable messes—can mean the difference between a family visiting a church one time only and a family finding a church home.

Elementary Children

Educational space for children includes all the activities that a church provides with children—children's church, Sunday school, vacation Bible school, after-school programs, clubs, and weekday events and childcare.

It is ideal to keep children's classrooms together on the first floor by grade level, with outdoor access for emergencies but away from unsecured pubic entries. These classrooms should have access to restrooms that are for children only. The system for signing a child in and out of a classroom should be established with a thoughtful plan for caregivers to recognize the person who will pick up the child.

Theme-based rooms are popular for young children and can provide a friendly environment, but it does limit the use of a room. Adult groups that use rooms that are clearly for children may feel out of place. The environment may not be suitable to talk about deep spiritual subjects and needs when a big fuzzy character is smiling down on the group.

A centrally placed closed circuit monitor of the worship services near children's rooms can allow for teachers to monitor the service and anticipate when to prepare children for their parents. This help can eliminate concerns about services that might go longer than anticipated or finish sooner than expected. Consideration should also be given to placing a monitor of the service in or near toddler rooms.

Youth

In many churches, the youth get whatever is left after the children get the safest spaces and the older adults get the spaces that have easy access. Of course, youth groups are also known for making and enjoying messes, noise, and a place away from their parents. For these reasons, youth spaces are often found in the basement, on a top floor of a building, or in a distant location. The challenge for youth leaders is to consider the needs of other groups without sacrificing safety and accessibility for the youth.

Youth need space to meet as a large group, indoor and outdoor areas, and small group meeting space that is private but not secluded. Youth are still young and vulnerable to the same dangers as children. In fact, with the wide age range of many youth groups, youth are more vulnerable as their bodies mature physically.

Adults

Many adults prefer the traditional Sunday school format, either lecture style or discussion style. A variety of flexible meeting spaces would accommodate these needs well. Easy access to a well-stocked kitchenette is also an asset. Other adult groups prefer more relaxed atmospheres more similar to a living room or coffee shop. They might be more comfortable in informal spaces that are designed more for conversation and food.

One of the most difficult challenges with adult groups is tenure. Many adult groups have existed for decades, often in the same spaces. As groups age, membership may decline from relocation, divorce, and death. Finding ways to help these groups transition not only in the emotional process of growing older but also to allow space for growing groups to meet is an ongoing process. When a group is honored by being listened to and heard, and when they feel cared for in the relocation, it can be a time of healing and recognition of the spiritual journey they are on.

Special Needs and Universal Access

Every child is a gift from God, and each child is truly unique. While it is easy to use traditional forms of education, those forms may not be adequate to meet the educational needs of many students. Some students many need extra assistance, different teaching methods, or customized space to learn most effectively. While these needs are often met in the public or private school system, the church is often not as well positioned to meet the needs of some children.

What many churches do not recognize is that when a church fails to minister to the whole family, it impacts the whole family. This has an effect on the way a family sees the church and God. Without intending to do so, the church sends a message that there is no room in the family of God for those with special needs.

If a church wants to begin including those with special needs, it should begin meeting with the family. Often families are very willing to help a church meet their children's needs with little or no additional need for staffing, resources, or finances. And over time, needs change for each child, so allowing flexibility for space and providing basic accessibility prepares a church to meet a variety of needs. Some needs, like wheelchair access to youth areas or in restrooms, can help children feel like an important part of the community.

Multipurpose Spaces

If the space is shared, the church should consider creative ways to change the room's personality for the different groups that will use a space. For children's toys or adult's books, wheels may be attached to book shelves so they can be easily turned to face the wall when not in use or moved to a storage area. Curtains can be installed that can either define different spaces in a room or cover age specific artwork.

Community Gathering

Holiness is not only a way of following God but is also naturally expressed in community. Finding a way for the body of Christ to meet together in one place outside of worship is an important way to live out the love of God. Whether it is outdoors on a patio or in a huge fellowship hall style, people will enjoy meeting others, sharing food, and hearing the stories of faith from people they don't normally meet.

Going Outside the Walls

For nearly two hundred years, the early Christians did not have a formal meeting space, but the transmission of Christianity continued. With every property comes maintenance, management, and need for upgrades. Churches may need to think more about how they can attract new members by going out into the world. There are several viable formats for meeting outside of a facility for education and/or worship.

A house church meets in a local house for worship, fellowship, mission, and spiritual formation. So necessarily it should be small, less than twenty people. If it grows larger than twenty, the house church could split into two or more churches, and then all of them could continue to grow. With this multiplication principle, a community of faith touches many people with the gift of salvation.

House churches are found around the world and have been seen throughout the centuries. Wolfgang Simson quotes the research of Christian Schwarz that churches under one hundred in attendance grow 63 percent over five years. Churches that were larger than one thousand members grew by only 4 percent. The result is that the larger the group becomes, the slower the growth of new members.[23]

Alternatively, churches with established structures may find that a ministry focused on being engaged with the culture is a positive direction for the spiritual formation of their community. In a missional church, the congregation makes

23. Simson, *Houses That Change the World*, 248.

intentional steps to reach out from a formally structured congregation. The church may release a small percent of its members who are well connected to culture to engage it. For example, these members may create nontraditional meetings in local apartment complexes or restaurants. This paradigm helps congregations begin to see how the community could use the building they have and how their faith community could make profound changes for good.

Online education and new uses of technology can also be important tools for education. Traditional educational models of sitting in a classroom listening to an instructor are being replaced with more interactive formats that engage students. With attention spans shrinking and the fundamental ways that people learn changing, offering opportunities that use familiar technology can meet emerging needs.

Summary

Nothing done in the church should be done to serve only the needs of the building. And going into debt to develop a facility creates a burden that is not necessary to carry out the mission of the church. In fact, many alternate forms of education can be explored that do not require dedicated space.

Regardless of how a congregation decides to meet the needs of the body of Christ and the community, the central reason that a church maintains a facility is to care for people. A facility should be about meeting hospitality needs, safety needs, developmental needs, and relational needs. It should reflect and enhance the mission of the church and even share what is most important to a congregation.

Bibliography

Berryman, Jerome W. *Teaching Godly Play: How to Mentor the Spiritual Development of Children.* Denver, CO: Morehouse Education Resources, 2009.

Brotherton, Marcus. *Teacher: The Henrietta Mears Story.* Ventura, CA: Regal Books, 2006.

Couchenour, William L. *Churches...Before You Build.* North Lima, OH: Cogun, Inc., 2003.

Fernandez-Armesto, Filipe and Derek Wilson. *Reformations: A Radical Interpretation of Christianity and the World 1500–2000.* New York: Scribner, 1996.

Halter, Hugh and Matt Smay. *AND: The Gathered and Scattered Church.* Grand Rapids, MI: Zondervan, 2010.

Johnson, Luke Timothy. *Among the Gentiles: Greco-Roman Religion and Christianity.* New Haven, CT: Yale University Press, 2009.

LeFever, Marlene D. *Creative Teaching Methods: Be an Effective Christian Teacher.* Colorado Springs, CO: NexGen, 2004.

May, Scottie, Beth Poterski, Catherine Stonehouse, and Linda Cannell. *Children Matter: Celebrating Their Place in the Church, Family, and Community.* Grand Rapids, MI: William B. Eerdmans Publishing Company, 2005.

Montessori, Maria. *The Montessori Method.* Mineola, NY: Dover Publications, Inc., 2002.

Simson, Wolfgang. *Houses That Change the World: The Return of the House Churches.* Waynesboro, GA: Authentic, 1998.

PART THREE

PRACTICE

CHAPTER EIGHTEEN

A Church Cannot Not Teach

KEITH DRURY

> Day after day they met together in the temple. They broke bread together in different homes and shared their food happily and freely, while praising God.
>
> Acts 2:46–47a

Everything the church does teaches something—a church cannot not teach. Even if a church tried to do nothing at all, that would teach something. This sort of casual teaching is sometimes called the "informal curriculum" of teaching. It is the sum total of everything the church does and says together. Church life is curriculum—what it teaches by who it is and what it does together. This chapter focuses on this informal curriculum and how it augments, expands, implements (and sometimes even reverses) the formal printed curriculum.

Formal and Informal Curriculum

The church's *formal curriculum* usually refers to a planned sequence of learning experiences designed on a long-term basis to achieve learning objectives. Usually it means printed curriculum that has been planned by professionals. An example of highly developed formal curriculum is Sunday school curriculum that is designed to cover all the basics of the faith over, say, three years. But the church also has an *informal curriculum* that is the sum total of everything happening beyond the formal curriculum instruction. This informal curriculum includes what happens at carry-in dinners, during lock-ins, in the worship services, and even what people learn by observing how church attendees treat each other. The informal curriculum can ratify and multiply the effect of the formal curriculum, or it can veto and reverse what the formal curriculum has tried to teach.

There are two sayings Christian educators sometimes repeat describing the role of the informal curriculum. "More is caught than taught" is sometimes quoted to imply that students often "catch" learning from informal modeling more than from formal instruction. The informal curriculum of a church deals with this "catching" kind of learning—what students catch from who the church is and what it does, not just from what is said. The other saying is, "What you are speaks so loudly I can't hear what you are saying." This statement implies that a teacher's informal modeling carries a kind of veto power over what he or she teaches formally. If she or he teaches love but acts unloving, the unloving action negates the formal instruction. What is true for an individual is also true of the church collectively. No matter what is taught formally, the informal curriculum of a church quietly verifies or vetoes the formal instruction. This is why it is so important that the church *be* what it plans to teach.

Holiness: Individual and Corporate

The work of Christian education is both personal and corporate. The Christian educator works for the spiritual formation of individuals in order to help them become more like Christ. This is the goal of individual holiness. But there is more to Christian education than making holy persons—God calls the church to fashion a holy *people*. Christian education attempts to build the church—the body of Christ—into a people of God that, combined together, reflects the image of Christ. This "corporate holiness" is not achieved by adding up each of the individual holy lives; rather it is something larger and bigger, for "the whole is greater than the sum of the parts." A *holy church* is what Christian education seeks to fashion. The process of bringing a group to holiness involves more than individual instruction. It involves "doing life together" in such a way that the church grows in love together. This is why the informal curriculum of a church is so important. In living and loving together, Christians learn to become the body of Christ—the visible manifestation of Christ's holiness to the world.

Instruction in Righteousness

A proper approach to Christian education cannot be content with the simple transfer of information. While it is important to know the facts of the Bible and the content of theology, knowledge is not the only outcome the church seeks. Christian educators are not in the *info*rmation business so much as the *trans*formation business. And it is the Holy Spirit who does the transforming. The task of Christian education is to instruct people in righteousness so that they become a holy people by the transforming work of the Holy Spirit. Accomplishing the robust vision of developing a holy people cannot be done in a one-hour Sunday school class each week. It takes a far more comprehensive approach than that. It will take a 24/7 year-round plan that includes everything the church does together, all aimed at the same goal: producing a holy people of God. Essentially, it should require the Christian educator to see everything the church does together as curriculum. Thus, the curriculum is both formal and informal, and it includes both planned and unplanned experiences. This comprehensive approach sees *church life as the curriculum for spiritual formation*. This model sees everything the church does (and those things left out) as having a teaching function—a church cannot not teach. This raises the question, *what* is the church teaching, through the formal and informal, planned and unplanned curriculum of church life? A related question is, can some sense of planning and purpose be brought to the informal curriculum?

Teaching Through Church Life

Maria Harris has helped Christian educators see this larger picture of church life as curriculum, focusing on five core activities of the church that accomplish teaching in this larger sense.[1] They are loosely based on the life of the early church described in the book of Acts. The five activities are *teaching, fellowship, worship, preaching,* and *serving*. Her argument is that the church teaches and forms the congregation through all of these activities, not just through the formal classroom teaching. While the other four activities of the church seem more random and less curricularized, they could be organized and sequenced into a macro-curriculum that fashions a godly people. The following section explores how the church teaches through these five activities, though only the first has traditionally been considered the curriculum of Christian education.

Teaching

The people of God have always been involved in teaching each other and instructing new generations. God could implant in a new baby all the learning they would ever need, but he doesn't. He leaves the teaching to the church, providing it with the Holy Spirit's help. Thus, God's people have always done some sort of instruction. Chapter 5 offers a more comprehensive treatment of the history of Christian education, but this section brings the reminder that God's people have always had some system of instructing new converts and the emerging generations. In the patriarchal period, family heads like Abraham, Isaac, Jacob, and Joseph served as chief teachers and storytellers. As the Israelites formed into a nation, "the law" emerged and Jewish parents taught the Ten Commandments to their children in the home. As time passed this story was

---

1. Harris, *Fashion Me a People*.

written down, so that by the time Israel was taken into captivity, the local syna-gogue emerged as a place for prayer and study of these written Scriptures. The early Christians founded local congregations and introduced catechesis for new converts and children. In the 1500s Martin Luther reenergized the catechism. The German Pietists deployed a small group strategy, as did John Wesley when he launched his "class meetings" for formal instruction, spiritual growth, and accountability. About the same time as Wesley, Robert Raikes launched the Sunday school, which swept England and America as a formal means of educa-tion and spiritual formation. All of these efforts were formal attempts to instruct converts and the emerging generations in matters of faith and practice. In fact, the term *Christian education* often brings to mind *only* these formal approaches, and Harris aims to correct that misunderstanding.

The church today uses a variety of formal teaching approaches. Sunday school is the most significant formal teaching effort for many denominations. With little attention and almost no encouragement, it plods on, gathering a number of people for formal ongoing instruction every week. Small groups periodically make a comeback and add to the Sunday school's formal spiri-tual formation efforts. Beyond these two there are children's church, vacation Bible school, midweek clubs, youth ministries, adult groups, summer camps, and a host of other formal programs where written curriculum offers a formal approach to teaching.

When hearing the term *curriculum*, most Christians think first of the Sunday school, VBS, or similar educational efforts that have printed curriculum resources. This section will not dwell on this first means of spiritual formation. The mistake is when the church thinks of these formal means of instruction as the *only* means of Christian education. This is the error that Harris attempts to correct. She does not argue that the church should pay less attention to formal instruction but that the church should *also* think of the other ways it instructs: how it teaches through fellowship, worship, preaching, and service.[2]

Fellowship

Is learning happening when Christians are eating at a carry-in dinner or playing volleyball together outside the church building? It is. Christian educators have long incorporated fellowship elements as part of formal classes. Sunday school teachers sometimes invite their students to their homes for pizza, or midweek club leaders take their students on an all-day hike. These fellowship gatherings

---

2. Maria Harris uses five Greek words to represent these five areas of church life as follows: *Koi-nonia* (community, fellowship); *Leiturgia* (prayer, worship); *Didache* (teaching); *Kerygma* (proclamation, preaching); *Diakonia* (Service). I am presenting them in a different order here with adapted titles, but the areas are generally the same. Harris's contribution to our thinking about curriculum is that these other areas of church life beyond our formal schooling are at least equal in their impact and perhaps need greater attention in planning for the spiritual formation of the body of Christ.

might look like extras or rewards for being good and listening well, but actually fellowship is a primary means of spiritual formation.

In the Western world where radical individualism prevails, people tend to think of a Christian as an *individual* who has been born again or saved. Westerners imagine that a single person can be a solitary Christian. Some have even gone so far as to imagine that a person might never go to church, never gather with other Christians, and claim to be a Christian on a solitary basis. The Bible knows no such kind of Christian—in the Bible a Christian is always a member of a *group*. Harris puts it this way, "One Christian is no Christian; we go to God together or we do not go at all."[3] An individual can no more be a Christian alone than she could be a Canadian alone. To be a Canadian implies *belonging*—so does being a Christian. This is why Christians are pictured in the Bible as members of the body of Christ—an eye or an ear or a hand. No person can be the body of Christ without others. Indeed the body of Christ cannot exist when there is only one person—it only exists when the parts are together.

Fellowship is vital as a means of teaching because *love* is so central to the Christian message. God is love, and the world will know the church is Christian by its love. To love Christ is to love others. Becoming a disciple of Christ is learning to love. How can Christians love their brothers and sisters if they are not with them? Fellowship brings us together so Christians can express love. Sure, most Christians have day jobs so they cannot live together 24/7 like the monks did in medieval times. But Christians must spend time together beyond sitting in pews for worship or lined up in rows for Sunday school. Fellowship offers those times to be together in a learning-living community.

It is a human trait to hunger for community. Humans yearn to bond with others. They want to be part of a group, a clan, a club, a church. Modern life tends to fragment relationships, and because of this, humans are hungry for real *koinonia*. Christian fellowship offers this kind of community. This is why mission trips are so transformative for Christians. In one study of college students and adults, both groups listed mission trips as the number one transformative impact in their spiritual life.[4] Perhaps the reason is that on such trips these Christians experienced *loving community* like they never had before. On a highly relational mission trip, they were "doing life together."

The vast majority of the virtues Christ exhibited and taught are relational: becoming merciful, forgiving, avoiding judgmentalism, being considerate, caring, compassionate, hospitable, and scores of other virtues. Certainly these are virtues people should practice at work and with the world, but they are especially suited for practice in a hyper-relational environment of a believing fellow-

---

3. Harris, *Fashion Me a People* 77.

4. Data are from personal interviews by a Christian Education course at Indiana Wesleyan University during November 2004. This was asked of 264 adults and 269 college students: What has had the most impact on your spiritual life so far in your life? The most frequent answer was "Mission Trip" for both groups.

ship. How will the world see the love Christians have for each other if they are seldom with each other?

This means that car washes, carry-in dinners, retreats, and traveling together are a core element of the church's macro-curriculum. People learn as they live together. They learn when they laugh together. They learn when they lovingly kid each other and tell jokes. They learn as they listen to others and accept their strange foibles. When they are together informally, they practice what it means to be forbearing, forgiving, and kind. In fellowship, they model informally what they teach formally. New converts and children see what is meant by being a loving and caring community—not just in words, but incarnated in community life.

One challenge with seeing fellowship as an important arm of curriculum is the fast pace of modern life. Many Christians attend church like they go to a movie. They show up to watch the one-hour performance and then slip out without interacting with others. If the church is not together much, it cannot model what a Christian community is supposed to look like. A second challenge is forgetting that fellowship is a teaching activity. Christians gathered are not always *Christian* in behavior. Someone can make harsh jokes at another's expense and teach the exact opposite of what was said in formal teaching. Seeing fellowship as part of the macro-curriculum of the church reminds the Christian educator they are never off-duty. Every time the church is together, teaching is happening. Influencing and channeling the behavior and speech of Christians as they eat together is just as important as preparing formal curriculum for a class session—perhaps more so.

Worship

Worship—especially prayer—may be the oldest form of teaching. A person is constantly learning in worship. In worship, the entire body is gathered to ascribe worth to the King of Kings and to speak with him in prayer. Worship is a conversation with God. If strangers from another planet attended worship and studied it carefully, they would be able to tell what that group believed before long.

The architecture of a church teaches. Such interplanetary visitors mentioned above would see the unique kind of buildings designed especially for worship. They would draw conclusions from how the platform is arranged or if it called a platform or a chancel or stage. They would notice what was central to the front of the worship center: a Communion table, a pulpit, or the band's instruments. They would note the location of the Communion table and learn from what was on it—a Communion set, an open Bible, or a spread of flowers. They would notice the cross and its placement, and even the material used to make the cross. Or they would notice no cross at all. Like the interplanetary visitors, attendees are learning before a word is spoken in worship. The nonverbal visual cues are constantly teaching in a quiet way.

The people are also learning from the songs sung, especially from the lyrics of the songs. Congregational singing is the way Christians emphasize doctrine, singing most what they believe most. Singing provides emotional contact with God and each other, bonding the body of Christ together.

A church's prayers reveal even more what they believe about God—not just what they *say* they believe. Do they believe God is majestic and almighty? It will be seen in the prayers. Do they believe God hears and answers prayer? This is revealed in how they pray. If they use prayer as a segue so musicians can move to new spots on the stage, it teaches the people more about prayer than they learn in most formal lessons on prayer. No matter what is taught in formal classrooms, more is caught in worship services.

Worshipers might hear testimonies of how God worked in someone's life. If a church teaches that God changes lives but people rarely hear any actual testimonies to life change, what are they left believing? Testimonies and stories in worship are powerful teaching tools.

A worshiper might see an altar call where people go forward to repent and be born again. Or they might witness the baptism of a new Christian. These events are teaching the church's doctrine on conversion and baptism beyond any formal lessons. If people have not seen such things for several years, what are they led to believe in spite of what was taught in class?

Some churches celebrate the church year, at least some seasons. While many evangelical churches are not serious about the liturgical calendar, even evangelicals at least celebrate Christmas and Easter. Even twice-yearly Christmas-Easter attendees get the two basic truths that God became incarnate in Christ and Christ died and rose for sinners. Other churches adopt a more robust approach and include an annual cycle of Advent, Christmas, Epiphany, Lent, Palm Sunday, Good Friday, Easter, and Pentecost so that the church calendar offers the most ancient curriculum of the story of redemption on an annual cycle. The church year forces a focus on the core events of the story of redemption, thus avoiding trying to teach so much; in the words of Josh Hunt and Larry Mays, "We teach so little because we try to teach so much."[5]

In worship, are scriptures read in a way that shows reverence for God's Word and assumes he speaks through those words? If a church teaches that the Bible is important yet seldom reads it in worship, the practice vetoes all the formal teaching—people *know* the Bible is not really as important as they have been told or it would be more important in worship. An increasing number of churches are returning to the ancient pattern of several Bible readings: one from the Old Testament, another from the Epistles, and a third from the Gospels, showing that Scripture speaks to Christians today. But when a church crowds out Scripture for other elements of worship, the people learn that Scripture can be treated as ancillary in their own lives just as it is in worship.

---

5. Hunt and Mays, *Disciple-Making Teachers*, 114.

When worshipers take the Lord's Supper together, they learn. Every time the church celebrates the Lord's Supper, they proclaim the gospel in action. Here Christians experience the bonding and transformation that comes through this means of grace. The Lord's Supper provides a ritual sign and symbol for each stage of faith.[6] The ritual itself does not bring change, for only God can bring about some changes. He does this through the *means of grace*—ordinary channels through which God works to sanctify a people. Scripture and the Lord's Supper are two primary means of grace that God uses to transform his people, thus both must have a prominent role in worship. However, when a church sidelines Scripture by reading only a few verses because of the limited time and avoids offering the Lord's Supper more than a few times a year, they are still teaching, because a church cannot not teach. That church teaches by what it omits, just like it teaches by what it includes, because it cannot not teach.[7] People are always learning through the curriculum of worship.

Preaching

A prominent part of Protestant worship is preaching or proclamation. The church proclaims the gospel in deed through the Lord's Supper and proclaims it in word by preaching. Preaching has a teaching effect.

Preaching has changed significantly in the last fifty years. Today's preachers *teach* more. They might even label themselves "teaching pastor," and if there are several staff ministers who preach, they might be called the teaching team. Morning preaching sometimes feels like a large classroom, complete with note-taking sheets tucked in the worship folder. Overhead transparencies first appeared in the 1970s, and PowerPoint presentations emerged later, outlining the lesson of the day.

By the turn of the twenty-first century, the teaching pastor model was common, and the morning worship became the largest teaching venue in many evangelical churches of a Wesleyan persuasion.[8] Where this teaching format

---

6. Browning and Reed, *Sacraments in Religious Education*.

7. The learning that comes by what we omit is sometimes termed the "null curriculum." That is, we learn by what is missing, not just by what is present. For instance, when a church that believes a woman can be ordained to the ministry just like a male can be, but the children and youth never actually *see* a woman preaching or presiding at the Lord's Supper, they learn something from that null curriculum—that the ministry is (actually and practically) reserved for males only. The null curriculum may indeed be the most powerful curricular tool of informal teaching.

8. In the 1950s, it was common for churches to have more people attending Sunday school than attending the morning worship service, which almost always followed Sunday school. Sunday school in the 1950s was often the "side door" entry-level event for newcomers. Churches in those days tried to persuade Sunday school attendees to stay for the "after service," by which they meant morning worship. In the morning worship service, the "preacher" would, well, *preach*. Proclamation at that time was often a persuasive sermon seeking a decision, often ending with an altar call to be born again or to receive an experience like sanctification. By the 1970s and 1980s, this attendance pattern reversed in many denominations, and the roles began to reverse as well. The morning worship became the larger gathering, and now church leaders tried to persuade those attending worship to come early for Sunday school (or, as multiple services increased, to *stay* for Sunday school, which was

continues, the implication for the teaching ministry of the church is momentous. In many churches, the preaching is now the primary educational effort for adults, with Sunday school and small groups serving as the second step.[9]

This shift means that the teaching in morning worship is now the primary Christian education curriculum for adults in many churches. An increasing number of pastors now plan their sermon cycle like they are designing curriculum—with a scope and sequence and outcomes, even for some on a ten-year plan. Unfortunately, many other pastors have not yet caught up to the implications of this shift. Thus, an educational leader in the local church must consider the Sunday preaching-teaching as a primary avenue of the comprehensive curriculum for Christian education. Some Christian educators are now expected to write curriculum for implementing the preaching outcomes in classes and small groups based on the core curricular plan of the teaching pastor's sermons.

The rise of the teaching pastor in morning worship has greatly expanded the Christian education efforts of the local church, though it does take some of the curricular planning out of the hands of the laity and the Christian educators and curriculum publishers. Nevertheless, this shift has significantly increased the educational efforts of the church. It is obvious that proclamation is increasingly performing a teaching function, and thus Christian educators must consider proclamation part—perhaps even the primary element—of the macro-curriculum for making a godly people.[10]

Serving

Christians have always been expected to serve one another and the world. Service takes people beyond themselves into mission. Missional churches do not hide in their churches waiting to get beamed up by the second coming, but they attempt to bring the kingdom of God to pass here and now by serving this present age. It should be obvious that teaching Christians to love and care for one another and the world should result in actual acts of mercy and service. Christian education is more than learning the importance of service—it should result in actual acts of service to the world. Thus, when the church mobilizes to

held after worship or simultaneously with multiple worship services). The church had something new on its hands: an increasing number of people attending only the worship service who were not in any Sunday school class at all. This may have fed a shift to greater teaching in worship, since for many, it was the only teaching they ever received.

9. This chapter does not deal with small groups but it is important to note that by 1980, under the influence of Paul Cho of South Korea (who was pastor of the largest church in the world at the time) and channeled through the American church growth movement, churches began to launch small groups as yet another alternative to Sunday school. This move was especially promoted by the model church of the period, Willow Creek Community Church, and its pastor, Bill Hybels.

10. It is not yet clear how the more recent shift by some pastors to "narrative preaching" will affect this situation. The notetaking guide style of preaching is beginning to be replaced by a narrative style in some churches. Yet a narrative approach has been an important method of teaching anyway, so even if this style of proclamation prevails it will still have a significant teaching influence.

build a Habitat for Humanity house, or bands together to drill a well for fresh water in an African village, it is implementing the beyond-the-classroom outcome of learning. It is narrow to view Christian education as primarily about classroom learning. Rather, the church gathered to serve is the end result of learning, since Christianity itself is not just something to be believed but is something to *do*. For Christians learning does not end with knowledge alone, but action.[11]

Implications of Church Life as Curriculum

When one sees the above five elements of church life as the macro-curriculum for developing disciples, a new way of thinking emerges. The greatest implication of this line of thought is the need for more careful *intentional planning*.[12] For generations, Christian education has been one of the best models in the church of long-range planning. Long before strategic planning and ten-year plans became popular, Christian education curriculum was designed over a decade or more. Sunday school curriculum materials are planned over a decade or more with a carefully cycled and graded approach. Yet many other areas of church life still have virtually no planning at all that is greater than a year in length. If preaching-teaching is going to be the primary effort at educating the people, then pastors cannot just grab a sermon off the shelf because it appeals to them or fits that week's news flashes. If fellowship is an important venue for training disciples in love, then a schedule of fellowship events needs to be planned with the overall goals in mind. If worship—even the architecture and set-up—is teaching people about God, then greater thought must be put into designing and redesigning the space with theological and practical educative outcomes in mind. The formal curricular teaching has been a good model of long-range planning. It is now time to share the wealth—helping these other arms of informal education bring greater planning and sequence to the combined efforts since church life is the macro-curriculum for making a holy people of God.

11. Pagitt, *Reimagining Spiritual Formation*.
12. Stanger, *Spiritual Formation in the Local Church*.

Bibliography

Browning, Robert L. and Roy A. Reed. *The Sacraments in Religious Education and Liturgy*. Birmingham, AL: Religious Education Press, 1985.

Harris, Maria. *Fashion Me a People: Curriculum in the Church*. Louisville: Westminster/John Knox Press, 1989.

Hunt, Josh and Larry Mays. *Disciple-Making Teachers—How to Equip Adults for Growth and Action*. Loveland, CO: Vital Ministries, 1998.

Pagitt, Doug. *Reimagining Spiritual Formation: A Week in the Life of an Experimental Church*. Grand Rapids, MI: emergentYS, 2003.

Stanger, Frank Bateman. *Spiritual Formation in the Local Church*. Grand Rapids, MI: Francis Asbury Press, 1989.

CHAPTER NINETEEN

Do as I Do *and* as I Say: Intentional Discipleship

LEON M. BLANCHETTE

> Go to the people of all nations and make them my disciples. Baptize them in the name of the Father, the Son, and the Holy Spirit, and teach them to do everything I have told you. I will be with you always, even until the end of the world.
>
> —Matthew 28:19–20
> (The Great Commission)
>
> He put some water into a large bowl. Then he began washing his disciples' feet and drying them with the towel he was wearing.
>
> —John 13:5

Christ's last word and command to the church before his ascension was to "make disciples" (Matthew 28:19). Not only did he speak of the importance of training faithful followers, but he himself showed those who followed him how to make disciples. Even in the final moments of his life, he was aware of the importance of modeling for others how they were to live. As he washed the disciples' feet, not only was he being a servant to those who followed him, but more importantly he was modeling for them the intentionality that is necessary to nurture one of his children to be a disciple. The last words of Christ, according to Matthew, shout loudly the imperative to make disciples intentionally.

Discipleship Defined

In his commentary on Matthew, Donald Hagner identifies a disciple as a "pupil" or "learner" and the act of discipleship occurs as a disciple is being nurtured in the teachings of his/her master.[1] Here begins a change from a traditional understanding of disciples as only the twelve that served with the Master for three years to everyone in all places who confess Jesus as Lord and serve him as Master. In the context of the church, a disciple is understood best as any person who is nurtured to "absolute commitment to the person of Jesus as one's sole Master and Lord."[2]

The act of discipleship is the process by which disciples are trained. This act of "making disciples" is commanded in Matthew 28:19 and is not presented as optional on the part of the follower. Michael Wilkins notes that the phrase "make disciples" is an imperative that is supported by three subordinate terms: "go," "baptize," and "teach."[3] These subordinate terms function as the means by which the imperative is accomplished. In essence, Jesus is commanding that his followers must lead others to a personal relationship with him and equip them to follow his teachings, thus making them disciples. The way that is to be done is by going to where they are, baptizing new believers, and teaching them to obey what he has taught.

Most modern English translations of the Great Commission begin with instructions to "go." Unfortunately, this translation tends to misrepresent the intention of the text. In Robert Smith's critique of the Great Commission, he warns that while the subordinate command "go" does have an evangelistic element to it, the main intent of the Greek word in this context is to be understood more as being "busy constantly making disciples of all nations."[4] Roger Hahn supports this interpretation and notes that "go" is not an imperative and should be understood as, "when you go, make disciples."[5] Smith further notes that these instructions deal not only with making disciples outside the church but within the church as well.[6] It becomes clear that the call to make disciples is an imperative to nurture those within the church to faithful obedience to God

---

1. Hagner, *Matthew 14–28*, 887.
2. Wilkins, *Matthew*, 952.
3. Ibid., 951.
4. Smith, *Matthew*, 338.
5. Hahn, *Matthew*, 346.
6. Smith, *Matthew*, 338.

while also evangelizing those outside the church and bringing them into an obedient relationship with God. Making disciples requires sacrifice and is not a temporary commitment.[7] Those who disciple others must be committed for the long road and faithfully teach others as they live out the faith in the ordinary routines of life.

A uniqueness of this call is that it is for all Christians. Throughout the Old Testament, it was understood by the followers of God that their avenue to God was through the priest. These men of God held significant roles in the life of the Hebrew people. They were honored, respected, and sometimes worshiped because they were mediators between God and the people. Following the death and resurrection of Christ, and symbolized by the tearing of the curtain in the temple (Matt 27:51), every believer now has full access to God directly. In 1 Peter 2:8–9, Peter says to the church, "But you are God's chosen and special people. You are a group of royal priests and a holy nation. God has brought you out of darkness into his marvelous light. Now you must tell all the wonderful things that he has done." As members of the priesthood of believers, followers of Christ are to function as priests who have direct access to God and whose responsibilities include going and sharing the wonderful things God has done with those who do not know.

The second participle in the Great Commission text is *baptizing*. Hahn simply calls it "the entry marker."[8] The sacramental act of baptism upon one's conversion becomes the symbol of entrance into the Christian community and serves as a public profession of faith. It is for this reason that in the early days of the church, those who believed in Christ as Savior were immediately baptized. Water was viewed as a symbol of purification and, therefore, became a lasting image of one who was committed to Christ and thereby became a child of God. Thomas Long puts the process in perspective when he says, "To become a Christian is not to be converted to an ideology; it is to be drawn into kinship with God and with all those who love God. To be baptized is to know that we are no longer slaves, but children of God."[9]

What is the relationship between the participle of *baptizing* and the third participle, *teaching*? In Scripture, it seems that believers were baptized immediately and teaching followed. In many churches today, baptism often follows teaching, the rationale being that one should not be baptized until a solid understanding of the meaning of baptism is reached. In the case of children, some churches set an age limit or require children to attend classes that help them reach a cognitive level of understanding that is acceptable to those in leadership. While this is understandable and practical, if one is honest about reaching a level of knowledge that is acceptable, the question must be asked, Does anyone

7. Long, *Matthew*, 326.
8. Hahn, *Matthew*, 346.
9. Long, *Matthew*, 327.

fully understand what occurs in baptism to an acceptable level? While many can explain the symbolism and meaning of baptism, is it ever possible for anyone to fully understand the work of the Holy Spirit in the act of obedience that is called baptism? It seems that there is much that happens in a person's spirit when baptism occurs that cannot be fully explained. Douglas Hare makes an interesting observation about the relationship between baptism and teaching, "The tense of the participles ("baptizing," "teaching") does not indicate that the Gentiles must be discipled before they are baptized, or baptized before they are taught.... Mathew perceives baptism as occurring in the middle of a discipling-and-teaching process that must continue indefinitely."[10] Perhaps a practical response to this interpretation is to recognize that the teaching of disciples, whether leading up to baptism or following baptism, must be an ongoing practice. Disciples of Jesus must be constantly taught how to live a life of faithfulness to God.

Formal and Informal Teaching

In chapter 4, formal and informal teaching was discussed in detail as it relates to how Jesus taught his students. The subject will be discussed here as well, because formal and informal teaching is an important element in understanding how discipleship occurs. Formal teaching generally takes place in formal environments, such as in a classroom or in any structured setting, and usually includes the use of a curriculum. This is in contrast to informal teaching, which usually occurs during the everyday activities of life. This informal learning often occurs without realization on the part of the teacher that teaching is taking place or by the student that learning is occurring.

Formal teaching has a role in discipleship in that it allows for important empirical information to be learned; however, for purposes of life-change, informal teaching is much more effective. The most familiar and, in the opinion of many, the most effective form of informal teaching is modeling. Modeling occurs most often in families as children are learning how to speak, act, and relate to others by observing adults, their own parents, in particular. Albert Bandura and Richard Walters identify the informal learning that takes place within the family context as an exemplary model of learning.[11] An exemplary model is identified as a form of modeling that is done by those with whom the learner has a personal relationship. This can include family members, friends, or any acquaintance of the learner. These relationships provide a platform for learner imitation that is influenced more by what the model does then by what the model says.

Bandura and Walters identify a second model of informal learning that can be observed in the influence of persons with whom the learner has no personal connection but, nonetheless, has influence due to his or her cultural popularity.[12]

---

10. Hare, *Matthew*, 334.

11. Bandura and Walters, *Social Learning and Personality Development*, 50.

12. Ibid., 49.

The symbolic model includes athletes, movie and television personalities, as well as any person who is culturally popular. An example of this form of influence can be seen any time a celebrity becomes a spokesperson for a particular product. The popularity of the spokesperson can have a significant influence on the success of product sales.

While there is no inherent spiritual development found in these two models, an observant disciple-maker will quickly recognize the applicability of these models to the disciple-making process. Those to whom the disciple is personally connected have a significant place of influence in the life of the disciple. There are also "spiritual giants" in the Christian community who have power to influence in the disciple-making process. Truth be told, all Christians have influence in the lives of numerous people, often when they are unaware of their influence. This influence is not limited to children alone but is effective in the life of any disciple no matter the age. It is for these reasons that living a life in right relationship to God has influence that reaches beyond a personal responsibility to God to a corporate responsibility to God's people. Living a life consistent with the biblical call to holiness is critical for the good of those who are watching how life is to be lived.

Role of the Family

If it is true that discipleship is helping those inside and outside the church to live in a faithful, obedient relationship with God, then the first place in which discipleship must take place is in the family. Diana Garland proposes that the family be understood as both structural and functional.[13] The structural family is the traditional family: parents, children, and relatives. In some circles, this is referred to as the nuclear family. In today's culture, the understanding of structural family extends beyond the traditional family to any structure of family that includes blood or marital relationships. The functional family is made up of those who are not related due to blood or marriage but are intimately connected to persons with whom they have close relationships. These definitions of family will be discussed in relation to their role in the discipleship of followers of Christ.

No role has greater impact upon the discipleship process than that of the structural family. Deuteronomy 6:4–9, known as the *shema*, lays out the responsibilities of parents to nurture their children in the love and admonition of the Lord. The text describes discipleship as taking place after the parents have made God first in their lives and are living in obedience. As they live faithful lives themselves, they become models for their children. The order of this directive is significant, because children cannot be taught what parents have not experienced and do not live out themselves. The next step in the *shema* directs parents to "talk about them all the time, whether you're at home or walking along the road or going to bed at night, or getting up in the morning" (Deut 6:7b). Parents need to

---

13. Garland, *Family Ministry*, 35–38.

recognize that the everyday occurrences of life become opportunities for education. As children observe parents' responses to the frustrations and joys of life, they learn what it means to serve God faithfully. It is in these informal moments, while life is occurring in everyday activities, that significant nurture occurs.

Parents have the opportunity to share life with their children in formal ways. There are key significant times in the regular schedule of life when important formational moments occur. These moments may include setting time aside for the family to read God's Word together, regularly eating a meal together, or praying together before bedtime. These structured times of nurture are important parts of the process of discipleship. Children need to have these formal teachable moments to learn the essentials of the faith. One word of warning: the ritual of repetitive structured moments may have little impact if parents are not demonstrating faithfulness to God in the everyday moments of life. Both informal and formal teaching must occur in the lives of families who desire to walk faithfully with God.

Role of the Church

The church basically has two roles in the disciple-making process: to equip parents to be the spiritual leaders in their families and to "fill the gaps" when parents are unable, on their own, to meet all the spiritual needs of the family. Unfortunately, too often the church has taken upon itself the role of disciple-maker. The church has said, "Bring your family to our church and we will disciple them." Perhaps a renewed focus on the biblical function of the church, to equip the saints and to provide a place for community, will result in a new generation of disciples who understand the call to live holy lives and live out that life in the present kingdom of God. Or said another way, to love God and love others as themselves, the Great Commandment. The best way to develop a new generation of disciples who understand what it means to be followers of Christ is for the church to understand its role in the disciple-making process.

Developing Parents to Be "Just Good Enough"

So, the family plays a key role in the discipleship process of children. In fact, the *shema* instructs parents to walk faithfully with God before they begin the responsibility of training their children in the faith. The difficulty here is that parents often feel inadequate in their own spiritual ability, leading to parents who are intimidated by the thought of adequately instructing their children in spiritual matters. This sense of inadequacy often leads to abandonment of responsibility in an attempt for parents to find a place of safety. By abandoning responsibility, parents think they have avoided any spiritual influence when, in fact, they continue to have influence, even if the influence is negative. Parents need to be assured that they do not need to be perfect in their parenting abilities nor in their depth of personal spiritual development. Scottie May and her colleagues encourages parents with this wonderful proclamation, "Children do not need perfect parents, simply good enough parents."[14] It is in the process of helping parents to be "just good enough" that the church finds itself in one of its most significant roles.

Those who love children and want to see the family be successful in living for God must focus their efforts on helping parents to grow right along with their children. Many pastors who work with children are discovering that as spiritual truths are being taught to children at church, parents are also acknowledging their desire to learn what is being taught to their children. It does not take long before one begins to realize that the church has done a poor job of teaching biblical truth and the beliefs that stem from those truths. There seems to be a generation of adults who are longing to be instructed, possibly for the first time. A renewed interest in raising up a generation who understands what the church believes, and owns its own faith, has become the focus of many pastors. Training moments provide opportunities to help parents understand the significance of the role they play in the spiritual formation of their children and to train them to understand the beliefs of the church, which will help them to have a personal walk with God that is real and active.

In addition to helping parents grow in their own walk with God, the church must provide training for parents that helps them to know how to disciple their children. Systematic plans must be developed to address these needs. A wise leader will not assume he or she knows the needs of parents. While some needs are intuitive, it is a sound strategy to ask parents what they need. What might it look like if a ministry leader asked a group of parents what they needed from the church rather than the leader presenting a plan of what will be provided? Not only will parents be more interested in being involved in ministries that meet their immediate needs, but they will recognize that the church desires to partner with them in helping them to raise their children. *Partnership* is a key word.

With the rise of consumerism in the 1950s and 1960s, parents seemingly began to demand that the church take a leading role in the spiritual development of children. In response, the church told parents that all they needed to do was bring their children to church and the leaders of the church would teach the children what they needed to know. This decision by the church stemmed from a realization that parents are the key spiritual leaders, but because they were not "doing their job" and required the church to provide ministries for their children, the leaders of the church chose to take the place of parents. Although the church chose to replace parents, the role of parents as the spiritual leaders of their families could not be thwarted. Parents will be the spiritual leaders of their families; the only question is what kind of leaders they will be. Churches

---

14. May et al., *Children Matter*, 158.

must acknowledge the role of parents and ask what can be done to help parents become faithful to God in their formation role.

Filling the Gaps

In addition to equipping parents to be the spiritual leaders of their families, there is a second important role that the church must play in the discipleship process. The church must step in and fill the gaps that parents are unable to fill themselves. Many spiritual needs of the family can and should be met by parents, but there are some needs that only the church can fulfill. The church is able to provide ministry to and for the family that cannot be provided by the family. The church can also provide support and opportunities for service that the family needs.

One important role the church plays in filling the gap is providing opportunities for growth that families cannot accomplish fully on their own. Many ministries that are designed for spiritual growth take place best in a communal environment. Take for instance a sex education class that is provided for preteens. Many parents know that they need to discuss a biblical view of sex education with their preteens so they will be prepared for the challenges that are ahead. Yet many parents do not know how to start or what to say. The results are parents who neglect to discuss difficult topics with their children and hope there has been enough Christian training that they have learned to abide by biblical principles. An alternative to this approach of hoping for the best might include a church saying to parents, "We know this is difficult for you. We want to help. Would it help you if we provided classes that you and your preteen could attend together? We could provide a biblical foundation, open up the conversation so it is easier to talk about difficult topics, and provide you with information that will assist you in continuing the conversation beyond our meeting." Parents would then discover that the church really does want to help. They would also realize that we are in this together and that there are other parents in similar situations. This is only one example of the important role the church plays in filling the gap for families.

Families need the church to fill the gap because it is impossible to parent alone. The old African proverb, "It takes a village to raise a child," is very true when it comes to the spiritual nurture of children. Families need other adults to contribute to the spiritual nurture of the family. The church is a place that other adults can speak into the lives of family members. These adults have opportunities to teach in formal and informal settings within the life of the church. As the family of God experiences life together, members of the family are able to model for those who watch them and show them how to live faithfully. Sunday school teachers have a prime opportunity to teach students the truth of Scripture while showing them how to live it out in the course of daily life. These models, no matter who they are or what role they play, become significant contributors to the spiritual nurture of the family.

The church also provides opportunities for the family to engage in service to others. Service occurs both within the church and outside the church. The church provides family members an atmosphere that encourages them to be involved in service to others. This may include serving on the worship team, being a greeter, or working in the nursery. There are also opportunities for the family to serve the community through service projects, school sponsorship, and other outreach ministries. The goal is to assist the family to become a family of life service. Helping the family learn the importance of service to others is a direct response to the second portion of the Great Commandment: love your neighbor as yourself.

The church and families must partner together if the ultimate goal of discipleship of the family is to be achieved. Both the church and families have attempted to be intentional in discipleship, but unfortunately they have often attempted to do it alone. It is time that these two important organizations that were created by God himself partner together to disciple those who have responded to God's amazing grace. When the church and families work together, the possibilities are endless. Reuben Welch was right when he wrote *We Really Do Need Each Other.*[15]

An apropos conclusion to the call to intentional discipleship is stated by Rodger Hahn in his commentary on Matthew:

In Matthew's gospel, the life of discipleship is always the journey of following Jesus. Even the final words of the Gospel, the Great Commission, are framed in terms of discipleship as the Christ-formed life. We do not need new techniques or marketing skills to be the followers Christ envisioned. If we will allow ourselves to be formed, informed, and transformed…, we will discover ourselves on a journey with Jesus into the heart of obedience to God the Father. God requires nothing more—or less—of us.[16]

---

15. Welch, *We Really Do Need Each Other.*
16. Hahn, *Matthew*, 347.

Bibliography

Bandura, Albert and Richard H. Walters. *Social Learning and Personality Development.* New York: Holt, Rinehart and Winston, 1963.

Boring, M. Eugene. *The Gospel of Matthew. The New Interpreter's Bible.* Nashville, TN: Abingdon Press, 1995.

Garland, Diana R. *Family Ministry: A Comprehensive Guide.* Downer's Grove, IL: InterVarsity Press, 1999.

Hagner, Donald A. *Matthew 14-28.* Vol. *33B, Word Biblical Commentary.* Dallas, TX: Word Books, 1993.

Hahn, Rodger L. *Matthew. A Commentary for Bible Students.* Indianapolis, IN: Wesleyan Publishing House, 2007.

Hare, Douglas R. A. *Matthew. Interpretation: A Bible Commentary for Teaching and Preaching.* Louisville, KY: John Knox Press, 1993.

Long, Thomas G. *Matthew. Westminister Bible Companion.* Louisville, KY: Westminster John Knox Press, 1997.

May, Scottie, Beth Posterski, Catherine Stonehouse, and Linda Cannell. *Children Matter: Celebrating Their Place in the Church, Family, and Community.* Grand Rapids, MI: William B. Eerdmans Publishing Company, 2005.

Smith, Robert H. *Matthew. Augsburg Commentary on the New Testament.* Minneapolis, MI: Augsburg Publishing Company, 1989.

Welch, Reuben. *We Really Do Need Each Other.* Nashville, TN: Impact Books, [1973].

Wilkins, Michael J. *Matthew. The NIV Application Commentary.* Grand Rapids, MI: Zondervan, 2004.

CHAPTER TWENTY

Camps and Retreats

MICHAEL D. SANDERS

> But so many people were coming and going that Jesus and the apostles did not even have a chance to eat. Then Jesus said, "Let's go to a place where we can be alone and get some rest."
>
> —Mark 6:31

Within the sixth chapter, Mark records several events that Jesus and his disciples experienced that led to his invitation in verse 31. In verses 1–6, as Jesus and his disciples come into his hometown of Nazareth, they experience rejection that prompts Jesus' words: "Prophets are honored by everyone, except the people of their hometown and their relatives and their own family" (v 4).

In verses 7–12, Jesus sends out the disciples to minister with specific instructions. They go out and according to verses 12 and 13 have great success. However, even with great success, ministry depletes physical and spiritual energy and the disciples need renewal and refreshment after such ministry experiences.

Then in verses 14–29, Mark records the events leading up to the beheading of John the Baptist. And in verse 29, Mark says that the disciples took the body of John and gave him a proper burial. This event must have depleted their emotional energy as they buried their ministry colleague and the one who had come to proclaim the coming Messiah.

Rejection, the demands of ministry, and emotional stress had taken a toll on the disciples and Jesus knew they needed retreat, quiet, and rest. The invitation was laid before them and they went away. However, the crowds followed, and the compassion of Jesus (v 34) led to further ministry: the feeding of the five thousand.

Ministry demands had preempted the retreat. However, Ruth Haley Barton comments, "But before the miracle is even cleaned up, Jesus is back on mission and says to them, 'I'll finish up here. You go ahead to that solitary place, because it is still what you need most' (Mark 6:45)."[1] Mark then states that after Jesus sends the disciples away and dismisses the crowd, he himself goes to the mountain to pray (v 46).

The invitation of Jesus to his disciples to retreat, quiet, and rest was rooted in his own habit. Luke's Gospel records how Jesus often found a solitary place (Luke 4:1–13; 4:42–44; 5:12–16; 6:12–16; 9:18–20; 21:34–38 and 22:39–46). It was during these times that Jesus communed with his Father as he made decisions, faced ministry tasks, and ultimately gave his life. Jesus' example points to the importance and necessity of these times in a disciple's life and ministry.

Gordon MacDonald, in *Restoring Your Spiritual Passion*, relates a wonderful story from Lettie Cowman's book *Springs in the Valley*:

> In the deep jungles of Africa, a traveler was making a long trek. Coolies (natives) had been engaged from a tribe to carry the loads. The first day they marched rapidly and went far. The traveler had high hopes of a speedy journey. But the second morning these jungle tribesmen refused to move. For some strange reason they just sat and rested. On inquiry as to the reason for this strange behavior, the traveler was informed that they have gone too fast the first day, and that *they were now waiting for their souls to catch up with their bodies.* Then Mrs. Cowman concludes with this penetrating exhortation: This whirling rushing life which so many of us lives does for us what that first march did for those jungle tribesmen. The difference: they knew what they needed to restore life's balance; too often we do not (196–97).[2]

Mark's narrative, Jesus' example and this devotional illustration set the stage for the needed "Come away" time in one's life. The NRSV translates Jesus' words in Mark 6:31, "Come away to a deserted place all by yourselves and rest a while." Whether in full-time professional ministry or not, hectic schedules deplete resources—physical, spiritual, emotional—and humans need time for renewal and refreshment. Jesus' instructions to his original disciples and the

---

1. Barton, *Sacred Rhythms*, 39.

2. Mrs. Charles E. Cowman, *Springs in the Valley* (Los Angeles, CA: Oriental Missionary Society, 1939), 196–97; as quoted in MacDonald, *Restoring Your Spiritual Passion*, 26 (emphasis added).

example of his own life give permission to modern-day disciples to seek out that "Come away" time and place for holistic health.

Sabbath

The concept of "Come away" is rooted in the Sabbath principle taught in Scripture. There is always a temptation to equate Sabbath with the commandments given to Moses on Sinai. However, upon further reflection, this principle actually originates in the creation story of Genesis. "So the heavens and the earth and everything else were created. By the seventh day God had finished his work, and so he rested. God blessed the seventh day and made it special because on that day he rested from his work" (Gen 2:1–3).

God rests on the seventh day, not from being tired and worn out after all of the creating, but as an example and out of compassion for all of creation. After God's creative actions, a rhythm of work and rest is established and the seventh day is set aside as a special and holy day in order to emphasize this needed rhythm. Even the commandment that comes later alludes to the creation account of Genesis:

Remember that the Sabbath Day belongs to me. You have six days when you can do your work, but the seventh day of each week belongs to me, your God. No one is to work on that day—not you, your children, your slaves, your animals, or the foreigners who live in your towns. In six days I made the sky, the earth, the oceans, and everything in them, but on the seventh day I rested. That's why I made the Sabbath a special day that belongs to me. (Ex 20:8–11)

One might say that Sabbath is a weekly "Come away" time established by God for his people to be refreshed and renewed. Our busy world and lives many times keep us from Sabbath experiences that really accomplish those purposes. Ruth Haley Barton contends:

The point of the Sabbath is to honor our need for a sane rhythm of work and rest. It is to honor the body's need for rest, the spirit's need for replenishment and the soul's need to delight itself in God for God's own sake. It begins with the willingness to acknowledge the limits of our humanness and take steps to live more graciously within the order of things."[3]

According to Barton, this Sabbath experience is so important for a person's well-being, she quotes Wayne Muller's powerful statement; "If we do not allow

---

3. Barton, *Sacred Rhythms*, 137.

for a rhythm of rest in our overly busy lives, illness becomes our Sabbath—our pneumonia, our cancer, our heart attack, our accidents create Sabbath for us."[4]

The call of Jesus for his disciples to "Come away" is rooted in the Sabbath principle of Scripture. This lays a foundation for an emphasis on weekly experiences as well as extended Sabbath time in the form of retreats and other venues, such as Christian camping. Seeking healthy rhythms, disciples choose to leave behind busy schedules, to seek places of solitude, to be in God's creation and to have focused time with God in order to be renewed and refreshed.

Retreats

According to *The Upper Room Dictionary of Christian Spiritual Formation,* retreats are "intentional times alone with God to listen and to respond to the Holy, possibly interspersed with individual or communal guidance or spiritual direction."[5] This definition identifies important concepts that are necessary for the establishment of a spiritual retreat. First, intentionality is required to set aside the necessary time and space. These kinds of things rarely happen without planning and preparation. Second, the need to identify a place for solitude, such as a favorite chair, an afternoon in the backyard, a day in the park, or an extended time in a retreat center. And third, a simple plan for the actual retreat time.

Emilie Griffin, in *Wilderness Time*, answers the question, "What is a retreat?"

Spiritual retreat is simply a matter of going into a separate place to seek Christian growth in a disciplined way. Retreat offers us the grace to be ourselves in God's presence without self-consciousness, without masquerade. Retreat provides the chance to be both physically and spiritually refreshed. It is the blessed opportunity to spend time generously in the presence of God. In such a time, God helps us to empty ourselves of cares and anxieties, to be filled up with wisdom that restores us.[6]

Griffin's description focuses on seeking a place for growth. It is finding a place from the normal routines of life so that one can concentrate on being in God's presence without interruption and over an extended period of time. Out of this time comes refreshment, both physical and spiritual.

Throughout church history, "Christian spirituality retreats have played a primary role for those who seek a deepening relationship with the Creator."[7] These times have been critical for extended time with the Holy, spiritual refresh-

---

4. Ibid., 131.
5. Canham, "Retreats," 236.
6. Griffin, *Wilderness Time*, 17.
7. Canham, "Retreats," 236.

ment and growth. Any yet "we often feel so harried that we can barely imagine leaving our whirl of responsibility behind, even for a short time."[8]

Griffin asks the question, "Why should I make a retreat?" She answers: "You should make it because your heart demands it, because a definite yearning calls you to something better, something more...Because the stirrings of grace are prompting you, because the Lord is inviting you to spend time in the courts of praise."[9]

Jones gives an initial reason for going on a retreat:

People are discovering that the din of daily life can drown out what one ancient spiritual sage called a still, small voice. The weight of duty can flatten us and squeeze us dry of energy. Only getting free from the press of distractions lets us recover our senses. Only as we pull apart for a time can we allow God to put us back again.[10]

Combined, these authors give valid reasons for making retreat a part of one's spiritual journey and formation. Griffin focuses on *the heart's demand...a yearning for something more...the prompting of grace...and the Lord's invitation.* Jones reminds one of *the weight of life, the loss of energy, the distractions that drown out the "still small voice."* As people begin to recognize the invitation and their own life condition, plans need to be made for needed refreshment.

Types of Retreat

Once one has identified the value and need for retreat, what are the options? Canham identifies several categories of retreats: "preached retreat, directed retreat, private retreats, and at home retreats."[11] Jones identifies traditional offerings: "Preached or conference-style retreat, Married or engaged couple's retreats, Guided retreats and Directed retreats."[12] He also shares other possibilities, such as "a prayer retreat, a vocational discernment retreat, a special-need retreat, a working retreat, a retreat spent with classical spiritual-life writings, a group retreat, a holy vacation and a retreat spent with a spouse or friend."[13]

One begins to see that there are traditional offerings that have met the needs of persons and groups down through the years. But retreat experiences can also be tailored to the specific needs of an individual or group in reference to their season or need of life. Following are some simple descriptions of retreat types identified in *The Upper Room Dictionary of Christian Spiritual Formation:*

---

8. Jones, *Place for God*, 3.
9. Griffin, *Wilderness Time*, 17.
10. Jones, *Place for God*, 19.
11. Canham, "Retreats," 236–37.
12. Jones, *Place for God*, 77–78.
13. Ibid., 71–76.

A "preached retreat" is usually offered in a church or monastic setting in conjunction with regular worship times or "offices." The conductor gives addresses followed by silence for personal prayer. There is no group interaction, but individual conferences and/or confession are available.

A "directed retreat" provides regular meetings between the retreatant and her or his "director," whose role is to listen, guide and support the retreatant's developing relationship with God.

"Private retreats" may benefit those who have experienced retreats in the past and are ready to choose time alone in a context conducive to contemplation. This type of retreat has no director, but a rhythm of regular worship and simple accommodations, food, and lifestyle supports the retreatant's desire to place herself or himself simply in the presence of God.

"At home retreats" are an important alternative for those unable to attend retreats due to infirmity or childcare responsibilities. Often a book will be used to offer an outline, and the retreat leader will meet in person or by telephone with the retreatant.[14]

With a variety of retreat options, Griffin and Jones continue to give reasons and simple instructions for participating in a corporate retreat or planning a personal experience. Jones even provides a *Directory of Retreat and Guest Houses* in the United States and Canada. Broken down into regions, each entry provides contact information (including address, phone number, and Web site), a simple description of the retreat center, accommodations and reservation information, and points of interest in the nearby area.

Planning a Retreat

The Christian Camp and Conference Association (CCCA) provides *Seven Steps for Effective Retreats* by John Pearson. This is a valuable resource for anyone planning a corporate retreat for a Sunday school class, small group participants, a choir retreat or an entire congregation. The steps identified are: (1) purpose, (2) promotion, (3) personnel, (4) program, (5) place, (6) price, and (7) post-retreat evaluation and follow-up.[15] This resource can also be modified for an individual who seeks a personal experience.

While all steps are important, steps one and seven seem to be pivotal for a successful retreat, whether corporate or individual. Establishing a clear purpose is essential so that plans can be made to concentrate the experience. And post-retreat evaluation will let one know if indeed the purpose has been achieved. A

---

14. Canham, "Retreats," 236–37.

15. Pearson, *Seven Steps for Effective Retreats*.

student responded in a paper that her experiences growing up attending camps and retreats lacked this very ingredient. Significant decisions were not followed up, and in her case, the spiritual high of the experience quickly faded. Had there been more effective planning and follow-up, who knows how much farther along she might be in her spiritual journey?

Intentionality is the key: to set aside needed time for retreat, to establish healthy rhythms for spiritual growth, to break away from the ruts and routines in order to be refreshed and renewed, for these things will not happen on their on. In *A Guide to Prayer for Ministers and Other Servants,* Rueben P. Job and Norman Shawchuck speak of this intentionality when they identify their commitment to "solitude and prayer…at least one hour each day, one day each month, and one week each year."[16]

Within the Christian community, there are many offerings of retreats, conferences and workshops. Ministers are inundated with invitations to the latest conference and the newest hot topic. These are good and important events for gaining new information, honing skills, and networking. However, they are usually scheduled with little down time, quiet, and rest. It is necessary to find the time and place for real retreat so that disciples can be refreshed and renewed in their lives and ministries.

Early in the book of Acts, Peter and John are arrested and brought before the Council (Acts 4). In their deliberations and interaction, Luke gives an amazing insight in verse 13. As the Council is demanding a response from the disciples as to their authority, they were well aware that these men were followers of Christ. Luke states, "The officials were amazed to see how brave Peter and John were, and they knew these two apostles were only ordinary men and not well educated. The officials were certain that these men had been with Jesus" (Acts 4:13).

This statement could be understood that they were simply associates of the man called Jesus. However a deeper understanding could be the miracle, the proclamation of the gospel, the bravery of these ordinary, uneducated men, all were the result of being in the presence of Jesus. There is something supernatural and extraordinary that happens when disciples spend time in the presence of the divine.

Establishing a clear understanding of retreat, knowing why they are needed in one's spiritual journey, determining the type of retreat that is needed, and knowing how to plan an experience from start to finish: these are the ingredients disciples need to chart effectively the course for refreshment and renewal in their spiritual journeys and lifelong formation.

Christian Camping

Many Christians can give testimony to significant decisions made during a "Come away" time at a Christian camp. Whether during a response time in a

---

16. Job and Shawchuck, *Guide to Prayer*, 12.

service, a Bible study/conference, or around a campfire, decisions for Christ are made that impact lives and eternity. These decisions to follow Christ have led to further discipleship experiences, leadership development, and responding to God's call to full-time professional ministry.

The Vision of the Christian Camp and Conference Association (CCCA) states the following:

> The Christian Camp and Conference Association will increasingly become a support ministry for Christian camp and conference leaders who will be encouraged, trained, resourced, and motivated to make their ministry-driven organizations vital in the process of raising up millions of followers of Jesus Christ. These followers will have a noticeable impact within the church and secular society worldwide. The time has come for Christian camps and conferences to be at the forefront of making disciples who will enter the fray of a post-Christian world to make a difference.[17]

CCCA is an organization that supports many denominational and independent church camps throughout North America. Particular camps have specific visions, purposes, and programming, and it is CCCA's desire to invest its knowledge and resources to help these camps succeed. The association's vision points to what many give testimony to in their camping experience: coming to know Christ, being discipled in the faith, experiencing God's call, and moving out into a world in need to make a difference.

Within CCCA's vision, one sees the goal of preparing leaders for the "raising up millions of followers of Jesus Christ." On its Web site CCCA reports:

> Every year, nearly eight million people are involved in the programs of CCCA member camps and conferences, and tens of thousands come to faith in Jesus Christ...What's more, 120,000-plus churches in America are served by CCCA member organizations, and more than 420,000 adults are now involved in full-time Christian work as the result of decisions made at CCCA member camps and centers.[18]

Christian camping has and continues to make an incredible impact upon those who participate. Providing opportunities for students to leave their routines and responsibilities for a period of time, placing them in a setting where focused attention can be given to specific topics and themes, and creating experiences where everyday distractions can be reduced to allow for communion with

---

17. Christian Camp and Conference Association. "Our Vision, Mission and Values." http://www.ccca.org/public/about/visionmissionvalues.asp (accessed March 19, 2010).

18. Ibid.

the divine, this is where transformation can happen. These three elements are critical in providing a "Come away" experience for campers.

First, leaving routines and responsibilities behind allows participants to lay aside school, jobs, home chores, and other activities that keep one busy, distracted, and often just plain exhausted. The excitement of leaving home and going to a different setting with friends and other similar students allows for the anticipation of something special to happen.

Second, the new setting allows for camp directors, counselors, special speakers, and conference leaders to focus on specific topics and themes that students are facing. In the midst of all the fun (and it should be fun), the camping experience offers focused attention through devotions, conferences, services, and other planned activities that can impact students' discipleship journeys.

Third, leaving and focusing allows participants the opportunity to commune with the divine, where true transformation occurs. Being in nature, participating in experiences that have been intentionally designed for campers, and allowing time for thought, interaction, and reflection allows participants to "Calm down and learn that I am God" (Ps 46:10).

When these three elements are combined with competent leaders, a beautiful camp setting, and intentionality in planning that takes advantage of the "Come away" moment, possibilities for transformation are heightened.

However, Mike Yaconelli claims that "Christian camping is dead." He states, "I don't mean camps aren't thriving across America. What I do mean is that many have sold their souls to American culture."[19] He gives a vivid description of his meaning:

> What do people want today in their camping experience? They want a high-tech, activity-filled experience complete with all the comforts of home. They want high-profile, dynamic speakers with Powerpoint presentations, worship bands, and the latest audio equipment. They want Internet access, cell phone capabilities, and easy parking close to their cabins. They want jet skis, boats, ATV's, snowmobiles, go-karts, mountain bikes, ropes courses, and mountain climbing equipment.[20]

Within this article he describes an experience of Christian camping that had a schedule from 6:30 AM until midnight. Within this quiet, serene, and pristine setting, activities were planned for every minute of the day, and at the end of the day, he noticed how tired and worn out everyone was. Their camping experience had not slowed them down and given them opportunities for quiet walks to listen for the voice of God. It had just replicated their daily lives in another setting.

---

19. Yaconelli, "Is This Christian Camping?," 11.

20. Ibid.

In his usual way, Yaconelli challenges the reader to step back and reconsider the need for camping to be a place where one breaks away from the hectic routines of life and spends time in the presence of God. His challenge is to be a "risk-taker" and "take a hard look at how it [Christian camping] has been secularized."[21] He concludes:

> Are camps truly places of spirituality, refuge, quiet, risk, and imagination? Instead of racing toward the latest twenty-first century technological and recreational trends to make the camping experience more meaningful, it's time to take a look backward at the heritage of Christian camping and the timeless truths of God's Word.[22]

Five Values of Christian Camping

In its Focus Series 6, the CCCA has identified five significant values that are realized in the Christian camping experience. They are: "1) Genuine community is experienced, 2) Ministry to the whole person takes place, 3) Relationships are built with God and others, 4) Memories and major life commitments are made and 5) Tomorrow's leaders are developed today."[23] As churches are providing camping experiences, these values can guide their planning.

Each individual Christian group, camp, and retreat center has its values, vision, and purpose statement. A quick search of the Internet produces a significant amount of valuable information as camps and retreat centers share their programming. These CCCA values are simply guidelines they have established in working with the many and various camps and retreat centers over the years.

Bud Williams believes that as campers leave the familiar routines and surroundings of home and come into contact with other campers, counselors, and leaders, the ingredients for experiences of genuine community are heightened.[24] This means that camp personnel must intentionally plan and program for the enhancement of community experiences.

Citing Luke 2:52, where Luke gives the synopsis of Jesus growing as a young man, mentally, physically, spiritually, and socially, Williams claims, "Camp, in the midst of God's glorious creation, is an ideal environment for whole person ministry."[25] The setting, physical activities, conferences and services, quiet times, and late night cabin conversations all contribute to this value of wholeness.

There are many campers who can point to lifelong friendships that resulted from their camping experiences. Year in and year out, these friendships were formed and developed. From peers to mentors, the camping experience lends

21. Ibid., 13.
22. Ibid.
23. Williams, *Five Values of Christian Camping*.
24. Ibid.
25. Ibid.

itself to the building of relationships. And, of course, the most important relationship that most Christian camps want to see experienced is a relationship with Jesus Christ as Savior and Lord.

Out of this most important relationship, other relationships and mutual experiences, memories are made for a lifetime. Williams asserts, "Camp is a distinct and intensive experience that will forever stand out from other life experiences in campers' memories."[26] In a Christian college setting, it is not unusual to hear students speak of their summer days at camp that will always include their friendships, their memorable experiences (some of camp lore), and the spiritual impact that camp had on their life and ministry calling.

The last value that Williams identifies is that of leadership development. Camp chores, cabin devotions and experiences, group activities and competitions, and speakers and services challenging students to step up and make a difference, all set the stage for the development of leadership skills. Shown above, CCCA's own statistics point to thousands who are in full-time ministry and other leadership positions who have passed through camps and retreat centers affiliated with that association.

The values of CCCA are meant to give guidance to association members as each camp and retreat center attempts to provide quality experiences for its constituents. These values are not automatic. They must be guiding principles that leaders use as they plan and implement their individual camps and retreats. As leaders better understand the value and purpose of a camping experience, not only in the life of a student, but also for the church, community, and world, values must lead to planning significant experiences that are truly life transforming.

Conclusion

Jesus called his disciples to a "Come away" experience for rest and renewal. This invitation was rooted in Jesus' own habits and the Sabbath principle that finds its genesis in the creation story. As modern and postmodern disciples, one finds this need more and more as the demands of ministry and the world seem to grow more complex and exhausting.

This chapter has focused on the "Come away" times of historic and traditional offerings within the Christian community of retreats and Christian camping. These have been and continue to be significant experiences for disciples on the journey of spiritual transformation and growth. There are agencies that have been identified that can provide resources from significant commitment and experience in order that "Come away" times can be planned in whatever setting and format one would desire.

The call of Christ is a call to growth and maturity, not for personal glory or adulation, but for the glory of God! It seems as though growth and maturity are assumed in the life of the disciple of Christ, but not automatic. It is of utmost

26. Ibid.

importance for Christians and their organizations to leverage all of the resources and opportunities that are available so that disciples can grow and mature.

The apostle Peter closed his second letter with an appeal for continued growth in the lives of those receiving his words of encouragement and instruction. He states, "Let the wonderful kindness and the understanding that come from our Lord and Savior Jesus Christ help you keep on growing. Praise Jesus now and forever! Amen" (II Peter 3:18).

In the midst of the rush, routines and the distractions of a postmodern culture, whether in the church or world, can one stop, step away for a moment and hear the compassionate call of the Master to his current disciples: *"Come away?"*

Bibliography

Badke, Jim. *The Christian Camp Counselor.* Crofton, BC, Canada: Qwanoes Publishing, 2004.

Barton, Ruth Haley. *Sacred Rhythms.* Downer's Grove, IL: InterVarsity Press, 2006.

Canham, Elizabeth J. "Retreats." In *The Upper Room Dictionary of Christian Spiritual Formation,* edited by Keith Beasley-Topliffe, 236–37. Nashville, TN: Upper Room Books, 2003.

Church of God Ministries, Inc. *Retreat Handbook.* Anderson, IN: Church of God Ministries, Inc., 2001.

Graendorf, Werner C. and L. D. Mattson. *An Introduction to Christian Camping.* Chicago: Moody Press, 1979.

Griffin, Emilie. *Wilderness Time: A Guide for Spiritual Retreat.* San Francisco, CA: HarperSanFrancisco, 1997.

Job, Rueben P. and Norman Shawchuck. *A Guide to Prayer for Ministers and Other Servants.* Nashville, TN: The Upper Room, 1983.

Jones, Timothy. *A Place for God.* New York: Image Books Doubleday. 2000.

MacDonald, Gordon. *Restoring Your Spiritual Passion.* Nashville, TN: Thomas Nelson, 1986.

MacKay, Joy. *Creative Counseling for Christian Camps.* Wheaton, IL: Scripture Press Publishing, 1975

Mattson, Lloyd. *Christian Camping Today: A Complete Handbook for the Short-term Staff.* Wheaton, IL: Harold Shaw Publishers, 1998.

_____. *Camp Counseling Today.* Saskatchewan: K & K Camping Publications, 1990.

Pearson, John. *Mastering the Management Buckets.* Ventura, CA: Regal, 2008.

———. *Seven Steps for Effective Retreats.* CCCA Focus Series 4. Colorado Springs, CO: Christian Camp and Conference Association, 2007.

Williams, George "Bud." *Five Values of Christian Camping.* CCCA Focus Series 6. Colorado Springs, CO: Christian Camp and Conference Association, 2009.

Yaconelli, Mike. "Is This Christian Camping?" *Christian Camp and Conference Journal*, July / August 2003, 11–13.

Web Sites

Christian Camp and Conference Association, www.ccca.org
Christian Camping International, cciworldwide.org
The American Camp Association, www.acacamps.org

CHAPTER TWENTY-ONE

Christian Education Across the Lifespan

JOHN H. AUKERMAN

> I also remember the genuine faith of your mother Eunice. Your grandmother Lois had the same sort of faith, and I am sure that you have it as well.
>
> —2 Timothy 1:5

In the twentieth century, Christian educators began applying the insights of the new science of human development. Taking developmental differences into account, they modified their approaches to teaching and learning. For example, the format of the Uniform Series when it was created in 1872 was for students of all ages to study the same passage of Scripture on Sundays; this was modified in 1922 in favor of a graded curriculum that provided age-appropriate biblical content for all students. Today, many curriculum plans direct children to one set of Bible stories, teens to another set, and adults to a third set (a common pattern is a three-year or six-year cycle of Bible study).

As churches increased in size and educational sophistication, they began to build educational facilities that took human development issues into consideration. Churches today commonly provide a nursery with cribs, rocking chairs, changing tables, and running water. For toddlers, churches have rooms with age-appropriate toys (large motor-skill toys, made of materials that are safe for young children), and plenty of space for movement. As a child continues to grow into preschool, early elementary, middle elementary, and later elementary years, churches regularly provide age-appropriate teaching-learning spaces and equipment. The same is true for teens and adults. (Chapter 17 presents these issues in depth.)

The alert reader has already noticed that this book does not have separate chapters on children's ministry, youth ministry, and adult ministry, because the authors made the judgment that Christian educators should see their teaching ministry in the lifelong framework. Learning begins *in utero* and continues through a dying person's final breath. Chapter 18 explores the reality that everything the church does teaches, which includes the way it relates to and ministers with pregnant mothers and their preborn children at one end of life and dying great-grandfathers at the other end.

Developmental Tasks and the Teachable Moment

In 1948, Robert J. Havighurst published a small pamphlet on developmental tasks for use in his teaching at the University of Chicago. He traced the genesis of this concept back to the 1930s and credited others with giving birth to the idea. In 1952 he elaborated the concept and republished it; he then did a major revision for his 1972 edition. Nothing more important has been published in the intervening decades to supplant Havighurst's foundational contribution to teaching and learning. In his words, "A developmental task is a task which arises at or about a certain period in the life of the individual, successful achievement of which leads to his [or her] happiness and to success with later tasks, while failure leads to unhappiness in the individual, disapproval by the society, and difficulty with later tasks."[1]

Developmental tasks are important for Christian educators because they give valuable clues about when is the right time for a person to learn important biblical truths. An obvious example would be the nursery worker trying to use a fill-in-the-blank worksheet on the birth of Jesus: Infants are not ready to learn to read and write. But older children are learning reading and writing and can benefit from simple worksheets. Another example would be biblical guidelines for dating and sexual purity: The obvious time for learning that material is in the preteen and early teen years. No thoughtful Christian educator would delay those lessons to age 18. Similar insights pervade the whole concept of developmental tasks and impact the teaching ministry of the church at all times, in all places, and during all events.

Havighurst summarized these concerns: "Efforts at teaching, which would have been largely wasted if they had come earlier, give gratifying results when they come at the *teachable moment*, when the task should be learned."[2] It is also important to realize that teaching efforts should not be delayed until months or

---

1. Havighurst, *Developmental Tasks and Education*, 2.
2. Ibid., 7.

years after the teachable moment. The teachable moment is when need meets opportunity. The learner, of whatever age, needs to learn certain ideas, attitudes, or skills, and the alert teacher recognizes the need and has an opportunity to teach.

Therefore, Christian education across the lifespan will value and use the insights of developmental tasks and the teachable moment. Most published curriculum material is based on these concepts, and the wise church teacher will not only be aware of them but will recognize them when they appear in the curriculum and will use them in the classroom at the appropriate times.

Following is a summary of Havighurst's developmental tasks, all taken from the third edition of his book. Across the list, a few implications are suggested as illustrations of how a particular developmental task can and should affect Christian teaching. The practitioner will be the best one to identify appropriate implications for teaching. Best teaching practices would maintain awareness of the developmental tasks, would be alert for teachable moments, and would take advantage of every opportunity to teach and nurture all across the lifespan.

1. Developmental Tasks of Infancy and Childhood

- **Learning to walk:**
  Teachers in a church nursery can assist, but not force, an infant in her first attempts at walking. This is opposed to ignoring the child while talking to other adults or listening to the music that is being piped in from the worship service.

- **Learning to take solid foods:**
  Nursery workers can offer appropriate snacks, with parental permission.

- **Learning to talk:**
  Nursery attendants can repeat key words, beginning with one-syllable words, and encourage the infant to mimic the sound.

- **Learning to control the elimination of body wastes:**
  The parents will inform the nursery staff when potty training begins, and the staff will support parents in this important developmental task.

- **Learning sex differences and sexual modesty:**
  Infants will wear appropriate clothing so as to protect their modesty. Boys go in the boys' restroom, and girls go in the girls' restroom.

- **Forming concepts and learning language to describe social and physical reality:**
  Christian educators can point to a picture and teach the young child to say, "Jesus." Teachers can also say things like, "Mommy will be back when worship is over."

- **Getting ready to read:**
  The nursery teacher can hold a child on the lap and read age-appropriate books aloud, pointing to key words, encouraging the child to repeat words.

- **Learning to distinguish right and wrong and beginning to develop a conscience:**
  Workers can share Bible stories about right and wrong, offering overt teaching about doing the right things and avoiding the wrong things.

2. Developmental Tasks of Middle Childhood

- **Learning physical skills necessary for ordinary games:**
  Teachers choose games that are within the skill set of children ages five to nine, games that are neither too easy nor too difficult for middle children to play.

- **Building wholesome attitudes toward oneself as a growing organism:**
  Educators teach lessons on self-esteem; help children know that their growing and changing bodies are good—it is as God planned.

- **Learning to get along with age-mates:**
  Helping children learn to treat everyone as a child of God.

- **Learning an appropriate masculine or feminine social role:**
  (See comments on this developmental task under #3, Adolescence, below.)

- **Developing fundamental skills in reading, writing, and calculating:**
  Using the academic skills that children are learning in school; making sure the lessons are not too simple or too difficult.

- **Developing concepts necessary for everyday living:**
  Having a play house or a play kitchen, and pretending to have a tea party or serve imaginary cookies.

- **Developing conscience, morality, and a scale of values:**
  When a child takes a toy away from another child, intervening and helping the offender to know that this was not the right thing to do. Helping children learn to apologize and forgive. Prizing Christian values and avoiding worldly values.

- **Achieving personal independence:**
  Saying something like, "Yes! You put on your coat and buttoned it up all by yourself! I'm so proud of you!"

- **Developing attitudes toward social groups and institutions:**
  Helping children understand and value that people who are "different" (Black, White, Hispanic, Chinese) are all made in the image of God and are just as loved as they are.

3. Developmental Tasks of Adolescence

- **Achieving new and more mature relations with age-mates of both sexes:**
  In early adolescence, it is important to have friends who are girls and friends who are boys. These relationships need to be on a deeper level than earlier relationships—planning projects together, learning to trust and be trustworthy, and so forth.

- **Achieving a masculine or feminine social role:**
  When Havighurst identified this developmental task, there were certain assumed roles for women and men in society. Many of those assumptions have proven false and have broken down. For twenty-first-century Christian educators, one path of wisdom might be to assist teens to achieve the gender roles that they feel comfortable with and are accepted in the local context, and to offer loving and caring support to teens who experiment with countercultural gender roles.

- **Accepting one's physique and using the body effectively:**
  Physical development and body image are key issues for both boys and girls during adolescence. Because of the simple fact that there is not much one can do about the body they have been given, it becomes critically important for teens to know that they are loved by significant adult Christians, regardless of the size, shape, or color of their body.

- **Achieving emotional independence of parents and other adults:**
  Perhaps church educators have more opportunity to assist teens with this developmental task than many others in society. Lessons can be offered, counseling can be done, and supportive relationships with teens and their parents can help tremendously in this important task. For many adolescents, earning their driving license is a milestone event; there would be nothing wrong with the church's recognizing this and affirming them in an appropriate public setting.

- **Preparing for marriage and family life:**
  This was written in 1972, when societal assumptions were that "everyone gets married." Those assumptions were wrong then and are still wrong today. In place of this developmental task, one might say something like, "Preparing either for independent living or for marriage and family life."

- **Preparing for an economic career:**
  Christian leaders should be on the lookout for young people who might have gifts and/or a call to ministry. In previous generations, this was the norm, but it has ceased to be the practice in many quarters. The author of this chapter was planning a career in electrical engineering when he was sixteen years old, until his pastor put an arm around his shoulder and suggested that he consider the ministry.

- **Acquiring a set of values and an ethical system as a guide to behavior. —developing an ideology:**
  Teens decide who they are (their self-identity) in relationship with their peers and adult mentors, so it is vitally important that they be in a sound youth ministry in relationship with authentic Christian adults; they are making choices right now that will have lifelong and life-changing ramifications.

- **Desiring and achieving socially responsible behavior:**
  Even though one of the chief concerns of adolescence is self-identity (an answer to the question, Who am I?), they must also learn to relate to others in socially responsible ways. For instance, teens need help from the church to accept cooperative values and to reject gang-oriented behaviors and bullying.

4. Development Tasks of Early Adulthood

- **Getting started in an occupation:**
  Unfortunately, it is during the young adult years that many have separated themselves from the church. But Christian leaders need to be aware of the young adults and the vocational choices they are making, and do whatever is in their power to encourage them to pray and seek God's will in choosing a career.

- **Managing a home:**
  When surveyed, many young adults say that one of the major things the church can do is to offer training for this developmental task. They are ready to learn, and this is a teachable moment.

- **Taking on civic responsibility:**
  Sermons and lessons can be offered on what it means to be a good citizen of one's country. Care must be taken to avoid mixing love for country with love for God and making an idol out of the nation and its symbols, but there are many valid points to be made about a Christian's responsibility in society.

- **Finding a congenial social group:**
  Most young adults do not find such a group in church, so they find friends elsewhere. It would be much better for them, and for the church, if the church would proactively plan friendship events and activities for young adults, with biblical and spiritual content.

- **Selecting a mate:**
  This is another value from the 1970s, when it was assumed that everyone got married. This developmental task and the next three seem to be true for most, but not all, adults. It would be best if young adults who marry

were to choose marriage partners from the same faith; when they are young and in love, they see no problem mixing faiths, but when children come along, so do the problems.

- **Learning to live with a marriage partner:**
Churches are in possession of much powerful information about building and sustaining deep, meaningful relationships. Young married couples need classes, seminars, and marriage enrichment opportunities, because learning to live with an "other" is no small task.

- **Starting a family:**
When those who choose to marry are blessed with offspring, the church can support them in many ways: baby showers, baby dedications/baptisms (depending on the church's tradition), babysitting service, and much more.

- **Rearing children:**
Again, the biblical basis for building and sustaining relationships applies to young parents who are learning to relate to their children in meaningful and life-changing ways. Churches can offer child-rearing classes and parent support groups.

5. Developmental Tasks of Middle Age

- **Assisting teen-age children to become responsible and happy adults:**
Obviously, this task applies only to those who had children. But it is a crucial developmental task. "Cutting the apron strings" is one of the most difficult things for many parents, particularly mothers, and through preaching, teaching, and support groups, the church can be of immense help.

- **Achieving adult social and civic responsibility:**
It is during midlife that many women and men find great personal fulfillment in doing volunteer work at the church. They can be teachers, youth sponsors, board and committee members.

- **Reaching and maintaining satisfactory performance in one's occupational career:**
Not many churches give formal public recognition when someone takes on a new job or receives a promotion, but such practices would do much to affirm and support middle-aged adults.

- **Developing adult leisure-time activities:**
With the decades-long decline of Sunday school attendance, the wise Christian educator will find other days during the week to gather groups of midlife adults for study, sharing, and support.

- **Relating oneself to one's spouse as a person:**
Obviously, this developmental task applies only to those who chose to marry. After the children move out of the home, this middle-aged man and middle-aged woman are face to face with one another and need to learn new ways of relating to each other.

- **To accept and adjust to the physiological changes of middle age:**
In a culture that prizes youth and beauty, it is not an easy thing for many midlife adults to accept the aging process. The Bible contains much wisdom about growing older, and Christian educators can be of great assistance to adults by sharing these teachings in a variety of venues.

- **Adjusting to aging parents:**
A strange yet inevitable thing happens: parents who once cared for their children now need their children's care. It is an unfamiliar, uncomfortable, yet necessary reversal of roles. At the very least, midlife adults who find themselves in this awkward position need Christian friends with whom they can share and process their feelings.

6. Developmental Tasks of Later Maturity

- **Adjusting to decreasing physical strength and health:**
During the first three decades of the twenty-first century, the fastest-growing segment of the American population is expected to be those over age sixty-five. They are not interested in sitting in a rocking chair awaiting the arrival of the Grim Reaper. They wish to remain active and healthy, and many do. However, they must adjust to a slower pace and eventually to declining health. A key role for the church is to walk with its older adults along these new paths.

- **Adjustment to retirement and reduced income:**
Biblical preaching and teaching, support and study groups, and inexpensive leisure activities (including volunteerism) can do much to assist in these important adjustments.

- **Adjusting to death of a spouse:**
The only one who knows what it feels like to lose a life partner is the one who has experienced it. No words can adequately describe the grief, the emptiness, after living with another for forty, fifty, or more years. The surviving spouse should not have to be alone on this journey. Faithful friends can walk alongside and offer empathetic listening and support.

- **Establishing an explicit affiliation with one's age group:**
This is an extension of previous developmental tasks. Churches often neglect older members, who complain of loneliness. Many meaningful activities can be created for senior adults; the key here is that the activities be relational.

- **Adopting and adapting social roles in a flexible way:**
  Obviously, social roles change across the adult lifespan. The watchword here is *flexible*. Older adults are often denigrated as inflexible, set in their ways. This is far from reality, because they are actually quite adept at making adjustments as needed. The key for Christian educators is to provide meaningful social activities at times and places that meet the needs of older adults. That is to say that it is not good for them to sit home alone; they need to be with each other.

- **Establishing satisfactory physical living arrangements:**
  Often, older adults are left to their own devices in locating their own places to live. The fortunate ones have family members to assist them, but others may need the church to step in and help. In either case, once an older adult is appropriately situated, the church can help by conducting a brief service of dedication of the home, by providing regular visits, and by sending periodic gifts (such as flowers on a birthday).

Beyond Age-Graded Classrooms: Intergenerational Christian Education

While twentieth century advances in human development and age-appropriate considerations were good, healthy, and necessary, Christian educators in the twenty-first century are being drawn ever closer to intergenerational models of ministry. The schooling models of the past segregated children, teens, young adults, and older adults; and while developmental tasks and the teachable moment rightly assert that some content is best learned in age-graded classes, churches are beginning to discover other things that are best learned intergenerationally. Some observers have noticed a return to the educational values of the one-room schoolhouse on the American frontier, with older learners serving as role models for younger ones, and sometimes even becoming teachers' helpers (and sometimes even learning from the younger students).

This chapter is not suggesting that graded classes be discontinued, only that they be supplemented with intergenerational learning. Generations can worship together, they can learn from each other during a meal, they can meet together a few times a year during the Sunday school hour, and they can have regular weekly interaction on a midweek evening. There seems to be no end to creative ways that generations can learn together; the only limitation is a church's imagination and willingness to work hard.

Examples of Intergenerational Ministry

Mark DeVries, author of *Family Based Youth Ministry*,[3] maintains that teens learn best in a family setting. He calls the church back to an earlier time in which mothers and fathers, grandparents, siblings, and cousins all participated in the spiritual formation of adolescents. In fact, the very concept of adolescence is a twentieth-century invention; in previous centuries, a person moved directly from childhood to adulthood, and it is in many ways unnatural to segregate teens from the older and younger generations. Through the services provided by DeVries's Youth Ministry Architects, hundreds of churches all across the United States have received coaching, consultations, assessments, and parenting seminars.[4] Many of the beneficiaries of this model of youth ministry have endorsed it publicly.[5]

In a similar vein, Brenda Seefeldt established "Church Family Based Youth Ministry" and has posted free resources on her Web site.[6] She is a strong advocate for churches that want to do youth ministry intergenerationally.

The Evangelical Lutheran Church in America has prepared several helpful documents and complete programs for intergenerational Christian education.[7] Churches in the Wesleyan Holiness tradition can access and download these programs and adapt them for use in their own settings.

Dale Milligan founded The LOGOS Ministry in Pittsburgh to train congregations that wish to promote generations learning together.[8] Hundreds of churches in more than twenty-five denominations have implemented this midweek model, which engages adults in authentic relationships with youth and children in Bible study, recreation, worship skills, and family time dinner hour. LOGOS is more than just a midweek program; it is a complete system of Christian nurture that engages the whole church in cross-generational relationships and ministry.

A Christian educator who does an Internet search for "Intergenerational Christian Education" will find more than thirty thousand Web sites. Many of them are philosophy papers, books, and local churches that have some form of intergenerational ministry. Many useful ideas can be gleaned in this manner.

The bibliography at the end of this chapter provides many helpful books and articles. It is provided with the hope that interested readers will pursue the topic and find appropriate ways to do intergenerational ministry in their local ministry contexts.

---

3. DeVries, *Family-Based Youth Ministry*. See the Web site at http://www.familybasedym.com/ (accessed July 13, 2010).

4. Youth Ministry Architects, http://www.ymarchitects.com/ (accessed July 14, 2010).

5. Youth Ministry Architects, "Who We've Helped," http://www.ymarchitects.com/endorsements.php?id=6 (accessed July 14, 2010).

6. Brenda Seefeldt, http://familybasedyouthministry.org/ (accessed July 14, 2010).

7. Evangelical Lutheran Church in America, "Plan Programs," http://archive.elca.org/christianeducation/programs/ (accessed July 14, 2010).

8. The LOGOS Ministry, http://www.thelogosministry.org/ (accessed July 14, 2010).

Conclusion

For churches to do their best lifespan Christian education, they should pursue two paths: age-graded learning and intergenerational learning. Neither alone is sufficient, and both are necessary.

Bibliography

Albom, Mitch. *Tuesdays with Morrie: An Old Man, a Young Man, and Life's Greatest Lesson*. New York: Doubleday, 1997.

DeVries, Mark. *Family-Based Youth Ministry: Reaching the Been-There, Done-That Generation*. Downers Grove, IL: InterVarsity Press, 1994.

Harkness, Allan G., "Intergenerational Education for an Intergenerational Church." *Religious Education*, 93, no. 4 (Fall 1998): 431–47.

Havighurst, Robert J. *Developmental Tasks and Education*, 3rd ed. New York: Longman, 1972.

Loper, Edward A. *Building an Intergenerational Church*. Louisville, KY: Geneva Press, 1999.

Meyers, Patricia Ann. *Live, Learn, Pass it On!: The Practical Benefits of Generations Growing Together in Faith*. Nashville, TN: Discipleship Resources, 2006.

Molrine, Charlotte N. and Ronald C. Molrine. *Encountering Christ: An Intergenerational Faith Experience*. Harrisburg, PA: Morehouse Publishing, 1999.

Ratcliff, Donald and Marcia G. McQuitty. *Children's Spirituality: Christian Perspectives, Research, and Applications*. Eugene, OR: Cascade Books, 2004.

Roberto, John. *Becoming a Church of Lifelong Learners: The Generations of Faith Sourcebook*. New London, CT: Twenty-Third Publications, 2006.

_____. *Generations of Faith Resource Manual: Lifelong Faith Formation for the Whole Parish Community*. Mystic, CT: Twenty-third Publications, 2005.

Roller, Patricia Kay. *Grand Friends, Young Friends: A Mentoring Program for Older Adults and Older Children: Leader's Guide*. Louisville, KY: Bridge Resources, 1998.

Stoner, Marcia Joslin. *Seasons of Faith: Teaching the Christian Year: For Intergenerational Use*. Nashville, TN: Abingdon Press, 2003.

_____. *Symbols of Faith: Teaching Images of the Christian Faith. For Intergenerational Use*. Nashville, TN: Abingdon Press, 2001.

CHAPTER TWENTY-TWO

Meeting Special Needs in the Christian Education Setting

SARAH BLAKE

> Jesus said, "Let the children come to me, and don't try to stop them! People who are like these children belong to God's kingdom."
>
> —Matthew 19:14

Aaron's family attends a large church, but five-year-old Aaron is the only young person with a physical disability who attends this church. A few elderly people in wheelchairs travel down hallways on the first floor to their Sunday school classrooms. Aaron's mother carries him down a flight of stairs to the children's classrooms in the basement; the church is old and has no elevator. Aaron is growing and getting heavier, and his mother wonders if she will be able to get him to his classes in a couple of years.

Eleven-year-old Angie is excited about getting her new Bible. It is taking a long time—the Braille Bible comes one volume at a time and will take up several feet of shelf space. Angie has memorized the books of the Bible, and she knows exactly which volumes have not arrived yet. She hopes they will arrive soon. She will not be able to participate in the contests that her Sunday school class holds, which require children to search through the Bible as fast as they can to find and read a particular passage; but at least she will be able to read the passages at home. Angie's mother says that she is eager to grow spiritually and sometimes goes to the altar in response to a message. Sadly, people don't seem to realize that Angie is responding to the message. When praying with her at the altar, they assume that she is there to pray for the healing of her eyes. At home, her mother works diligently to support her spiritual growth. It would be a blessing to the family, she says, for the church to recognize her trips to the altar as steps toward spiritual maturity.

Marcy is twenty-three years old, but she has difficulty dressing herself, remembering what day it is, and remembering all of the things she needs to do every day as part of her self-care routine. She lives with a support person and receives therapeutic services to assist her in continuing to learn new skills. She cannot read, but she loves going to church and singing the songs. One day a week, she goes to the church and helps fill bags for the food pantry. She believes in God, and when her friends are sick, she cannot rest until she calls and tells them she will be praying for them. Every day she calls and checks to see how they are doing, and she is comforted when she learns that they are feeling better. Despite the fact that she cannot remember what day it is, she becomes distressed when a familiar person is absent from her life for a long period of time.

These scenarios illustrate the need for awareness of special needs in the church. In the first case, the challenge is to get Aaron into the children's classrooms without placing strain on his mother's body. He should be able to use his wheelchair to travel through the building to his classroom. In the second scenario, one can identify several problems facing Angie's relationship with the church. She cannot participate in the activities that her class is using to build familiarity with the Bible, and people are not responding effectively to her prayers at the altar. The third scenario may present the most challenging situation for church educators. How is it possible to educate a person who cannot read and, it may seem to some people, cannot learn? Is the answer the creation of a special class with lessons designed for her intellectual level? Marcy enjoys vibrant relationships with church members. How would the creation of a special class affect her relationships?

Churches have resolved questions concerning special needs in many ways. This chapter provides an overview of special needs that church educators may encounter, some of the ways that they may impact people's learning processes, and some examples of ways that special needs can be met in various educational settings. Resources listed at the end of the chapter provide further information.

How the Church Teaches

Discussions of the church's educational program often focus on children's ministries, youth activities, and adult Sunday school classes. John Westerhoff discussed the church's historic tendency to equate education with schooling. He explained,

While admitting that learning takes place in many ways, church education has functionally equated the context of education with schooling and the means of education with formal instruction. The public schools have provided us with our model of education, and insights from secular pedagogy and psychology have been our guides. A church school with teachers, subject matter, curriculum resources, supplies, equipment, age-graded classes, classrooms, and, where possible, a professional church educator as administrator, has been the norm.[1]

In many churches, educational approaches also include role plays, discussion groups, service projects, and many other innovative strategies. Education also occurs within the total church program, for the life of faith is not only learned about; it is learned by doing.

When addressing special needs, leaders must attend to three areas: the accessibility of "schooling" settings and materials, the accessibility of other educational activities that require innovative adaptations, and the general accessibility of the building, worship services, and relationship building.

What Are Special Needs?

The term *special needs* is used in this chapter to describe conditions that may affect the way that a person learns or participates in a church's educational activities. While it is impossible to discuss every kind of special need in this limited space, several categories of special needs are important to understand. Within these categories are numerous conditions that affect people in various ways. Relationship building is very important in understanding how a given person's special needs affect learning.

Sensory Impairments

Sensory impairment is a term that refers to a degree of loss of vision or hearing. A person may be able to see or hear some things or may be totally blind or deaf. People may prefer to use the terms *deaf* or *blind* even if they have usable hearing or vision.

Accommodations for a blind person will depend on how much the person can see, whether the person can read large print or Braille or prefers material to be read aloud. A person who is blind will often be eager to learn the layout of the church building and will be able to navigate around it without assistance once oriented.

When thinking about accommodations for a person who is blind, it is important to understand that the impact of blindness depends on the amount of vision the person has, the age the person was when blindness occurred, and the skills

---

1. Westerhoff, *Will Our Children Have Faith?*, 9.

the person has that allow for doing things in alternative ways. The dilemma of the child in the Sunday school classroom that uses a combination of workbooks and flannel boards illustrates the impact of early-onset blindness.

Coloring books, workbooks, and other visual craft projects are common tools in children's educational programs. Not only can the blind child not see to fill in the materials, but she also misses certain key concepts in the curriculum. One adult recalled that her childhood teachers addressed this dilemma by having an adult sit with her and color the pictures for her. Sandy explained, "The room was very loud, and I was very bored, just sitting there. The lady asked what color I wanted Joseph's shirt to be, and I had no idea because I didn't really understand clothing colors. I also wondered if people really wore the same clothes back then and would have had the same colors to choose from. I felt very stupid and was afraid the other kids would laugh at my picture, but I had to choose something. But then I was afraid the teacher would think I was silly for not knowing."[2]

Other problems may occur when children are allowed to touch tactile representations of drawings, flannel board figures, and so on. To a sighted person, this accommodation may seem appropriate. A very young blind child who cannot yet connect the two-dimensional representations with real objects may not be able to make a connection with biblical story figures. Use of three-dimensional manipulative objects in Bible story time can be an effective alternative.

Youth and adults who are blind may be tolerant of having workbooks read to them; however, Sandy explained that it was uncomfortable for her to dictate her answers aloud while everyone else was writing, even when the answers were shared later.[3] If the blind person uses a personal note-taking device, it is possible for the person to write his or her own answers and share them along with the rest of the group. Alternatively, free-flowing discussion can be an equalizing format.

Marshall Lawrence provided some suggestions for including a person who is deaf in a small group setting. Differentiating between people who consider themselves part of Deaf culture and those who are deaf but consider themselves part of hearing culture, he explains:

> The separation from the" intellectual company" of others makes the challenge of deaf people different from blindness and difficult to address within the church. And it's not just the spoken words of the leader of a group that the deaf miss; it's discussion, the fellowship, the essence of the shared worship or teaching experience. So my first piece of advice is to remember that the deaf person experiences people so dramatically differently from the hearing, so their perceptions, and even their core values, will be profoundly affected by that truth. Secondly, remember that deaf people "hear" with

---

2. Sandy, telephone interview by author, April 29, 2010.

3. Ibid.

their eyes. It seems obvious, but when one considers the full ramifications of that, it affects nearly everything.

The next thing to determine is the primary communication method used by the d/Deaf person. Those methods are quite different if we are talking about a deaf person or a Deaf person. A deaf (small "d") person does not hear but uses English as a primary language and relies on lip-reading for interpersonal communication. This might be someone who became deaf later in life, or a person who was educated in a totally oral environment. A Deaf person (large "D") does not hear but uses a signed language as a primary language and considers him/herself as a member of the Deaf culture. In the United States and Canada, that language would typically be American Sign Language (ASL).

In both cases, there are some specific things the leader will want to do. For example, the room should have plenty of light, and if possible, the chairs should be placed in a circle rather than a row. The leader should not wear clothes that are too bright and should not stand in front of a window or other bright light source, for those would add to the visual noise and cause eye fatigue. Also remember that lip-reading becomes increasingly difficult the further the d/Deaf person is from the one who is speaking. Another technique that will assist the d/Deaf person is for the leader to call on and point to members of the group who wish to make a comment in the discussion. Since the d/Deaf person cannot hear who is speaking and simply turn their head to look in the speaker's direction, by the time they notice that others have turned to look at a new speaker, they have missed several key visual cues as to what that person is saying. Leaders should also be sure that videos used in the meeting are captioned or subtitled!

If the person is culturally Deaf, the best option by far would be to find a skilled ASL interpreter to facilitate communication with the Deaf person, for this will give the Deaf person the best opportunity to join in the intellectual life of the group. Even though virtually all Deaf people have acquired the ability to read lips, even the best lip-readers under ideal conditions can be confident of only six or seven words out of ten. The rest is guess work. ASL is a very rich and complex language, and a good interpreter can make the difference between understanding and not understanding. In the small group setting, the interpreter can help the Deaf person interact with the other members of the group, making real fellowship possible.[4]

If a person uses a communication system that requires a microphone to be passed to the person who is speaking, it is important that the group facilitator take responsibility for seeing that this is done. Otherwise the person remains isolated from the discussion and the group does not gain sensitivity to the need.

---

4. Marshall Lawrence, e-mail interview by author, April 30, 2010.

Mobility Impairments

Mobility impairments include damage to the arms and legs that affect a person's ability to move around in the environment. Elderly people may experience mobility impairments due to age-related limitations. Young people are also affected by mobility impairments for a variety of reasons: some have cerebral palsy; others have been in accidents that caused injuries to the back or neck resulting in paralysis. In some cases, the same condition that causes the paralysis also causes difficulty with speaking.

People who use wheelchairs or scooters often have difficulty getting into churches because of lack of ramps or because of narrow doorways. A prominent ramp, generous doorways, accessible rest rooms, and accessible seating in the sanctuary help to create a welcoming atmosphere.

When planning classroom seating, the impact of a wheelchair's location on the experience of community needs to be considered. If a person is seated alone at a table and the rest of the group is seated together, the person seated alone may feel isolated even if she is free to participate in group discussion.

Home groups often form a part of the church's educational ministry; and many homes feature steps or narrow doorways. If a group needs an accessible environment, the group should consider meeting at another home or at the church.

Learning Problems

Learning problems include conditions such as dyslexia, which affect a person's ability to read, and problems with attention. Since so many educational programs use written material, it is important to develop strategies to accommodate people with reading disabilities. These include reading content aloud in classrooms, not requiring all participants to read, and reading Scripture aloud during the worship service. The reading of Scripture during worship is particularly important, for Scripture is the cornerstone of Christian faith, and if a worshiper cannot access the passages, the church has failed to deliver the Word to all in attendance.

Some people are unable to sit through long presentations. Most people associate attention deficit disorder with children, but adults are also subject to attention problems. Many older youth and adults with learning disabilities and attention deficit disorder cease going to church. One parent of a teenager with attention deficit disorder explained, "I don't think he feels welcome anymore. He is questioning a lot of things that we believe. He may come to believe those things himself, and he may not."[5]

---

5. Susan, telephone interview by author, April 13, 2010.

Adult Sunday school classes and small groups struggle to meet the needs of people with learning disabilities and attention deficit disorder. These groups often study from books and hold discussions lasting from sixty to ninety minutes. Even in a group where members are welcome to get up and fix a cup of coffee or a snack, a member with special needs may feel embarrassed to do so if no one else has moved from their seat. When people move around randomly during the group meeting, an atmosphere of relaxation and hospitality is created for the person who may feel self-conscious about a disability that causes difficulty sitting still.

Developmental Disabilities

Developmental disabilities include what has traditionally been called mental retardation as well as autism and related disorders. Some people with autism are very intelligent, but many also have cognitive difficulties as well as problems with social relationships and communication. Whether to serve people with developmental disabilities by starting a special class is a challenging question. Some churches have found this to be a positive solution, but some families do not want their children to be in special classes. The children often desire to participate in educational programs with their peers, but they may at times need a place to calm down when they have become overstimulated by too much noise or activity.

People with severe or profound developmental disabilities sometimes vocalize randomly and may display mannerisms in reaction to certain stimuli or emotions. Leaders can assist in creating a welcoming environment by helping the congregation to develop a positive attitude toward these behaviors. Speaking in a normal tone of voice, even when using simple language, is especially important when relating to adults with developmental disabilities.

Mental Illness and Dementia

The neglect of mental illness in discussions about special needs has contributed to a great lack of information in the church. One of the greatest educational needs is to learn how to persevere through great pain and depend on a love that cannot always be seen or felt. Mental illness presents a tremendous challenge to faith, but people with mental illness experience great woundedness when their symptoms do not abate quickly enough to satisfy the church community's expectation. Confused churchgoers assume that they must have sinned, or lacked faith, since they have not been healed. The combination of lack of understanding and flawed theology adds to the torment that the person already experiences because of mental illness.

Most people with mental illness do not disclose the details of their situations to the church. Acquaintances may not become aware that they experience difficulties unless symptoms interfere with their lives and cause them to become absent or need assistance. This involuntary disclosure can strain relationships between the person and the church community.

Though grouped together for the sake of discussion, it should be understood that dementia differs from other forms of mental illness in one important respect: it affects primarily older people, while other forms of mental illness can affect people of all ages. Dementia causes loss of cognitive abilities, personality and behavioral changes, and loss of communication skills. A common cause of dementia in elderly people is Alzheimer's disease (other causes of dementia exist as well). Dementia can affect people in a variety of ways: some become hostile and suspicious, while others become docile. Some churches hold special classes for adults with dementia.

Chronic Illness

Chronic illness covers a wide variety of needs, including epilepsy and arthritis. Illness can affect a person emotionally in ways that interfere with learning. It can also keep a person from being present in the learning environment. Understanding how a person's illness affects learning can allow a teacher or pastor to assist in spiritual formation. However, the church leadership will not necessarily know that a person has a chronic illness unless the person volunteers this information. Often this will not happen unless the person experiences symptoms while at church or is absent for an extended period and receives a follow-up call.

When surveyed, several leaders said that they did not consider chronic illnesses disabling. Others said that they recognized that the impact of illnesses and medications could interfere not only with spiritual formation but also with the development of relationships within the church.[6] Because of this, it is important that chronic illness be understood within the category of special needs.

Barriers to Inclusion

Some barriers exist that keep churches from meeting special needs. One is self-deception: some churches truly believe that they are including people to the best of their ability, especially if one or two people with special needs attend church regularly, smile, and know everyone's name. The tests of inclusivity in these programs lie in whether the lessons are being retained and applied outside the church setting and whether the community that is built in the educational setting continues at other times. One of the most common complaints among people with and without disabilities is that nobody calls during the week, that they see each other on Sunday and then seem to forget about each other during

---

6. Sarah Blake, "Finding Common Ground: Setting the Stage for the Welcome of People with Disabilities into the Welcome of the Church," independent study under Guy R. Brewer (Anderson University School of Theology), August 17, 2008.

the week. For people with disabilities, this "community" is often the litmus test of whether they are genuinely a part of the fellowship or are simply a member of the church in name. The danger of nominal inclusion is that the person with special needs may eventually cease involvement with the church due to lack of true fellowship.

Some churches openly admit failure to include people with special needs, especially those with hidden disabilities. John Baron provides two possible reasons for this. Some people believe that there is no need, that things like attention deficit disorder and autism are today's buzz words for laziness, bad parenting, or emotional problems that can be controlled if a person just tries hard enough. Others believe that including people with special needs requires expert training and that volunteer teachers would not attend classes or make the effort.[7] Such comments are generally followed up with, "I care ... but it just wouldn't work."[8] These comments are discouraging for the person who attempts to launch a special needs ministry. When they are spoken to a person with special needs who requests accommodations, they are heart-breaking and can push the person away from the church.

Making It Work: Inclusion in the Church Community

The challenge of creating awareness about special needs often arises because a person with special needs has recently begun attending a church. An awareness event can help to open the way for church members to learn how people with special needs live and to provide avenues for dialogue. Tami, who has two blind children and attends a mid-size church in a large urban area, planned an awareness event to assist her church members in learning about blindness, titling it "Walking by Faith."[9] Thinking that it may be helpful to senior citizens, who are often at risk of losing their vision, she invited rehabilitation professionals to come and work with volunteers from the church to teach groups of church members to prepare dishes while wearing glasses that simulated varying degrees of visual impairment. The professionals also taught church members how to serve as a guide to a person who is blind. The event culminated with a worship service at which Tami's daughter read scripture from a Braille Bible and a lay minister who is blind provided the message.

Awareness events are most successful when they are repeated from time to time and when the church follows up with intentional inclusive practices. In the early weeks of follow-up after the "Walk by Faith" event, Tami was uncertain of its impact. She said that it provided some church members with exposure to information that they did not seem to have previously. One child who was a few years older than Tami's daughter said, "I didn't know she could read!"

---

7. Baron, *Place for All*, 24.

8. Ibid, 25.

9. Tami, interview by author, April 27, 2010.

In the ongoing journey with special needs, everyone learns. Susan, a mother of two children with special needs, shared a portion of her family's journey.[10] Her son, Ethan, was born prematurely and suffered a brain hemorrhage shortly after birth. These events left him blind, unable to walk, unable to speak other than a couple of words, unable to take food or drink by mouth, and prone to seizures. When he reached confirmation age, Susan and the pastor of the church discussed at length the question of whether to have him sit in the confirmation class. The decision was made that he would attend the class with his brother, who was a year younger.

The pastor gave Ethan a Bible on cassette so that he could listen to the passages. Ethan's cognitive ability is unknown, but Susan believes that he understands many things. She explained that when the Bible is read or someone is praying, he becomes quiet and still; and at the end of a prayer, he says, "Na na," as if saying, "Amen." The pastor was also able to give Ethan a sip of Communion without problems. Susan said that there were very few churches with accessible entrances in her area, and she appreciated the opportunity to attend one, even if they had to go in through a back door.

Holiness churches face dilemmas concerning people with developmental disabilities. When several children in attendance have similar needs, parents sometimes form a class so that they can use teaching methods that meet the children's special needs. However, when one child has unique needs, churches find it helpful to mainstream the child. Mike, whose daughter had developmental disabilities during the years when he served as pastor of a small church, explained, "We didn't want her in a room by herself with an adult. We wanted her to be with other children."[11]

Thinking Outside the Box

The presence of people with special needs offers an opportunity for the church to learn to fellowship with those who are different, to rejoice with those who rejoice and weep with those who weep (Romans 12:15), and to communicate the gospel message clearly. Many creative relational strategies require no specialized training; and the whole church learns as they practice community together. When Emily's son, Andrew, attended a new church and his class came into worship together, Emily was still wounded from the attempt to find an accessible church. The accessible entrance was located in the back of the church, and using this entrance was a painful reminder of the feelings of exclusion that pervaded the search for a welcoming church.[12] Andrew's confirmation class solved the problem creatively: the entire class used the back entrance, accompanying Andrew for the service instead of having him go through the accessible entrance

---

10. Susan, telephone interview by author, April 13, 2010.

11. Mike, interview by author, 29 May 2008.

12. Emily, e-mail interview by author, April 13, 2010.

alone. This not only included Andrew, but it also enabled the rest of the class to learn what it means to provide community for one another.

The worship service offers opportunities for educating the congregation about how to live in community with all of its members, including people with special needs, as well as opportunities to model educational strategies. Churches that offer times of testimony may plan opportunities for people with special needs to share their stories. This can be an important step in helping a person or family to integrate into the church. Melanie, who is blind and uses a dog guide, appreciated the opportunity that her church provided for her to introduce herself and her dog, say a few words about the work that her dog did, and explain her needs to the congregation.[13] Following her introduction, members of the congregation were invited to join her at the altar to pray for her to experience growth and to welcome her to the church. These opportunities for people to share their stories and communicate their needs can be vital. Many people struggle with lack of knowledge about how to communicate with people with special needs. Mary McClintock Culverson put the dilemma into words:

> As I approach the man in the wheelchair, my body feels suddenly awkward and unnatural. When I get in his immediate vicinity, I realize I do not know where to place myself. My height feels excessive and ungainly. I tower over this pale man strapped in the wheelchair. Do I kneel down? Bend down to be face level with him? Speaking to him from above feels patronizing. Or is it the crouching down that would be patronizing?[14]

Pastors and worship leaders have numerous opportunities to model inclusive strategies in the conducting of worship services. This not only assists educational leaders in learning to use inclusive strategies; it also assists the whole congregation in learning to worship together. A few things to think about when planning worship include:

- Those who cannot see the hymnal or projector screen may benefit from having lyrics provided in advance, perhaps via e-mail. The availability of large print bulletins or assistive listening devices should be announced at the beginning of the service.
- Instruments and vocals should be balanced so that words can be clearly heard and understood.
- When Communion is served, the community should be served so that no one partakes alone.

---

13. Melanie, telephone interview by author, April 25, 2010.
14. Culverson, *Places of Redemption*, 5.

- Description should be integrated into visual presentations.
- Positive special needs theology should be modeled in sermons and other teachings.

The modeling of positive theology about special needs is especially important. Theology about special needs may not be something that people think about academically, but it underlies the way that people respond to various situations. The healing narratives are often interpreted literally, but they also provide contexts for teaching about relationships in the community of God. Kathy Black challenged traditional interpretations of these narratives:

Will the community be one that brings healing through acceptance, support, and encouragement, or will the community of faith establish boundaries to protect itself from those considered unclean or cursed? Will our preaching imply that one has to be physically and mentally "whole" (based on the preacher and congregation's definition of "wholeness") through miracle or medicine in order to be an active participant in the life of the church, or will difference be honored and accepted? Will our preaching nurture an interdependent community where we are agents of the daily miraculous transformations God wills for each of our lives?[15]

Equipping People with Disabilities to Serve as Leaders

The church's educational tasks include not only teaching the gospel to people but also equipping them to teach others. Questions sometimes arise concerning whether people with special needs can participate in the church's educational leadership and how this can be made possible. Churches have responded to this question in various ways, sometimes prohibiting people from serving at all and sometimes enabling them and assisting them to locate resources to accomplish leadership tasks more easily.

People with disabilities experience difficulty in entering places of ministry at both the lay and professional level for a variety of reasons. Nancy Eiesland explained that there is a common linkage between Leviticus 21:17–23 and policies prohibiting people with disabilities from serving in positions of public leadership:

These and similar passages have historically been used to warrant barring persons with disabilities from positions of ecclesiastical visibility and authority. The specific physical standards of this passage may not be retained as criteria for today's religious leadership, but the implicit theology that repre-

---

15. Black, *Healing Homiletic*, 53–54.

sents disability as being linked with sin, marring the divine image in humans, and preventing religious service persists in church actions and attitudes.[16]

Other barriers also exist. People with disabilities often encounter barriers when seeking to work in children's educational programs. Leaders who are unfamiliar with the capabilities of people who are blind may have questions concerning the ability of a person to supervise children effectively, the safety of service animals around children, and the methods that the person will use to work in the children's educational setting. When Jennifer Jones Wilson hired a blind person to work in the children's ministry at her church in 1999, she addressed these questions by taking the person on a hands-on tour of the facility, asking questions, and listening openly to the person's answers. Some solutions were found during the process of adjustment to employment.

Addressing Safety Concerns

Liability issues are common concerns raised by church leaders when considering the impact of meeting special needs, particularly in educational settings for children. Addressing safety concerns is important in the care of all children. While liability is an important concern, it is also important to understand that the special needs alone do not necessarily increase liability. For example, there is no published research demonstrating increased risk of injury to blind children in a setting with sighted peers when proper precautions are taken to ensure that the child is oriented to the environment.

When evaluating safety procedures in educational programs, it is wise to review the safety procedures for all children and not only those concerning the disabled child. A review of safety procedures should also be conducted in the event that a worker with special needs is hired to ensure that the procedures are both accessible to the worker and safe for everyone involved.

- Are there adequate check in and check out procedures so that the child and parents or guardians are properly identified? Is appropriate health-related information on file? Is there a way to contact parents if necessary?

- How are children taken out of the room in the event of a fire or other disaster? Are there enough adults in the room to evacuate all the infants in a nursery without making multiple trips?

- Are adults left in classrooms alone with children? If so, can another staff member see into the room at all times via a half-window or open door?

- How is discipline handled if a child is endangering other children? Are parents properly informed of the disciplinary policy?

---

16. Eiesland, *Disabled God*, 71.

- Is policy and parent contact information in an accessible format if a worker is visually impaired?

Check-in and check-out procedures need not be complex. R. W. Moody, associate pastor at Parkgate Community Church in Pasadena, Texas, explained that after considering technological options, the church settled on a simple sign-in procedure, and the children wear nametags on lanyards.[17] The church is small enough, he explained, that if a sibling (instead of a parent) picks up a child, the workers generally recognize the sibling. Larger churches may need more innovative solutions, including ways to reach parents during worship in case a child is ill.

A safety plan should also be in place in the event that adults need intervention for health-related incidents. These plans benefit people with chronic illnesses as well as older adults who may experience age-related emergencies. If a person in the church is affected by chronic illness, that person may wish to offer assistance in drawing up a plan for responding to emergencies, especially their own. Many churches are blessed to have medical personnel in attendance, and these people can also provide assistance. Planning ahead will help to reduce anxiety in the congregation in the event of an emergency situation.

Bibliography

The resources listed here represent a small selection from the material which can assist leaders in learning about special needs ministry, theology, and so forth. Books and curricula often go out of print. Libraries and used bookstores can be helpful places to find resource material.

Books and Articles

Baron, John. *A Place for All: Ministry for Youth with Special Needs*. Winona, MN: Saint Mary's, 2008.

Black, Kathy. *A Healing Homiletic: Preaching and Disability*. Nashville, TN: Abingdon Press, 1996.

Block, Jennie Weiss. *Copious Hosting: A Theology of Access for People with Disabilities*. New York: Continuum, 2002.

Carter, Erik W. *Including People With Disabilities in Faith Communities: A Guide for Service Providers, Families, & Congregations*. Peoria, IL: Paul H. Brookes Publishing Co., 2004.

Culverson, Mary McClintock. *Places of Redemption: Theology for a Worldly Church*. New York: Oxford University Press, 2007.

---

17. R. W. Moody, telephone interview by author, March 29, 2010.

Davie, Ann Rose and Ginny Thornburgh. *That All May Worship*, 7th ed. National Organization on Disability, 2005

Eiesland, Nancy. *The Disabled God: Toward a Liberatory Theology of Disability.* Nashville, TN: Abingdon Press, 1994.

Hager, Joseph W. "Providing a Pastoral, Caring Ministry to People Suffering with Alzheimer's Disease." *Lutheran Partners*, July/Aug 1999, 15. http://www2.elca.org/lutheranpartners/archives/provid.html (accessed November 18, 2010).

McKim, Donald K. *God Never Forgets: Faith, Hope and Alzheimer's Disease.* Louisville, KY: Westminster/John Knox, 1997.

Newman, Barbara J. *Autism and Your Church: Nurturing the Spiritual Growth of People with Autism Spectrum Disorders.* Grand Rapids, MI: Friendship Ministries, 2006.

Rapada, Amy. *The Special Needs Ministry Handbook: A Church's Guide to Reaching Children with Disabilities and Their Families.* CGR Publishing, 2007.

Reinders, Hans S. *Receiving the Gift of Friendship: Profound Disability, Theological Anthropology, and Ethics.* Grand Rapids, MI: Eerdmans, 2008.

Tada, Joni Eareckson. *Barrier-Free Friendships.* Grand Rapids, MI: Zondervan, 1997.

Westerhoff, John H. *Will Our Children Have Faith?* San Francisco, CA: Harper and Row, 1976.

Web Sites

Silent Blessings Deaf Ministries: www.silentblessings.org
Joni and Friends: www.joniandfriends.org
Rest Ministries: www.restministries.org
The Center for Religion and Disability: www.religionanddisability.org

CHAPTER TWENTY-THREE

Why the Church Needs the Family

AMANDA J. DRURY

> You must be very careful not to forget the things you have seen God do for you. Keep reminding yourselves, and tell your children and your grandchildren as well.
>
> —Deuteronomy 4:9

Pastor Elizabeth gave her confession at the first parents' meeting of the year in the form of a simple math lesson: "I long to see your children transformed into the image of Christ," she said, "This is my passion. This is my job. And yet I can't do it by myself. I see your kids for 1.2 percent of the week. I'm up against the 40 percent for the Internet, texting, and Hollywood. If you desire to see your children transformed into the image of Christ, they need more than two hours a week. I need you to be pastors, too."

All too often parents shuttle their children to Sunday schools and youth groups in hopes that their children will develop into godly individuals. "Christian education is the job of the pastor" is often the assumed position of parents desiring their children to mature in the faith. What these parents fail to realize, however, is what Sunday schools are up against. According to a study by the Kaiser Family Foundation, "8–18 year-olds devote an average of 7 hours and 38 minutes (7:38) to using entertainment media across a typical day"—32 percent of a twenty-four-hour day.[1] This is in comparison with the average 29 percent of time spent sleeping and the average 28 percent spent in school. For a teenager who attends church for an hour on Sunday morning and an additional hour for a midweek service, that means two hours a week at church—as Pastor Elizabeth said, those two hours account for 1.2 percent of that teenager's week. While certainly the Holy Spirit can transform people into the image of Christ in any given frame of time, the point stands: parents cannot expect a local church to provide a sufficient life-changing ministry in only two hours a week.

This was a particularly self-aware pastor who recognized that she alone could not provide what was needed for these children and teenagers. She recognized faith formation as a partnership between the church and the family. Many Christian educators, however, are overwhelmed with their position to the point that they do not think they have the time to plan for tomorrow's lesson, much less how the *family* might be involved.

The thesis of this chapter is simple: parents matter in spiritual formation. What is not so simple, however, is *why* parents matter nor *how* to convince parents that they matter. The remainder of this chapter will assess the current problem of lack of familial involvement in Christian education in North America as well as challenges the church faces when seeking to nurture the faith lives of families under their care. This chapter will draw from John Wesley's writings on this topic as well as a broader understanding of Wesleyan theology. Again, while it is impossible for families to create faith, when parents understand the amount of influence they hold over their children, understand what true Christian faith looks like, and are empowered to put this knowledge into action, then families within the church will be better poised to recognize and respond to God's gifts of faith and grace.

Assessing the Problem: Why Education Is Not Enough

In his sermon "On Family Religion," John Wesley asks, "If family religion be neglected?—if care be not taken of the rising generation? Will not the present revival of religion in a short time die away?"[2] This high esteem for the family's role in religious education most likely springs from his own religious upbringing.

His mother, Susanna, certainly knew the importance of "family religion." In addition to learning Greek, Latin, and other classical studies common in England at the time, John was raised as a young child to say prayers, sing psalms, and read Scripture. But it was not merely a rote memorization that shaped Wesley. His mother routinely announced that religion was only real if expressed through daily living. In a letter to her daughter, she explained, " 'Tis not learning these

---

1. Kaiser Family Foundation, "Generation M2: Media in the Lives of 8- to 18-Year-Olds," The Henry J. Kaiser Family Foundation, http://www.kff.org/entmedia/mh012010pkg.cfm (accessed December 17, 2010).

2. Wesley, "On Family Religion," 77.

things by rote, nor the saying a few prayers morning and evening, that will bring you to heaven; you must understand what you say, and you must practice what you know."[3] So rigorous and edifying was Susanna's training that others soon attended the formal lessons and prayers she had intended for her family in the community. Scholars estimate that at times she had up to three hundred in attendance.[4]

As an adult, Wesley continually commends the family as a place of spiritual nurture. Holding the family in high esteem, Wesley is critical of the average religious education programs of his day: "What is commonly called a religious education frequently does more harm than good; and…many of the persons who were so educated are sinners above other men, yea, and have contracted an enmity to religion, which usually continues all their lives."[5]

Obviously, Wesley is not a modern educational theorist, and yet contemporary Christian educational theorists echo his critique of church educational programs. John Westerhoff explains that the church has been neglecting family religion in favor of "schooling-instructional paradigm[s]."[6] American Christian educators have modeled the church educational system after the American school educational system, operating under an education-solves-everything mindset. If there is a problem in the church, the general solution has been to add a class or a sermon addressing the issue. The church has too easily linked ways of secular education with religion.[7] Westerhoff's critique of the church is brutal: you can teach religion, but you cannot teach faith. At best you can produce educated atheists.[8]

Nurturing Faith in the Family: Why It Matters

God is the author and giver of faith. One cannot earn her own salvation much less the salvation of her child. And yet God often seems to work through others to nurture faith in such a way that the child might be able to recognize and name God's work. God works both directly and indirectly to form his people into his likeness. God works through particular people to nurture faith in others. This divine indirect work takes place through churches, cultures, peer groups, and families.

Statistically speaking, this kind of nurturing is most effective within the family. In 2005 the National Survey of Youth and Religion (NSYR), under the direction of religious sociologists Christian Smith and Melinda Lundquist Denton, sought to uncover the sources and content of adolescent religious understand-

---

3. Best, *Charles Wesley.*

4. Ibid., 18.

5. Wesley, "The Manner of Educating Children," 475.

6. Westerhoff, *Will Our Children Have Faith?*, 15.

7. Ibid., 17.

8. Ibid., 18.

ing. What they discovered was, "For better or worse, most parents in fact still do profoundly influence their adolescents—often more than do their peers."[9] This is despite "their children's apparent resistance and lack of appreciation."[10] This may sound suspicious, especially to those who would point to typical images of teenage rebellion and generation gaps. Smith and Denton claim these images may have been the experiences of teenagers in prior generations, "but they do not accurately portray the religious realities of most teenagers in the United States today."[11]

The correlation that Smith and Denton found between a parent's faith and a child's faith is worth exploring at length:

> Parents for whom religious faith is quite important are thus likely to be raising teenagers for whom faith is quite important, while parents whose faith is not important are likely to be raising teenagers for whom faith is also not important...Hence, of parents who report that their faith is extremely important in their daily lives, 67 percent of their teens report that faith is extremely or very important in their daily lives...Likewise, of parents for whom faith is somewhat important in their daily lives, 61 percent of their teens also report that faith is somewhat or not very important in their daily lives...Finally, of parents for whom faith is not at all important in their daily lives, 47 percent of their teens also report that religious faith is not at all or not very important in their lives...**most parents most likely will end up getting religiously of their children what they themselves are.**[12]

The type of influence that is exerted by parents comes about by simply "living and interacting with their children."[13] In everyday living and interacting, "most parents establish expectations, define normalcy, model life practices, set boundaries, and make demands—all of which cannot help but influence teenagers."[14] Parents affect their children's religiosity. But simply knowing this is not enough. While many people might agree that parents make a difference in faith development, many do not know what to do with this information. And as the church strives to figure out how to best reach families, the verbalized faith of children appears to be more and more anemic.

The key discovery in the NSYR is that, with exception of Mormons and some conservative evangelicals, most adolescents seem unable to talk about their religious beliefs, practices, and why these matter to them. Specific con-

---

9. Smith and Denton, *Soul Searching*, 56. (Emphasis added.)

10. Ibid.

11. Ibid., 120.

12. Ibid., 57.

13. Ibid., 56.

14. Ibid.

cepts such as sin, holiness, justification, and church were replaced with generic language about niceness, happiness, and merit-based heavenly rewards. Smith and Denton coined the phrase "moralistic therapeutic deism" to describe the religious condition of America's youth and identified five aspects of moralistic therapeutic deism: "1) A God exists who created and orders the world and watches over human life on earth. 2) God wants people to be good, nice, and fair to each other, as taught in the Bible and by most world religions. 3) The central goal of life is to be happy and feel good about oneself. 4) God does not need to be particularly involved in one's life except when he is needed to resolve a problem. 5) Good people go to heaven when they die."[15] Their study suggests either (a) that religion is unimportant to North American teenagers, (b) that the church has been woefully inadequate in teaching Christian beliefs, or (c) that at the very least, the church has been inadequate in passing on a language for adolescents to speak of what they have been taught. If parents are so influential in the religious lives of their children, the NYSR study raises the question, Just what kind of faith are these parents exhibiting?

How to Move Forward

A church seeking to nurture family-based faith has three challenges: (1) Informing and convincing parents of their important role, (2) helping a parent understand what true faith looks like (as opposed to the moralist therapeutic sentiments echoed above), and (3) empowering parents and families to model and nurture faith within their homes.

Challenge 1: Informing Parents of Their Valued Role

"My kid doesn't want anything to do with me."
"Every time I open my mouth my daughter rolls her eyes."
"I can't compete with the influence of his friends."
"What's the use? Whatever I do my daughter just does the opposite."

Perhaps a pastor's greatest challenge will be in convincing parents that they actually play an important role in the spiritual development of their child. Smith and Denton are clear: for better or worse, parents exhibit an enormous amount of influence on the spiritual lives of their children. They recognize, however, that often this fact is difficult to believe. They joke that children seldom come to their parents saying, "Thanks so much for steering me in the right direction.

---

15. Smith, "Is Moralistic Therapeutic Deism the New Religion of American Youth?," 64. Moralistic Therapeutic Deism (MTD) holds a "primarily instrumentalist view of religion...[where] faith and practice become redefined as instrumental therapeutic mechanisms to achieve personal goals" (ibid., 61). Expounding upon the dangers of MTD, Smith explains, "It is ultimately a parasitic religious faith. It cannot sustain itself as an autonomous living entity over time. Rather, as far as I can tell, it survives by feeding upon the denigrating bodies of other, particularistic religious faiths" (ibid., 67).

I really appreciate it. I really want you to know that you are a big influence."[16] While the research shows the importance of parental influence, a child seldom articulates this sentiment to his parents.

What is more, when Smith and Denton asked teenagers what they would most like to change about their family, the most common response was, "I wish I was closer to my parents."[17] When asked why they were not closer to their parents, they responded, "I don't know how to do it."[18] Despite current culture's assumptions of generation gaps and the desire of teenagers to have autonomy from their parents, the research reveals just how influential parents are and a desire on the child's part to be closer.

Single parents and parents who do not share similar faith with their spouses may doubt their own influence. While research shows that religious influence flows most easily from stable, two-parent homes where both parents share a common faith,[19] God is certainly not limited to working within the boundaries of Christian wedded bliss. Consider the multiple scriptural instances of one parent having an influence on a child. Hannah presents Samuel to Eli alone, her husband very much in the background. David grows up in the household of Jesse without any biblical reference to a mother (though this certainly does not mean she was not present). Esther was raised by a loving uncle. Timothy blossomed under the prayers of his mother and grandmother. And the Shunamite woman went to the Prophet Elisha on behalf of her son in spite of her husband's vocalized reluctance to do so. While in a perfect world children would be nurtured by two parents sharing a common Christian faith, the Holy Spirit is not limited by such idealistic pictures.

Parents make a difference in the spiritual lives of their children. So how does the Christian educator inform and convince parents of their crucial role? Of course, the most straightforward way to inform and convince parents of their important role in a child's spiritual development is simply to present them with the research at hand at various parents meetings or in newsletters. Perhaps parents could come to understand their important role through something more informal like a testimony from a teenager on the power a parent can have in building up one's spiritual identity. Perhaps a pastor preaching a sermon could regularly point out the influence of the family in various texts when appropriate. However this information is presented, churches must find a way to inform and convince parents that they matter in the spiritual lives of their children. Parents focusing only on the physical, emotional, and mental needs of their children are missing out on something key.

---

16. Cromartie, "What American Teenagers Believe."
17. Ibid.
18. Ibid.
19. Boyatzis, Dollahite, and Marks, "Family as a Context, 297–309.

Challenge 2: Help Parents Understand What True Faith Looks Like

Of course, many of these parents are skittish for good reason. Some wonder, "How can I pass on something that I don't have myself?" John Wesley wrestled with this question when he asked Peter Bohler how he could possibly preach faith when he does not feel as if he has faith himself. Bohler's response was, "Preach faith till you have it; and then, because you have it, you will preach faith."[20] A parent may also find that there is something reciprocal in this kind of spiritual nurturing. A parent speaking of faith to her child may find that her own faith is strengthened in the process.

It may also be that the child's response to faith will be edifying for the parent. There is no reason to think that there is a strict unilateral formative effect from parent to child. It could be that the faith of the child will challenge and strengthen a parent's understanding of faith. Consider the relationship between Eli and Samuel. While Eli was the one responsible for Samuel's spiritual formation at the synagogue, Eli was the one learning from Samuel when God choose to speak to him at a young age.

Research shows that parents matter in the spiritual development of their children. But before addressing *how* parents might influence their children, it is important to grasp the *content* of their influence. Parents will influence their children one way or another. The question Christian parents must grapple with is whether or not they are modeling what Wesley calls "true religion," whereby individuals are transformed into the image of God. This kind of transformation comes about by the Holy Sprit who may or may not use human agency for such a change.

In "The Manner of Educating Children," Wesley begins his explanation on true religion by stating what true religion is not. He speaks of those who suppose "it to be barely the doing no harm, the abstaining from outward sin; some, the using the means of grace, saying our prayers, reading good books, and the like; and others, the having a train of right opinions, which is vulgarly called faith."[21] In his sermon "The End of Christ's Coming," Wesley warns, "Do not suppose that honesty, justice, and whatever is called *morality*, (though excellent in its place,) is religion! And least of all dream that orthodoxy, right opinion, (vulgarly called *faith*,) is religion. Of all religious dreams, this is the vainest."[22] True religion is not something that one is merely trained in and then recites. And it certainly is not a kind of generic niceness. Over two hundred years before Smith and Denton published their findings in *Soul Searching*, Wesley appears to speak out against a kind of moralistic therapeutic deism of the eighteenth century.

---

20. *John Wesley's Journal*, Saturday, March 4, 1738.

21. Wesley, "Manner of Educating Children," 475.

22. Wesley, "End of Christ's Coming," 276.

True religion, Wesley explains, must "be described as consisting in holy tempers; in the love of God and our neighbor; in humility, gentleness, patience, long-suffering, contentedness in every condition; to sum up all, in the image of God, in the mind that was in Christ."[23] This is further expounded upon in "The End of Christ's Coming":

> Here then we see in the clearest, strongest light, what is real religion: A restoration of man by Him that bruises the serpent's head, to all that the old serpent deprived him of, a restoration, not only to the favour but likewise to the image of God, implying not barely deliverance from sin, but the being filled with the fulness of God. [24]

For Wesley, the primary deviance from true religion occurs when the part is mistaken for the whole.[25] Wesley longs to see a restoration to the image of God—a transformation that involves more than a deliverance of sin, but a being filled with the fullness of God which leads to holiness.

Challenge 3: Empowering Parents to Put Knowledge into Action

Wesley identifies two reasons why this "true religion" might not be passed on to the next generation. First is the problem of the religious instructor or parent not comprehending the nature of true religion.[26] Second, even if the instructor does grasp the meaning of true religion, he "may still be mistaken with regard to the manner of instilling it into children."[27] In other words, he knows *what* to teach but not *how* to teach it. While Wesley does not bluntly state what he means by "proper instillation" in his letter, much can be inferred from other writings. Again, while Wesley is not an educational theorist, his thoughts on how the family can serve as the Holy Spirit's agent to teach toward true religion are nevertheless enlightening.

If parents are convinced that they matter in the spiritual development of their children, the next challenge is to empower them to do so or, as Wesley would say, that they know how properly "to instill" this knowledge. Too often pastors are met with the understanding, "I don't know what I'm doing, *you're* the pastor." In "On Educating Children" and "On Family Religion," Wesley clearly lays out small steps for parents to undertake in teaching toward faith.

---

23. Wesley, "Manner of Educating Children," 476.

24. Wesley, "End of Christ's Coming," 276. Wesley uses the terms "real religion" and "true religion" interchangeably to speak of *genuine* religion.

25. Ibid., 277.

26. Wesley, "Manner of Educating Children," 475.

27. Ibid., 476.

Instruct early

Appealing to parents, Wesley gives the charge to begin faith formation early: "You should particularly endeavour to instruct your children, early, plainly, frequently, and patiently. Instruct them *early*, from the first hour that you perceive reason begins to dawn. Truth may then begin to shine upon the mind far earlier than we are apt to suppose."[28] This instruction is worthless, however, unless it is delivered to the children in an age-appropriate manner: "Use such words as little children may understand, just such as they use themselves. Carefully observe the few ideas which they have already, and endeavour to graft what you say upon them."[29] Wesley's advice supposes a kind of familiarity with a child—knowledge of the words and concepts the child might be familiar with.

Speak regularly of God

Wesley also gives the charge to speak regularly of God. He notes how rarely even God-fearing parents mention the name of God. "Meantime," he writes, "they talk of a thousand other things in the world that is round about them." Wesley explains how talk of God is replaced with words like "nature," "happening," "chance," and "fortune."[30] Part of what it means to be holy is to love and recognize that God is the creator and giver of all that is good.

Speaking regularly of God is not just acknowledging where God is active today; it is also remembering where God has been active in the past. Deuteronomy 4:9 reads, "You must be very careful to not forget the things you have seen God do for you. Keep reminding yourselves, and tell your children and your grandchildren as well." Often times, when there is conflict between God and the people of Israel, it is when the people of Israel have forgotten their past interaction with God.

Faith over knowledge

According to biographer Charles Best, in Wesley's "Lessons for Children," Wesley declared it essential to avoid "making children parrots" that simply regurgitate information.[31] Instead, he instructed that "they should be made to question everything they read so as to better understand 'the true meaning of Christianity.'"[32] Speaking specifically of the school he helped found with his brother Charles, Wesley writes that the instructors were to imitate holiness for the students. He draws upon William Law's description of the student imitating the teacher: "An education under Pythagoras or Socrates had no other end,

---

28. Wesley, "On Family Religion," 81.
29. Ibid., 81–82.
30. Wesley, "On the Education of Children," 91.
31. Best, *Charles Wesley*, 195.
32. Ibid.

but to teach children to think and act as Pythagoras and Socrates did."[33] So too, Christian education should have no higher end than to teach children "how to think, and judge, and act according to the strictest rules of Christianity."[34] Taking this to heart, parents would be advised to encourage questions concerning faith, all the while modeling true religion.

Additional options for churches today

Building on Wesley's base, Christian educators today have multiple options to explore. Churches that operate with multiple programs in their curriculum often segregate adults and children. While there might be pedagogical function in teaching toward a particular age group, there are downsides to continual and complete segregation.

A youth group in Pennsylvania attempted to overcome part of this segregation by making a regular practice of once a semester hosting what they called The Bridge. This event was designed for teenagers and their parents. These evenings often consisted of teen and parent panels for questions and answers, a short teaching time, and small group times for families to talk through guided questions. Occasionally the youth group brought in licensed therapists to be on call during these sessions. The goal of these sessions was simply to bring parents and their teenagers together so that they could talk about their faith. Both parents and teenagers might answer questions such as

> At what point did you most sense God's presence?
> When has God seemed absent to you?
> If you could ask God one question, what would it be?

Ideally religious conversations between parents and teenagers would happen on a regular basis in a more organic fashion, and certainly teenagers could benefit from more than one religious conversation a semester. But what this youth group found was that it was easier for them to talk about God at home once the ice had already been broken.

Another church has begun by asking its children to participate in parts of the worship service, whether reading Scripture, giving a testimony, or offering a few thoughts in a children's sermon. This church has required that the parent(s) of the child rehearse the child's role together at home. While this is a rather formal structure, it nevertheless opens the door for further faith conversation within the home. While many churches today send home stories and questions for parents to ask their children around the dinner table, the church would be wise to attempt more creative means to empower a parent to speak of faith.

---

33. William Law, as quoted in Wesley, "On the Education of Children," 88.
34. Law, *Serious Call*, 250.

Conclusion: The Role of the Holy Spirit

With all of his instructions on what role humans play in the transformational process, Wesley is very clear concerning our dependence upon the Holy Spirit. He desires that it be "carefully remembered all this time, that God, not man, is the physician of souls...But it is generally his pleasure to work by his creatures: to help man by man."[35] The Holy Spirit is working *through* other persons.

Wesley is more blunt on the limits of human agency in his commentary notes on 1 Corinthians 3:6–8, "Ministers are still barely instruments in God's hand, and depend as entirely as ever on his blessing, to give the increase to their labours. Without this they are nothing; with it, their part is so small, they hardly deserve to be mentioned."[36] While the adult might play an important role that Wesley is all too willing to expound upon, Wesley nevertheless desires to place the emphasis upon the workings of the Holy Spirit.

Wesley understands the Holy Spirit to be the one who "should both enable Christians...to live unto God, and fulfil precepts even more spiritual than the former; and restore them hereafter to perfect life, after the ruins of sin and death."[37] Wesley goes on to explain that it was "the incarnation, preaching, and death of Jesus Christ...[that] designed to represent, proclaim, and purchase for us this gift of the Spirit."[38] From a Wesleyan theological standpoint, it is impossible to speak about true transformation without acknowledging it as a profound work of the Holy Spirit. To his credit, he does desire that it be "carefully remembered all this time, that God, not man, is the physician of souls... But it is generally his pleasure to work by his creatures: to help man by man."[39] The Holy Spirit is working *through* other persons: he is the one who blesses with gifts of faith, and quite often God uses the Holy Spirit to work through others, *most notably, parents.*

There is a sense of peace and surrender that comes with this realization. Yes, a parent holds vast influence over her child's faith, but she is not the creator of that faith. She cannot earn her own salvation, and she certainly cannot earn the salvation of her child. As difficult as this kind of relinquishment may be, a parent is called to be faithful to the task at hand. He is neither responsible for nor capable of creating faith; his charge is simply to be faithful.

35. Wesley, "On the Education of Children," 88.

36. Wesley, *John Wesley's Commentary on the Bible*, 512.

37. Wesley, "Holy Spirit," 509.

38. Ibid.

39. Wesley, "On the Education of Children", 88.

Bibliography

Best, Gary. *Charles Wesley*. Norwich, England: Epworth, 2006.

Boyatzis, Chris J., David C. Dollahite, and Loren D. Marks. "The Family as a Context for Religious Spiritual Development in Children and Youth." In *The Handbook of Spiritual Development in Childhood and Adolescence*, edited by Eugene C. Roehlkepartain et al, 297-309. Thousand Oaks, CA: Sage Publications, 2006.

Cromartie, Michael. "What American Teenagers Believe: A Conversation with Christian Smith." *Books and Culture*, Jan/Feb 2005. http://www.ctlibrary. com/bc/2005/janfeb/4.10.html (accessed March 24, 2010).

Law, William. *A Serious Call to a Devout and Holy Life*. Edited by Kevin A. Lynch. New York: Paulist Press, 1978.

Smith, Christian. "Is Moralistic Therapeutic Deism the New Religion of American Youth? Implications for the Challenge of Religious Socialization and Reproduction." In *Pass on the Faith: Transforming Traditions for the Next Generation of Jews, Christians, and Muslims*, edited by James L. Heft, 55–74. New York: Fordham University Press, 2006.

Smith, Christian, and Melinda Lundquist Denton. *Soul Searching: The Religious and Spiritual Lives of American Teenagers*. New York: Oxford University Press, 2005.

Wesley, John. "The End of Christ's Coming." In *The Works of John Wesley*, edited by Thomas Jackson, 2:267–77. Grand Rapids, MI: Baker, 1979.

———. "The Holy Spirit." In *The Works of John Wesley*, edited by Thomas Jackson, 3:508–20. Grand Rapids, MI: Baker, 1979.

———. *John Wesley's Commentary on the Bible*. Edited by G. Roger Schoenhals. Grand Rapids, MI: Zondervan Publishing, 1990.

———. "The Manner of Educating Children." In *The Works of John Wesley*, edited by Thomas Jackson, 13:474–77. Grand Rapids, MI: Baker, 1979.

———. "On Family Religion." In *The Works of John Wesley*, edited by Thomas Jackson, 3:76–86. Grand Rapids, MI: Baker, 1979.

———. "On the Education of Children." In *The Works of John Wesley*, edited by Thomas Jackson, 3:86–98. Grand Rapids, MI: Baker, 1979.

Westerhoff, John H. *Will Our Children Have Faith?* New York: Seabury Press, 1976.

CHAPTER TWENTY-FOUR

Intercultural Education

KRISTIN D. LONGENECKER BULLOCK

> I will give instruction and explain the mystery of what happened long ago. These are things we learned from our ancestors, and we will tell them to the next generation. We won't keep secret the glorious deeds and the mighty miracles of the Lord.
>
> Psalm 78:2–4

In following Christ, Christians may serve among many different cultures and people groups. Sometimes these groups will be across town and others may be around the world. And many times Christians will find themselves unprepared or at a loss about how to relate even basic Christian concepts.

There is no question that God's word is for all people. Perhaps the most visible and memorable scripture is John 3:16, "God loved the people of this world so much that he gave his only Son, so that everyone who has faith in him will have eternal life and never really die." A study of all possible ways to relate to others would be a lifetime pursuit and no one approach works with all people. A Christian educator must, therefore, learn basic principles of how to relate with new unfamiliar cultures.

What Is Intercultural Education?

Education is "the instrument both of the all-round development of the human person and of that person's participation in social life."[1] This definition can be used around the world and is inclusive of any culture, age, and specific environment. The term *multicultural* is a description of the "culturally diverse nature of human society"[2] It includes things like language, socioeconomic factors, and religious distinctions. Whenever groups relate that have different expressions of culture, the relationship could be described as "intercultural."[3]

For the second half of the twentieth century, the primary operational principle of many churches in the United States was known as the homogeneous unit principle.[4] The basic premise was that groups that were composed of the same kinds of people would grow the fastest. While many churches in the United States grew using that principle, it also made relationships with different cultures more difficult and has perhaps unintentionally reinforced certain stereotypes.

Biblical Basis for Intercultural Church Education

In the first chapters of the book of Acts, the Christian church was shaped and formed. In Acts chapter one, the early Christians gathered in Jerusalem to wait for the Holy Spirit. Men and women from many places were gathered together praying. After the Holy Spirit came down at Pentecost, the church was described as teaching and spending time in fellowship[5]. During this time the church continued to grow.

In chapter five and six of the book of Acts, early Christians still met in the temple in Jerusalem. They focused their evangelism on those who were most like them, and many priests became followers of Jesus. What was emerging in the followers of Christ was different from the Jewish traditions they had come from. But despite intense persecution, the early Christians still only shared salvation within Jewish communities.

The vision that Peter realized in Acts 11 led him to understand that the gift of salvation was for all people. People from all over the region began to worship God, hear the good news of Christ, and receive the Holy Spirit. It was in Antioch that people from many countries, languages, and religions came together. There in this multicultural environment the followers of Christ were first called Christian.[6]

---

1. UNESCO, *UNESCO Guidelines on Intercultural Education* (Paris: UNESCO, Section of Education for Peace and Human Rights, n.d.), 12. http://unesdoc.unesco.org/images/0014/001478/147878e.pdf (accessed December 16, 2010).

2. Ibid, 17.

3. Ibid.

4. Deymaz and Li, *Ethnic Blends*.

5. See Acts 1 and 2.

6. See Acts 11 where Peter returns to Jerusalem and the church in Antioch is established.

Gilbert Bilezikian identifies early forms of churches found in Acts 1:13–14, Acts 2:42–47, and Acts 5:42 and 6:7.[7] These models are consistently used throughout Christian churches as small groups, missional communities, and structured churches. Notably all three models come from within the homogeneous Jewish community. Mark Deymaz and Harry Li suggest that the Acts 11 church in Antioch is what Christ envisioned for the church in John 17:20–23:[8]

> "I am not praying just for these followers. I am also praying for everyone else who will have faith because of what my followers will say about me. I want all of them to be one with each other, just as I am one with you and you are one with me. I also want them to be one with us. Then the people of this world will believe that you sent me.
>
> "I have honored my followers in the same way that you honored me, in order that they may be one with each other, just as we are one. I am one with them, and you are one with me, so that they may become completely one. Then this world's people will know that you sent me. They will know that you love my followers as much as you love me.

This is a call to find unity, not in uniformity, but in loving one another as Christ first loved us. This is the foundation of intercultural education in the Christian church. Because of the power of the Holy Spirit, Christians everywhere can love, teach, and live in community with all who follow Christ.

A Guide for the Local Church: Making the Connection

Whether an educator is serving in a local community or across the world, they should take time to develop an appreciation for the culture they are entering. It is important to remember a framework for approaching unfamiliar cultures and people groups. Take time getting to know the community and people by name. Where do people like to gather? What does a typical household look like? What is most important to the people of the community?

Relate

Gaining the trust of a new community takes time. For some cultures it may take a few years before the community trusts someone new. Spend time where the people spend time. Listen to the needs of the community and invest time where the people spend time.

> On one Native American reservation, a church group would visit year after year. The group would emphasize that the children accept Christ during

---

7. Gilbert Bilezikian, Anderson University chapel address, Anderson, IN (February 2002).

8. Deymaz and Li, *Ethnic Blends*, 38.

their one-week stay. During one visit, the local pastor confronted the leaders of the trip and suggested that instead of trying to "save" the children, perhaps they should play with them. The pastor pointed out that most of the children had heard and accepted Christ every time a missions group came to the reservation. But the children did not know that they were loved. On that trip not a single child was officially "saved," but countless kids had spent the week playing with the group.

Building a relationship with the people where you serve is loving God through "loving your neighbor as yourself."

Learn

Just as the Good Shepherd knows the sheep by name, a good teacher learns the names of the students. Learn how to correctly pronounce the name as much like it is intended as possible.

Listen

What are the stories, traditions, holidays, and songs of the culture? The goal is not to transpose one culture on another but to inspire a life of worship and a desire to love God and others in the way that people have been gifted.

A new pastor was placed in an inner-city church. His first observation of this new church was that they sang the same song each Sunday about how God had brought them to the church again. The pastor thought the song was old and uninspiring. He loved creative worship and wanted to suggest using some new music. But he waited since he was still very new to the church.

Through the course of his ministry, he visited the homes of the people in the congregation. During one trip he described walking to the apartment and down the hallway to a parishioner's door. He had to push past drug dealers and people with guns while stepping over alcoholics passed out on the side of the hallways. But as he walked, he realized that the song the church sang each week was a statement of defiance to the culture they lived in. Their song was a reminder that no mater how bad things were in their community, God had triumphed by bringing them to worship again. The pastor realized an important key to the culture he served and sang joyfully with the congregation their song of deliverance.

Look

While it may be difficult, suspend judgment of the culture, good or bad. What do you see when you look at the context without judging it? What would Jesus see? What would Jesus respond to? Are there barriers to learning or even to coming to church? Are children being fed before they come to class? Are people working during typical church hours? Is there a social stigma surrounding church?

There was a church on the West Coast that was struggling with its numbers. A new pastor began to discover that there was a long history of the church inviting the "right people" like a social club more than inviting all people. Additionally, there was a legacy that many West Coast churches noticed of being reliant on the history of the pioneers who had arrived. It took over ten years of relationships and creating new ministries, but the church was able to begin to welcome people to the church. They also realized that mission did not mean sending money but going themselves.

Share

You have experiences that are unique and a personal story that is meaningful. Share your story with your students. Opening up yourself may allow them to open up with you more.

Reflect

Reflect on the gifts you have and how you could uniquely minister in the place where you are. Just as each person has been given gifts, each ministry has unique gifts of the people in them. Not every formula will work in every place. As new people with different gifts join the ministry, it is the Holy Spirit moving the direction of the ministry.

Learning from Differences

The majority of the people in the world still live in clusters with those of similar values and beliefs. Perhaps the first intercultural experience for many individuals is going to school with children from different parts of town. Through this immersion into culture, children begin to discover varieties of family structures, religious expression, sexual orientation, political views, and any number of potentially difficult conversations with adults.

Children can begin to learn more about their own faith as other children ask questions. Teachers may be asked to answer questions that are difficult or confusing. The Christian faith is a journey, and many of the "answers" are found in unexpected places throughout life. Sometimes the best way to answer a question is to ask students how they might answer the question. This creates a safe space for children to ask questions and wonder about what faith looks like in their own context.

Through these early interactions with the world, students begin to recognize the value of Christian community in their life. The congregation can provide a solid foundation of Christian community that is like belonging to a large family that cares and extends grace because of the love of God.[9] It is not as much about the right answers as it is about relationships with God and others. And when other students come into contact with Christian community, their lives may very well be changed.

For many educators, generational differences will be significant. It is not uncommon for teachers to express that students have changed over their years of teaching. When confronted with generational cultural differences, it is important to step back and observe the students. Educators should consider things that they appreciate about them and the way they perform in classes. An educator's understanding and interest in a student honors the student more than the highest quality of education.

Sometimes the teacher is younger than the students. This is often the case in senior adult ministries. For the teacher, finding a group of people who can guide the classroom plan and give input on class response is key. It is very possible that the student knows more than the teacher, but don't assume this is always the case. While many will know Scripture and the church's theology and positions on issues, many may be from other churches, other faith traditions, or may be new to religion entirely.

A teacher should lecture only when they have expertise in the topic. Discussion formats and more interactive presentations where participants can share their knowledge will honor the experience of the older student while engaging students with potentially new material.

Ethnic Diversity

The term *race* originated in the Old Italian *razza*. It is a family, tribe, people, or nation belonging to the same stock.[10] The term *race*, however, does not adequately describe groups of people for educational purposes, especially if the goal is to find ways to build a relationship. To learn more about an individual, learning about the people and stories they identify with might be a way to connect and understand more about how they see themselves and the world. Contrasted with the term *race*, these shared stories and self-identity are part of the ethnicity of an individual.

When speaking of ethnicity, there are three layers of understanding. The first is the group with which the individual identifies. While someone may be of a certain race, they may more readily identify with a different community because of birth location or parental ethnicity.[11]

The second component of ethnicity is a collective history that is treasured. The self-identity carried in stories and memories of important events may differ significantly from the dominant culture's historical narrative or even from other

---

9. Dawn, *Is It a Lost Cause*, 135.

10. *Merriam-Webster Collegiate Dictionary*, 11th ed., s.v. "race."

11. Nieman and Rogers, *Preaching to Every Pew*, 25.

groups within the same race. It includes the homeland with which someone identifies and the stories of what that group overcame, whether it was wars, famines, oppression, or persecution.[12]

Cultural distinctives are the third way groups identify with each other. The focus is on the commonality of shared practices. It would include customs and holidays that are unique to a group, or values that the group holds.[13]

It is a gross overstatement, even in primarily homogeneous churches, to say that they are all of the same ethnicity, even if they are of the same race. Variations in accents, country of origin, and shades of skin color, to mention a few, can represent significant ethnic differences.

> Mina was clearly from another culture. While she spoke just like all of her co-workers, her name, her dark hair, and small stature set her apart from the others who looked Asian or Hispanic. She had been born in California but said her family was from the Philippines. Her family was a part of the Filipino community in their city, and it was expected that she would marry a Filipino man. But their family was also a part of a tight-knit church community, which meant that her selection of mates was limited. She was groomed to take over leadership of the community in the future, learning to preach and lead worship, but discovered that she was not as thoroughly Filipino as others in her community. She decided not to marry a Filipino man and found a job outside of the church. While she celebrates all the traditions and identifies with being Filipino, she does not consider herself to be only Filipino. That is only a part of her identity.

Ethnicity is not about classification or stereotyping individuals or groups. Ethnicity is about the story, the people, and the places that are meaningful to who the individual is and how they view the world. Spending time learning the stories of individuals and the broader communities reveals much more than stereotypes or demographics ever could.

Socioeconomic Differences

Socioeconomic differences can be a challenge to congregations that are trying to reach people with the love of God. Most people hide their finances well. Even if the congregation members seem to be similar in their financial standing, it is probable that even the most wealthy in a congregation have some load of debt, and those who live very frugally may have a great deal of personal wealth.

It can be difficult to know whether someone is stable and doing well or about to lose their job or, even worse, their home. Debt reduction courses and money management certainly help individuals move beyond critical stages. But

---

12. Ibid., 26.
13. Ibid., 27.

of course the goal of the gospel is not to make sure everyone drives a newer car and has a new outfit each Easter and meets friends to play golf. Part of the ministry of the educator is find ways to encourage hope and faith in people of all socioeconomic levels.

Nieman and Rogers point to common values held among people no matter what their class experience. These values are those things that people strive to achieve and give them a sense of fulfillment but when lacking remind them of their failure. These values include personal and social order, maintaining health and freedom from addiction, security of having social supports and tools to use. When present these three things create hope in individuals. When absent, an individual experiences fear and, over time, a diminishing of the individual's ability to see possibilities.[14]

And people of all social and economic and cultural backgrounds experience this feeling of diminishing possibilities. It is not just those who need food pantries or a free clinic. Often those who are wealthy beyond measure suffer from this diminishing hope. Mother Teresa once said, "We think sometimes that poverty is only being hungry, naked and homeless. The poverty of being unwanted, unloved and uncared for is the greatest poverty. We must start in our own homes to remedy this kind of poverty."

The ability to see possibilities is a vital part of being human. It is the core of what makes humans strong enough to keep going. It is the feeling of hope that above all makes someone get up and change their lives, love their families, work, and have faith in God.

> The Gonzales family worked at the local church. The father and six of his children and their spouses were contracted to clean the facilities and maintain the property. The church was in an affluent area and members were heads of multinational companies. Every day the pastor watched the Gonzalez family as they carefully cleaned and cared for every corner of the church. She watched as they graciously cleaned up every mess that congregation members made. The pastor noticed that this family could not afford to live in the area and had to drive nearly thirty minutes to church every day to work. And even though they did not have the seven digit salaries of the members and probably worked just as hard, the family was much happier than any of the families at church. Their secret was that they had family, job security, health, and they knew that by working hard they could make a better way for their kids. They had hope.

A key point to remember with every individual is that when hope is shaken from health concerns, a loss of daily order, or uncertainty in jobs or relationships, especially when there is not a strong base of extended support, individu-

---

14. Ibid., 71–72.

als become stressed and fearful.[15] The educator cannot always effect change on the environment or the circumstances that individuals choose, but being a consistent presence and offering prayer can be a stabilizing force in the most difficult situation.

Interfaith and Plural Environments

Many educators find themselves in richly diverse environments that may challenge the very basic assumptions of faith. Historically, there have been two major ways Christians have approached other faith groups. The faith is either compared to Christianity as a distortion of Christian practice or is seen as a false religion that is completely flawed. This assumption makes it difficult to live in proximity with other faith groups, especially when the observed practices are deeply meaningful for the believers.

A second approach is to attempt to discover religious differences. It must be assumed that the practice of comparing or contrasting two different things requires a basic system of values. These values are most profoundly shaped by the culture in which one was raised, which would include religion. So if one were to place value on one religious system over another, it would obviously be flawed by the bias toward one's own culture and religion.

An alternative to the aforementioned systems of extrapolating faith validity is to take a position of observing differences among religions. For example, different faiths have different core principles and beliefs that guide the religion and must be valued on their own merit. Religions are not just principles but are embodied by individuals who live out their faith. This faith orientation creates an order to life that sustains the individual. All of these observations together press the need to affirm that there is indeed religious substance to their beliefs.[16]

Since this approach is based on observation, it can only be studied through relationship and dialogue. While in Athens, the apostle Paul is called to the council of Aeropagus and asked to tell about the new teaching and explain it. In Acts 17:22, he recognizes the people as being very religious since they worship so many idols. Then he goes on to say that he noticed that they worship an "unnamed God." Paul could never have said these things or been ready to share about the story of Christ if he had not been aware of the differences that there can be in faiths. Not everyone was swayed by Paul that day, but still some were, because he was willing to observe the differences of faiths.

Every year the local church had a unity service with the local Jewish temple. At first the unity service was only during the week to avoid difficult situa-

---

15. For a theoretical list of what might threaten these values, refer to the 1967 University of Washington School of Medicine Social Readjustment Rating Scale by Thomas Holmes and Richard Rahe (revised and updated in 2009 at http://www.emotionalcompetency.com/srrs.htm).

16. Nieman and Rogers, *Preaching to Every Pew*, 115–16.

tions. But over time, the cantor of the temple and the worship leader developed a friendship that allowed them to learn from each other. They found that for Christians and Jews, God is a common factor. They found that the key to bringing the two groups together was finding commonalities, saving the specifics of each faith that would create tension for another service (an example is using scriptures pertaining to Jesus as the Savior). Honoring each faith's unique traditions of worship brought a level of friendship and communication that had not existed before. Even Jesus could be acknowledged as a wise Rabbi as in teachings in Matthew. One unexpected blessing was that many couples where one spouse was Jewish and one was Christian were worshiping together for the first time in their marriage and finding common ground for their own relationship.

This emphasis on observing faith differences to create understanding is helpful, especially when relating with congregations or individuals who are from diverse faiths. Christians are called to share the love of God with all humanity. Sometimes it may be through words; sometimes it may be through relationship. While it may not be obvious at first, it is possible to find common ground that does not question the humanity or basic respect for those to be educated.

Language Differences

While missionaries do in-depth preparation and study for new language environments, it is entirely possible that an educator may encounter students in their local congregation who speak other languages. The teacher may not have a basic knowledge of the culture or language of the student. The student may also be new to the culture and have little knowledge of the language.

If students speak more than one language, educators should try to provide resources in both languages whenever possible to support continued growth in both languages. Educators may also need to modify lessons with difficult words and find creative ways to reinforce the important points of the lesson through body language, gestures, pictures, and examples. Educators should also encourage the use of a common language with students as much as possible while affirming the student's preferred language. One opportunity with students of different languages is to have students teach each other new words and explain difficult subjects to each other. This not only affirms the students but helps the class discover ways to relate to those who speak different languages.

Amanda had been sent from Asia to live with her American family members. She was four years old and only spoke Mandarin. The Sunday school teacher did not speak Mandarin and found it difficult to include Amanda as she did her other students. To ease the situation, one of Amanda's relatives began to attend with her, to help her learn the language and know how to play with classmates. When the relative could not come to the class, one of the children began befriending her and would do many of the same techniques that the relative would do. She would act things out, draw pictures, and they would teach each other words. This was an important step in the child's growth in the new culture: to make a friend who wanted to communicate with her.

One of the most important principles with students is to allow students to learn at their own pace and in their own way. Students may need additional time to meet together to talk, play, or have coffee depending on their age. This will maximize the effectiveness of a teacher by leveraging the motivation of the student and the interest and curiosity of the other students. Teaching students who do not speak the language requires a great deal of patience on the part of the teacher, but it can be tremendously rewarding as the student not only discovers the language but the meaning of the lessons.

Summary

It is very possible that Wesleyan Holiness churches will increasingly find that their context of ministry will have not just one or two but all of these multicultural dimensions. It is inevitable that there will be misunderstandings, rejection, and disagreements that arise from being together. Some people and groups value and actively maintain distinctions that provide orthodoxy or boundaries. Others may discover injustices that should to be resolved before relationships can continue. But Christian educators should not be discouraged. Leonard Sweet proclaims:

> The gospel doesn't "counter" cultures but "crosses" culture with the gospel...piercing the heart of every culture with the divine so that we can be human again. In fact, Christianity is cultureless. The gospel is not a culture; the gospel does not have a culture. But the gospel is an incubator in every culture. Disciples of Jesus don't have a 'culture'. What we do have is relentless availability to other languages, other contexts, other cultures, other people.[17]

As people who believe that the Christ came for everyone, his followers can walk the streets of their neighborhoods and befriend the people they meet, no matter who they are, because Christ followers are willing to listen and learn from everyone. Christians can see God at work in the lives of those around them through being present with others and building relationships with them. Above all, a relationship with God that is led by the Holy Spirit is the most important

---

17. Sweet, *So Beautiful*, 178.

cross-cultural technique. The Holy Spirit can make connections possible that formulas of teaching could never deliver.

In spite of all limitations, we simply must study God, because God has touched our lives and has become our very life. There is no period of Christian history in which the attempt to study God has been completely disregarded or has entirely ceased.
—Thomas C. Oden, *The Living God*, 323

Bibliography

Blomberg, Craig L. *Contagious Holiness*. New Studies in Biblical Theology 19. Downers Grove, IL: InterVarsity Press, 2005.

Dawn, Marva. *Is It a Lost Cause: Having a Heart of God for the Church's Children*. Grand Rapids, MI: William B. Eerdmans Publishing Company, 1997.

Deymaz, Mark, and Harry Li. *Ethnic Blends: Mixing Diversity Into Your Local Church*. Grand Rapids, MI: Zondervan, 2010.

Hines, Samuel George, and Curtiss Paul DeYoung. *Beyond Rhetoric: Reconciliation as Way of Life*. Valley Forge, PA: Judson Press, 2000.

Kung, Hans, Josef Van Ess, Heinrich Von Strietencron, and Heinz Bechert. *Christianity and World Religions: Paths to Dialogue*. Translated by Peter Heinegg. Maryknoll, NY: Orbis Books, 2002.

Nieman, James R., and Thomas G. Rogers. *Preaching to Every Pew: Cross-Cultural Strategies*. Minneapolis, MI: Fortress Press, 2001.

Oden, Thomas C. *Systematic Theology*. Vol. 1, *The Living God*. Peabody, MA: Prince Press, 1987.

Sweet, Leonard. *So Beautiful: Divine Design for Life and the Church*. Colorado Springs, CO: David C. Cook, 2009.

CHAPTER TWENTY-FIVE

Church and Public Education

SHANNON NEW-SPANGLER

> Listen, Israel! The Lord our God is the
> only true God! So love the Lord your God
> with all your heart, soul, and strength.
> Memorize his laws and tell them to your
> children over and over again. Talk about
> them all the time, whether you're at home
> or walking along the road or going to bed
> at night, or getting up in the morning.
>
> —Deuteronomy 6:4–7

Christian education is vital to the formation of youth. There is now, and has been for some time, an earnest debate on the proper mode of education for Christian children. Specifically, whose job is it to teach young people what it means to be Christian? And more specifically, where is the best place for Christian education to take place? Ultimately, Christian parents have to make these decisions for themselves and for their family, but this chapter will look at several sides of the issue of Christian education from kindergarten through grade 12.

Human beings were created with capacities surpassing all of creation in thinking and learning; therefore, in the words of Vernon S. Broyles, "education is an essential ingredient in our capacity to become what God has created us to be."[1] The aptitude for knowledge is a precious gift given to creation by the Creator to be seized with intentionality.

Within the realm of education, there are a plethora of possible foci. This chapter will deal specifically with Christian education or spiritual formation. Broyles continues, "The opportunity to develop to fullness the potential that God has given us requires education and nurture."[2] Untended, human cognitive potential is wasted and intellectual capacities decline. As with maintenance of body and spirit, the mind must be sculpted and shaped proactively, meticulously, and perpetually. Freda A. Gardner maintains that Christian education "is the church's intentional way of responding to people's search for understanding of the gift of faith that has been bestowed by God."[3]

Whose Job Is Christian Education?

The first question that becomes apparent in Christian education is the matter of where the responsibility to educate rests. Three main options come readily to mind: the home, the faith community, and the more civic sector, schools.

Home/Familial Community

The most obvious and traditional place for Christian education is in the home. Considering that each family has its own set of beliefs and that children spend a majority of their time with family, this seems to be the most obvious choice for the main thrust of Christian education. Biblically, Christians are told in Deuteronomy 6 to teach children, to tell them over and over again, so that they know the tenets of the faith. Historically, Jewish children were taught at home, and the task of religious education was the father's.

Teaching at home comes in a variety of forms: verbal instruction, teaching through action, and teaching both intentionally and passively. Children watch what their parents do and say. Ultimately, the main responsibility for Christian education lies with the parents. In the words of Holly C. Allen, "Children's spiritual growth and development are heavily dependent on God's truths being both modeled and intentionally taught by parents."[4]

Many parents do not feel educated or equipped to teach their children. However, the faithful, consistent behavior of a Christian parent will have significant impact on a child, even when the parent is unable to give extensive verbal instruction. Christian parents can rely on the Holy Spirit to work in them as they lead their household in the ways of the Bible.

---

1. Broyles, "Presbyterians and Education," 14.
2. Ibid., 20.
3. Gardner, "Current Situation in Christian Education," 75.
4. Allen, *Nurturing Children's Spirituality*, 264.

Faith Community

One of the first events in the life of a child whose family is involved in a Holiness church congregation is a dedication ceremony. This is a three-way covenant among parents, congregation, and Creator. At this moment, the faith community covenants to participate actively in the development of the young person. More specifically, they profess that they will be a vital aspect of this child's journey of faith.

Obviously the faith community has a deep responsibility for spiritual formation. In fact, it is one of the main goals in any faith community. Churches teach in three ways: **explicitly,** those things the church teaches directly and intentionally; **implicitly,** those things that the church teaches through actions or indirect means; and the **null,** those things that are taught by avoiding them.[5] It is of great importance that the church be aware of this educational paradigm, because Christian education will occur no matter what. Education happens in many different ways, and the church teaches in everything it does.[6] Christian education in the faith community has long been the basic mode of transferring biblical, spiritual, and faith knowledge. According to Vernon S. Broyles, "Nothing is more basic in the life of any community of faith than the transmittal of that faith from generation to generation."[7]

The concern here is that while children spend roughly 30 percent of their waking hours at school and about 60 percent of their waking hours with family, they only spend about 5 percent of their time in church. Thus, there is an extremely small window for the faith community to have a significant impact in the arena of Christian education. The positive side is that Christian education is the faith community's main role. Therefore, the church is justified in having laser focus on the primary task of Christian education.

Civic Sector/Schooling

Christian education in schools is where the debate ignites. In general, there is agreement that Christian education ought to take place in the church and in the home, but there is a fierce debate regarding whether or not Christian education ought to be included in schools. This debate will be spelled out more thoroughly in the following section.

Private Schools, Public Schools, and Home Schooling (K–12)

On all sides of this three-pronged debate, for private education, public education, and home schooling, there exists passionate allegiance. Who is right? The primary question in this debate is twofold: are children getting a well-rounded

---

5. Gardner, "Current Situation in Christian Education," 75.

6. See chapter 18 of this volume.

7. Broyles, "Presbyterians and Education," 14.

academic education in preparation for college and the real world? And are they being taught to fulfill the ministry of the gospel in every part of their lives?

Private Education

For centuries church-sponsored educational centers have been commonplace.[8] The option of a faith-centered private education is available to nearly every American family that so chooses. These centers offer many similar classes to a public school but provide a second, vital focus on Christian formation. In many areas these schools provide a safe, stable place for children and teens to learn. Still, not all Christian families opt for the private school.

Pros

On one side of the debate are those who believe that private schools work the best in providing a holistic education for their children. Edward Gilbreath and John Wilson write that Christian parents "are convinced that their children need an explicitly biblical framework for their education, a countercultural grounding that will prepare them for life in a resolutely secular society."[9] The idea is that if Christian children are prepared in a Christian environment, they will have the necessary skills and strength to live in the secular world and not be consumed by its temptations.

There is the view that Christians should not compartmentalize their lives, keeping schooling separate from faith. As explained by Paul D. Spears and Steven R. Loomis, "Within education (and most fields and disciplines, in fact), it is easy to separate ourselves into what are nearly two separate existences: one that works within the boundaries of the educational guild, and the other that pursues a life of following the teaching of Jesus Christ."[10] This separation can cause a great deal of confusion to children: if Christians are to be Christian throughout their existence, why must they leave faith at the door for academic purposes?

From the perspective of the educator, it is important to see a child as more than just a brain. Spears and Loomis contend, "To be successful educators we must understand our students as more than just their physical selves; their identities transcend the limitations of the empirical realm."[11] Advocates of this position believe that Christian education has every right to be placed in school so that children are educated both academically and spiritually and have an understanding of how those two realms function together.

---

8. See chapter 5 of this volume.

9. Gilbreath and Wilson, "Two Schools of Thought," 51.

10. Spears and Loomis, *Education for Human Flourishing*, 30.

11. Ibid., 57.

Cons

Brian Victor Hill writes:

> Christian school theory often embodies a logic alien to Scripture. It accords validity to the activity of the Christian teacher only within the context of teaching in a Christian school, the premise being that only there can a curriculum built on Christian presuppositions be sustained. Logically, then, Christian teachers who remain in the public sector are compromising their calling.[12]

Certainly, there are those who think that private institutions focus too adamantly on the spiritual and leave the academic education wanting. Logically, if the private schools need to include chapel and classes that are focused on Christian content, they will have to cut other areas. What is eliminated is very dependent on the school and what they deem unimportant.

It appears that Christian schools passively devalue large groupings of professions by simply not offering classes that develop those trades. In a study of Catholic schools versus public schools, 89 percent of public schools offered wood/machine shop, while only 4 percent of Catholic institutions did so. The numbers are similarly lopsided for home economics and auto mechanics.[13] These classes not only teach children simple skills that they will incorporate the rest of their lives, but they also allow the young people to make decisions regarding their gifts and desires on their own in terms. Failing to offer children every opportunity for their career path is inadvertently saying that some career choices simply are not legitimate.

Public Education

The roots of compulsory education in the United States go back as far as the seventeenth century. The public option has a long history throughout the country. For some families, public education is the only option for financial reasons. Others believe that children are better served in such a setting. Still, Scripture demands that a Christian, called out of the world, must still be a part of that world. However, for young people in public schools, there is not just the challenge of being Christian in a secular world but also the task of doing so in a place where the teaching of religion is restricted.

Pros

Edward Gilbreath and John Wilson cite the resurgence of "Christians who believe that now more than ever the public schools need the active support and

---

12. Hill, *Faith at the Blackboard*, 86.
13. Bryk, Lee, and Holland, *Catholic Schools and the Common Good*, 76.

participation of committed believers."[14] A good example from the Holiness tradition is Church of God author Linden Boggs, who has served for several decades as a high-school teacher and public school administrator in northern Indiana. He writes:

> Let's begin building bridges between the home and the school—bridges of understanding and cooperation. Parents and teachers could travel in both directions upon [these bridges]. We can tell school teachers our ideas and aspirations for our children, and they can tell us theirs. Together we can forge a partnership to train our children—academically, morally, and spiritually—to become mature adults.[15]

Boggs encourages congregations to establish scholarship funds for their young people who wish to train for careers in public education. He advises Christian parents to become actively involved in their schools' textbook selection process, volunteer to serve as classroom aides, and so on.

An interesting experiment was attempted at the Community Church of Greenwood, Indiana, a nondenominational church founded by Dr. Charles Lake, a graduate of Asbury Theological Seminary. In the early 1980s, Dr. Lake guided this congregation to establish a Christian summer school program. Here is how he stated the rationale for the program:

> Community Church recognizes that the public schools do a good job of developing academic skills…and educationally preparing our youth for the world in which they will live.
>
> But most of the time, this educational experience is not put in the Christian perspective and, occasionally, may even be presented denouncing the Christian perspective. Each family individually and the church collectively have a responsibility to help our youth put their educational experience into a Christian perspective.[16]

For one month each summer, the Greenwood church gave its fifth graders a Christian orientation to information they would receive about scientific theories, sociological trends, and many other subjects in the public schools. Dr. Lake has since retired and this program has been discontinued, but parents and local school leaders commended the quality of the summer school experience.

Christian advocates of public schooling believe that the family and the worshiping community are primarily responsible for a young person's spiritual

---

14. Gilbreath and Wilson, "Two Schools of Thought," 51.

15. Boggs, *Concerned Parents*, 18.

16. Boggs, *Concerned Parents*, 186.

formation and Christian education. Without giving careful attention to this, a void can be created where Christian education should take place.

Cons

Christian schools employ teachers to inform children on the Bible, theology, and Christian ethics. Parents spend their money to ensure that professional attention is given to Christian education. The most obvious downside for public education is that children have no guarantee of any kind of Christian education. Even if they have Christian teachers or Christian friends, the regulations regarding discussion of religion are very restrictive.

Another possibly devastating drawback to public education is the exposure to the secular elements that can corrupt forming minds—drugs, language, sex, aggression. Furthermore, some believing parents must make peace with the distinct possibility that a public school will teach theories and materials that directly contradict what the parents teach about Christianity. Issues of creation, history, and science can threaten some family faith structures.

Recently, another issue has arisen, that in a financial downturn, public schools are failing along with the economy. Schools are becoming understaffed, underfunded, and the students pay the price. For many parents, this makes private schooling the only responsible option.

Home Schooling

As previously discussed in this chapter, Deuteronomy 6 states that parents are to teach their children in the ways of the faith. This task, arguably the most important task a human can be trusted with, ultimately is left to the parents. For this reason, many parents take the entire education of their children as their mission. This great responsibility certainly has its benefits. However, as with all three options, there are certainly shortcomings as well.

Pros

Home schooling, involves taking children out of the public-education arena altogether. This option allows parents and their church community to exercise more control over what the children learn, how they learn, and where they learn. Home-schooled students are often taken out of an environment where they do not receive enough attention and are potentially held back by "problem" students. Home schooling gives parents the opportunity to teach their children more adequately, based on their child's specific needs.

Within the home, spiritual formation can easily be incorporated into the schooling process. Parents are able to provide their own perspective on the important issues of life instead of having to re-teach where schools would compromise the tenets of their faith. The home school teacher can very readily blend academic and spiritual education.

Cons

Home schooling can develop adults who are out of touch with society. It can fail to develop well-rounded citizens. For this reason, home-schooling parents must deliberately involve the child or children in social activities outside of the home schooling environment, even beyond the larger home schooling society. All children need a chance to develop their character in secular civic society, since that is where they will spend most of their adult lives.

Another problem with home schooling is a lack of consistent educational standards for the teachers themselves. While some states stipulate that only a parent or guardian may home-school, many states place no requirements on who may teach. And according to the Home School Legal Defense Association (HSLDA), forty-one out of fifty states have *no* educational requirements on those who home school; in the other nine states, only a High School Diploma or GED is required.[17] Many states have no basic curriculum requirements and no testing of educational outcomes for home-schooled students.

Christians believe that every child has the right to receive a high-quality holistic education. While home schooling affords a unique opportunity to obtain such an education, it poses some risks of its own.

Summary

Whichever side a person agrees with, the problem that remains is that Christians are called to be in the world, to reach the lost, and to love one another. When Christians are separated from the public arena, there is a deep neglect of the call of Christ.

Perhaps a lens for assessing the question of schooling should be, which of these options promotes reconciliation of humanity to the Creator? Public schools mingle the nonbeliever and the believer, providing an obvious opportunity for reconciliation. However, one limitation is the inability of teachers and administrators to speak overtly about religion in the classroom. Private schools equip students with much more concrete biblical and theological education, but students are not easily involved in the community. Home schooling varies greatly, which makes it difficult to make generalizations about the quality of education or spiritual formation. What is likely, though, is that its relationships with the community are much like that of the private school.

---

17. Home School Legal Defense Association, "Summary of Home School Laws in the Fifty States," http://www.hslda.org.

Making a Prudent Decision

Ultimately, each family must choose for itself what is best. Certainly there are circumstances that will make the decision easier or more necessary. There is no definite right answer, because one must take into account many factors. However, what is obvious is that Christians must be careful in their choice, that they must consider the importance of a well-rounded education and the mission of God.

Though many years pass from the dedication of a child to the time a young person enters the educational system, the memory of that dedication within the community of faith is something parents must remember as they make this difficult decision. This covenant between the worshiping community, parents, and God will provide the framework for deciding what is best for the youth and hopefully not the selfish desires of any human party involved.

The Christian Ghetto

An overarching concern within Christian education and the debate over public, private, or home schooling is the idea of a Christian ghetto, which is a segregation of sorts. A Christian ghetto is created when Christians exist as a separate culture, with a different language and a unique mentality. Christian ghettos have their own music, television, books, and stores, and those in it have no contact with outsiders. Christians can very easily create a place where nonbelievers are not comfortable or welcome. Christians can create a subculture that envelops their whole life.

When Christians create these communities, they lose sight of the biblical mission to go out into the world, for the safety of not being influenced by the "evil" outside world. This is neither biblical nor compassionate; it is certainly not what Christians are called to. Looking at Jesus' example, one would easily see his daily interaction with sinners, tax collectors, and the like.

The question is, are Christian schools and home schools creating a type of Christian ghetto, where Christians are not in contact with the world and are not involved in the call to be "in the world" as Jesus commands? Private Christian schools and home schools can create an environment where children are never exposed to "the others." Consequently, they learn that there is no need to be involved outside of their Christian bubble.

Since God so loved the world, Christians also ought to love the world. Because Jesus told the disciples to "go and preach the good news to everyone in the world" (Mark 16:15), Christians ought to go. Since Jesus came to seek and save the lost, Christians ought to get out of their safe Christian communities and minister to a lost and dying world.

Hill asserts, "The Christian's primary mission is evangelism, and it is in evangelism that the biblical notion of reconciliation is imbedded."[18] A major recurring theme throughout the entirety of Scripture is reconciliation. For this reason, it must be a concern to all believers that their actions be in accordance with what will bring about reconciliation. To avoid the secular world out of selfishness is to act divisively. This contradicts reconciliation and, therefore, the mission of God.

Not only are Christians taking themselves out of the arena of society, they are also depriving society of ministers of the gospel. If teachers choose to teach in a private Christian school, they are depriving the public schools of their gift of ministry. If parents choose to keep their students out of public schools, they are depriving their children of the opportunity to both witness to and experience the world that God calls believers to be a part of. In the words of Broyles, "Christian responsibility requires us to work to provide [the] opportunity [for education and nurture] to all of God's children, not just our own."[19] Are not Christians called to be in the world, to minister to the world, and to love their enemies? Watkins proclaims, "The church at its best is a model for inclusivity. The family of God does not include just the brightest and best. Our responsibility as a community is to insure that all children have the basic education skills they need to succeed in today's rapidly changing world."[20]

Christians need to be involved in public education. They can run for school boards, be public school teachers, work together with schools, lift up public education in worship, and look at ministries through public education eyes.[21] There are ways to be involved that can fulfill God's ministry and mission without cutting off communication.

The role of Christian teachers and students in public schools is to reach the community and nonbelievers in that context, not to compartmentalize their faiths. For those in home school and Christian educational programs, there must be a more adamant charge to the world. Turning inward can happen in either context, and the educators and students involved must be aware of the shortcomings of their own context and be willing to overcome them in the name of Christ.

Parachurch Organizations

Parachurch organizations are faith-based organizations, generally Christian, which work apart from and across denominational lines and serve a wide range of purposes, goals, and means of functioning (e.g., Young Life, World Vision, Campus Crusade for Christ, Habitat for Humanity). These organizations func-

---

18. Hill, *Faith at the Blackboard*, 129.

19. Broyles, "Presbyterians and Education," 20.

20. Watkins, "Church and Public Education," 26.

21. Ibid., 26–27.

tion in ways that church faith communities are unable to function, they are welcome in places that churches are not welcome, and they serve an important and valuable purpose in the realm of Christian education. Parachurch organizations are a useful place for Christians to get involved with other believers in coming together for kingdom mission. These are groups that can function along with public education to create an outlet for both discipleship and evangelism. These action-based groups promote Christian education principles through participation and community involvement. Parents who want their children to be more involved missionally might look at these organizations as an alternative.

Conclusion

Looking at Christian education, believers have the responsibility to teach and the responsibility to be a part of the world God created. This can be done most effectively by being a part of the society to whom Christians are called to minister. They can administer the most change from the inside. Watkins proclaims, "When you get right down to it, the separation of church and state protects the church as well as the state and forces the church to take seriously its own educational ministry."[22] No matter the choice, the Christian education of young people must be pursued and chosen deliberately by their parents. These parents have to recognize the shortcomings of whatever path they choose and make every possible effort to counteract them.

Spiritual formation is something that is most appropriately done in the faith community and by the parents. Broyles challenges his readers: "To neglect the development of our minds and the minds of all of God's other children is to waste one of God's most precious gifts and to abdicate one of our most basic responsibilities as Christians."[23]

Bibliography

Allen, Holly C. *Nurturing Children's Spirituality: Christian Perspectives and Best Practices*. Eugene, OR: Cascade Books, 2008.

Boggs, Linden. *Concerned Parents*. Cincinnati, OH: Standard Publishing, 1986.

Broyles, Vernon S., III. "Presbyterians and Education." *Church & Society* 88 (1998): 14.

Bryk, Anthony S., Valarie E. Lee, and Peter B. Holland. *Catholic Schools and the Common Good*. Cambridge, MA: Harvard University Press, 1993.

Gardner, Freda A. "The Current Situation in Christian Education." *Church & Society* 88 (1998): 75.

---

22. Ibid., 25.
23. Broyles, "Presbyterians and Education," 14.

Gilbreath, Edward, and John Wilson. "Two Schools of Thought." *Christianity Today* 45 (2001): 51.

Hill, Brian Victor. *Faith at the Blackboard: Issues Facing the Christian Teacher*. Grand Rapids, MI: Eerdmans, 1982.

Olsen, Glenn, and Mary Lou Fuller. *Home-School Relations: Working Successfully with Parents and Families*, 2nd ed. Boston: Allyn and Bacon, 2003.

Spears, Paul D., and Steven R. Loomis. *Education for Human Flourishing*. Downers Grove, IL: IVP Academics, 2009.

Watkins, Jim. "The Church and Public Education." *Church & Society* 88 (1998): 24.

CHAPTER TWENTY-SIX

Contemporary Holiness Living

SHANNON NEW-SPANGLER
AND BRETT A. SPANGLER

> Finally, my friends, keep your minds on whatever is true, pure, right, holy, friendly, and proper. Don't ever stop thinking about what is truly worthwhile and worthy of praise. You know the teachings I gave you, and you know what you heard me say and saw me do. So follow my example. And God, who gives peace, will be with you.
>
> —Philippians 4:8–9

History is filled with stories of humanity straying from God. As time marches on, the things that cause people to drift from intimacy with the Creator change. However, this constant remains: humans struggle to live what God has revealed to them as a holiness lifestyle. Society today faces Christians with a plethora of opportunities to step away from holiness living. In a postmodern context, temptations are only a mouse click away. How can Christians be holy when the temptation is so easily achieved? How can believers stay strong in the face of the attraction of the secular ideals? This chapter will deal specifically with several of these contemporary challenges to holiness living, which is by no means an exhaustive list, and will discuss what holiness really is all about.

An important discussion regarding holiness is the change that is coming in how holiness living is perceived. Traditionally, holiness living has implied, and even been described, as a list of activities that make a person Christian or un-Christian. In contrast to this rather legalistic, confining view of holiness living, many Christians are starting to consider a very different set of holiness ideals. As younger generations gain a voice, perceptions are changing and a new understanding of holiness is emerging.

This "new" view of holiness is not new at all. In fact, it is a calling back to Christian roots. Christians are beginning to consider holiness as Christlikeness. Contemporary views of holiness move more toward Beatitude holiness and away from Ten Commandments holiness. In this view, holiness is about what the Christian does and not what the Christian is forbidden to do. In this light, holiness is viewed as liberating rather than confining. Christians are identified by who they are uniquely created to be in Christ rather than what they abstain from doing.

The call to holiness is the initial call; it is the call that God makes that sets the Christian life in motion. No other call can be fulfilled without first accepting the call to holiness. Stewardship is unreasonable without first accepting a call to holiness. Likewise, mission is a waste of time without first accepting a call to holiness. Life in community with other believers is a hassle without first accepting a call to holiness. Life ethically shaped and spent alongside Jesus, empowered by the Spirit, and intended by the Father, is illogical without first accepting a call to holiness.[1]

Holiness is foundational to the Christian life. And if this is the case, then a clear understanding of what holiness is, will be required.

Modern Hindrances to Holiness Living

God continues his self-revelation throughout human history. As believers walk alongside the Creator, they learn more about God and more about who they are created to be. Therefore, holiness is a dynamic venture. How the people of God live holy lives is constantly shaped by a deepening understanding of the triune God and an ever-changing culture. Holiness living in a pre-messianic culture was far different from holiness in a society redeemed by the Messiah. Along the same lines, modernity understands holiness far differently from postmodernity. This twofold movement presses the believer to constant growth and reassessment. Static living is impossible.

Ultimately, in this discussion of *modern* hindrances to holiness living, the discussion is more about modernity's hindrances to holiness living. What this means is, a primary hindrance to living a holy life in the world today is the manner in which modernity has handcuffed Christians to a rigid life that is not

---

1. Greenway and Green, *Grace and Holiness*, 62–75.

at all free. Many concepts tied to modernity and its interpretation of holiness hinder holiness living.

Perfection

A major concern within the Holiness Movement is the idea that holiness equates to behavioral perfection.[2] Some Christians think that if they do anything wrong, they are unworthy to serve in the church, so they are unwilling to confess their moral failures and the lines of communication shut down. This lack of confession hinders holy living in many churches. People are not free to bring their failures to the community, to their pastor, or even to God. How can believers say that they love God if they refuse to be honest with God?

In a paper presented to the 1996 convocation of the Association of Nazarene Sociologists and Researchers, Richard Benner underscored the problem of perfectionism in the Holiness Movement. Despite a traditional aversion to sacramental theology, he suggested that Holiness people make confession an integral part of their worship as it is in sacramental churches:

> Nazarenes are in deep need of confession and opportunities to ask forgiveness. Whatever we need to do as a part of our growth in sanctifying grace, we need to ask forgiveness and pray personal and collective prayer[s] of forgiveness. Here are some of the issues about which I would hold that even sanctified Nazarenes need to ask forgiveness:

- Our self–indulgent appetites and ways,
- Our exploitation of other people,
- Our anger at our own frustration,
- Our envy of those more fortunate than ourselves,
- Our intemperate love of worldly goods and comforts,
- Our negligence in prayer and worship,
- Our failure to commend the faith that is within us,
- Our neglect of human need and suffering,
- Our indifference to injustice and cruelty,
- Our lack of compassion and caring,
- Our belief that we no longer need to ask forgiveness.

---

2. When John Wesley preached perfection, he meant something far different than contemporary Christians understand perfection to be. For Wesley, Christian perfection was a condition of the heart—loving God perfectly; contemporary Christians think of perfection as absolutely perfect behavior. For more information, see Wesley, *Plain Account of Christian Perfection*, or Outler, *John Wesley's Sermons*.

What would happen and what would we be teaching our people if we had a prayer of confession in our services as is the tradition in many Christian groups?[3]

Often holiness is seen as not much more than vehement avoidance of all perceived sins because of the intense guilt and shame that accompany them. However, this understanding causes Christians to gradually add to their substantial list of sins, tangible and otherwise, until they are handcuffed by "holiness," unable to live in a world that God created and proclaimed good. Christians fear the God they have created. This is not the God of grace exemplified in the ministry of Christ or the witness of Scripture. No, this is a vengeful God who exists outside of scriptural witness. Too often believers choose this created God over the God of grace. How much freer would believers live if they simply accepted that God *knows* humankind is going to fail? Christians think failure is more avoidable than God does, so when it happens, they are far more disappointed and shocked than the One who loves them the most.

Pastors are fine telling people from the pulpit that they do not need to be perfect to give their life to Christ. However, once someone has been a Christian for a "good enough amount of time" (whatever that is), the expectation of perfection creeps in. Michael Yaconelli reminds us that the church is not truly being the church until it expects incompetence.[4] Because God did not create perfect human beings ("all have sinned," Romans 3:23), Holiness Movement churches must remember that perfection is not a virtue; holiness is. And the two are not the same.

Jesus prefers the people who are immersed in their incompleteness. He came to save the lost, not those who believed they were found. He healed cripples, not marathon runners. The holy predecessors described in the stories of the pioneer people of God in the Bible are not "holy" people according to a man-made code of holiness. These are people who lie, cheat, kill, drink, and perpetually battle depression. They are holy because, in the midst of all of the mess of life, they are fervently seeking community with believers and with God. These are people longing to love God with all of themselves and are not willing to damn themselves for what they once did.

Holiness is, in fact, the opposite of perfection; it is the continued life in faith and pursuit of God in the face of days, months, years, and decades of imperfection. Reconciliation is the business of God, and business has been good for thousands of years. Logically humanity cannot be perfect, but the business of reconciliation is still thriving.

God knows the human condition more intimately than humans know it. God knows grace far deeper than humans can. The Creator loves, even marvels,

---

3. Benner, "Naming the Silences," 4–5.

4. Yaconelli, *Messy Spirituality*, 30–33.

at the created when they stumble toward him like infant toddlers. When the teetering and tottering, the falling and toppling, is over and the young one is in the arms of the Father, the tumbling makes no difference. Instead, the Father marvels at the dedication and persistence of the journey and the love shown as the tike tumbles into a well-deserved hug.

Legalism

A common hindrance to holiness living is living by law rather than by grace. While the two are not mutually exclusive, law without grace loses sight of Jesus.[5] Legalism, too, is often confused with holiness; legalism is an overemphasis on law or codes of conduct. It is the belief that salvation can be earned by obedience to laws. It is also known as works righteousness. Legalism forgets that God is graceful and loving and that God knows the heart.

Holiness groups in their early conception were much more legalistic than they are now. There was a vast list of don'ts having to do with clothing, actions, and attitudes. Christians could not watch movies, dance, smoke, drink, or go to places that served alcohol, and they had to be in before 10:00 PM. This list is from a list of rules that were implemented at one Holiness school in the mid-twentieth century.[6] Holiness had become to them a form a legalism.

Legalism is asking what must be done; holiness is asking what can be done to glorify God. Legalism is comparing oneself to others; holiness is comparing oneself to God. Legalism is trying to save oneself; holiness is asking God to save. Legalism is works; holiness is faith. While it needs to be said that the actions of the Christian are important, Christians have to break out of trying to do the "right thing" and move on to imitating Jesus. It is a matter of changing a mindset.

A major concern with legalism is what it implies about God. "The God of the legalistic Christian…is often unpredictable, erratic, and capable of all manner of prejudices. This God expects people to be perfect and to be in perpetual control of their feelings and thoughts. When broken people with this concept of God fail, they expect punishment. So they persevere in religious practices as they struggle to maintain a hollow image of a perfect self. The legalists can never live up to the expectations they project on God."[7] But who wants to serve this God? And where does this God come from? Certainly this is not the biblical God of love and grace.

Living by rules and guidelines and calling it holiness is wrong. There is no way around that. However, living in love and being *guided* by rules, understanding that the rules are not God, is helpful. Life without rules, according to

---

5. Ibid., 75.

6. Rebecca New-Edson, e-mail message to authors, November 2009.

7. Manning, *Ragamuffin Gospel*, 40–41.

Thomas Jay Oord and Michael Lodahl, "would be chaotic and destructive."[8] The issue is that the rules cannot ever be more important than God or the love that God would have all of humanity to know.

Comfort

On the subject of comfort, Michael Yaconelli writes,

> All of us tend to seek comfort, to structure predictability, to eliminate the new and different from our experience. The word *messy* strikes fear into the hearts of the comfortable. According to the comfortable, God does what he always does…There are those in the church who honestly believe God is a nice and neat God. One quick run through the Bible gives you a different picture. The God of the Bible is the master of surprises…No one can follow God and be comfortable for long.[9]

An often overlooked issue with personal holiness is falling into the idea that holiness or godliness is meant to be comfortable, that holiness can be attained and held onto without much effort. God is not nice and neat, and neither is holiness. Those who wish to be holy must be willing to move and grow, to get messy and dirty, and to take risks. Comfort falls into the sin of sloth, which is spiritual apathy. When Christians get comfortable, they are not living in holiness.

A mistake of modernity is a desperate need for answers and completion in order to feel whole. Christianity cannot be boiled down to a formula that fits all people. Holiness is a constant state of incompletion and process. Holiness means that the believer is under construction, allowing God to work in and on them.[10] But modernity wants definite answers, right here and right now. Holiness, as Christ would have us know it, is attractive to postmoderns more concerned with the journey than the destination.

Another way that Christians get comfortable is in their unwillingness to go out and share holiness with their neighbor. So comfort, or a completely internal and personal understanding of faith, becomes a hindrance to holiness living. Holiness is more than a personal walk with Christ and an inward transformation or a remission of sins. Holiness is also the call to be involved with others, the mission to share God's love with those in need of hope.

Elitism

Another modern hindrance to holiness living is the corporate rejection of those Jesus so openly accepted: the outcasts of society. However, elitism is not so much

---

8. Oord and Lodahl, *Relational Holiness*, 129.

9. Yaconelli, *Messy Spirituality*, 42.

10. Ibid., 29.

a modern hindrance to holiness as it is a human condition. The Pharisees were guilty of it in Jesus' time, the clergy were guilty of it in the Middle Ages, and the churches of the Holiness Movement are often guilty of it today. When are Christians going to recognize that the Messiah was anything but elitist? When will we realize that Christ opened his arms to all people, every shape and every size, every religion, every race? Jesus Christ was the very opposite of elitist. But Christians throughout history have taken this attitude, forgetting the muck and the mire that they themselves were saved from. In this they keep salvation from the poor, the weak, and, ultimately, the ones who need it the most.

Looking into the Bible, it becomes clear that God loved all people, that Christ worked with even prostitutes and tax collectors, and that Christians are told to go into the entire world. In the words of Yaconelli, "Christianity proclaims that it is an equal opportunity faith."[11] But in practice, many Christians do not uphold these ideals.

A Different View of Holiness

Holiness is about what a Christian does, who they love, how they live, and how they believe. Holiness is not perfection, legalism, comfort, or elitism. Holiness is a process that moves the believer toward God. Holiness is not something that can be accomplished alone or out of sheer willpower; it requires the Holy Spirit to work within the believer to change the heart, the mind, and the soul.

Relational

Holiness is, above all else, relational. It requires a deep relationship with God and an active relationship with humankind. Holiness works when Christians are genuinely involved in both of these relationships. The core function of holiness is love. It is impossible to "love one another" without relationships.

Holiness is love in action. Holiness is love for God in the way God taught us to love. Holiness is loving humankind the way God loves humankind. Oord and Lodahl write, "We are holy as God is holy when we love as God loves."[12] When faced with persons who are a different gender or race, holy Christians must love as Christ loved. When confronted with a homosexual, the holy Christian must love deeply. When met with a divorced person, an unwed mother, or an alcoholic, the holy Christian loves without judgment. Holiness is relational, learning to love humankind truly and purely as beloved creations, just as God loves them without agenda or bias.

Christians must exchange their religion for relationship. Only then will their self-righteousness become holiness. In 1 John 4:17 we read, "As we live in God, our love grows more perfect." Human nature is to imitate those with whom

---

11. Ibid., 76.
12. Oord and Lodahl, *Relational Holiness*, 72.

there is the most intimate relationship. If God is the one known most intimately, as a child mimes her mother, followers will begin to resemble their Creator. However, as relationships grow shallower, the tendency is to try to imitate holiness. What results is a hollow performance void of any true knowledge of why anything is done the way it is. Yaconelli asserts, "Spirituality is not a formula; it is not a test. It is a relationship. Spirituality is not about competency; it is about intimacy."[13] When choices are made because of the abundance of God's love and knowledge of God, Christians are living in holiness.

Christlikeness/Godliness

The main focus for the believer working toward holiness is Christlikeness. If there is any question as to how the believer ought to act, they can simply look to Jesus. Several years ago, WWJD (What Would Jesus Do?) bracelets were very popular among Christians.[14] While this phrase may seem trite, it does show what the holiness mindset is all about. In any given situation, believers may ask themselves, What would Jesus do? Whatever the answer, Christians ought to do the same.

Jesus is the believer's teacher and guide. He is one to look up to and to work to imitate. But the Bible does not simply give believers the example of Jesus Christ; it shares the triune God: Father, Son, and Spirit. Throughout the Bible, humankind is given evidence of God and of God's character. While Christians must strive to be like Christ, they also were created in God's image (Gen 1:27). Being holy then also means reflecting the image of God.

The process of refining silver and other precious metals involves putting the metal through intense heat that literally burns and consumes all the impurities in the metal. One silversmith was asked, "How do you know when the silver is ready?" He said, "That's simple, I heat it until I can see my reflection in the metal, and when I see my reflection, I know it's ready."[15] That is exactly how God works in the believer's life. When one becomes a Christian, God fires the soul and then begins to cleanse and purify the believer's life. When Christians have been fully cleansed and purified, the image and holiness of God is reflected in their hearts and lives.

A List of Dos

As the Holiness Movement has grown, it has come to realize that holiness is more than a checklist of don'ts. In the Sermon on the Mount, Jesus recites what are known as the Beatitudes. These statements challenge Christians in what should be done rather than what should be avoided: blessed are the meek,

---

13. Yaconelli, *Messy Spirituality*, 13.
14. The source of this fad is Sheldon, *In His Steps*.
15. Story based on Malachi 3.

blessed are the merciful, blessed are the pure in heart, blessed are the peacemakers.[16] This is not a list of don'ts; it is a list of dos: Do be meek, do be merciful, do be pure, do be peacemakers. This is what believers are called to, an invitation in how to function in holiness.

Christianity is not about works-righteousness. Grace cannot be earned. Relationship with God, however, will bear its fruit in a list of holy dos that bless neighbor, self, and God. As the believer grows in relationship, the dos will simply become the way of being. Christ's mission, in the eyes of many, is liberation. This does not merely mean liberation at the end of life but also liberation in the midst of life. The Beatitudes liberate believers from the confines of static holiness.

Along with the Beatitudes, Christians are given another list of dos: the fruit of the Spirit, which is love, joy, peace, patience, kindness, goodness, faithfulness, gentleness, and self-control (Gal 5:22–23). The believer is called to exemplify these attitudes and behaviors. Christians might ask themselves, Am I acting in love? Patience? Gentleness? And if the answer is yes, than they can be assured that they are being holy.

Living a dynamic holiness envelops all of Christian life. When attention is given to the relationship with Father, Son, and Spirit, the list of dos will overwhelm the list of do nots. The product of this relationship, of wholly doing, is holiness. Jeffrey E. Greenway and Joel B. Green write, "Holiness should mean wholeness, the integrity of heart and life."[17] When following these lists of dos, the believer will automatically be changed in their heart and in their actions. Most importantly, Christian life will be dominated by doing. Beatitude holiness is active holiness. There is no time for stagnation when living in the fruit of the Spirit.

What Holiness Was

Rather than a way of relating to God, humanity, and self, holiness became, over the years, a way of ensuring salvation, social standing, and peace of mind. As holiness became less about relationship, it lost its entire purpose. Instead of blessing others through the overflow of healthy relationships with God, believers spilled guilt onto each other for how imperfect their lives were.

---

16. Matthew 5:3–12. "Blessed are the poor in spirit, for theirs is the kingdom of heaven. Blessed are those who mourn, for they will be comforted. Blessed are the meek, for they will inherit the earth. Blessed are those who hunger and thirst for righteousness, for they will be filled. Blessed are the merciful, for they will be shown mercy. Blessed are the pure in heart, for they will see God. Blessed are the peacemakers, for they will be called sons of God. Blessed are those who are persecuted because of righteousness, for theirs is the kingdom of heaven. Blessed are you when people insult you, persecute you and falsely say all kinds of evil against you because of me. Rejoice and be glad, because great is your reward in heaven, for in the same way they persecuted the prophets who were before you" (NIV).

17. Greenway and Green, *Grace and Holiness*, 61–62.

Works-holiness sounds absurd, but that is what holiness became. Humanity was the gauge for holiness. People fooled themselves into believing that they could be good enough for God, that they could fool others into believing they were perfect, and that they could fool themselves into thinking that such was a Christian lifestyle. This went on for quite a while. The result was generations of believers who lived in fear of God and were afraid to do or say anything that may lead people to believe they were not holy.

The key change in the concept of holiness ultimately boils down to movement. Previously conceived notions of holiness confined the believer, paralyzing him or her to the point that life was consumed by fear. God wants people to live! Humanity is to be the ever-moving, ever-changing vehicle of reconciliation that conveys divine love in a broken world. That vehicle struggles to move when the passengers will not ease off of the brake.

What Holiness Is Becoming: A Definition

Holiness remains tremendously important to the life of the believer; however, that does not mean it will look the same as it did in the modern age. Holiness in the postmodern era is still a very important principle. Choosing to partake in a traditionally taboo event that is in no way sinful according to any biblical witness does not mean that Christian people have thrown away holiness. It means they view it differently. Much can be learned about holiness through the history of Christianity. That the definition of holiness may change does not take away from the validity of past human experience.

Holiness is a journey that includes becoming comfortable with self. Believers walk with God and begin to understand in an infinitesimal way how much God loves and cares for them. This leads to a love for self that is comfortable with who God created each individual to be. Love for self spills out into love for the community. This includes believers and nonbelievers. Holiness grants the believer a lens that discloses the abounding potential in every created person. A person journeying in holiness sees God in self and neighbor. Holiness is a reciprocal process that continues throughout the lifetime of a believer.

Holiness is love. It is a love for God that is so deep that the believer cannot help but work toward God's purposes and be formed in God's image. It is a love for others that sees them as beautiful creations of a good God. It is a love for self that allows the believer to be loved by a graceful God. Though it sounds simple, there is little more to say. God's desires of humanity are simple: love me, love each other, and love yourself. That sounds too easy. It is not. Mastering that is a lifelong task that every believer must pursue.

Holiness as Christian Education

One of the major problems of holiness living is the fact that holiness is either not being taught or not being taught well. Many churches do not even delve into the topic, leaving holiness to be discovered by the wayward reader of the Bible, leaving each one to his or her own interpretation. According to Oord and Lodahl, "It is not uncommon for a person to grow up in the Holiness tradition, attend a Holiness college or university, and proceed even to a Holiness seminary, all the while finding that theologians in the Holiness tradition have come to differing conclusions about what holiness means."[18]

The church is teaching constantly. Christian educational systems are teaching constantly. In both silences and lectures, in the doing and the resting, teaching is happening. Modeling holiness is a significant way in which spiritual formation is promoted. People learn how to be in relationships by watching others who are involved in successful relationships. The saints of the church model their successful relationship with God for nonbelievers and new believers to see. Howard A. Snyder puts it well:

> God wants to fill the church with His Spirit so that it walks and talks like Jesus, doing the work Jesus left for it. This is holiness. A Spirit-filled church draws the holy love of the Trinity into itself and spreads it all around, releasing an epidemic of healing.
>
> Holiness is not only friendship with God. It is deep, nurturing, question-answering, heart-warming, soul-satisfying friendship with Jesus' sisters and brothers on the pilgrim road to the kingdom… "Whoever does the will of my Father in heaven is my brother and sister and mother" (Matthew 12:50).[19]

Finally, as Snyder indicates, holiness in Christian education sees the God-given potential of each person. A Spirit-led teacher is blessed to get a glimpse of the potential that God sees in every person. Christian education is profoundly set apart from secular education in that every single student is a fount of seemingly limitless potential. The Creator has blessed every person with gifts. The role of Christian education is to nurture those whenever possible. Holiness enables Christian educators to recognize these gifts and take part in the holy work of developing them.

Conclusion

The parable of the talents[20] teaches what God perceives holiness living to be. Had those servants invested the talents and lost them all, the offense would not

---

18. Oord and Lodahl, *Relational Holiness*, 36.

19. Snyder, "Good News of God's Holiness," 8.

20. Matthew 25:14–30.

have been nearly as serious as that of the servant who buried his talent in the ground. Holiness grants Christians the freedom to take drastic risks. Timidity and holiness may as well be antonyms. Relationship, sought fervently and honestly with God, will not end in failure, of course. Perhaps that is a subtle lesson in this parable. Jesus is saying that all who invest wisely by betting their lives on him will reap great gains.

God is calling humanity to an active relationship. Active faith is the sign of holiness living. Relationship with God is freeing. It grants the believer a new perspective for viewing self, community, and Creator. Holiness enables, frees, and binds the believer to the Creator—and not to certain works. This holy binding is freeing, unlike the restrictive bindings of a guilt-motivated holiness code. It is never completed, never comfortable, never stagnant. Christians are invited to journey with one another and their Creator in a process that has been happening throughout human history. The way that it is executed and understood changes, but the intent, pleasing God, is unchanging.

There are certainly many things that holiness is *not*: it is not legalistic, static, selfish, or negatively binding. Holiness *is* a love and relationship between humans, neighbor, and Creator. When asked the greatest commandment, Jesus gave humanity the guide for holiness living: *Love the Lord your God with all your heart and love your neighbor as yourself.*[21] This is, ultimately, the most concise and thorough description of holiness living available.

---

21. Luke 10:27.

Bibliography

Benner, Richard. "Naming the Silences: The Doctrine of Holiness." Paper presented at the Annual Conference of the Association of Nazarene Sociologists and Researchers, 1996. http://www.nazarene.org/files/docs/Naming%20 the%20Silences_%20the%20Doctrine%20of%20Holiness.pdf.

Greenway, Jeffrey E., and Joel B. Green. *Grace and Holiness in a Changing World.* Nashville, TN: Abingdon Press, 2007.

Manning, Brennan. *The Ragamuffin Gospel.* Sisters, OR: Multnomah Press, 2000.

Oord, Thomas Jay, and Michael Lodahl. *Relational Holiness: Responding to the Call of Love.* Kansas City, MO: Beacon Hill Press, 2005.

Outler, Albert. *John Wesley's Sermons: An Anthology.* Nashville, TN: Abingdon Press, 1991.

Sheldon, Charles M. *In His Steps: What Would Jesus Do?* New Kensington, PA: Whitaker House, 2004.

Snyder, Howard A. "The Good News of God's Holiness." *Light and Life,* September/October 2010, 6–9.

Wesley, John. *A Plain Account of Christian Perfection.* In *The Works of John Wesley,* edited by Thomas Jackson, 11:366–446. Grand Rapids, MI: Baker, 1979. (Reprinted by many publishers. Available online from the Christian Classics Ethereal Library: http://www.ccel.org/ccel/wesley/perfection/formats/ perfection.txt.)

Yaconelli, Michael. *Messy Spirituality: God's Annoying Love for Imperfect People.* Grand Rapids, MI: Zondervan, 2002.

CHAPTER TWENTY-SEVEN

Christian Education in the Emerging Church

JERRY HICKSON

> [God] knows what is in everyone's heart. And he showed that he had chosen the Gentiles, when he gave them the Holy Spirit, just as he had given his Spirit to us. God treated them in the same way that he treated us. They put their faith in him, and he made their hearts pure.
>
> —Acts 15:8–9

In every age, the church has had to cope with change and address cultures with different values. In the New Testament, this was the case as the gospel bridged from the Jewish people to the Gentiles. Recent years have brought a phenomenon known as the emerging church. For many, this is the latest wave of reformation, changing the way ministry is done to address more adequately the reality of the present culture.

Defining the Buzz Word

Who is this emerging church? The emerging church is a loose collection of people who refuse to be identified as a uniform movement but rather who work among the postmodern environment (itself not uniform) to develop new approaches to ministry. The emerging church is largely a counter to modern rationalism and the methods of the seeker-sensitive approach that first became popular in the 1970s. D. A. Carson sees five characteristics of the emerging church.

- a sensitivity to the changing culture;
- a profound desire for authenticity;
- the recognition that we all interpret life and faith out of a social framework;
- a genuine desire to evangelize the unchurched;
- the adaptation of traditional worship forms.[1]

An informed discussion of the emerging church requires an understanding of **postmodernism**. To a large degree, the twenty-first century is defined by the values of the postmodern mindset. Chapter 7 contains an in-depth definition of this mindset, but in brief, postmodernism is an adaptation to the excesses of the modern age or the Enlightenment. Not everyone in the emerging church responds to postmodernism in the same way. As Doug Pagitt says, some work against postmodernism, some work with postmodernism, and some work as postmoderns.[2] Those who work against postmodernism tend to take reactionary stances, trying to hold the line against further erosion of the values once held. Others see postmodernism as neither all good nor all evil, working to make connections where possible and to correct excess and error where required. Then there are some who unashamedly identify themselves by postmodern values, seeking to bring the rest of the church into the light of day. Those of the emerging church tend to work with or as postmoderns.

Perhaps the most controversial issue surrounding the emerging church and Christian postmodernism is the question about absolutes. Many understand that postmodernism rejects all absolutes, and surely there are some who fit this description. Many, however, would agree that absolutes exist but that great caution should be exercised in asserting that one understands what they are. Modern experience has shown the limitations of logic and rationalism for finding absolute truth. Life is full of mystery and paradox. God is bigger than any assertions about him. What has become objectionable is not so much absolutes but the power plays that are mounted by those who believe they are armed with the proven facts.[3]

Most of the leading examples of the emerging church so far have come from a particular Christian tradition. These persons tend to come from a background of the Reformed church, Calvinism, evangelicalism, or fundamentalism.

---

1. Burns, Review of *Becoming Conversant*, 122. Burns is summarizing Carson's second chapter.
2. Attributed by McKnight, "Five Streams of the Emerging Church, 37.
3. Hampton, et al, "Is There Room at the Table?"

Their thinking is naturally flavored by the theology of their tradition. Persons who work in the Holiness tradition frequently find value in the ideas offered by emerging writers while having to steer around theological issues that do not fit their environment. Surely the emerging church will take on a slightly different flavor among those who come from a background in the Holiness Movement.

Practitioners of this new wave distinguish between the labels *emerging* and *emergent*. To be sure, some use the terms synonymously. Where they are distinguished, **emergent** usually refers to a select portion of the emerging church represented by Tony Jones, Brian McLaren and others and is represented by the Web site www.emergentvillage.com. This chapter will use the broader label of *emerging church*.

In spite of all the excitement over the emerging church, most congregations continue to operate in a modernist mindset. Postmodernism is often viewed as a villain. Implementation of methods used in the emerging church in such settings will likely result in conflict and division. Among the most progressive, the emerging church is already viewed as a passing fad. A satirical blog offers an obituary for this trend.[4] While working to understand and engage with the emerging church, no trend should be enshrined as the "end all." While learning from this movement, the wise will always keep their eyes open for still newer developments.

Characteristics of Emerging Christian Education

While emerging writers have been prolific in writing articles and books, little has been written specifically about Christian education from this perspective. Most of the writing concerns philosophy or worship style. When the discussion moves into educational areas, other terms (discipleship, spiritual formation, mentoring) are often used in place of Christian education. Discussion of Christian education must be extrapolated from these discussions.

A key value is **cultural sensitivity**. Instead of beginning with a foundational truth and fitting everything into that framework, the practice is to appreciate the nuances of the different values of different communities. These communities are defined not only by ethnicity but also by generational characteristics. Christian education in the emerging context is profoundly conditioned by understanding the perspective of the learners.

At the same time, the emerging church emphasizes the larger world of **Christian tradition** over the particularities of various specific **denominational traditions**. Emerging ministry reaffirms vintage faith and practices, reaching beyond the revivalism of the 1950s or nineteenth century to Celtic Christianity and medieval spirituality. A label used by some is "Ancient/Future,"[5] reaching back several centuries to mine the heritage of the faith. Resources found in this

---

4. Bennett, "Obituary for the Emerging Church."

5. Robert Webber is best known for the label.

storehouse include *lectio divina*, use of creeds, and other spiritual formation practices (e.g., labyrinths, stations of the cross, a rule of life).

A predominant theme is **missional** ministry. The attractional approach, which is characterized by the misquoted movie line, "If you build it they will come,"[6] is rejected in favor of the words of Jesus, "Go into all the world." This aspect of emerging mindset is particularly an affinity for those in the Wesleyan tradition. Social holiness has always been characteristic of those who follow the lead of John Wesley. Missional ministry seeks to be holistic rather than just addressing spiritual concerns. In missional thinking, every program and method is evaluated by its effectiveness in engaging persons in the surrounding culture with the gospel message.

The emerging church values **authenticity** above theological precision. Emerging Christian education works to major on majors and minor on minors. Where some emphasize systematic theology, the emerging emphasize experiential and application-oriented theology. Emphasis is placed on living right lifestyles more than on articulating right doctrine. In the words of John G. Stackhouse:

> [S]ince the Christian message is fundamentally an invitation extended to human beings—not just human brains—to encounter the person of Jesus Christ rather than to adopt a doctrinal system or ideology, it is only obvious then that establishing the credibility and plausibility of that message will depend on more than intellectual argument. It will depend instead upon the Holy Spirit of God shining out through all the lamps of good works we can raise to the glory of our Father in heaven.[7]

While *authentic* may sometimes become something of a buzz word, the intent is to be relevant and meaningful to actual behavior.

Emerging ministry takes an **incarnational** approach. This is what Webber calls "the apologetics of embodied presence."[8] Every effort is taken to express through action the very presence of God. The expectation is that persons will experience God as they interact with Christians.

Another key value is an **egalitarian** approach to process as opposed to hierarchical systems. With the democratization of the Internet comes a preference for networking as opposed to command and control. This influences interaction within a small group or classroom and the structure of programs like a children's ministry. Power and authority are decentralized as trust is extended to those who participate in the process.

---

6. *Field of Dreams*, 1989.

7. As cited in Carson, *Becoming Conversant with the Emerging Church*, 66. Carson uses the quote to illustrate the tendency of the emerging to practice the same things they criticize in modernity.

8. Webber, *Younger Evangelicals*, 69.

Among the emerging, the use of **images** has become a key medium for communication. To a large degree, this represents a return to premodern practices. Some ancient practices are being renewed, including stained-glass, icons, and candles. Technology allows these to be accentuated with video presentations, interactive computer software, and graphic arts.

Narrative is becoming a predominant vehicle for communication instead of propositional presentations.[9] Story offers a richness of nuance and individualization. Much of the Bible is made up of stories. To these are added historical and fictional narratives of various kinds. Hal Knight explains:

> Proclamation and teaching in emerging churches finds truth more in biblical narrative than a rational/propositional reading of scripture...In this way they reject both the claim of rationalism that truth can only be found in clear and distinct ideas, and of romanticism that it is found in subjective experience. Instead, they find truth in biblical narratives and images and express it through story and art as well as in propositions.[10]

This shift leads to significant change in the structure of lessons (and sermons). Neat three-point outlines give way to amorphous story lines that may lead to multiple understandings.[11]

Dogma has given way to **questioning**. This sometimes results in a reversal of order as the lesson moves from the problem to the solution in a more inductive manner than has been the case before. One method is the use of a "doubt box," where learners are encouraged to prompt discussion with their concerns. In what he calls "The World's Most Dangerous Bible Study," Eric Eines begins youth meetings with pop songs to provide the grist for discussion of Christian themes.[12] Among the things commonly questioned are modernist mindsets, including use of categories and the dualism that sees everything as right/wrong or good/bad.

This new approach tends to **reverse the order** of the overall process. Often the old order was to get converted and then join the church. Many are advocating that the welcome net be cast out to receive persons into the community so that they can come to belief. Robert Webber took this a step further, saying, "The old paradigm for modernists was 'behave, believe, belong' while the paradigm adopted by many in the Emergent church is 'belong, believe, behave.'"[13] This change in thinking influences expectations for membership and for leader-

---

9. Hampton et al, "Is There Room at the Table?"

10. Knight, "John Wesley and the Emerging Church," 5.

11. See chapter 9 of this volume.

12. Eines, "World's Most Dangerous Bible Study," 201–6.

13. Webber, *Younger Evangelicals*, 48.

ship. How far can one go with incorporating a person into leadership roles who has not yet assimilated the values of the community?

In some cases, **alternative communities** have arisen as contexts for learning. These are sometimes like the monastic communities of medieval times. These communities may be a group of single men sharing a condo or more than one family sharing a house or living in close proximity and sharing resources. A lesser scale would be the house church, where all ministry, including Christian education, takes place in the relational dynamic of a few families and singles who meet together in intentional covenant.

Concerns Related to Emerging Ministry

To a large degree, the emerging movement arose on the West Coast of the United States. Some of the product of this group has an eccentric flavor that will not connect well with other cultures. As this movement evolves, it is taking diverse flavors influenced by the cultures of the different regions.

Some find objectionable certain aspects of the emerging church. With its proclivity to postmodern thinking, some find an excess of relativism that demeans the uniqueness or authority of the Christian faith. Some are concerned about the anti-institutionalism that pervades the present generation. The emerging church may be more relevant to house churches or large churches in urban settings than to small churches in small town or rural settings. Still, the emerging church represents a concerted effort to translate the timeless message of Jesus into the current context.

Bibliography

Bennett, Rick. "An Obituary for the Emerging Church." Blog: Cheaper Than Therapy. http://djword.blogspot.com/2010/01/obituary-for-emerging-church.html (accessed November 19, 2010).

Burns, Bob. Review of *Becoming Conversant with the Emerging Church*, by D. A. Carson. *Presbyterion: Covenant Seminary Review* 31, no. 2:122.

Carson, D. A. *Becoming Conversant with the Emerging Church: Understanding a Movement and Its Implications*. Grand Rapids, MI: Zondervan, 2005.

Eines, Eric E. "The World's Most Dangerous Bible Study." *Direction*, Fall 2004:201–6.

Hampton, James K., et al. "Is There Room at the Table? Emerging Christians in the Church of the Nazarene." http://didache.nts.edu/index.php?option=com_docman&task=doc_view&gid=794&Itemid=.

Knight, Hal. "John Wesley and the Emerging Church." *Preacher's Magazine*, Advent/Christmas 2007–2008, 5.

McKnight, Scot. "Five Streams of the Emerging Church: Key Elements of the Most Controversial and Misunderstood Movement in the Church Today." *Christianity Today*, February 2007:34–39.

Webber, Robert E. *The Younger Evangelicals: Facing the Challenges of the New World.* Grand Rapids, MI: Baker Books, 2002.

CHAPTER TWENTY-EIGHT

Trends in Christian Education

JERRY HICKSON

> ...teach them God's laws and show them
> what they must do to live right.
>
> —Exodus 18:20

There may have been a time when a congregation's Christian education ministry could consist of a Sunday school program and maybe a children's church program. However, many churches are moving away from both of these. What are the trends in Christian education in the twenty-first century?

A New Mindset

Methodology is a reflection of a changing context. The last century has brought a tidal wave of cultural change with radically different perspectives. Those who are attuned to the realities of the present are taking new approaches to Christian education.

Christian education is moving from *content mastery* to *life transformation*. The objective is more formation of character than transmission of information. If *knowing* had been the objective, the trend is toward *doing and being*. Curriculum increasingly includes an orientation to practical acts of service. Increasingly, evaluation of Christian education methods includes the question, What difference did this make in the way the learners are living their lives? The primary objective is leading persons into practical holiness as they reflect the personality of Jesus. Many are opting for "discipleship" or "spiritual formation," or "small group ministry," or "apprenticeship" as preferred descriptions instead of "Christian education."

Where the old approach was based on the model of the school with a set curriculum, graded classes, teacher/student roles, and achievement/reward, the new approach is "life along the way." As Doug Pagitt says, "These changes call us to rethink the value of the education model in spiritual formation. The heartbeat of our efforts within Solomon's Porch is to pursue a way of life in harmony with God created from means far beyond what educational formation can provide."[1] If the old model valued propositions of fact or truth, the new model values **personal application**: What does this have to do with me? Gone is the day when learning was its own reward; the learner today often must see an immediate benefit or payoff to investing in the process.

Story is replacing principle (or proposition) as the primary element of study. The Bible offers a rich mine full of stories for a starting point. Where stories once provided illustration material for the lesson points, **narrative** is increasingly becoming the heart and structure of the lesson. The narrative approach provides greater fluidity that both makes the content more approachable and increases the likelihood of contrasting outcomes. An important narrative component is "my story," the life experience that each learner brings into the learning setting.[2]

Christian education methods are increasingly emphasizing **experience and mystery**. A cornerstone of modernity and the Enlightenment was foundationalism, where one fact could be neatly stacked on another. This usually involved a deductive process whereby conclusions were drawn from sure data. Today, many are finding a complexity to reality that is often described in terms of paradox. Even those who are convinced that ultimate absolutes exist find that truth is usually clouded in uncertainty. An inductive process is often a better approach, encouraging the learner to observe and engage with various experiences from which conclusions may be drawn. While the outcome may not be as predictable, it is likely to be more relevant.

The new apologetic is embodied in lifestyle in an **incarnational** message. Relationships have grown to primary status as a means for teaching. Teachers must themselves represent the values that are to be instilled in the student. Learners catch the message as a contagion more than accept a convincing logical argument. Instead of studying facts or principles, the key is modeling a lifestyle wherein the power of Christ is displayed. Lessons are not easily contained in one hour units but are woven into a journey as life becomes a path walked together.

Christian education methods are increasingly using the arts and visual communication. **Imagery** was always important, even if the media was limited to drawings and flannel boards. Sculpture, video, and images (often photographic) are important delivery media today. This is art for its own sake, not just an

---

1. Pagitt, *Reimagining Spiritual Formation*, 19.
2. See chapter 9 of this volume.

adjunct to propositions. Ministry in the twenty-first century is returning to the Middle Ages where methods like stained glass were designed to communicate with a nonliterate populace. The younger generations of the twenty-first century have been trained by television and other media to be responsive to visual forms of communication. A lesson that relies entirely on textual communication is likely to fail.

The rapid evolution of **technology** has dramatically increased the options available for Christian education. No longer is the teacher restricted to face-to-face encounters and concrete objects to create a learning experience. The microchip has altered history in much the same scale as did the printing press. Many are harnessing the computer, the Internet, and other technologies as vehicles for doing the work of Christian education. The widespread use of such technology also opens up relational opportunities as people crave for authentic face-to-face encounters with other persons. The church has a unique capability to deliver the "high touch" that a high-tech world demands.[3]

The **nature of learning** has changed. Persons tend to have shorter attention spans: where music performances once lasted twenty to thirty minutes for a symphonic orchestra, popular music rarely exceeds two or three minutes. The younger generation is accustomed to rapid shifts of thought, whether from hypertexting on the Web or from the camera shifts of MTV or from the incessant interruptions of the cell phone with another text message. Lessons need to be planned in short units and may be more disjointed than in the past. Other changes reflect the changes in the learners. The model is moving from learning in large groups to learning in small groups where interactivity is maximized. If lecture ever was the most effective model, it rarely is today.

Spirituality is now defined as *who you are* rather than *what you do*. Character matters more than skill. Old expectations that sometimes led to legalism are giving way to a more ephemeral sense of spirituality. Classic techniques of spirituality are finding new interest. Many are returning to ancient practices of spiritual formation like *lectio divina*.

Many churches are finding a new sense of purpose in defining themselves in **missional** terms. The focus here moves intentionally beyond the church facility and the internal network of relationships to providing an incarnational presence in the community. Partnerships are created with almost anyone who shares at least some of the same values to accomplish acts of service. Many of the activities involve simple and pragmatic attempts to "show the love of Jesus with no strings attached."[4] The emphasis is on extending the kingdom of God rather than building an institutional program.

---

3. Naisbitt, *Megatrends*.

4. One source for ideas in Sjogren, *101 Ways to Reach Your Community*, and Sjogren, *101 Ways to Help People in Need*.

Instead of talking about Christian life, the new motto is, "Let's do it." Theory is replaced by **praxis**, and observation with active **service**. Christian education becomes the establishment of a community in which persons are molded in Christian character. Even in a traditional classroom setting, lessons must include practicums, either during the class time or between classes. Today's learner learns experientially. On the job training is a significant method in today's Christian education.

Christian education is becoming more **holistic and inclusive**. It is becoming difficult to tell the difference between Christian education and "doing ministry." One option is the classic approach of apprenticeship as learners observe and replicate the work of their mentor. Learning also occurs in group settings, like the youth group that engages in activities of service to the community. Worship, music, and prayer are increasingly utilized as parts of Christian education.

Methods are being **decentralized**. Not only is administrative structure becoming more of a democratic network, but the large class is giving way to small groups and online study. The classroom may not be eliminated, but it is not the only vehicle for Christian education. Alternative settings to the classroom include small groups meeting in homes, one-on-one mentoring at a coffee shop, working together in various settings, and sitting in front of a computer or television. Mentoring or coaching may use a combination of individual study online or reading a book or article and time spent face-to-face applying the lessons learned.

Increasingly, effective churches must learn to operate across cultural lines. Society is becoming more and more diverse, and churches must decide whether to isolate themselves to one culture or to reach several. Crossing generational lines is in itself a matter of **intercultural** ministry. Cross-cultural dynamics are present when persons come from different educational backgrounds or different economic levels. Of the various ethnic groups, Hispanics present the fastest growing segment of population in the United States. The Asian population is growing faster than ever before in regions of the United States east of the Pacific coast states. Urban areas are finding significant growth in Muslim and Buddhist populations. Churches that choose to be holistic in their ministry must develop an approach to Christian education that connects with the contrasting values of these diverse cultures. A model that fits only a white suburban world will be ineffective in reaching much of the harvest field.

A major challenge is presented in the changes in the concept of the **family**. In most settings, households have frequent contact with little more than the persons in their nuclear family, because grandparents and cousins live in distant locations. The number of families with two parents living in the home has fallen to minority status. Often, children are being raised by their grandparents or other relatives due to issues such as parental irresponsibility or commitment to military service. Societal expectations present conflicts, with children facing demands from sports involvements or other activities that compete with church programs. A church that is engaged with its community must overcome the challenges of ministering with individuals whose families do not come to church with them.

A growing problem is a neglect of **teacher training**. The growing complexities of Christian education demand quality training more than ever: teachers cannot be left to their own resources. The basics of Christian education—including human development, learning styles, lesson preparation, and the other topics covered in this text—need to be learned by volunteer workers as much as ever. The new challenges presented by a changing context raise additional training needs. Teachers deserve to be provided with continuing education in the philosophy and methodology of their craft.

Methods for the Twenty-First Century

In some places, the **Sunday school and/or children's church** are still in use. This is especially true in the small town/rural area and the smaller church. Churches with existing facilities often have the needed classrooms and sometimes find that the method remains effective for discipling at least the children, if not also the teens and adults. Special challenges are presented to those ministering in small town/rural settings as much of the curriculum is designed more for the suburban environment than the small town. In the small town, the church is still part of the social fabric. Change comes at different speeds, and some can still use many of the techniques of yesterday.

Alternative models to the graded curriculum of the classic Sunday school are under development. In some cases, graded classes are interspersed with large group activities for children where various types of presentations and interactive activities are offered. Some churches are following the lead of progressive schools in offering classes without walls where isolation is replaced by a flow between various learning stations. Smaller churches often find it necessary to group several age levels together.

In many churches, the **worship service** is where most of the teaching (at least of adults) is happening. This is usually a large group format where the focus is on the pulpit (often a metaphor rather than a piece of furniture!). Larger churches tend to find Sunday school to be cost prohibitive, especially when they offer multiple services or are building new facilities. Often, a special program for the children continues during the worship service. These may be structured like a traditional Sunday school or may themselves be large group formats with presentations of children's sermons, videos, or stage productions.

Small group ministries have become a predominant vehicle, especially among adults. These are increasingly taking place throughout the week in locations other than the church building. In more traditional settings, the methods of the small group process are used to make adult Sunday school classes more effective. Besides the adult Sunday School classes, women's Bible studies often happen in the church facility.

The scale of small group use should not be overstated. Careful reporting often reveals that churches that are featuring small groups as a keystone of their ministry are only involving a small minority of their adults in actual group involvement. Rather than judging themselves a failure, congregations that involve as many as 25 percent of their adults in small group ministries should consider themselves to be among the most successful.

Small groups take a variety of models. Many last for four to six weeks, with others lasting up to two years or indefinitely. Some groups are designed to be open to visitors or new attendees, while others are restricted (closed groups) to the group that initially started. Some are structured to emphasize Bible study and/or prayer, while others make accountability or service a focus.

Small groups are designed to address a variety of topics or concerns. Some are designed to present the basics of the faith to persons who are new to the church. Some focus on spiritual gifts to equip persons for ministry. Some are designed as evangelistic tools to train persons to share their faith or to provide a setting where seekers can explore the faith. Some are primarily designed to teach Bible content, while others are primarily designed to strengthen the relationships of those who attend. Some groups are primarily focused on a specific type of ministry activity, whether the rehearsal of the worship team or a group that works to serve the poor.

A specialized type of ministry is the recovery ministry that is being tailored not only for alcohol and drug addiction but also for issues like divorce, domestic abuse, and sexual addiction. In many settings, this is an expression of small group ministry. Most of these are based on the 12 Step Program founded by Alcoholics Anonymous.

Some churches offer **seminar type classes** that offer instruction for adults in a more didactic setting. These may last for three weeks or more and may take 90 to 120 minutes each week on a Sunday evening or at other times. Marriage enrichment and parenting classes are a popular option for such seminars. Some churches offer courses on personal financial management or job hunting skills.

In most programs of the past, persons were segregated by age level. In some settings, good results are occurring with an **intergenerational** approach to Christian education. Here, the family unit becomes a major element in structuring program. The house church is structured around an inter-generational dynamic unless everyone present is of the same age group: often the focus is on a communal meal with intentional dialogue. Some larger churches have explored intentionally working together across generational lines as nuclear families are woven together in a larger family context that once occurred naturally in the old village setting. Creative Bible studies are developed to include adults with children of all ages.[5] Even in programs that segregate by age group, some are making connections as retired persons "adopt" teens and/or children to develop mentoring relationships.[6] Service ministries like Habitat for Humanity are becoming intergenerational, with older adults serving meals while children participate.

Some churches are using **daycare, preschool, and private school** programs as significant elements of their Christian education ministry. These ministries offer the children far more hours of exposure to Christian education than the traditional Sunday school program. Families that might be resistive to recruitment to a Sunday morning class find child care and education more fitting to their needs. Some churches continue to offer private schooling through grade school and beyond.

Some churches are offering support to families that practice **home schooling**. Centralized facilities devoted to the Christian faith offer the prospect of corporate learning environments for portions of the home school curriculum. Support ministries for the parent/teachers can also be offered.

Computers and the Internet offer new resources for Christian education. Video presentations often provide a component in classroom lesson plans. Besides the ever-growing library of DVDs, sources like YouTube offer a diversified choice of material to incorporate into a lesson. With Skype or similar software, persons from distant locations can be brought into the classroom. Some local churches are using software to build classrooms where the students are dispersed to several different locations. These may involve video cameras that share pictures of the participants or may be limited to simpler sharing of text messages. Class presentations that are more content-oriented than relational can be recorded for future viewing by interested individuals. Besides storing lessons on DVD, churches can stream educational material via Web video or podcasts. People do not just learn in classrooms and scheduled programs: technology offers new options for decentralizing the learning process. Blogging has become a popular medium. Twitter provides a way of sending out short devotional thoughts. Using group e-mails, groups can work together without physically meeting to share prayer requests or discoveries made in Bible study.

Christian education is increasingly an **experiential** phenomenon. This generation learns by doing. Interaction is everything! Even in the traditional classroom setting, the wise teacher will offer "field trips" within and beyond the scheduled class time to complement the traditional curriculum. "Homework" takes on a new dynamic as learners are encouraged to implement concepts discussed in class. Experiential discipleship is possible in a variety of contexts apart from the traditional class.

---

5. One example is the FaithWeaver curriculum available from Group Publishers. http://sunday-school.group.com/faithweaver.

6. One resource is the Christian Association of Senior Adults. http://gocasa.org/.

Christian education with **senior adults** is changing as the Boomer generation moves into their sixties and beyond. As always, this oversized generation is making its mark with different expectations than those who went before. As a rule, Boomers expect higher levels of participation in the design and implementation of ministry. More than ever, senior ministry must be done *with* rather than *for* the persons involved. Fellowship activities like dinners and parties must be supplemented with service opportunities such as construction of buildings or preserving the environment.

What Happened to Christian Education?

Christian education in the twenty-first century looks much different than any of the models of the twentieth century. Careful investigation will show that this ministry has not disappeared but has multiplied into a plethora of expressions. What remains is the core imperative: teach the Word of God so that people know how to live.

Bibliography

Naisbitt, John. *Megatrends*. New York: Grand Central Publishing, 1988.

Pagitt, Doug. *Reimagining Spiritual Formation: A Week in the Life of an Experimental Church*. Grand Rapids, MI: Zondervan, 2003.

Sjogren, Steve. *101 Ways to Help People in Need*. Colorado Springs, CO: NavPress, 2002.

———. *101 Ways to Reach Your Community*. Colorado Springs, CO: NavPress, 2000.

Index

A

ABCD lesson outline pattern, 225
Abraham, 41–42, 106–8
Abstract Experience (Kolb), 213
accommodator learner, 214
Active Experimentation (Kolb), 213
Adler, Mortimer J., 62
administration: Christian education committee, 148–50; education pastor's role, 147–48, 156; key considerations overview, 151–52; leadership development, 156–58, 162; Ministry Action Plan, 156–59, 173–77; personnel issues, 152–54; volunteers, 154–56
adolescence, 285–86, 290, 312–13. *See also* children and youth
adults: early adulthood developmental tasks, 286–87; new trends in educating, 371–72; preparing parents for teaching, 263; seniors, 374; spaces for teaching, 238; and transmissive vs. dialogic approaches, 221; wisdom and development of, 88
advance organizer, 220
affective/attitudinal learning domain, 194, 204, 206–7, 210–11
age-level educational ministries, 53
Allen, Holly C., 334
alternative communities in emerging church, 364
Anabaptists, 46
analytic learner, 213–14
Andover seminary, 51, 52
Anthony, Michael J., 61, 64, 67

anthropology, 15
apocalyptic books of Bible, 186
apologists, Christian, 47–48
Apostles' Creed, 45–46
apprenticeships for volunteers, 157
area, curriculum, 195
Aristotle, 57–58
Arminius, 9
Arthurs, Jeffery, 98
assimilator learner, 213–14
at home retreat, 272
attention deficit disorder, 298–99
attitudinal/affective learning domain, 194, 204, 206–7, 210–11
auditory learner, 214
Ausubel, David P., 220
authenticity focus of emerging church, 362
authority, biblical, 4, 23–25

B

Babbie, Earl, 77, 82
background element of story, 103
Bagley, William C., 63
Bandura, Albert, 260–61
baptism, 47, 259–60
Baron, John, 301
Barton, Ruth Haley, 268, 269
Beatitudes, 208–11, 352–53
behavioral/psychomotor learning domain, 194, 204, 211–12
behaviorism, 65–67, 69
being and doing, balance of, 12
Bell, M. Robert, 33, 175–77
Benner, Richard, 347
Benson, Warren S., 61, 64–65, 67
Best, Charles, 317

Bible: authority of, 4, 23–25; Beatitudes, 208–11; as central to Christian education, 59, 167, 169, 170–71; choosing for lesson plan, 223–24; as curriculum, 192–93; expansion of access to, 231; family structure variety in, 314; foundational role of, 4–5, 25–27, 59; God's covenant with Abram, 41–42; inerrancy issue, 4–5, 24–25; as inspiration, 4, 23–25; instructors as students of, 27–28; and intercultural education, 322–23, 329–30; origins of religious teaching in, 247–48; overview of educational role, 23–25; primacy of, 7, 84; reading in worship as form of teaching, 251; and Reformation, 79; rest and retreat imperative in, 267–69; verse markings, origins of, 27. *See also* Jesus Christ; storytelling
Bible study, 26, 109–13, 179–88
biblical literacy, 27
biblical literature, genres of, 185–86
biblical mission, identifying, 174
biblical narrative, 97–101, 99n10, 103n20, 185. *See also* storytelling
bibliolatry, 23–24
Bilezikian, Gilbert, 323
Black, Kathy, 304
blind persons, accommodations for, 293–94, 295–96
Bloom, Benjamin, 204–5, 208
Boggs, Linden, 338
Bohler, Peter, 315
Bradbury, William B., 51
brainstorming a story, 106–8
Branson, Robert, 29–30
Brinton, Crane, 79
Broyles, Vernon S., 334–35
Bruner, Jerome, 221

Burgess, Harold, 60, 61–62
Byrum, Russell, 136

C

calling, concept of, 151–52, 170
Calvin and Hobbes (Watterson), 75
Camp and Conference Association (CCCA), 274, 276–77
camps, 273–77
Canham, Elizabeth J., 271
Carson, D. A., 360
catechism, 38
catechumens, 46–47
CCCA (Camp and Conference Association), 274, 276–77
centurion's servant, healing of, 103–6
change, learning's equivalence to, 204–5
"changing grace," 7
character element in story, 102
character studies, Bible, 187
children and youth: developmental tasks of, 283–86; discipling, 139–40; educational spaces for, 236–38; engaging in worship roles, 318; intellectual development phases (Piaget), 88; intergenerational ministry, 290; and power of story, 100–101; and public education, 52, 333–43; special needs, 293–94, 295–96; teaching methods, 35, 221; trust and faith relationship for, 92. *See also* parents
Cho, Paul, 253n9
Christian Camp and Conference Association (CCCA), 272
Christian education: Bible as central to, 59, 167, 169, 170–71; and call to be in the world, 342; defined, 70; discipleship role of, 58, 59–60, 72, 97, 167; early seminaries' neglect of, 51–52;

evangelism training, 136; location of responsibility for, 334–35; objective of, 166–73, 246; vs. religious education, 166; salvation role of, 168–69, 171–72; sanctification role of, 21; trends in, 367–74; worldview consideration, 84. *See also* history of Christian education; local churches

Christian education committee, 148–50

Christian ghetto issue, 341–42

Christianity, defining, 132–33

Christlikeness/Godliness: as central objective, 169–70; as essential to salvation, 20–21; fostering, 10–11, 97–98; holiness as, 346, 352; relational nature of, 249–50

Christology, 15–16

chronic illness, educating those with, 300

churches. *See* local churches

church life, teaching through, 247–54

Church of God (Anderson), revised Christian education objective, 168–69, 170

Church of the Nazarene, 24n3, 169, 170

civic sector as locus of educational responsibility, 335. *See also* public education

climax element of story, 103

cognitive development theory, 36

cognitive/intellectual learning domain, 194, 204, 206, 208–9

comfort, 350

commission to ministry (Jeremiah story), 115–17

commonsense learner, 214

communion of saints, 19

community of believers: camping as relational adhesive, 276–77; as center of Christianity, 249; early Christian communities, 45–48; emerging church's alternative communities, 364; holiness in, 5–6, 11, 246; Holy Spirit as uniter of, 19; importance in Christian education, 167, 246; and learning from difference, 325–26; as locus of educational responsibility, 335. *See also* holiness living; local churches

comprehensive Bible study, 180–81

Concrete Experience (Kolb), 213

Concrete Operational Period (Piaget), 88

Cone of Experience, 221–22

confession for forgiveness, 347–48

conflict element of story, 103

Conjunctive Faith stage (Fowler), 94

consequences of sin (David and Bathsheba), 110–13

Constantine, Emperor, 230–31

content and convergence in story, 106–8

Conventional Moral Reasoning (Kohlberg), 91

converger learner, 214

conversation as teaching tool, 37–38

conversion process, 92, 134, 137–41. *See also* salvation

Cooperative Curriculum Project, 166, 167

"corporate holiness," 5–6, 11, 246

covenants for educational ministry roles, 155, 162

covenant with Abram, God's, 41–42

Cowman, Lettie, 268

creator, God the Father as, 14–15, 77–78, 80, 269

creeds in early Church, 45–46

Criticism and Questioning Orientation (Kohlberg), 91
cross-cultural discipling, 101n13
Culbertson, Howard, 142
cultural context of education ministry, 101n13, 167–68, 361. *See also* intercultural education
Culverson, Mary McClintock, 303
Cummings-Bond, Stuart, 150
curriculum: definitions, 192; of fellowship, 250; formal vs. informal, 245–46, 248; grab-bag resourcing, 196; historical perspective, 192–93; introduction, 191–92; Jesus', 38–39; new trends in, 371; null, 252n7; preaching as, 252–53; selecting, 196–202; service as, 253–54; teaching planning, 217–28, 254; terminology, 193–96; worship as, 250–52

D

Dale, Edgar, 221–22
David and Bathsheba, story of, 110–13
daycare programs, 373
Dayton, Donald, 171
d/Deaf persons, accommodations for, 296–97
Decalogue, 42
decentralization in Christian education, 370
decision-makers, curriculum, 197
dementia, educating those with, 300
Denton, Melinda Lundquist, 311–14
Dettoni, John, 67
developmental disabilities, educating those with, 294, 299, 302
developmentalism, 67–68

developmental perspectives: cognitive development theory, 36; conclusion, 291; faith (Fowler), 92–95; intellectual (Piaget), 87–88; intergenerational ministry, 289–90; introduction, 281–82; moral reasoning (Kohlberg), 89, 90–91; psychosocial (Erikson), 88–89, 90; space considerations, 236–39; tasks and teachable moments, 282–89
DeVries, Mark, 290
Dewey, John, 60, 62
Deymaz, Mark, 323
dialogical / discovery teaching approach, 43, 44, 219–21
Didache, 230
didactic passages of Bible, 185
directed retreat, 272
discipleship: centrality to Christian education, 58, 72, 167; children and youth, 139–40; and content of Christian education, 59–60, 97; defining Christianity, 132–33; definition, 258–60; and holiness expectations, 58–59, 140–41; intentional, 257–65; introduction, 131–32; Jesus Christ on, 58, 136; juggling identities, 142–43; mature, 58–59, 70, 172, 174; nominal Christians, 138–39; overview of educational, 10–12; safe atmosphere for, 141–42; stages of, 133. *See also* evangelism
discovery / dialogical teaching approach, 43, 44, 219–21
disequilibrium, learning as taking place through, 36
diverger learner, 213
doctrine. *See* holiness living; theology
door-to-door evangelism, ineffectiveness of, 134

Downs, Perry, 33, 65–66, 67, 68, 169
Drucker, Peter, 154
Dunn, Kenneth and Rita, 214–15
dynamic equivalence version of
    Bible, 183, 184
dynamic learner, 214

E

early adulthood, developmental tasks
    of, 286–87
early Christian Church, 45–48, 78,
    193, 230, 322–23
ecclesiology, 18. *See also* theology
educational mission, curriculum, 194
educational philosophies:
    behaviorism, 65–67, 69;
    content, 59–60; definition
    of Christian education,
    70; essentialism, 63–65, 69;
    Groome's shared praxis,
    70–71; humanistic education,
    67–68, 69, 70; introduction,
    57–59; perennialism, 62–63,
    69; progressivism, 60–62, 69;
    summary of, 68–70; and Sunday
    school development, 71–72
egalitarian approach of emerging
    church, 362
Eiesland, Nancy, 304–5
Eines, Eric, 363
eisegesis, 26
elementary school children, spaces
    for, 236–37
elitism, 350–51
Elkind, David, 82–83
Elliott, William, 49–50
emergent vs. emerging church, 361
emerging church, 359–64
emotional stimuli strand of learning,
    215

Enlightenment, 11, 48–50, 80–81
environmental stimuli strand of
    learning, 215
environments for learning. *See*
    facilities
Erikson, Erik, 88–89, 90
errantist view of the Bible, 25
eschatology, 21–22
essentialism, 63–65, 69
ethnic diversity, 326–27, 370
evaluation: curriculum materials,
    197–202; educational ministry,
    11, 158–59; volunteers'
    performance, 155–56, 163–64
Evangelical Lutheran Church in
    America, 290
evangelism: and Christian camping,
    274–75; and Christian education
    objective, 168–69; discipleship
    role of, 134; educating the church
    for, 134–36; and intentional
    discipleship, 258–59; origins in
    Wesleyan revival movement,
    50; private/home schooling as a
    subversion of, 341–42; as process,
    136–38. *See also* discipleship
Everest, Norma Cook, 134, 135
evil, problem of, 15
example, teaching by, 34–37, 45,
    260–61, 352, 355. *See also* holiness
    living
exegesis, 25–26, 113–14n23, 113–17
experience, personal, and
    postmodern worldview, 81, 84
experiential focus of Christian
    education, 373. *See also*
    transformation
expository approaches to
    Bible study, 26
Ezra, 218

F

facilities: community gathering, 239; creating new space, 233–34; developmental needs, 236–39; historical roots, 230–32; hospitality, 235; introduction, 229–30; media equipment, 236; meeting needs of congregation, 233; multipurpose spaces, 239; nursery, 234; policies, 236; safety, 234–35; universal access, 234, 238–39, 293, 298; use of community, 239–40; utilization study, 232–33; weekday schools, 234; worship space as teaching tool, 250

faith community. *See* community of believers

faith development (Fowler), 92–95

faithfulness of God, 106–8

family: educational role of, 35, 41–42, 264–65, 309–10, 334; Holy Spirit's role in, 319; implications of changes in, 370–71; importance of, 310–11; intentional discipleship role, 261–62; nurturing faith in, 311–18. *See also* parents

Family Based Youth Ministry (DeVries), 290

fellowship, teaching through, 248–49

final judgment, 21

Ford, Gerald R., 53

foreign faith in Scripture, 104

forgiveness of sins, 19–21, 347–48. *See also* salvation

Formal Operational Period (Piaget), 88

formal teaching: discipleship role of, 260–61; in family, 262; vs. informal, 245–46, 248; by Jesus, 32–33, 34; schooling approach, 34, 71–72, 294–95, 311, 368; as transmissive approach, 219–20, 221

Foster, Richard, 97

Fowler, James, 92–95, 167

free will and grace, 9–10

full salvation, 19–21, 172

functional family, 261

G

Gardner, Freda A., 334

Garland, Diana, 261

generational cultural differences, 326

Genesis 17:1–17, 18:1–15, and 21:1–8 (brainstorming narrative), 106–8

Gibbs, Eddie, 138–39

Gilbreath, Edward, 336, 337–38

Gilligan, Carol, 91–92

goals and objectives: curriculum, 193–94; introduction, 165–66; learning objectives, writing, 224–25; local church level, 173–77; objective of Christian education, 166–73, 246

God: as beyond denominational boundaries, 6; as change facilitator, 7–8; as creator, 14–15, 77–78, 80, 269; direct access to, 259; and free will for humans, 9–10; holiness and relationship to, 356; importance of speaking regularly of, 317; as initiator of relationship with humanity, 166–67; nurturing relationship with during retreat, 270–71; rest after creation, 269; salvation role of, 19–21; surrender to, 119–21; as teacher, 41–44, 218; triune, 4, 13–18

Godliness as focus of holiness living. *See* Christlikeness/Godliness
God of grace vs. God of laws, 348–49
God's messengers, teachers as, 218
God the Father, 13–15, 14. *See also* God
God the Holy Spirit, 14, 16–18. *See also* Holy Spirit
God the Son, 15–16. *See also* Jesus Christ
Golden Rule, 91
Good Boy/Nice Girl Orientation (Kohlberg), 91
grab-bag resourcing for curriculum, 196
grace: "changing grace," 7–8; and forgiveness of sin, 19; and free will, 9–10; as major attribute of God, 348–49; means of grace, 20, 252; prevenient, 8, 20; sanctification role of, 20–21; vs. works-holiness, 353
Great Commission (Matthew 28:19–20), 258–60
Green, Joel B., 353
Greenway, Jeffrey E., 353
Griffin, Emilie, 270–71, 272
Griggs, Donald, 218, 220
Groome, Thomas, 70–71, 167
A Guide to Prayer for Ministers and Other Servants (Job and Shawchuck), 273

H

Hahn, Roger, 258, 265
hamartiology, 19–21
Hare, Douglas, 260
Harper, A. F., 169, 170
Harper, William Rainey, 52
Harris, Maria, 247, 248n2
Hauerwas, Stanley, 101
Havighurst, Robert J., 282–89

Hebrew education, ancient, 41–44
hemispheric dominance in the brain, 208
Hendricks, Howard, 221, 222
Hill, Brian Victor, 337, 342
hippocampus, 206–7
history as interpretation, 43
history of Christian education: early Christian communities, 45–48, 78, 193, 230, 322–23; Enlightenment influence, 11, 48–50, 80–81; future path of, 54; Jesus' contribution, 44–45; medieval period, 48, 78, 193, 231, 361; 19th century, 50–52; Old Testament contribution, 41–44, 192–93; Renaissance and Reformation, 48–49; 20th century, 52–53
holiness living: Christlikeness/Godliness in, 346, 352; communal nature of, 5–6, 11, 246; conclusion, 355–56; and discipleship, 58–59, 140–41; as educational content, 59–60, 355; and evangelical relationship to secular world, 135–36; expectations for, 140–41; and importance of Jesus' full humanity, 15–16; and informal teaching, 246; introduction, 345–46; modern hindrances to, 346–51; positive perspective on, 352–53; postmodern version, 354; relational aspect of, 351–52; Wesley on importance of, 315–16; works-holiness, 20, 353–54
Holiness Movement, 19, 59, 347–49
holistic perspective, 32, 370
holy people of God, 6. *See also* community of believers

Holy Spirit: and biblical inspiration, 4; as church creator, 18, 19; educational role of, 5, 16–18, 167, 170, 319; and triune God, 14, 16–18

home as source for Christian education, 334. *See also* family

home schooling, 335, 339–40, 373

homogenous unit principle, 322

Hook, Book, Look, Took lesson outline pattern, 225

house church, 239

human and divine natures of Jesus, 15–16

human development. *See* developmental perspectives

humanism, 48–49, 80–81

humanistic education, 67–68, 69, 70

Hunt, Josh, 251

Hunter, George, 132, 133

Hutchingson, Robert Maynard, 62

Hybels, Bill, 138

Hymans, Diane, 142

I

idolatry, biblical, 23–24

imagery focus in Christian education, 363, 368–69

imaginative learner, 213

imaginative retelling method, 121–27, 187

imago dei, 32

incarnational approach, 362, 368

inclusivity, 300–304, 370

individualism, 11, 49, 140, 249

Individuative-Reflective Faith stage (Fowler), 93–94

inductive Bible study, 109–13, 182–83

Industrial Revolution and child labor, 49

inerrancy, biblical, 4–5, 24–25

infants, education and development, 236–37, 283–84

informal teaching, 32–35, 245–54, 260–62

initiation of seekers, 141–42

inspiration, biblical, 4, 23–25

Instrumental Relativist Orientation (Kohlberg), 89

intellectual / cognitive learning domain, 194, 204, 206, 208–9

intellectual development (Piaget), 87–88

intentional discipleship, 257–65

intentionality in retreat, 273

intercultural education: biblical basis for, 322–23, 329–30; ethnic diversity, 326–27, 370; interfaith and plural environments, 329–30; introduction, 321–22; language differences, 330–31; learning from differences, 325–26; local church connection, 323–25; socioeconomic differences, 327–29; summary, 331–32

interfaith and plural environments, 6, 329–30

intergenerational education, 289–90, 318, 372–73

Internet resources, 373

Intuitive-Projective Faith stage (Fowler), 92–93

J

Jefferson, Thomas, 81–82

Jeremiah 1:1–10 (synthesizing / retelling), 115–17

Jesus Christ: as authority over Bible, 24; as Christian education's focus, 97–98, 167; commitment to retreat and rest, 267–69; as exemplar of holiness, 352; historical overview, 44–45; introduction, 29–30; and making disciples, 136; on mature discipleship, 58–59; Passover supper, 121–27; resurrection of, 21–22; as teacher, 31–39, 218; temptations in the wilderness, 119–21; and triune God, 14, 15–16

Job, Rueben P., 273

John 13:1–32 (paraphrasing), 121–27

Johnson, Ben Campbell, 134, 142

Johnson, Leona, 98

Jones, Timothy, 271, 272

Joshua, 42–43

journaling, 188

justification vs. sanctification, 20

K

kinesthetic learners, 214

kingdom of God, 10–11, 172–73

King James version, 185

Kneller, George, 60, 62, 64

Knight, George, 61, 62, 65, 66

Knight, Hal, 363

Kohlberg, Lawrence, 89, 91–92

koinonia, 249

Kolb, David, 213–14

L

Lake, Charles, 338

language choice and evangelism, 135

language differences and intercultural education, 330–31

later maturity, developmental tasks of, 288–89

Law, William, 317–18

Law and Order Orientation (Kohlberg), 91

Lawrence, Marshall, 296

Lawson, Kevin, 165–66, 168, 170

leadership development: at camps, 277; pastors, 147–48, 156, 252–53, 303–4, 328–29; processes and resources, 156–58, 162; for special needs persons, 304–5; teaching planning, 217–28

learning: as change, 204–5; Christian perspective on, 205; defined, 204–5; domains of, 175, 204–12; introduction, 203; local church activities, 174; modalities, 214; modern value of, 80; and personal transformation, 47; postmodern influence on, 82; sensitive periods for, 207–8; shifts in attitudes toward, 369; spectrum of approaches, 219–20; styles of, 82, 213–14; symbolic model of, 260–61; Taxonomy of Experiential Learning, 33; through disequilibrium, 36; 21 elements of learning, 214–15

learning objectives, writing, 224–25

learning problems, educating those with, 298–99

lectio divina, 78, 117–21, 182–83

lectionaries in Bible study, 180–81

Lee, Mary E., 80

left brain / right brain theory, 208

legalism, 349–50

lesson plan design, 223–27

Levine, Daniel, 61

Li, Harry, 323

liability concerns and special needs, 305

liberalism, theological, 62

liberation theology, 139

life everlasting, 21–22

limbic system, 206–7

liturgical calendar, 251

local churches: assimilating into community, 142–43; discipling role of, 262, 263–65; emerging church, 359–64; goals and objectives, 173–77; house church, 239; intercultural education, 323–25; missional, 239–40, 253, 362, 369; unspoken expectations, 132; and worldview expression, 84. *See also* administration; small-group ministry

Lodahl, Michael, 350, 355

LOGOS Ministry, 290

Long, Thomas, 259

Loomis, Steven R., 336

Lord's Supper as teaching tool, 252

love, message of, 249, 351–52, 354

Luke 4:1–15 (*lectio divina* approach), 119–20

Luke 7:1–10 (Sermon on the Plain), 103–5

Luther, Martin, 79

Lynn, Robert W., 50–51

M

MacDonald, Gordon, 268

main idea formation, 224

Managing the Non-Profit Organization (Drucker), 154

MAP (Ministry Action Plan), 158–59, 173–77

Maslow, Abraham, 67

Matthew 8:5–13 (Sermon on the Mount), 103, 105–6

Matthew 28:19–20 (Great Commission), 258–60

mature discipleship, 58–59, 70, 172, 174

May, Scottie, 263

Mays, Larry, 251

meaningful learning, 220, 221–22

meaning making and Christian education objective, 167

means of grace, 20, 252

medieval period, 48, 78, 193, 231, 361

memorization, Bible, 186

mental illness, educating those with, 299–300

mentoring of volunteers for leadership, 157–58

middle age, developmental tasks of, 287–88

middle childhood, developmental tasks of, 284

Milligan, Dale, 290

Ministry Action Plan (MAP), 158–59, 173–77

ministry description, 154–55, 161

missional church, 239–40, 253, 362, 369

mission trips, 249

mobility impairments, educating those with, 293, 298

modeling as teaching tool, 34–37, 45, 260–61, 352, 355

modernity, 49–53, 79–81, 82, 83–84, 346–51

modes of thinking and being, 75–84

monasteries, 48, 231

Moody, R. W., 306

moralistic therapeutic deism, 313, 315

moral reasoning (Kohlberg), 89, 91–92

Moses, 42, 148–49, 218

Mother Teresa, 328

Mulholland, Robert, 118

Muller, Wayne, 269–70

multicultural perspective, 322

multipurpose spaces, 239

Mythic-Literal Faith stage (Fowler), 93

N

narrative, biblical, 97–101, 99n10, 103n20, 185. *See also* storytelling

narrative preaching, 253

Nathan, prophet and advisor to King David, 110–13

naturalism, 80

needs, community, and education planning, 152

neurons and learning in the brain, 206–8

Nicene Creed, 14, 46

Niebuhr, H. Richard, 92

Nieman, James R., 328

19th century, Christian education in, 50–52

nominal Christians, nurturing, 138–39

null curriculum, 252n7

nursery space, 234

O

obedience and mature discipleship, 172

objective of Christian education, 166–73, 246. *See also* goals and objectives

objectivity vs. subjectivity and worldview, 82

Old Testament contributions to education, 41–44, 192–93

The One Year Bible, 180

online education "facilities," 240

Oord, Thomas Jay, 350, 355

ordo salutis, 20

Origen, 14, 80–81

Ornstein, Allan, 61

outcomes, curriculum, 194

Outler, Albert, 80–81, 83

outline, lesson, 225

P

Pagitt, Doug, 23, 360, 368

parables as teaching tools, 35–36

parachurch organizations, 342–43

paraphrase version of Bible, 184

paraphrasing Scripture, storytelling mode, 121–27, 187

parents: church support for, 262, 264–65; discipleship role of, 261–65; educational role of, 35, 42, 316–18, 334; and home schooling, 339–40; spiritual formation role of, 309–19

parochial schools, 52

Passover supper with Jesus, 121–27

pastors, 147–48, 156, 252–53, 303–4, 328–29

Pazmiño, Robert, 168, 170, 225

Pearson, John, 272

peoplehood, 6

perceiving dimension of experience (Kolb), 213

perennialism, 62–63, 69

perfection, 347–49

performance evaluations for volunteers, 155–56, 163–64

periodic assessments of curriculum, 202

personal application of spiritual knowledge, 368

personnel, calling, 152–54

Peterson, Eugene, 121

physiological stimuli strand of learning, 215

Piaget, Jean, 36, 87–88

plot element in story, 103

Pneumatology, 16–18

poetic passages of Bible, 185

Post-Conventional Moral Reasoning (Kohlberg), 91

postmodernity: as educational philosophy, 68; emerging church, 359–64; historical development of, 81–83; holiness lifestyle, 354; importance of personal experience, 81, 84; influence on learning, 82; and Scripture interpretation, 26

praxis, emphasis on, 70–71, 370

prayer: in Bible study, 179, 181–82; Jesus' use of, 45; in lesson plan design process, 223; and retreats, 273; in teaching-learning transaction, 250, 251

praying the Scripture, 186, 187

preached retreat, 272

preaching as teaching, 252–53

Pre-Conventional Moral Reasoning (Kohlberg), 89

premodernity, 77–79, 82, 83

Preoperational Period (Piaget), 88

preschool programs, 234, 373

presence, ministry of, 136–37

prevenient grace, 8, 20

Primal Faith stage (Fowler), 92

Princeton Seminary, 51–52

Pritchard, G. A., 138

private education, 335–37, 373

private retreat, 272

processing dimension of experience (Kolb), 213

progressivism, 60–62, 69, 70

promise and fulfillment (God's promise to Abraham), 106–8

prophetic books of Bible, 186

propositional knowledge, moving beyond, 11, 18, 34, 363, 368–69

Protestant Reformation, 48–49, 79, 193, 231

providence, 15

psychological stimuli strand of learning, 215

psychomotor/behavioral learning domain, 194, 204, 211–12

psychosocial development (Erikson), 88–89, 90

public education, 52, 333–43

Punishment and Obedience Orientation (Kohlberg), 89

The Purpose Driven Church (Warren), 151

Q

questioning approach in emerging church, 363

R

rabbis, 43

race vs. ethnicity, 326

Raikes, Robert, 49, 151, 231, 248

reader response value in Bible study, 26

reason and rationality in modern thinking, 79, 84

reciprocity and faith development, 93

reconciliation, 20, 342, 348

recovery ministry, 372

reflective devotional reading, 181–82

Reflective Observation (Kolb), 213

Reformation, 48–49, 79, 193, 231

regeneration vs. sanctification, 20

relational aspect of holiness, 351–52

relationship-building in evangelism, 134–35

Renaissance, Christian education during, 48–49

resolution element of story, 103

Restoring Your Spiritual Passion (MacDonald), 268

resurrection of the body, 21–22

retreats, 267–69, 270–73

righteousness instruction, 246–47

rising action element of story, 103

Rogers, Carl, 67

Rogers, Thomas G., 328
Roman Catholicism, 78

S

Sabbath principle, 269–70
safety issues, 234–35, 305–6
salvation: as central to Christian education, 168–69, 171–72; conversion process, 92, 134, 137–41; defined, 8; and discipleship of children and youth, 139–40; nature of, 11; reconciliation, 20, 342, 348; and sanctification, 19–21. *See also* transformation
sanctification, 8, 20–21
Sanner, A. Elwood, 169, 170
Sarah (Abraham's wife), 107
Sawicki, Marianne, 47
schooling approach to Christian education, 34, 71–72, 294–95, 311, 368
scientific study, modern beginnings of, 79–80
"scientific theology," 47–48
scope and sequence, curriculum, 194–95
Scripture. *See* Bible
second coming, 21, 173
secular humanism, 48–49, 80–81
Seefeldt, Brenda, 290
seminaries, 51–52, 54
senior adults, educating, 374
sensitive periods for learning, 207–8
Sensorimotor Period (Piaget), 88
sensory impairments, educating those with, 293–94, 295–97
Senter, Mark, 152
Sermon on the Mount (Matthew 8:5–13), 103, 105–6

Sermon on the Plain (Luke 7:1–10), 103–5
service as teaching, 253–54, 265
setting element of story, 102
The 7 Laws of the Learner (Wilkinson), 31, 36–37
Seven Steps for Effective Retreats (Pearson), 272
shared praxis approach, 70–71
Shawchuck, Norman, 273
shema, 261, 262
Simson, Wolfgang, 239
sin, doctrine of, 19–21
singing the Scripture, 187
Sire, James W., 76
small-group ministry: effectiveness of, 239; growth of, 53, 253n9; Jesus' use of, 44; and safe atmosphere for discipleship, 141–42; trend toward, 371–72
Smith, Christian, 311–14
Smith, Robert, 258
Snyder, Howard A., 355
Social Contract Orientation (Kohlberg), 91
social networking, 373
society, call to action in, 11, 12, 135–36, 139–40, 342
socioeconomic differences, intercultural education, 327–29
sociological stimuli strand of learning, 215
songs in worship, 187, 251
soteriology, 19–20
Spears, Paul D., 336
specialization in education ministry, 165–66

special needs individuals: chronic illness, 300; dementia, 299–300; developmental disabilities, 299; inclusion, ensuring, 300–304; introduction, 293–95; leadership from, 304–5; learning problems, 298–99; mental illness, 299–300; mobility impairments, 298; safety issues, 305–6; sensory impairments, 295–97; universal access, 234, 238–39, 293, 298

spiritual formation, Christian education as, 97, 309–19

spiritual gifts and education planning, 152

spirituality, shift to identity from behavior, 369

Stackhouse, John G., 362

staffing issues, 152–54

Steinaker, Norman, 33, 175–77

story-in-a-sentence, 113–17

storytelling: as central to Christian education, 98n5; characters, 102; conclusion, 127–28; content and convergence, 106–8; elements of, 103–6; as emerging church focus, 363; Fee and Stuart's levels of, 114n24; increased adoption of, 368; inductive Bible study, 109–13, 182–83; and Jesus' teaching style, 44; *lectio divina*, 117–21; paraphrasing Scripture, 121–27, 187; plot elements, 103; scriptural use of, 97–101, 99n10, 103n20, 185; setting, 102; synthesizing and retelling, 113–17

strategic planning, 150–52, 173–77

structural family, 261

students: as active participants in education, 71; nurturing relationships with, 32, 37–38, 45, 218; as primary focus of teaching, 31–32; progressivism's approach, 61

students of the Word, teachers as, 27–28

study Bibles, using, 181, 183

subjectivity vs. objectivity and worldview, 82

Summers, Georgianna, 44–45

Sunday school: contemporary demise of, 165; curriculum development, 193; historical development, 49–53, 71–72, 231–32, 248; niches for continuation of, 371; teachers' meeting, 156; vs. worship service in popularity, 252–53n8

Sweet, Leonard, 331

symbolic language as teaching method, 38

symbolic model of learning, 260–61

synagogue, establishment of, 43

synthesizing and learning taxonomy, 209

synthesizing and retelling, 113–17

Synthetic-Conventional Faith stage (Fowler), 93

T

tactile learners, 214

Taxonomy of Experiential Learning, 33

teachable moments, 34, 282–89

teachers' meetings, 156

teacher training, neglect of, 371

teaching: dialogical/discovery approach, 43, 44, 219–21; by example, 34–37, 45, 260–61, 352, 355; as fundamental to the church, 247–48; informal, 32–35, 245–54, 260–62; planning process, 217–28, 254; preaching as, 252–53; relationship to baptism, 259–60; worship as, 187, 250–52, 371. *See also* Christian education; formal teaching; learning

teaching pastor model, 252–53

teaching strategy, curriculum, 195–96

team concept in educational ministry, 148–49

technology contributions, 369

temptations and surrender to God, 119–21

Ten Commandments, 42

Tertullian, 14

theist, 15

theme, curriculum, 195

theme studies, Bible, 187

theodicy, 15

theology: communion of saints, 19; conclusion, 22; contribution to education, 59; eschatology, 21–22; and human development theories, 92; liberation, 139; salvation and sanctification, 19–21; "scientific," 47–48; Trinitarian, 4, 13–18, 218

Thorsen, Donald, 25, 83

Tillich, Paul, 92

time schedule for Bible study, 188

toddlers, educational spaces for, 236–37

topical approaches to Bible study, 26

Torah, 42

tradition, church, role of, 59, 78, 80, 84

transformation, personal: and catechumen's learning experience, 47; Christian education's focus on, 59–60, 167, 171–72, 367–68; and discipleship, 10, 12, 58–59; educator's role in, 19; as purpose of Jesus' teaching, 31, 34, 39; righteousness instruction, 246–47. *See also* salvation; storytelling

translation issues, Bible study, 183–85

transmissive/traditional teaching approach, 219–20, 221. *See also* formal teaching

Trinitarian theology, 4, 13–18, 218

triune God, 4, 13–18

trust and child's faith, 92

truth, ascertaining, 7, 83–84, 94

20th century, Christian education in, 52–53. *See also* modernity

21 elements of learning, 214–15

2 Samuel 11–12 (inductive Bible study), 110–13

U

unity of life, 11, 323

universal access to educational space, 234, 238–39, 293, 298

Universal Ethical Principle Orientation (Kohlberg), 91

Universalizing Faith stage (Fowler), 94–95

V

value system and emotional engagement with learning, 211

verse markings, biblical, 27

Virgin Mary, 15

vision, local church, identifying, 174

visualization of biblical passages, 187–88

visual learners, 214
vocation, 151–52, 170
volunteers, 153–58

W

Wallace, Jim, 140
Wallerstein, Immanuel, 79
Walters, Richard, 260–61
Ward, Ted, 57
Warren, Rick, 151
Watkins, Jim, 342, 343
Watterson, Bill, 75
Webber, Robert, 363
Webinars, 157
weekday schools, 234, 373
Wesley, John: class meetings, 50, 193, 248; on education, 68; vs. Enlightenment thinking, 80–81; on family's role, 310, 311; on full salvation, 172; on Holy Spirit's role, 319; on parents' role, 316–18; on perfection, 347n2; on preaching without having it, 315; quadrilateral of, 7, 83–84; Scriptural focus of, 171; on true religion, 315–16; worldview of, 83–84
Wesley, Susanna, 310–11
Wesleyan Holiness: as educational approach, 3–12; vs. humanism, 48–49, 80–81; and modes of thinking and being, 83–84; and staffing decisions, 152–53. *See also* Christian education

Wesleyan Quadrilateral, 7, 83–84
Westerhoff, John, 139, 294–95, 311
wilderness, Jesus and temptations in, 119–21
Wilderness Time (Griffin), 270–71
Wilhoit, James, 67, 68
Wilkins, Michael, 258
Wilkinson, Bruce, 31, 36–37
Willard, Dallas, 97
Williams, Bud, 276
Williams, Dennis, 168
Wilson, Jennifer Jones, 305
Wilson, John, 336, 337–38
wisdom and adult development, 88
women and Kohlberg's Moral Reasoning, 91–92
works-holiness, 20, 353–54
worldviews, 75–84
worship service: coordinating space with education, 232–33; engaging children in, 318; integrating special needs persons, 303; vs. Sunday school in popularity, 252–53n8; as teaching, 187, 250–52, 371
Wright, Elliott, 50–51

Y

Yaconelli, Mike, 275–76, 348, 350, 351, 352
Yount, William, 67
youth. *See* children and youth

Z

Zacharias, Ravi, 135, 140–41